Shooter's Bible GUIDE TO TACTICAL FIREARMS

Shooter's Bible GUIDE TO TACTICAL FIREARMS

A COMPREHENSIVE GUIDE TO PRECISION RIFLES AND LONG-RANGE SHOOTING GEAR

ROBERT A. SADOWSKI

SKYHORSE PUBLISHING

Skyhorse Publishing books may be purchased in bulk at special discounts for sales promotion, corporate gifts, fund-raising, or educational purposes. Special editions can also be created to specifications. For details, contact the Special Sales Department, Skyhorse Publishing, 307 West 36th Street, 11th Floor, New York, NY 10018 or info@skyhorsepublishing.com.

Skyhorse® and Skyhorse Publishing® are registered trademarks of Skyhorse Publishing, Inc.®, a Delaware corporation.

Visit our website at www.skyhorsepublishing.com.

10 9 8 7 6 5 4 3 2

Library of Congress Cataloging-in-Publication Data is available on file.

Cover design by Owen Corrigan

Print ISBN: 978-1-63220-534-6
Ebook ISBN: 978-1-63220-935-1

Printed in China

There are times when wolves protect the lambs. Let us celebrate these punishers of evil for their courage, honor, and technique. Let us also remember and celebrate those who do not return. It is right and just.

"Only accurate rifles are interesting."
—Townsend Whelen

CONTENTS

Foreword   vii

Introduction   viii

Chapter 1. Top 10 Long-Range Rifles   1

Chapter 2. Anatomy of a Bolt-Action Rifle   26

Chapter 3. A Brief History of Military Snipers   32

RIFLE TESTING & EVALUATION

Chapter 4. Uberti 1874 Buffalo Hunter Sharps   44

Chapter 5. Savage Arms Model 25 Lightweight Varminter-T   50

Chapter 6. Savage Arms Model 11/111 Long Range Hunter   53

Chapter 7. America's Last Bolt-Action Combat Rifle: M1903A3 Springfield   57

Chapter 8. Mosin–Nagant M91/30 PU Sniper   64

Chapter 9. The Evolution of the USMC M40 Series Rifles   70

Chapter 10. SIG SSG 3000 Patrol   72

Chapter 11. Accurate-Mag's Multi-Caliber Rifle Chassis System   77

Chapter12. PTR91KC and Surplus Hensoldt Scope   82

Chapter 13. The Scout Rifle   88

Chapter 14. Mauser 98k-ZF 41 Replica   91

MAINTENANCE

Chapter 15. Precision Rifle Maintenance   96

Chapter 16. Optic Maintenance   99

OPTICS

Chapter 17. Anatomy of a Rifle Scope   100

Chapter 18. Ballistic Reticle Rifle Scopes   102

Chapter 19. Leupold Mark 4 LR/T 4.5–14x50mm   105

Chapter 20. U.S. Optics ER-25 5-25xT   107

Chapter 21. Unertl Target Scope   109

Chapter 22. Anatomy of a Binocular   110

Chapter 23. Rangefinder Binocular   111

Chapter 24. Anatomy of a Spotting Scope   114

Chapter 25. Leica APO-Televid 82   115

Chapter 26. Meopta MeoStar S2 82 HD Angled   116

Chapter 27. Laser Rangefinders   117

AMMUNITION

Chapter 28. Anatomy of a Cartridge   119

Chapter 29. 6.5 Creedmoor   121

Chapter 30. .300 Norma Magnum and .338 Norma Magnum   124

SHOOTING TECHNIQUE

Chapter 31. Anatomy of a Sling   128

Chapter 32. Shooting Positions   131

Chapter 33. Shooting Technique   136

Chapter 34. Shooting Drills   139

RIFLES, OPTICS, AMMUNITION & ACCESSORIES

Chapter 35. Custom Precision Rifles   141

Chapter 36. Factory Precision Rifles   191

Chapter 37. Vintage Precision Rifles   287

Chapter 38. Scout Rifles   295

Chapter 39. Suppressors   299

Chapter 40. Tactical Rifle Scopes   315

Chapter 41. Tactical Binoculars   343

Chapter 42. Tactical Spotting Scopes   349

Chapter 43. Tactical Rangefinders   356

Chapter 44. Ammunition   363

Chapter 45. Tactical Shooting Gear   381

References   406

Appendix A. Rifleman's Creed   406

Appendix B. Military Sniper Kill Counts   407

Appendix C. Rifle Scope Reticles   411

Foreword

*I*n my younger, more vulnerable years, when I roamed woods and abandoned farms, my father offered some advice: he would rather be lucky than good. Dad had been a bird and deer hunter and extolled the virtue of practice but would rather have luck on his side. It was only later on as I became more intimate with calibers and rifles and hunts that ended well or otherwise that I realized what he meant. I have in me what he had and what so many others have, too—the ability to create one ragged, hairy hole in a target at distance or cleanly kill a beast with a single shot. So in the end I, too, would rather be lucky, but I train and practice and study to ensure my bullet will fly true.

Robert A. Sadowski
East Haddam, CT
January 2014

Once again, to Deborah whom I love.

Introduction

Where the circles of the competitive rifle, hunting rifle, and military service rifle intersect is the area where the precision rifle lives. Since the days of the Springfield trapdoor rifle, service men have brought military service rifles into hunting camps. Military rifles like the Krag–Jørgensen, 1903 Springfield, and today's AR-15 have been transformed to do the work of a hunting rifle. Those same military rifles are also used in competitive shooting. Service rifle matches see the use of AR-15s, M1 Garands, and M14s. But while military service rifles provide good accuracy, in times of need (like during the Vietnam War), Winchester Model 70 hunting rifles mounted with scopes—grabbed off sporting goods store shelves—were used as makeshift sniper rifles.

In the early days of our nation, the rifle (more than likely a Kentucky, Tennessee, or Pennsylvania longrifle unless there was a musket liberated from one of King George's troops) was used to put food on the table and protect one's family. It was also the instrument through which our militia conducted our revolution. In times of peace, that same rifle gave the winning shooter bragging rights at turkey shoots and other informal contests. The longrifle was purpose–built by European immigrants to better fit the scenario offered by North America. A true student of longrifles can identify where and who built a rifle by knowing the caliber, lock work, and other details.

Since those early longrifles, firearms producers have been making improvements to every aspect of the rifle.

Better, heavier barrels; stocks built out of non-warping synthetic material rather than wood; triggers that break like that—I hate to say it—mythical glass rod. Optics and cartridge design has kept up with rifle development. Bullets that slip through the air with minimal friction. If they had taught ballistics in science class and trajectory in math class, I would have paid more attention. Optics that easily allow a talented shooter to hit a target at 500 or more yards.

Long range shooting in America is as old as this country is young. Shooters have always had a fascination with shooting at distance whether they are plinkers, competitive shooters, or hunters. The ability to place rifle bullets in the same hole of a target or kill an animal quickly are goals we all share. In recent years the interest in tactical precision rifles has increased with many factory and custom rifle makers plying their skills producing rifles that can easily outperform the ability of many shooters. This "Shooter's Bible Guide" will help new and experienced shooters make smart equipment purchases ranging from rifles and optics to ammunition and gear.

I thought I knew a thing or two about precision tactical rifles but writing this book has deepened my understanding of the nuances of rifles, optics, and ammunition. I know more today than I did when I started and as equipment evolves, I hope to evolve with it. I am forever a student of the rifle.

Acknowledgments

The author wishes to acknowledge the help from the following people and companies. Edwin Parry of Black Hart Long Arms, Michael Haugen from Remington Defense, Vin Bagalia from BML Tool, Doug Wicklund Senior Curator at the NRA NationalFirearms Museum, Gunsite Academy for images of the late Jeff Cooper, Eduardo Abril de Fontcuberta for his keen sniping experience, Stu Stoyanovich, and Neil Delmonico form Brooklyn Trading Post. I also need to thank some of the websites like dragunov.net and snipercentral.com for their insight and use of their data. All the custom gun builders for their help with images and specs and incessant questions, and all the factory built rifle companies especially Tom Dodge of Mitchell's Mausers, Bill Dermody of Savage, Kathy McQueen of SIG Sauer, and Uberti; optics manufacturers especially Bushnell, Hi-Lux Optics, Pat Mundy of Leopold, Reinhard Seipp and Shannon Jackson of Meopta, Kyle Brown of Nightforce Optics, Nikon, Dean Capuano of Swarovski, Leica, and John Williams III and George Syrengelas of U.S. Optics; ammunition manufacturers especially Hornady and Norma; and finally all the gear manufacturers especially Lou Schwiebert of Ballisticard Systems, BlackHawk!, Larry Weeks of Brownells, Dewey Rods, Do All Targets, Tony Gimmellie at Impact Data Books, Lenspen, LouAnn Robinson of Mildot Enterprises, Otis Technology and Traditions Performance Arms. Thanks to Harris Publications, a version of "Accurate-Mag's Multi-Caliber Rifle Chassis System" and ".300 Norma Magnum and .338 Norma Magnum" appeared in *Special Weapons for Military and Police*; a version of "America's Last Bolt-Action Combat Rifle: M1903A3 Springfield" appeared in *Military Surplus*; and a version of "Savage Arms Model 25 Lightweight Varminter-T" appeared in *Gun Annual*. A version of "Ideal Tool: Reloading Like the Buffalo Hunters"and "6.5 Creedmoor" are reprinted from *GunHunter Magazine* courtesy of Buckmasters LTD. Versions of "Ballistic Reticle Rifle Scopes," "Range Finder Binocular," and "Laser Range Finders" appeared in *Gun-Tests*.

1. Top 10 Long-Range Rifles

Precision Rifles of Historical Significance

A long-range rifle needs to be extremely accurate at distance, give consistent accuracy, and be reliable no matter the environment—humid jungle heat, corrosive sea water, dry grit of desert, or icy cold mountain. Over the centuries these weapons have evolved, adapting to environments and user needs. At times the line blurs between hunting rifles and sniper rifles, which illustrates how intrinsically entwined the two rifle types are and reaffirms their mission to kill, be it man or beast. It would be ignorant not to consider the influence rifle target shooting competition has had on the evolution of long-range rifles. Target shooters from the Creedmoor days to benchrest shooters of a generation ago have had an impact on rifle design from barrels and stocks to triggers and optics. Here is a countdown of the top 10 most significant and noteworthy long-range rifles in the last 300 years.

#10: Pennsylvania Longrifle

The Pennsylvania Longrifle is truly an American form of artistry, craftsmanship, and technology. Significant not only for the extended range it afforded its user, but also because it served both hunter and soldier. In centuries past as wars ramped up, a sniper rifle was merely a hunting rifle called into military service. This was true during the American Revolution, in World War I, as well as the Vietnam War.

When colonists arrived in the original 13 Colonies in the 1700s, experienced gunsmiths were among those new settlers from the old world. These gunsmiths were mainly from Germany, many were Moravians who had settled in Germany and then left to avoid religious oppression. They settled in Lancaster County, Pennsylvania, and later along the Appalachian Mountains in places like Kentucky, Tennessee, the Carolinas, and elsewhere. The rifles they had built in Europe were not well-suited for America and these gunsmiths would go on to make a new type of rifle specifically built for this new land and unique to the region he lived in. Mass production had not yet been imagined nor invented. Each longrifle was uniquely created and therefore recognizable as having been built in Kentucky, Pennsylvania, Tennessee, or another state. The *Foxfire Book* series (a series on Appalachian living) describes gunsmiths

▲ The heritage of the Pennsylvania Longrifle can be seen in this example of a *Jäger* rifle handcrafted by Edwin Parry of Black Hart Long Arms. Note the short barrel and wood patch box, which are characteristics of the *Jäger*. Courtesy of Black Hart Long Arms.

from that era as excellent craftsmen "required to be a master in tool making, ironworking, and blacksmithing, and the high arts of fine relief sculpture and inlay." It was the time when every item in your home, and even your home itself, was hand built. There were no corner markets or big box department stores.

In Europe these gunsmiths built rifles known commonly as a *Jäger* or *Yaeger,* which literally translates to "hunter." These were stout hunting rifles that featured a heavy, short barrel in a large caliber, wooden patch box, and raised cheekpiece. The evolution from the *Jäger* to the longrifle happened over decades to emerge by the late 1770s. Gunsmiths in Lancaster and elsewhere coaxed metal with the forge, hammer, and anvil to build a new rifle with distinct features. It differed from the *Jäger* by using a long barrel bored in smaller calibers that typically ranged from .32 to .45. It also had a slender, graceful stock of native curly maple that stretched to the muzzle. The patch boxes were made of metal. Often the locks were from England but later American gunsmiths began producing their own flintlock mechanisms. The rifles were decorated to an extent that matched the buyer's budget. Inlays, carvings, and engravings adorned many rifles, yet these beautiful weapons were technological marvels of the time. Not only did they have form, they had function.

▲ This is a Parry replica of a John Bonewitz rifle. Bonewitz was one of the very best gunsmiths in Reading, Pennsylvania, and this is an excellent example of a Pennsylvania Longrifle. Courtesy of Black Hart Long Arms.

▲ This Parry rifle was inspired by the famous 1793 Herman Rupp rifle. Rupp's use of wire inlay, raised patchbox lid, and curved buttstock make this Pennsylvania Longrifle distinctive. Courtesy of Black Hart Long Arms.

The design changes suited the American landscape of the time. A small-caliber weapon used less lead and powder, rare commodities on the frontier. Pennsylvania Longrifles were quite capable of taking small game—squirrel, rabbit, raccoon—as well as big game, ranging from deer and black bear to elk. The shooting distances in America also dictated that a rifle needed the long-range accuracy and power that the smaller calibers provided. The ignition system was a flintlock, where a piece of flint kept in the jaws of the hammer struck a frizzen to unleash a shower of sparks that ignited a small charge of black powder in a pan. A touch hole bored through the barrel allowed the powder in the pan to reach the large powder charge in the breech and ignite and fire a lead ball swathed in a cotton fabric patch. There is a discernible delay when the trigger is pulled and the bullet fires.

The rifle, along with some of its users, is ingrained in American folklore. Daniel Boone called his Longrifle "Tick-Licker," probably because he could shoot a tick off a deer's hide. Some speculate that Boone carried a *Jäger*-style rifle early on but he ended up with one of the best rifles of the day in the Pennsylvania Longrifle.

The colonists' rifles also proved to be valuable tools that offered extended range over the British army's smoothbore muskets. During the American Revolution, Morgan's Riflemen (under the command of Virginian Daniel Morgan) skirmished with British troops, sniping at them with rifles while out of range of the British army's smoothbore muskets. Previous encounters with other foes, like the indigenous tribes and enemies in the French and Indian War, had taught the colonists how to fight an overwhelming force with only a few.

The rifled barrels allowed shooters to accurately hit targets out to 200 yards. Smoothbore muskets were common weapons of the time and in use by militaries across the globe, with an effective range of less than 100 yards. The advantage of a rifled weapon over a smoothbore weapon is obvious. Sniping redcoats from behind trees and over stone walls proved to be an effective tactic. Davy Crockett and his fellow Texans held off a massive attack by the Mexican army at what is now San Antonio, Texas. During the Battle of the Alamo some 189 Texans fought about 1800 Mexican troops in a 13-day siege. In the end, most of the Texans were dead and some 600 Mexican troops were killed or wounded. Davy Crockett and his comrades used Longrifles.

As technology advanced, the percussion ignition system replaced flintlocks and many Longrifles were retrofitted with a percussion lock. As America expanded and moved farther west America's rifle evolved again as needs changed. The Hawken brothers of Missouri built a shorter, larger caliber rifle to handle the larger game encountered in the west, namely buffalo and grizzly bears. By the 1900s, cartridge guns had become the norm and Longrifles were hung up over fireplaces as a reminder of the old days.

Since the eighteenth century it is fair to say that the craft of building longrifles never really stopped. The trade was

▲ This is an example of a plain Tennessee-style Longrifle built by Parry with a curly ash stock and inlaid with ivory escutcheons. The iron hardware is browned. Courtesy of Black Hart Long Arms.

passed down from generations in small rural pockets of the Appalachians and elsewhere. True handcrafted longrifles are organic, formed of iron from mountain ore, forged in heat from local coal, and mated with native hardwood found in the region. Italian manufacturers like Pedersoli produce replicas that are mass-produced and provide a good example of a Pennsylvania Longrifle but true longrifles were custom ordered and built by hand. The buyer negotiated with the gunsmith and agreed on the rifle's features and price—lock, stock, and barrel. A handful of gunsmiths today produce stunning and quite functional rifles. One such gun builder is Edwin Parry of Eastford, Connecticut. At his shop, Black Hart Long Arms (blackhart-

▲ This is an award-winning copy of a 1787 Peter Neihart rifle stocked in a rare piece of "rope" figure cherry with carving similar to other eastern Pennsylvania schools such as Christians' Spring and Lehigh Valley. The patch box and wire inlay style is considered a forerunner of the Herman Rupp rifles. Courtesy of Black Hart Long Arms.

longarms.com), Parry has been building longrifles to customer specifications for over 30 years. His rifles have won numerous awards. To Parry it is a marriage of metal and steel. Typically Parry crafts about 12 rifles a year following the style of the Pennsylvania Longrifle originally made from 1740 to 1840 by master gunsmiths in Pennsylvania like J.P. Beck, Adam Ernest, Frederick Sell, and others. He also has made rifles in the manner of Connecticut gunsmiths like Benoni and Medad Hills. As fine a rifle as they are to look at, Parry still hunts with a rifle he made over 15 years ago.

▲ A Parry reproduction of a J.P. Beck rifle with a 46-inch barrel produced this group. Courtesy of Black Hart Long Arms.

Specifications	Longrifle
Manufacturer	Numerous gunsmiths
In Service	1700–1900
Caliber	.32–.45 (most common)
Magazine Capacity	None, single shot
Action	Flintlock (most common), percussion lock
OA Length	54 in.–70 in.
Barrel Length	32 in.–48 in.
Weight (unloaded)	7 lbs.–10 lbs.
Effective Range	200 yds.

#9: Sharps Model 1874

If the Pennsylvania Longrifle was the hunting rifle brought into military service, then the Sharps was the military rifle that became coveted by hunters, frontiersmen, and target shooters for its accuracy and power. The Sharps Model 1874 was America's first high-power cartridge rifle but it had its beginnings in the black powder era when most rifles were loaded from the muzzle. It was one of the first United States military rifles that successfully transitioned from the battlefield to hunters' camps just like the Springfield Trapdoor (a Sharps contemporary), as well as the Krag–Jørgensen, Springfield 1903, and AR-15 over the years. The Sharps was also one of the few rifle designs that successfully made the jump from percussion ignition to metallic cartridges.

The goal of Christian Sharps and his business partners was to build a sturdy, reliable rifle for the military and procure a lucrative government contract. They really had no idea that the rifle would become ensconced in the American lexicon as the "Buffalo Rifle," nor did they imagine the feats of accuracy these rifles would accomplish in the hands of target shooters.

Breechloaders made great sense from a military standpoint as they allowed troops to stay close to the ground or hidden behind cover during a reload. A muzzle-loading rifle is loaded muzzle first, necessitating the user to stand during the reloading process and thus exposing himself to enemy fire. The breechloader was not a new design in the mid-1800s, but Sharps developed a breechloader that improved the design and impressed the United States military. A percussion ignition system, in which a percussion cap is used to ignite a charge of black powder to fire the bullet, was used on Sharps models prior to the Model 1874. Sharps models like the 1851, 1852, 1853, 1855, 1859, and others progressed through design changes that laid the groundwork for the 1874. The Model 1874 actually came out in 1871. Frank Sellers, in his excellent book, *Sharps Firearms*, speculates the model name might have been used to commemorate the reorganization of the Sharps Company not the actual first production date.

▼ A Winslow Homer illustration from *Harper's Weekly* depicting a Union solider, one of "Berdan's Sharpshooters," using an optic equipped Sharps.

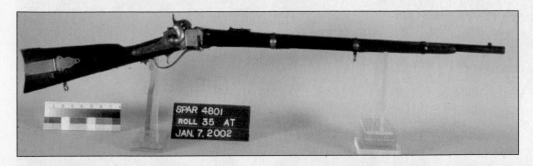

▲ A military Sharps breech-loading rifle manufactured in Hartford, Connecticut, chambered in .52 caliber and using a paper cartridge. Courtesy Springfield Armory National Historic Site.

▲ A buffalo hunter could easy kill up to 250 bison in one day. The hides were the main reason for the market scale hunting.

During the Civil War, Union marksmen under the command of Hiram Berdan employed percussion Sharps rifles with deadly results on Confederate troops. Some of these rifles were equipped with a high-tech piece of equipment—a telescopic sight. These nineteenth century snipers became known as "Berdan's Sharpshooters" and showed that breech-loading weapons equipped with optics could lay down a withering amount of precision firepower. Where a smoothbore musket commonly used by both sides during the conflict had a rate of fire of four shots per minute, the Sharps could fire eight to ten rounds per minute. A carbine version of the Sharps was used by both sides during the Civil War and it was known as a reliable weapon. The rifles proved to the military that breech-loading rifles were safe, reliable, and effective.

After the war, the US Army had about 50,000 Sharps percussion rifles and carbines in inventory or in use, and many of these were converted to use what was then another

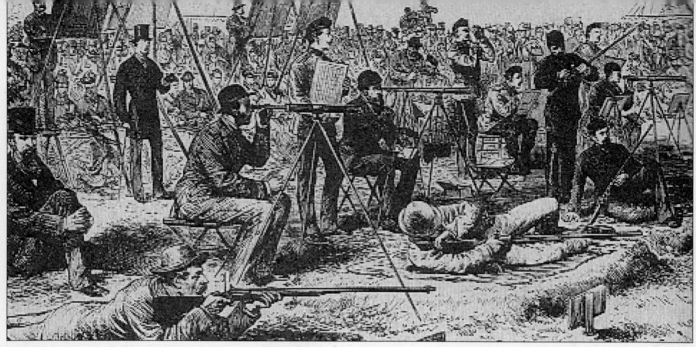

▲ At the Creedmoor shooting range on Long Island, New York, shooters came to test their marksmanship skills out to one thousand yards. Note the position of shooter, lying on his side with the barrel of his rifle resting on his leg.

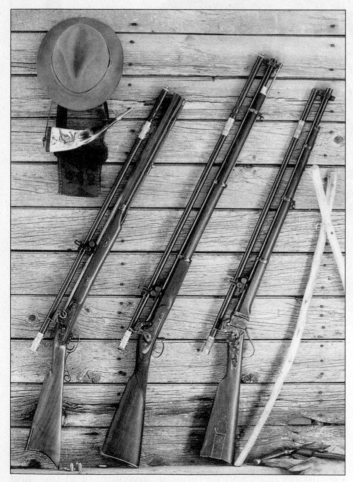

▲ These 6x power rifle scopes are manufactured by Hi-Lux Optics and are reproductions of vintage William Malcolm scopes. Malcolm started making scopes in 1840. Courtesy Hi-Lux Optics.

high-tech development—metallic cartridges. Sharps were "REPAIRED and ALTERED for Metallic Cartridges" according to labels shipped with the weapons to the US Ordnance Department. The .54-caliber percussion rifles and carbines were converted to handle .50/70 cartridges. At this time there was also a dearth of military orders, so the Sharps Company focused on the civilian market.

The Model 1874 won high favor with the shooting public partly due to soldiers returning to civilian life who were familiar with other Sharps models and the fact that Sharps rifles could take down big beasts at long range. The Sharps was also highly regarded as accurate long-range rifles with competitive target shooters. The Model 1874 was not a conversion gun but a new one designed to fire metallic cartridges. The operating mechanism on the Model 1874 is known as a falling block. As a lever is pulled downward the breechblock drops or falls down exposing the chamber and allowing the user to load or unload the rifle.

Model 1874s could be customized with features per the buyer's request. Everything from the stock, finish, barrel length, caliber, locks, trigger assemblies, sights, and butt plates to just about everything else could be custom ordered. According to Sellers, "The Sharps Model 1874 was made in many variations and most of the variations had their own sub variations." There were some twelve model variants of Sharps Model 1874, including a Sporting, Long-Range, Creedmoor, Mid-Range, Business, Military, Express, and Carbine, among others. Keeping track

▲ Bison hunting today is like it was back in the old west. A heavy caliber is needed to bring the giant beast down. Here a Hi-Lux Malcolm is mounted to a Sharps. Courtesy Hi-Lux Optics.

of the variations between these rifles has filled books. Of note are design changes for models built in Hartford, Connecticut, and those built in Bridgeport, Connecticut. Caliber choices included .40, .44, .45, and .50, and chamber lengths were specified. In Mike Venturino's very informative book, *Shooting Buffalo Rifles of the Old West*, he helps decipher black powder cartridge specs as they were used by buffalo hunters. "In their day cartridges were referred to most often by the much more specific method of giving their bore size and case length. How much powder the round carried varied enormously." The most common calibers for the Sporting Rifle were .44/77 and .45/70, which we shooters today understand as the ".44" referring to the bore diameter and the "77" referring to the amount of black powder charge. Buffalo hunters of the day knew the .44/77 as the .44 2-¼; a .44-caliber bullet and a 2-¼-inch chamber.

By the late 19th century Eli Whitney, among others, had created a production line process where parts were machine made then handfitted by skilled gunsmiths.

The Sharps were manufactured in factories, unlike the Pennsylvania Longrifle hand-crafted in small shops. They were in no way mass produced by today's standards, but many thousands of Model 1874s were manufactured for hunters and target shooters.

The Sharps and the term "Big Fifty" are closely associated with a Sharps Model 1874 chambered in .50 caliber. The two calibers that gave the Sharps the nickname "Big Fifty" were the .50/70 (1-¾-inch case) and the .50/90 (2-½-inch case). The rifle and caliber are closely associated with buffalo—actually bison— hunting and buffalo hunters for good reason as it was the most popular and most used rifle with the hunters. The Remington Rolling Block played second fiddle to the Model 1874. Sharps rifles in the hands of skilled hunters decimated the buffalo population. The desire back east for buffalo hides led to market hunters killing the beasts on an unprecedented scale. The Sharps proved an efficient instrument of choice for those hunters who nearly killed the buffalo herds to extinction. By the mid-1880s there were a few hundred bison remaining from herds that had once stretched as far as the eye could see.

According to Sellers, "in the early period of buffalo hunting, the .44/75 2-¼ inch and .50/70 Government cartridges were widely used." Bigger and heavier calibers were also used but Sellers notes that as the hunters moved away from Kansas and Nebraska and experimented with different loads, the herds became more wary and put more distance between themselves and the hunters. As a result, some calibers saw a decline in favor of others. Sellers notes "that the .44 caliber would shoot better at one thousand yards than the .50 would at six hundred." By 1884 the bison hunting had ended.

In the early 1870s on Long Island, New York, long-range black powder shooting competitions took place at the Creedmoor range. This was the predecessor to the Palma Matches of today. Typical matches at Creedmoor consisted of targets placed at extended ranges of 800, 900, and 1,000 yards. These matches were fired with no rests and no optics. Bull's-eyes on targets at these ranges were three feet square and originally the bull's-eye was an actual square; only later was the bull's-eye changed to a circle. As a target rifle the Sharps excelled and a rivalry developed betwen Sharps and Remington as to which was the better rifle. The Ballard and Maynard rifles were two of the other rifle makers at the time. The breechloaders also competed against old-school muzzle-loaders. John Browning's Model 1885 rifle manufactured by Winchester was designed to appeal to these long-range rifle shooters.

In the late 1870s Sharps introduced the Model 1878, which had a hammerless design. However, hunters were becoming more interested in repeating rifles like the Winchester Model 1876, which competed with the Sharps in power but completely trounced it with fast follow-up shots. Long-range shooting competitions became less popular, too.

Today building Sharps rifles is a niche business for a few Italian companies like Uberti and Davide Pedersoli, while some small American manufacturers like Shiloh Sharps and C. Sharps Arms Inc., both located in Montana, build reproductions of the grand old rifles used in black powder cartridge target shooting competitions. Today the rivalry among the Remington, Sharps, and Browning Model 1885 continues.

Specifications	Sharps Model 1874
Manufacturer	Sharps Rifle Manufacturing
In Service	1871–1882
Caliber	.40, .44, .45, .50
Magazine Capacity	None, single shot
Action	Falling block
OA Length	38.3 in. (Carbine model)–54.9 in. (Sporting model)
Barrel Length	21-½ in. (Carbine model)–36 in. (Sporting model)
Weight (unloaded)	7 lbs.–25 lbs.
Effective Range	1000 yds.

#8: Mauser Gewehr 98 Sniper

That strip of land between the Franco-British and opposing German forces was known as no man's land. Desolate and deadly, this area held the remains of villages and farms caught between the battling armies. The land was treeless, pockmarked with craters from artillery shells, and tangled with miles of toothy barbed wire. This is where the twentieth-century sniper was created. The *Scharfschützen,* or sharpshooter, was the Imperial German Army's solution to the entrenched conflict in the winter of 1914–1915. In Peter R. Senich's well-written book, *The German Sniper: 1914–1945,* he reveals how the Germans quickly grasped the importance and advantage of rifles mounted with optic sights: "The ability for the telescopic sights to function in subdued light was the principle reason for their adoption by the Germany army at this time." The rifles were only given to those soldiers who were excellent marksmen and acquainted with the outdoors. More than likely, they were hunters skilled in stalking and concealment. When the Germans first fielded the scoped rifles, the British and French at first attributed the resulting casualties to stray bullets and erratic fire. When the Allies discovered scoped rifles among captured Germans, they soon realized the Germans had changed the game.

In the beginning, the Germans issued hunting rifles with scopes, but soon realized hunting rifles could not hold up under the rigor of trench warfare. Regular army soldiers were issued the standard Model 98 rifles, also referred to as the Gewehr 98, G98, Gew 98, or M98. The Mauser was known as an excellent battle rifle; in fact, the rifle was a

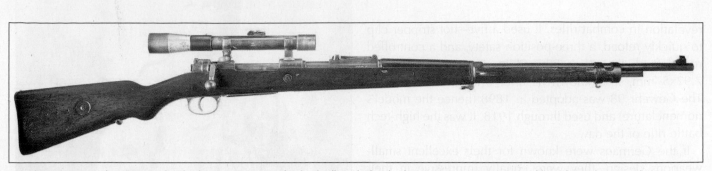

▲ The Mauser Gewehr 98 mounted with a hunting optic proved to be deadly in the hands of WWI German snipers. Most soldiers chosen for sniper duty were hunters and outdoorsmen.

▲ Here is a rare image of a German sniper during WWI about to ply his craft.

▲ German spotters take a step back as the shooter takes aim at the enemy during WWI.

revelation in combat rifles. It used a five-shot stripper clip to quickly reload, a three-position safety, and a controlled round feed. It was chambered in a potent caliber, the 7.92x57mm, also known as 8mm Mauser or 8x57mm. The Gewehr 98 was adopted in 1898 (hence the model's nomenclature) and used through 1918. It was the high-tech battle rifle of the day.

If the Germans were known for their excellent small-weapons design, they were equally impressive in their optics-manufacturing capabilities. According to Senich, the *Scharfschützen-Gewehr98* was a G98 mounted with a 3x or 4x power hunting scope. Modifications to the G98 included a turned down bolt handle to clear the scope. The standard G98 used a straight bolt. A clearance notch was cut in the rifle's stock to accommodate the turned down bolt handle. The new sniper rifle used optics from various scope manufacturers—Zeiss, Hensoldt, Goerz, Voigtländer, Busch, R. Fuess, and others—and as there was no specification at the time, mounting methods used by armorers varied. The Gewehr 98 Sniper is noteworthy as an excellent example of one of the first military bolt-action combat rifles to be modified as a dedicated sniper weapon. If the Germans were the first, the British and Americans were close behind.

The British in WWI were armed with the No. 1 Short Magazine Lee-Enfield (SMLE) Mk III rifle. It was an excellent combat rifle, but unlike the Mauser, the SMLE had a ten-round detachable box magazine. Sniper versions of the SMLE were typically mounted with a 2x power PPCo (Periscopic Prism Company LTD) scope that was calibrated to the trajectory of the .303 MkVII round. In American military ranks, the Springfield 1903 was called into sniper service. The M1903A4a was the US Military's first effort at

▲ Sergeant H. A. Marshall of the Sniper Section, the Calgary Highlanders, was instrumental in providing training to troops. He holds a SMLE Mk III sniper rifle. Courtesy Springfield Armory National Historic Site.

building a dedicated sniper rifle by replacing iron sights with a Weaver Model 330 scope on Redfield mounts. The M1903A4 was used by the Army and Marines from WWII through the Korean War.

By the end of World War I, most militaries forgot about sniper rifles and sniper training. The Soviet Union, what is today Russia, was one of the only countries to remember the impact snipers and sniper rifles had on combat. However, when World War II began, German sniper training recommenced and the rifle chosen for the task was the 98K, a variant of the G98.

▼ The Springfield Model 1903A4 was also a compromise sniper rifle taking the Model 1903 rifle and modifying it with an optical sight. Courtesy Springfield Armory National Historic Site.

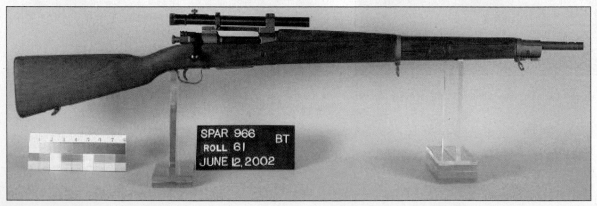

SPAR 966 BT
ROLL 61
JUNE 12, 2002

Specifications	Mauser Gewehr 98 Sniper
Manufacturer	Various
In Service	1915–1918
Caliber	7.92x57mm (also known as 8mm Mauser)
Magazine Capacity	5
Action	Bolt
OA Length	49.2 in.
Barrel Length	29.15 in.
Weight (unloaded)	9 lbs.
Effective Range	300 m (328 yds.)

#7: Mosin–Nagant Model 1891/30 PU

It is noteworthy that the Mosin–Nagant Model 1891/30 rifle was designed in 1891 and is still in service today. A look at the front page of *The New York Times* during the summer of 2013 showed a Syrian rebel using a Mosin–Nagant rifle

▲ The Mosin–Nagant M91/30 PU sniper rifle has been in constant military service since 1932. Note the bent bolt handle to allow scope clearance. Courtesy Mitchell's Mausers.

with a forward mounted scout-style scope. The design is old but very reliable and durable. Some thirty-seven million rifles have been built in the Soviet Union/Russia.

The rifle was adopted with what was then a new cartridge—the 7.62x54Rmm. This is one of the last rimmed cartridges still in military use. The Russian Army still uses the round in the Dragunov and SVD semiautomatic sniper rifles. Think of the 7.62x54Rmm cartridge as the Russian equivalent of the .30-06 cartridge. They are both old-school cartridges designed over one hundred years ago that use a .30-caliber bullet. The performance of the 7.62x54Rmm is comparable to the .308 Winchester. The 7.62x54Rmm originally came in a 210-grain round-nose bullet but the 7N1 sniper load uses a 151.2-grain boat-tail FMJ projectile with an air pocket, a steel core, and lead in the base. Sniper bullets have been modified over the years but most keep the bullet weight at 151.2 grains.

If the Mauser defined the bolt-action rifle then the Mosin–Nagant Model 1891 set the benchmark for longevity and adaptability. Numerous variations of the M91 were built from carbines to the M91/30 PU sniper.

When World War II broke out, Germany, the United Kingdom, and the United States scrambled to procure sniper rifles. The US military reissued the Springfield 1903A4. The Soviets, on the other hand, knew that precision rifle fire could turn a battle. The M91/30 was the standard issue rifle to Soviet troops. In 1932 the M91/30 was converted to a sniper rifle by modifying the standard 91/30 with a fixed, 4x power PE or PEM scope, a Soviet copy of a Zeiss design. Eventually the rifle was designated the 91/30 PU, which used a fixed 3.5x power PU scope. Like the German Mauser, British SMLE, and American Springfield, this rifle was a compromise that used a proven

▲ Across the Eastern Front during WWII, Russian snipers equipped with M91/30 PU rifles raised havoc with German forces.

▲ The Soviet Union deployed many female snipers during WWII, realizing that women made excellent snipers due to their patience.

battle rifle with a telescopic sight. The bolt handle on the Mosin–Nagant needed to be bent to avoid interfering with the PU scope.

The Russian city Volgograd (formerly Stalingrad) saw the effectiveness of the M91/30 PU in late August of 1942. The city was between the German army and the oil-rich region in southern Russia, and the Germans needed oil to fuel their war machine. Thus Stalingrad would turn out to be one of the decisive battles of the war. The *Luftwaffe* pummeled the city, turning it into rubble. As the *Wehrmacht* moved in, the fighting turned to close quarter combat, building by building, street by street. By November the Germans had pushed the Soviet defenders to the Volga River but the Soviets counterattacked. The combat was what we call today urban warfare, but at the time fighting like this had never been encountered before.

Both men and women were Soviet snipers. Armed with the M91/30 PU, these snipers provided troops with long-distance suppressive fire and took out high-value targets such as German officers. During the Battle of Stalingrad, the sniping prowess of Soviet shooter Vasily Zaytsev was used by the Soviet propaganda machine to raise morale among troops. As the (possibly apocryphal) story goes, the Germans were not to be outdone by the Soviets. Erwin König was sent to Stalingrad by the Germans to kill Zaytsev. The sniper-on-sniper battle was fought like a game of lethal chess in the ruined city. Checkmate was declared by Zaytsev after a long period of stalking his opponent. He killed König with a single shot from his Mosin–Nagant M91/30 PU. The Battle of Stalingrad was a turning point in World War II with Mosin–Nagant in the hands of Soviet snipers.

Specifications	Mosin–Nagant Model 91/30 PU
Manufacturer	Various
In Service	1930–Present
Caliber	7.62x54R
Magazine Capacity	5
Action	Bolt
OA Length	48.45 in.
Barrel Length	28.75 in.
Weight (unloaded)	9.7 lbs.
Effective Range	800 m (731 yds.)

#6: Winchester Model 70

Soldiers returning to civilian life after the Spanish-American War took Krag–Jørgensen bolt-action rifles to deer camp. The Krag, as it was commonly known, was not the best combat rifle but the .30-40 cartridge proved to be a good deer cartridge. By the end of World War I, American soldiers were accustomed to bolt-action rifles. The M1917 Enfield and, to a lesser extent in the Great War, the Springfield M1903, had proved their worth in reliability and accuracy, along with the stopping power of the .30-06 Springfield cartridge. The .30-06, commonly called "thirty-aught-six" or "thirty-oh-six," would become the most popular centerfire cartridge with American big game hunters. Countless Springfield M1903s were sporterized and made into hunting rifles. Both the Krag and the Springfield are good examples of a military rifle adapted for civilian life. By the early 1920s, the bolt-action rifle had a permanent place in the hands of hunters and target shooters.

In 1925, Winchester was the first American firearms company to come out with a successful bolt-action rifle for the civilian market, the Model 54. It used a Mauser-type action and three-position safety. It was expensive to produce and not well-suited for optics, which were becoming increasing popular on rifles. Winchester modified the design and in 1936 introduced the Model 70. The Model 70 proved to be extremely popular with hunters and target shooters and was a tremendous success for Winchester. It would be referred to as the "rifleman's rifle," becoming iconic around the world.

The Model 70 offered a quality rifle that most American hunters aspired to own. It used a controlled round feed system similar to a Mauser, a three-position safety, hand-cut checkering, and a machined floorplate, among other features. Over the years the Model 70 went through numerous design modifications and they

▲ The Winchester Model 70 is the "rifleman's rifle," and pre-'64 models are highly valued by collectors.

THE NATIONAL HIGH POWER RIFLE MATCHES
AT CAMP PERRY WILL PROVE IT AGAIN...

WINNERS COUNT ON *WINCHESTER*
TRADE-MARK

Shown is the Model 70 Heavy
Weight rifle. Model 70's also are available
in Standard Weight and Bull Gun grades. All
have a Marksman stock. Action and barrel
of Winchester Proof-Steel. Standard Weight
available in 30-06. Heavy Weight in 243
and 30-06. Bull Gun in 30-06
or 300 H&H Magnum.

Whenever it's "Commence Firing" for the country's greatest shots you see firing-line proof of their faith in Winchester.

At Camp Perry, at all Regional big bore matches, and wherever shooters demand the rifle that will help them deliver their top performance, you'll find that overwhelming choice is a Winchester Model 70 target rifle. The fact that it is the finest bolt action center fire rifle made anywhere in the world today makes the Model 70 the consistent and logical choice for big bore target shooting. In all positions, at all ranges, its feel, handling qualities, accuracy and smoothness of action make the great Model 70 the rifle of champions.

Next time you go to a large match, make one test. When the shooting is over, look for the competitors with satisfied expressions — chances are that most of them will be carrying a Model 70 target rifle.

▲ As a target rifle, the Model 70 was built with a heavy barrel and target sights. It excelled at long-range rifle competitions.

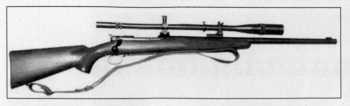

▲ With a reproduction Unertl 8x power scope mounted to it the Model 70 in .30-06 is a dead ringer for the sniper rifles used by USMC snipers during the Vietnam War. Courtesy of Hi-Lux Optics.

are generally grouped into three types: pre-'64, push feed, and current manufacture. The push-feed type was an attempt at making the rifle more cost-effective to build. The controlled feed was replaced with push feed. The rifle lost some of its allure as a push-feed rifle and Winchester eventually returned to the controlled-feed system. The Model 70 always had a high price point and faced with competition from other manufactures it saw sales decline. In 2006 the manufacturing plant in New Haven, Connecticut, closed. Since 2012 FN Herstal began building the Model 70 again in a facility in Columbia, South Carolina.

The Model 70 has been chambered in calibers that run from those used to tackle small ground rodents like prairie dogs to large, bone-busting calibers for pachyderms in Africa. It is still available in a popular Featherweight model, as well as Safari Express, Sporter, Super Grade, and others.

Gun writers like Jack O'Connor evangelized the Model 70 in the pages of *Outdoor Life* and numerous books. O'Connor's exploits with the Model 70 chambered in .270 Winchester are legendary, especially his tales about sheep hunting. In *The Art of Hunting Big Game in North America*, O'Connor says ". . . whenever I go out for the noble rams I'll take one of a matched pair of Model 70 Winchester featherweights in .270 caliber." O'Connor used a Redfield Bear Cub 4x scope on one and a Leupold 4x on the other. He could take shots out to 400 yards with these setups.

At long-range rifle matches like those held at Camp Perry many shooters used heavy-barrel Model 70s set up with target sights. Target models were known for their accuracy, smooth action, and consistent performance, with MOA and sub-MOA accuracy achieved.

Like the German Army during World War I, the Marines called upon a hunting rifle for combat service in World War II. The Marines had purchased some 373 Model 70 rifles for training but called the rifles into service in the Pacific Theater during World War II and later for the duration of the Korean War. They were chambered in .30-06 with 24-inch, hunting-style taper barrel. After Korea, many of the rifles were reconditioned and modified with a heavier barrel. The stocks were also bedded to free float the barrel and aid in accuracy. A Unertl 8x power scope, the high-tech optic of the day, was typically mounted on the Model 70s. During the Vietnam War these reconditioned Model 70s were issued to snipers, such as Marine Gunnery Sergeant Carlos Hathcock. Hathcock used a Model 70 to kill a North Vietnamese sniper in a legendary shot. He killed the enemy sniper by shooting him in the eye through the scope of the enemy sniper's Mosin–Nagant rifle. The US Army also utilized Model 70s during the Vietnam War, but the Remington Model 700 ousted the Model 70 in the military by the end of the Vietnam War.

Today the Model 70 uses the classic Pre-'64 controlled-feed, three-position safety, free-floated barrels. A new MOA trigger offers zero creep, no take up, and no over travel. Some models sport synthetic stocks with stainless steel receivers and barrels. Versions specifically set for varmint hunting to dangerous game. The Model 70 has come full circle: returning to the classic design, being manufactured by American craftsmen, and regaining its reputation as the rifleman's rifle.

▲ Circa the 1960s, US Marine Gunnery Sergeant Carlos Hathcock takes aim with a Unertl-equipped Model 70 during the Vietnam War. Courtesy Hi-Lux Optics.

Specifications	Winchester Model 70
Manufacturer	Winchester Repeating Arms Company, US Repeating Arms, FNH (current)
In Service	1936–1963 (Pre '64) 1964–2006 (push-feed/classic) 2008–present
Caliber	.22-250 Swift, .220 Swift, .243 Win., .257 Roberts, .25-06 Win., .264 Win. Mag., .270 Win., 7mm-08, 7mm WSM, .308 Win., .30-06, .300 Win. Mag., .300 WSM, .325 WSM, .338 Win. Mag., .375 H&H Mag., .416 Rem., .458 Win. Mag. (current catalogued calibers)
Magazine Capacity	3 (magnum calibers) 4 (larger calibers) 5 (standard calibers)
Action	Bolt
OA Length	39.5 in. (20-in. barrel), 42.75 in. (22-in. barrel), 44.37 in. (24-in. barrel), 46.37 in. (26-in. barrel)
Barrel Length	20, 22, 24, or 26 in.
Weight (unloaded)	6 lbs.–8 lbs. (depending on caliber and barrel length)
Effective Range	400 yds. (depending on caliber)

▲ The M24 was designed by the US Army to be a dedicated sniper rifle and was adopted by the Army in 1988. Courtesy Remington Defense.

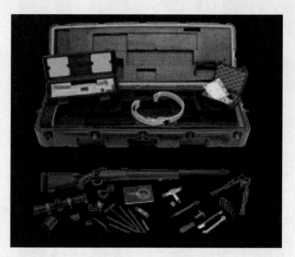

▲ The M24 is a Sniper Weapon System (SWS), which means numerous accessories like a Leupold scope, tools, spares, Harris bipod, hard case, and sling are included with the rifle. Courtesy Remington Defense.

#5: M24 Sniper Weapon System (SWS)

In 1962 Remington introduced the Model 700 bolt-action rifle. Since then more than five million Model 700s have been built in some forty calibers ranging from .17 Remington to the .458 Winchester Magnum. The Model 700 has an exceptionally strong action with "three rings of steel," as Remington advertisements touted. The first ring is the bolt face, which is recessed to enclose the base of the cartridge. The second ring is the chamber end of the barrel that surrounds the bolt face. The third is the front receiver ring, which in turn surrounds the chamber end of the barrel. It uses a two-lug bolt with a push-feed system.

With a reputation as an accurate rifle that is reliable and safe, the Model 700 is the most popular centerfire rifle with hunters across the United States. For long-range target shooters the Model 700 is a very popular platform. The Model 700 receiver is easier to accurize than Mauser-style actions. Countless competition shooters have used Model 700-based rifles to win matches.

When the US Army decided to create a dedicated sniper rifle they used the civilian Model 700 action as the platform. Eventually it would be designated the M24 SWS (Sniper Weapon System) when it was adopted by the Army in 1988. It is referred to as a Sniper Weapon System because numerous accessories like the Leupold scope, tools, Harris bipod, and sling are included. The M24 is significant because the US Army built it from the onset

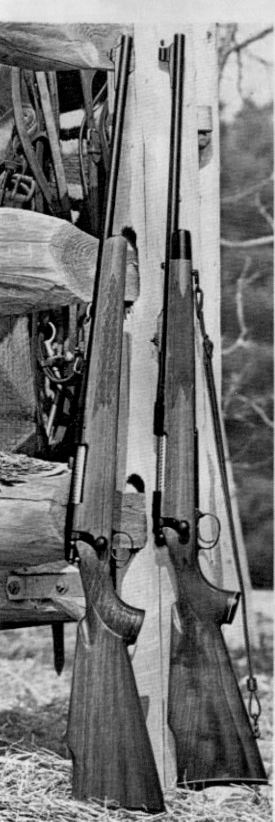

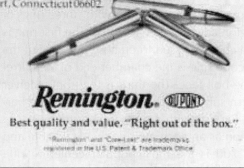
▲ The Remington Model 700 touted its "out-of-the-box" accuracy in an ad from the 1980s.

▲ The business end of the M24 shows the crowned muzzle. This particular M24 looks as if it has had hard use. Courtesy Remington Defense.

◄ An M24 is a maneuverable weapon, making it easy to use in tight places like this hide under an evergreen. Courtesy Remington Defense.

▲ A sniper takes aim from a rooftop somewhere in the recent past in the Middle East. Note the duct tape on the stock comb. The XM2010 has a fully adjustable cheekpiece. Courtesy Remington Defense.

▲ Operators have come to appreciate the M24 as a reliable rifle with an effective range to eight hundred meters. Courtesy Remington Defense.

as a sniper rifle. It was not a combat rifle reconfigured for sniping.

The M24 starts with a long-action Model 700 receiver, since the rifle was originally going to use .30-06 Springfield ammunition. The rifle's development was fast-tracked and, as the story goes, there was not enough .30-06 ammo of the same lot in Army storage to test the rifle. The decision was made to chamber the rifle in 7.62x51mm NATO (.308 Winchester), but the design remained the same.

There was not time to retool for a short-action rifle. The thought, too, was the rifle could be retrofitted in a caliber the same length as the .30-06 such as the .300 Winchester Magnum. Some fifteen thousand M24s have been built by Remington Arms to Army specifications. The M24 will most likely be replaced with the XM2010 Enhanced Sniper Rifle, but the M24 continued to be fielded.

The heart of the M24 is a Remington Model 700. The M24 shares many attributes with its civilian counterpart in terms of design. However, the M24 undergoes a significant number of quality checks and controls; plus the M24 uses a number of special components like the stock, barrel, trigger, and floor plate. The 24-inch barrel is made of 416R stainless steel with a twist rate of 1:11.2 and five radial land grooves. The stock is made by HS Precision using polymer foam reinforced with fiberglass, carbon fiber, and Kevlar. The length of pull is adjustable via a wheel with a lock ring. An aluminum bedding block is used to secure the stock to the barreled action. The bedding block provides rigidity while the forend free floats the barrel.

Each component of the rifle is inspected for conformance to the specifications and each assembled rifle is inspected for completeness of build. Rifles are "proofed" then targeted to ensure that they meet the accuracy standard. The specification the Army requires for performance is stated in MIL-R-71126(AR) that "the rifle and day optical sight shall withstand a 10,000 rounds endurance test. The rifle shall be capable of firing 10,000 rounds without the receiver requiring overhaul." The spec further dictates the type of accuracy required:

Range	Average Mean Radius (AMR)
200 yd.	1.3 in.
300 yd.	1.9 in.
200 m.	1.4 in.

The service life of an M24 barrel greatly depends on how the rifle is used and maintained. The Army specifies that the barrel is worn out when the average mean radius of five targets of ten shots exceeds the values listed below:

Range	Average Mean Radius (AMR)
200 yd.	2.6 in.
300 yd.	3.8 in.
200 m.	2.8 in.

The M24 system uses a Leupold Mark 4 LR/T 10x40mm (30mm) M3 fixed-power scope with a mil-dot reticle. At the time the M24 was being developed in the late 1980s variable power optics were inconsistent and problematic. Additionally there was a historical mistrust by snipers of variable power optics based on the experience with the ART series optics used on the M21 system. There were

problems with the loss of zero when the power was changed, internal breakage during hard use, and inability to seal the optic due to moving parts. Therefore, the new Leupold Mark 4 M3A Ultra was selected for the M24 and subsequently proved to be an exceptionally robust and capable optic. Detachable BUIS (Back-Up Iron Sights) can be attached to sight bases that are fixed at the muzzle end of the barrel and on the receiver.

The longest confirmed kill with the M24 was by US Army Staff Sergeant Jim Gilliland in 2005 during the Iraq War in the city of Ramadi. The distance was 1,367 yards. The M24 has served well and proven its capability in the worst conditions. There is no doubt the rifle is appreciated by users.

Specifications	M24 SWS
Manufacturer	Remington Arms
In Service	1988–present
Caliber	7.62x51mm NATO
Magazine Capacity	5
Action	Bolt
OA Length	43 in.
Barrel Length	24 in.
Weight (loaded with optic)	7.3 lbs.
Effective Range	800 m (875 yds.)

#4: Dragunov SVD

Officially the SVD-63 rifle is called *Snayperskaya Vintovka sistem'y Dragunova obraz'tsa 1963 goda*, which translates to "Sniper Rifle, System of Dragunov, Model of the Year 1963." For short it is called the Dragunov SVD, SVD, or the Dragunov after its designer, Yevgeny Dragunov.

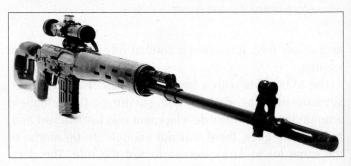

▲ The semiautomatic Dragunov SVD was introduced in 1963 as a squad support weapon, not specifically as a sniper rifle. It is still in widespread use by many militaries. Courtesy dragunov.net.

▲ The complete kit for the SVD includes a bayonet which is an odd feature to be built into a long-range rifle. Courtesy dragunov.net.

▲ A competitor takes aim with an SVD variant during team competition at a sniper match held outside of Moscow. Photo by Vitaly Kuzmin.

It is a semiautomatic rifle that can pull double duty either as a sniper or designated marksman rifle. The Dragunov was not originally designed as a sniper rifle but as a squad support weapon and has a bayonet lug—a distinct feature not found on sniper rifles. It also has adjustable iron sights that can be used in conjunction with or in lieu of optics.

The SVD may look like an AK-type weapon but it is a wholly different design than the AK-47 and AK-74 variants designed by Mikhail Kalashnikov. The SVD was designed to have similar controls—like the safety and selector levers and charging handle—to an AK platform so operator training time would be short and make an easier transition for a soldier familiar with the AK assault rifle.

The Dragunov uses a rotating three-lug bolt and a short-stroke gas system where a series of separate pistons in the gas system push the bolt carrier to the rear when fired. It also has a manual two-position gas regulator. The receiver is machined and has a removable trigger assembly. No

parts, not even the rear sight leaf, will interchange with an AK rifle. Internally the AK and SVD are ditinctly different.

A detachable 10-round, double stack magazine is used with the SVD and is chambered in 7.62x54mmR. This cartridge has similar performance as the 7.62x51mm NATO (.308 Winchester). Compared to other sniper rifles, the SVD has a thin barrel to reduce weight. The barrel is free-floated; it is connected to the handguard but moves with the barrel when the weapon is fired. A two-stage trigger with a short pull and weight is used. The stock was originally constructed of wood using a two-piece hand-guard and a skeletonized, thumbhole buttstock with a detachable cheekpiece rest. Current models use polymer furniture.

Standard equipment is a quick-detachable PSO-1 4x power telescopic sight that has a passive infrared-detection capability. The illuminated reticle has range-finding ability and the elevation knob has bullet drop compensation built in. Maximum range is out to 1,300 meters.

The current load for the SVD is 7N14 ammunition, which was designed in 1999 specifically for the SVD. It uses a 151-grain bullet that has a sharp, steel core. The SVD also chews through conventional military ammo. The maximum rate of fire is about 30 rpm (rounds per minute), which means the SVD can lay down suppressive fire.

Most former Warsaw Pact countries, like Albania, Bulgaria, Hungary, Poland, and Ukraine, among many others, use a variant of the SVD. It is a widespread weapon. Wherever one might encounter an AK, more than likely the SVD is around as well. The military in China licensed

▲ Sniper training exercises at the 467th Guards District Training Moscow-Tartu Red Centre located in the Kovrov Vladimir region of Russia. Photo by Vitaly Kuzmin.

production of the SVD and called it the Type 79 and Type 85. United States and coalitions troops have encountered the SVD in use by insurgent groups in Afghanistan and Iraq. The SVD and its variants have been used in conflicts beginning with the Vietnam War, the Soviet War in Afghanistan, the Gulf War, Chechnya, the war in Afghanistan, the Iraq War, and present day in Syrian Civil War.

Specifications	Dragunov
Manufacturer	Izhmash in Russia (originally)
In Service	1963–present
Caliber	7.62x54mmR
Magazine Capacity	10-round detachable
Action	Semiauto, gas-operated, rotating bolt
OA Length	48.2 in.
Barrel Length	24.4 in.
Weight (with unloaded magazine and scope)	9.48 lbs.
Effective Range	800 m (875 yds.)

#3: M21

During World War II, General George S. Patton called the semiautomatic M1 Garand "the greatest battle implement ever devised." The M14 that replaced the M1 Garand in 1959 and was anything but great. Officially called the United States Rifle, 7.62 mm, M14, it addressed some of the M1 Garand's limitations, like the fixed magazine and the telltale pinging sound that told the user—and the user's combatant—the clip was ejected and the rifle was empty. The M14 used a detachable box magazine. The piston system in the M1 needed frequent cleaning, but the M14's piston system was more robust. It was also slightly lighter and used the 7.62x51mm NATO (.308 Winchester) cartridge, which has less recoil than the M1's .30-06 cartridge.

As the way warfare was conducted changed, the selective fire M14 proved not to be the right rifle. In semiautomatic mode it was a pleasure to shoot, but in full automatic mode it was uncontrollable. The war in Vietnam showed the M14 to be too long and heavy for close jungle fighting. The wood stock swelled in the humid environment, knocking the weapon out of zero. A fiberglass stock

was a temporary fix, but the real solution was the M16 rifle, which was lighter, had less recoil, and was better suited to the close to mid-range combat encountered in Vietnam. What many grunts or soldiers of the day appreciated about the M14 was its utter reliability, accuracy, and knockdown power. The M14 was standard-issue from 1959 to 1970, making it the American combat rifle with the shortest service life; it may have faded out of memory if it were not needed by the US Army in Vietnam in 1969 for a specific mission.

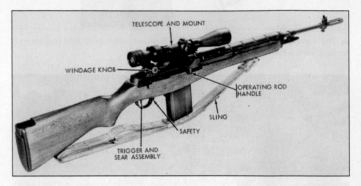

▲ The XM21 used a National Match Barrel for accuracy, original wood stock, and a high magnification scope. Courtesy Springfield Armory National Historic Site.

▲ The M14 platform is reliable and accurate and is still used by competitive shooters in service rifle class matches. Courtesy of Civilian Marksmanship Program.

The Army required a sniper rifle, and the military once again chose a combat rifle and modified it for sniper use. The M14 turned out to be a better sniper rifle than combat rifle. It was accurate, reliable, and provided a fast follow-up shot. The Rock Island Arsenal modified national match M14s with a Leatherwood 3-9x power scope and the new weapon was designated the XM21.

When the wood stock was replaced, the sniper rifle was renamed the M21. The M14-based sniper rifles like the XM21 and M21 use a rotating bolt operated by a gas piston. When a round is fired, gas from the round is siphoned from the barrel and used to move the piston. The XM21 is fitted with a national match barrel, which is heavier than a standard issue barrel and is match grade for better accuracy.

The Leatherwood optic in service during the Vietnam War used an Adjustable Ranging Telescope (ART) system that combines a rangefinding reticle with an adjustable cam built in. The scope automatically computes the bullet trajectory as the target is ranged, so the shooter only has to aim at the target dead-on with no holdover.

The US Army sniper with the most confirmed kills during the Vietnam War was Staff Sergeant Adelbert Waldron. Waldron used an XM21 to rack up 109 confirmed kills. The M21 was also used during the Invasion of Grenada in 1983. The bolt-action M24 replaced the M21.

The M25 is similar to the M21, but the M25 was built in a joint venture between the US Army Special Forces and the US Navy SEALs to produce a sniper rifle in late 1980s. The M25 uses an M14 national match action and barrel, McMillan fiberglass stock, and fixed- or variable-power scope. Since about 1991 the M25 has been in service and has seen action during the Gulf Wars and in Afghanistan and Iraq.

Newer variants on this design include the Enhanced Battle Rifle (EBR) used by the Army and the Marine's M39 Enhanced Marksman's Rifle (EMR). These rifles use the guts of an M21/M25 placed on a new chassis with a pistol grip and adjustable buttstock. With the increased use of body armor, the M21/M25 fiberglass stocks did not fit shooters comfortably. The EBR is fitted with a Leupold 3.5–10x power optic while the EMR uses a Schmidt & Bender M8541 Scout Sniper Day Scope, giving users the ability to engage targets out to eight hundred meters.

▲ Hi-Lux Optics makes an updated replica of the famed Leatherwood ART scope. The magnification zoom ring is actually fitted to a cam to achieve ranging without holdover. Courtesy Hi-Lux Optics.

▲ US soldiers in the Gulf War, Afghanistan, and Iraq have relied on the M21 for precision firepower. Courtesy Springfield Armory National Historic Site.

▲ Here a spotter and shooter team use an M25. Note the lightweight Harris bipod attached to the rifle. Courtesy Springfield Armory National Historic Site.

The M14 platform will most likely be replaced with an AR-style platform similar to the SOCOM Mk 11 Mod 0, or the M14 may continue its run.

Specifications	M21
Manufacturer	Springfield Armory, Rock Island Arsenal
In Service	1969–present
Caliber	7.62x51mm NATO
Magazine Capacity	5-, 10-, or 20-round detachable box
Action	Semiautomatic
OA Length	44 in.
Barrel Length	22 in.
Weight (unloaded)	11.6 lbs.
Effective Range	900 yds.

#2: L118A1

Accuracy International (AI) was formed in 1978 with one purpose: to design and build the best sniper rifles in the world. Unlike the many tactical rifles developed from hunting rifles, the rifles produced by AI have a history in competition shooting. AI was run by a two-time Olympic gold medalist, the late Malcolm Cooper. He and other international or national target shooters designed and manufactured a variety of tactical rifles. The L118A1 is a variant of the AI AW (Arctic Warfare) rifle system used by the British military. The AW weapon system offers a host of options and configurations. Every component is manufactured from corrosion-resistant material or given a protective finish prior to assembly, ensuring reliable and consistent performance in any environment—marine, desert, or arctic. A barrel can be replaced easily and quickly in the field using a barrel-change kit. All major parts are interchangeable between rifles of the same caliber.

The AW features a bonded action, meaning the flat-bottom, steel action is permanently bonded and bolted to a full-length aluminum chassis, affording rigidity and

▲ The Accuracy International AW rifle is offered in a variety of configurations and is in use in many European and Asian countries.

▲ Royal Marines snipers with L115A1 sniper rifles similar to the weapon used by British soldier, Craig Harrison, to make the longest confirmed sniper kill in combat.

stiffness. Unlike traditional rifles, where a barreled action is bolted to a stock, the aluminum chassis holds the action and barrel, and polymer stocksides encase the aluminum chassis. This construction means the barrel free-floats, and there is no effect on accuracy or zero, even in different climates. Some models offer a folding chassis, allowing the stock to be folded. A two-stage trigger is adjustable for pull weights of 3.3–4.4 pounds. The trigger assembly can be easily removed for maintenance. The AW also features a three-position safety.

AW rifles are typically fitted with a fixed or variable power Schmidt & Bender PM II telescopic sight. In addition to the United Kingdom, an AW variant is used by the militaries of Sweden, Spain, Russia, Italy, Greece, Belgium, and Australia, among other European and Asian countries.

In December 2011, Darrel Evans set three new United Kingdom benchrest records with an AI rifle. Evans used an AW chambered in 6.5x47 Lapua. To make a long story short, he broke the following three UK records: smallest group of the day (1.8 inches at 600 yards); smallest aggregate group (2.8 inches); and smallest aggregate group in the light gun class (2.8 inches). An AI rifle, an L115A3 with a Schmidt & Bender Military MKII 5-25x56mm scope, was used by Craig Harrison in the Blues and Royals RHG/D of the British army when he killed two Taliban insurgents from a distance of 2,474 meters (2,707 yards or 1.54 miles) in November 2009 in Afghanistan. After some calculations, it was determined the .338-caliber bullet took about three seconds to hit the targets, 914 meters (999 yards) beyond the rifle's recommended range. According to Harrison, it took about nine shots for him and his spotter to initially range the target. Then his first shot "on target" killed the first insurgent, and a consecutive shot killed the second enemy combatant. A third shot disabled the machine gun the two were carrying. Guinness World Records certified the record.

Specifications	L118A1
Manufacturer	Accuracy International
In Service	1988–present
Caliber	7.62x51mm NATO
Magazine Capacity	10-round detachable magazine
Action	Bolt, short throw, 60° lift
OA Length	46.5 in.
Barrel Length	26 in.
Weight (unloaded)	14.3 lbs.
Effective Range	1000 m (1100 yds.)

#1: Barrett M82A1

The Barrett M82A1, otherwise known as the M107 in US Army parlance or the M82A3 SASR in USMC speak, harnesses the power of a century-old cartridge in a modern, one-man, portable, shoulder-fired rifle. The .50 BMG was first introduced in 1910 and adopted into military service in 1921 for use in the heavy M2 Browning machine gun. Though other firearms designers have built weapons chambered in .50 BMG, Barrett was able to create a semiautomatic rifle design that was reliable and accurate.

For over two decades the M82A1 design was modified to perform in whichever environmental hell it might encounter—ice, snow, sand, humidity, heat, or seawater. Military agencies around the globe use this light recoiling rifle, which has the ability to deliver precise, rapid fire on targets out to 2,000 meters. The effective range of the M107 is far longer than the M24, XM2010, or M110. The Swedish Army was the first military organization to purchase M82A1 rifles. In 1990 the US Military chose the M82A1 as an anti-material weapon in operations Desert Shield and Desert Storm in Kuwait and Iraq, respectively.

The M82A1 effectively disabled vehicles, parked aircraft, and radar installations, among other high-value targets. In the hands of a sniper this heavy rifle can defeat enemy personnel at ranges where conventional shoulder weapons are ineffective.

Numerous long-range shots have been made with the M82A1. In 2004 during the Iraq War, Sergeant Brian Kremer of the 2nd Ranger Battalion used a Barrett M82A1 to neutralize enemy targets at a range of 2,515 yards. During the War in Afghanistan in 2008, US Army sniper Sergeant Nicholas Ranstad had a kill out to 2,288 yards with a .50-caliber Barrett. The range was 1,765 yards to an enemy machine gunner during Operation Iraqi Freedom in 2004 when USMC sniper Staff Sergeant Steve Reichert engaged and killed the enemy.

In operation the barrel recoils slightly backwards then the rotating bolt takes over and spits out the empty cartridge case and scraps a fresh round from the magazine. Similar to the AR platform, the M82A1 has upper and lower receivers. To mitigate recoil the M107 uses a dual-chamber, detachable muzzle brake. Standard optics include a Leupold 4.5-14x50mm day scope.

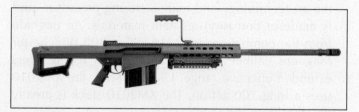

▲ The Barrett M82A1 was a commercial, off-the-shelf, .50 BMG shoulder-fired rifle that was first used by the military when the Swedish Army ordered one hundred rifle systems in 1989.

▲ A US soldier fires the M107; note the empty cartridge case being ejected. Recoil is very tolerable due to the rifle's design. Courtesy of US Army PEO Soldier.

Specifications	M82A1
Manufacturer	Barrett Firearms Manufacturing
In Service	1989–present
Caliber	.50 BMG
Magazine Capacity	10-round detachable box magazine
Action	Semiautomatic, recoil operated, rotating bolt
OA Length	48 in.
Barrel Length	20 in.
Weight (unloaded)	29.7 lbs.
Effective Range	1800 m (1969 yds.)

▲ At about thirty pounds, including the scope and loaded magazine, the M107 is still very maneuverable and easy to reposition. Courtesy of US Army PEO Soldier.

XM2010 Transition Q&A

The US Army has fielded the M24 since 1988, and has since identified the XM2010 rifle as a replacement. The XM2010 was designed and developed specifically for use in harsh environments. It is built using state-of-the-art technology and manufacturing processes, and is made of corrosion-resistant materials. An upgrade from the combat-proven M24 is the .300 Winchester Magnum caliber in the XM2010. This round offers extended effective range. Like the M24, the XM2010 uses a long 700 action. The XM2010 stock is greatly different from the M24's.

The Remington Arms Chassis System (RACS) features a folding stock that allows for adjustment of the length of pull and cheek height and captures the bolt handle when folded. This allows the user to configure his or her weapon to his or her personal physical requirements and transport the system more easily. The chassis also features a monolithic rail with removable rail pieces and cable routing guides to maximize rail insert space, co-align electroptics like day optics and night vision, and manage electric cables. The XM2010 has a five-round detachable box magazine unlike the M24 which an internal box magazine. The complete system includes a Leupold long-range variable powered optic and the Advanced Armament Corp TiTan quick-detach sound suppressor.

Michael Haugen from Remington Defense offered some insight on the transition from M24 to XM2010. Haugen is director of international military/law enforcement sales and holds the rank of CW3(R) in the US Army Special Forces.

Q: How did the performance of M24 influence the XM2010?
MHaugen: Soldiers were emotionally tied to the M24 due to its durability, accuracy, and ease of use. These attributes made the selection of the XM2010 very natural for them and an easy transition.

Q: What separates the M24/XM2010 barrel from other barrels, like those on hunting rifles?
MHaugen: Both the M24 and XM2010 barrels are 416R stainless steel 5R rifled barrels, whereas hunting line rifles typically use chrome-moly rifle barrels. The rifling for the hunting barrels is of conventional design.

Q: What is the barrel life of the M24 versus the XM2010?
MHaugen: For the M24, the barrel is guaranteed for 5,000 rounds; however M24s have been known to go in excess of 10,000 rounds. The XM2010 barrel is capable of firing 2,500 rounds before a degradation in accuracy is evident due to the .300 Winchester Magnum caliber.

Q: What are the differences between a chassis system and traditional stock? Pros/cons of each?

▲ The XM2010 is the slated replacement for the M24. It is more customizable than the M24 and has a farther effect range. Courtesy Remington Defense.

▲ A sniper team (shooter and spotter) exercise the XM2010. Courtesy Remington Defense.

▲ Note how the stock is folded on the XM2010, making the rifle more maneuverable and allowing this sniper to creep into position. Courtesy Remington Defense.

MHaugen: Much of this is opinion-based, but the M24 stock is simple, is easy to use, and withstands a significant amount of abuse; however it is very limited in its ability to be adjusted for different shooters and equipment. The XM2010 is exceptionally versatile and allows adjustment for any/all shooters and their equipment. The folding stock allows for easier carrying, configuring for jump and dive operations, as well as use in and out of vehicles. Additionally, the XM2010 chassis offers the user the ability to mount a wide variety of ancillary equipment in a multitude of locations and orientations.

2. Anatomy of a Bolt-Action Rifle

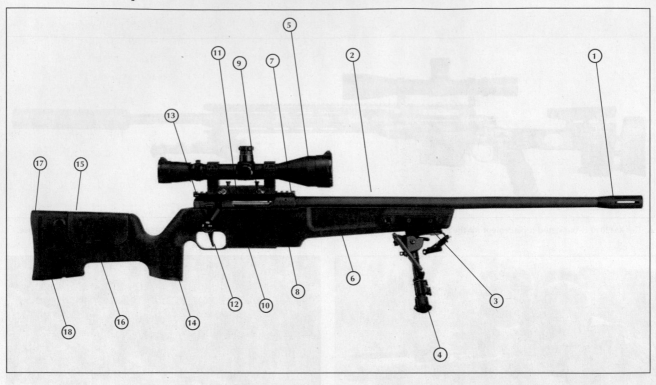

1. Muzzle Device: Modern tactical rifles and many hunting style rifles have a threaded muzzle that allows a user to attach a muzzle brake, flash hider, or a suppressor. Depending on the type of device, a user can expect decreased noise signature, reduced recoil, and lessening of the muzzle flash. In addition to providing sound suppression, attaching a suppressor to a barrel's muzzle actually enhances the performance of the rifle barrel through the dampening of barrel harmonics and the increase of muzzle velocity. Many muzzles are crowned, meaning they have a raised edge that protects the rifle at the end of the bore. Some muzzles are recessed. Either way, the rifling is protected in case the rifle is accidentally dropped muzzle first.

2. Barrel: Barrels on precision rifles are typically thicker than those on hunting rifles. The heavier weight gives the barrel a stiffness that aids in accuracy. Barrel weight is determined by the taper or barrel diameter, and ranges from 1 to 5. A number 5 taper is thick and stout; a number 1 barrel taper indicates a thin skinny barrel, such as may be found on a lightweight hunting rifle. A straight taper refers to the thickness straight from action to muzzle (such as barrels on varmint rifles); the less the taper, the stiffer and the heavier the barrel. Barrels are free-floated, meaning no portion of the barrel actually contacts the stock. Most barrels are made of either steel or stainless steel; some are made with a steel liner wrapped with a carbon fiber to reduce weight. The inside of the barrel or the bore is rifled and there are many types of rifling. Button rifling uses a spiral broach to cut grooves. When a rifle is fired the bullet is force fit into the grooves and is rotated by the grooves. A predetermined rate of twist is measured in a ratio depending on the caliber. For example, a .308 Winchester barrel may have a twist rate of 1:10" RH, which means the bullet makes one complete rotation every ten inches and it has a Right Hand (RH) rotation. Polygonal rifling forms a polygon bore and does not use grooves. Whitworth muzzle-loading rifles used during the Civil War had polygon rifling as did the German MG42 machine gun used in World War II. Rifling known as 5R uses a series of 5 lands in a twist pattern that applies a specific type of radiusing to the way the lands are shaped. This type of rifling does not

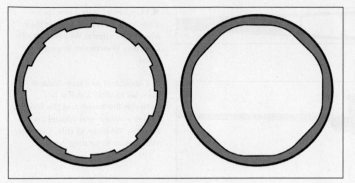

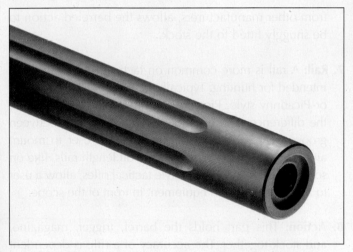

▲ This cross section of a rifle barrel shows two different rifling types; on the left is traditional groove rifling, on the right is polygonal rifling.

▲ Notice the ridge around the muzzle; this protects the rifling. This barrel is also fluted to reduce weight and enhance cooling. Courtesy Remington Arms.

deform bullets as much as grooved rifling. Some barrels are also fluted to help reduce weight and increase the cooling rate of the barrel.

There are several factors that contribute to decreased barrel life. Poor or improper maintenance can significantly contribute to decreased barrel life, including lack of cleaning, use of the wrong chemicals, and neglecting to utilize items such as bore guides. Sniper rifles, being precision instruments, require specific materials and items to properly clean and maintain them. Not using a bore guide with a one-piece rod, or using a stainless steel chamber or bore brush will directly decrease barrel life.

3. **Accessory Rail:** Modern tactical rifles typically have accessory rails that allow a user to attach tactical lights, laser sights, and night vision equipment. These are usually Picatinny or Weaver style and are located over the barrel or on the sides of the stock's forend.

4. **Bipod:** Heavy rifles require support and typically have an extra attachment point for a bipod that allows the users to quickly remove or attach the bipod.

5. **Optic:** An optic is chosen to perform a specific aiming function at a certain distance, whatever the shooter's requirement. The optic should be mounted as low as possible above the bore without the objective lens touching the barrel.

6. **Stock:** Modern precision rifles have stocks that are made of synthetic materials that resist moisture and will not warp in high heat or extreme cold. There are still many manufacturers equipping hunting rifles with traditional wood stocks. Wood can, however, swell and warp making contact with and putting pressure on the barrel, which will then throw off zero and accuracy. Three alternative stock materials are fiberglass, composite, and laminated wood. Some composite stocks are made from a combination of Kevlar and graphite. Weatherby Accumark rifles use composite stocks made by Bell and Carlson which consist of fiberglass, aramid fibers, graphite, epoxy gel coats, and laminating resins to construct very lightweight yet durable stocks. Ruger's GunSite Scout Rifle is an example of a rifle that uses a wood laminate. Wood laminate stocks are heavier than those made of synthetic material but they are strong and have a more traditional look. Fiberglass has been used in military rifles since about 1977 when the US Marines retrofitted their M40 rifles with McMillan stocks and is now the norm in US Marine and Army sniper rifles. Fiberglass stocks are less expensive than composite stocks and just as light and rugged. When a rifle barrel is free floated all material has been removed from the forend and the barrel does not touch the stock. An easy method to determine if a barrel is free floated is to slip a dollar bill between the stock and barrel and run the bill back toward the action. If the bill easily slides all the way back to the action the barrel is free floated.

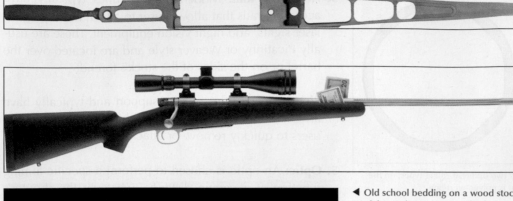

◄ Winchester uses a one-piece aluminum bedding block in their Model 70 Extreme Weather SS rifle. Courtesy Winchester Repeating Arms.

◄ Classic test of a free-floated barrel is to slide a dollar bill between the barrel and the forend. This is a Winchester Model 70 Extreme Weather SS rifle. Courtesy Winchester Repeating Arms.

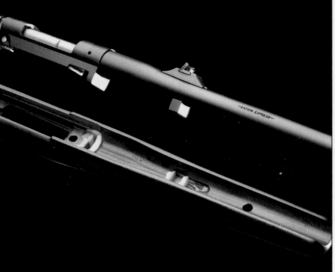

◄ Old school bedding on a wood stock shows the recoil lugs of this Winchester Model 70 Safari Express perfectly mated in the epoxy notches inset in the wood. Courtesy Winchester Repeating Arms.

A free-floated barrel is allowed to vibrate as harmonic waves travel down the barrel when a round is fired. Without any interference from the stock, the barrel is free to move.

Traditionally, bedding meant gouging out the inside of a wood stock, filling it with some sort of synthetic filler like fiberglass, and inserting the barreled action while the fiberglass is still wet. Once set, the action-to-stock fit is close and tight and the action does not move inside the stock when fired (an action that moves inside a stock will have inferior accuracy and a possibility of the stock cracking, especially with severe recoiling calibers). Savage Arms, for example, uses what they call the AccuStock which consists of a rigid rail firmly embedded in the stock throughout the length of the forend and action area of the rifle. This system, like bedding system

from other manufacturers, allows the barreled action to be snuggly fitted to the stock.

7. **Rail:** A rail is more common on tactical rifles than those intended for hunting. Typically the rail is either a Weaver or Picatinny style. Picatinny is MIL-SPEC, Weaver is not; the difference is a few thousandths of an inch between grooves. The grooves in the rail allow a user to mount an optic in a variety of positions. Full length rails, like on some AR rifles and chassis style tactical rifles, allow a user to attach night vision equipment in front of the scope.

8. **Action:** This part holds the barrel, trigger, magazine, and stock together. The accuracy of a rifle is dependent on the rigidity of the action or receiver. The thicker the receiver, the more rigid it is and the less it will flex when a rifle is fired. In rifles like the SIG SSG 3000, Savage 12 Palma, Steyr SSG 69, and others, the ejection port is small because extra metal is left on the top portion of the receiver and hidden inside the stock, which contributes to the weight of the tactical rifle. Hunting rifles like the Winchester Model 70, Remington Model 700, Sako A7, and others, have less metal which makes them lighter and more desirable in hunting situations. Actions are typically referred to as a short-action or a long-action, depending upon the length of the cartridge used in the action. A short-action can be used with cartridges like the .308 Winchester, .243 Winchester, and 6.5 Creedmoor; a long-action uses cartridge lengths like the .30-06, .300 Winchester Magnum, and 7mm Remington Magnum. Most tactical rifles use a push-feed system as opposed to a Mauser style control-feed system due to

▲ Picatinny style rails are very common on tactical bolt-action rifles. This is a Remington Model VTR. Courtesy Remington Arms.

▲ This is a front view of a Kimber action showing the bolt fully forward with locking lugs engaged. Courtesy Kimber.

the ease of manufacturing. Push feed systems are also proven to work well without the added components found in a Mauser style system. "Tuning the action" is a term used by gunsmiths to describe machining the action to ensure that the front of the action is exactly parallel as well as the recoil lug and barrel shoulders. This ensures that when the barrel is installed, it is completely bearing on the recoil lug and the lug on the action.

9. Bolt: The bolt encases the firing pin assembly and rams a cartridge into the chamber and withdraws and ejects the fired cartridge case. The two main types of bolt-actions are controlled feed and push feed actions. In a controlled-round action the cartridge is grasped by the bolt's claw-type extractor as soon as the bolt pushes the cartridge forward from the magazine and into the chamber. In a pushfeed action the round is not held by the extractor as it exits the magazine and enters the chamber. The controlled feed actions can be found in current rifles by CZ, Kimber, Ruger, Winchester (current models), and others. Push feed actions are used in rifles by Remington, Steyr, Weatherby, Savage, Howa, and Mossberg among others.

10. Magazine: Modern bolt-action rifles have two types of magazines, a detachable box magazine that can be removed from the rifle and a fixed or internal box magazine that is fixed to the rifle. A fixed box magazine is loaded with a stripper clip like the K98k, Springfield

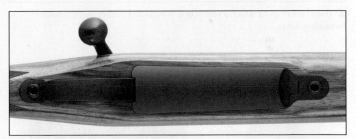

▲ This Dakota 97 Custom has an internal box magazine with a floorplate. Courtesy Dakota Arms.

▲ This is another Dakota Model 97 Custom with a blind box magazine. Courtesy Dakota Arms.

1903, and other military rifles, or each cartridge is loaded one by one as in a Winchester Model 70 and other hunting rifles. The fixed box magazine consists of two types, a blind box and a floorplate. The Howa Hogue Heavy Barrel Varminter is an example of a rifle with a fixed magazine. The other type of magazine is a detachable box magazine, utilized by rifles such as the SIG SSG 3000, for example. Detachable magazine kits are available for Howa rifles that replace the fixed magazine with either a 5-round or 10-round detachable box.

11. Optic Mount: The rings hold a rifle scope above the action and are attached to the receiver via a mount, also referred to as a base or bases. Many hunting rifles have either one- or two-piece basepieces. The base is screwed to the action's receiver and the rings

▲ These are rings in which a rifle scope is mounted. Courtesy Winchester Repeating Arms.

▲ This is an example of two-piece bases. Courtesy Winchester Repeating Arms.

▲ This is an example of one-piece base. Courtesy Winchester Repeating Arms.

are attached to the base. The mounts are as important as the optic is; they must be strong, simple, and robust.

12. Trigger: A trigger can be viewed by three characteristics: weight of pull, overtravel, and creep. Weight of pull is defined as the amount of pressure, measured in pounds and ounces, to make the trigger break and release the sear and allow the firing pin to hit the cartridge primer. This process is called lock time—the time when the sear releases the firing pin and the primer is ignited. In most precision rifles the trigger can be adjusted by the user. Competition rifles can be very light and measured in ounces, while hunting and tactical work rifles are higher and are set at between 4 to 5 pounds. A light trigger is not a good idea when hunting in cold climates where gloves are worn. With a cold, numb trigger finger a light trigger pull weight may mean accidentally firing the rifle before proper sight alignment. Overtravel is the distance the trigger travels after it breaks. Too much overtravel can impact shot follow-through and accuracy. On many precision rifles, overtravel can be adjusted. Creep is the movement of the trigger before it breaks. Military rifles have what is called a two-stage trigger where the first stage is initial take-up of the trigger which takes minimal trigger pressure. The second stage requires more trigger pressure to fire the weapon. A good trigger will have no creep and the pressure to fire the weapon will be crisp. Many times a good trigger—with no creep—is known to break like a glass rod. Try different triggers out and you will soon understand why triggers are so important to rifle accuracy.

13. Bolt Knob: The bolt knob is used to cycle the action. The size, shape, and texture of the knob varies with manufacturers. Tactical rifles typically have larger knobs.

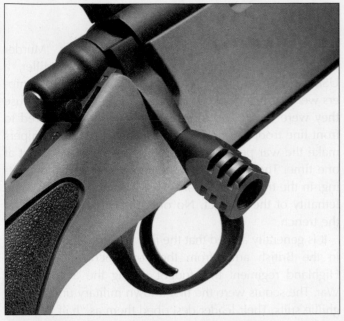

▲ The Remington Model 700 VTR is a tactical style knob that's large and knarly. Courtesy Remington Arms.

▲ The Kimber Model 84 knob takes a traditional hunting style, it is smaller and smooth. Courtesy Kimber.

14. Pistol Grip: More contemporary tactical rifle designs incorporate a pistol grip style. This grip of an M40A3 is more vertical compared to the grip of the M24, which is more traditional. The vertical grip provides better ergonomics in a variety of shooting positions and places less stress on the shooter's wrist.

15. Comb: The comb is where the shooter's cheek rests on the stock. The term "cheek weld" is used to describe the contact between a shooter's cheek and the stock. Since each shooter's stature and facial structure is different, as well as the size of optics mounted on the weapon, many manufacturers build in an adjustable comb, like on the Savage 11/111 Long Range Hunter. The adjustable comb allows shooters to customize the stock for their specific needs.

16. Butt Hook: The butt hook has a dual purpose for either riding sandbags or controlling the rifle with the non-trigger hand.

17. Butt Pad: The butt pad fits into the shooter's shoulder. It is contoured and typically made of a soft, flexible material to help absorb the recoil of the rifle when fired.

18. Buttstock: The buttstock on most rifles is fixed, creating a length of pull (LOP) the distance from the trigger to the end of the buttstock, buttpad, or recoil pad. The buttstock is measured in inches and varies slightly from rifle to rifle, and manufacturers tend to make the LOP fit most shooters' stature. Typical LOP is slightly over thirteen inches.

3. A Brief History of Military Snipers

Marksmanship, Fieldcraft, and Tactics

❝ It was the ultimate hunting trip: a man hunting another man who was hunting me," is how Charles Mawhinney described his experience as a sniper. Mawhinney holds the record for the most confirmed kills by a USMC sniper during the Vietnam War. "Don't talk to me about hunting lions or elephants; they don't fight back with rifles and scopes," he told the *Los Angeles Times* in 2000. In the simplest terms, a sniper is a hunter.

Most believe that King Richard was the first kill by a sniper in 1199. King Richard was hit with a bolt fired from a crossbow by a solider hidden in the ramparts of a castle under siege in France. Though there are centuries between a soldier in mail and armor firing a crossbow to a ghillie-suited solider with a .338 Lapua bolt-action rifle, the incident is a perfect example of how snipers operate. They are skilled marksmen using stealth to get close to, identify, and take out the high value target. Snipers have been treated over the centuries as a necessary evil.

THE WAR IN THE TRANSVAAL: THE BOERS' METHOD OF FIGHTING.—SEE PAGE 192.

▲ Lovat Scouts in the Second Boer War (1899–1902) were described as "half wolf and half jackrabbit" who lived by the credo "He who shoots and runs away, lives to shoot another day."

Regular grunts at times referred to snipers as "Murder Incorporated" according to accounts by Jim Miller, a USMC sniper during the Vietnam War. It's ironic that snipers were, at first, looked on with a bit of disdain because they were better and more efficient killers compared to front line troops. More than likely it was because snipers make the war personal, carefully aiming at one target at one time. The effect snipers have on morale is devastating. In the trenches of World War I, snipers increased the lethality of the conflict. No one dared lift his head over the trench.

It is generally agreed that the first sniper unit was formed in the British army from the Lovat Scouts, a Scottish Highland regiment that fought during the Second Boer War. The scouts were the first known military unit to wear ghillie suits. Their leader described them as "half wolf and half jackrabbit."

As sniping was given more credence in military circles and snipers were viewed as valuable tools in war, some common characteristics emerged in individuals best suited for the role. Not only do snipers excel in marksmanship, most had hunted when they were civilians. They were patient and calculating, waiting for the precise opportunity to fire a bullet. In his informative book, *The Ultimate Sniper*, John Paster identifies three components of military sniping: marksmanship, fieldcraft, and tactics. This is the basic skill set needed for an individual to excel at the craft of sniping. It is what hunters do naturally.

Today's sniper is viewed as integral to combat tactics. There are still those snipers who grew up learning the fundamentals by hunting rabbits and squirrels and navigating open, untamed areas with ease. They are also highly trained in camouflage, navigation, infiltration, reconnaissance, and observation. They typically work in pairs of one spotter and one sniper, operating independently or supporting a larger combat force. The sniper credo of "one shot, one kill" could not be more appropriate.

Here is a brief look at distinguished military snipers from past and recent history.

Name: Timothy Murphy
Confirmed Kills: Unknown
Date: 1777
Conflict: American Revolution

As a member of Daniel Morgan's Sharpshooter Corps, Timothy Murphy was one of five hundred handpicked men to travel to upstate New York to respond to the push from British troops. During the second Battle of Saratoga—two battles raged eighteen days apart—Morgan called on Murphy who is reported to have pointed out British General Fraser rallying British troops, and said: "That gallant officer is General Fraser. I admire him, but it is necessary that he should die, do your duty." Murphy was born in the Delaware Gap region and most likely used a Pennsylvania Longrifle handcrafted from that area of the colonies. Climbing a tree, Murphy fired from 300 yards away. On the third shot Fraser went down.

Name: Truman Head, a.k.a. "California Joe"
Confirmed Kills: Unknown
Date: 1861–1862
Conflict: American Civil War

Colonel Hiram Berdan commanded the 1st and 2nd US Sharpshooters who are reputed to have killed more Confederate soldiers than any other unit in the Union Army. Berdan armed his men with breech-loading, .52 caliber Sharps rifles. To be accepted into the Sharpshooters a candidate had to supposedly shoot ten consecutive shots at an average of five inches from the bull's-eye at 600 feet. Berdan himself could walk the talk and was an excellent marksman. A story is told that Berdan could score repeated head shots at life-size drawings of Confederate President Jefferson Davis from 200 yards. Truman Head, a hunter, was an old timer who enlisted. Head had travelled west from New York state to find his fortune but returned

▲ Hiram Berdan organized the 1st and 2nd US Sharpshooters in late November of 1861.

east, hence the nickname "California Joe." The Union needed good press to boost morale and latched upon California Joe who had a keen aim and was good fodder for newspaper stories. When California Joe's eyes started to fail him he was discharged, but not after helping to make Berdan's Sharpshooters legendary.

Name: John W. Hinson, a.k.a. "Old Jack"
Confirmed Kills: 100
Date: 1861–1862
Conflict: American Civil War

War has a way of making neutral parties take a side. When John Hinson's sons were suspected by Union troops as Confederate guerrillas and executed, Hinson took sides

▲ California Joe was a storied sniper in the Union Army during the Civil War.

shortly afterward and targeted Union troops using a .50-caliber Kentucky Longrifle with a 41-inch barrel. He owned the land and water along the Tennessee River and the Cumberland River and is alleged to have killed as many as 100 Union troops.

Name: Benjamin Powell
Confirmed Kills: unknown
Date: 1861–1862
Conflict: American Civil War

Union General John Sedwick's last words were: "What are you dodging for? They couldn't hit an elephant at this distance!" A moment later, Sedwick lay dead on the ground, killed by a sniper some 800 yards away. The place was the Battle of Spotsylvania Court House in May 1864 and Ben Powell is credited with the shot. Powell used a British manufactured .45-caliber Whitworth rifle with a hexagonal rifling. Mounted with a telescopic sight, the Whitworth had an effective range of 1,500 yards.

Name: William Edward "Billy" Sing, a.k.a. "The Assassin" or "The Murderer"
Confirmed Kills: 150
Date: 1914–1918
Conflict: World War I

During the Gallipoli Campaign in World War I, Billy Sing served as a sniper in the Australian Imperial Force. The battle took place on the Gallipoli peninsula of what was then part of the Ottoman Empire (today it is part of Turkey). Sing is credited with at least 150 confirmed kills during that campaign, but may have had over 200 kills in total. Sing plied his trade with a standard issue Lee-Enfield rifle chambered in .303 British. It was his comrades who gave him his nickname due to his great disdain for the enemy. So devastating was Sing's precision fire that the Turks sent out their own sniper who the Allied forces nicknamed "Abdul the Terrible." In the trenches Sing and his spotter noticed the Turkish sniper lying in wait. Sing fired first, killing the sniper and thus ending the duel.

▲ During WWI, Billy Sing had 150 confirmed kills in the Gallipoli Campaign using a standard issue Lee-Enfield, Mk. III rifle with iron sights.

Name: Francis Pegahmagabow, a.k.a. "Peggy"
Confirmed Kills: 378
Date: 1914–1918
Conflict: World War I

Pegahmagabow was a native Canadian who volunteered with the Canadian Expeditionary Force in 1914 and was deployed with the first Canadian troops to fight in Europe. Issued a Canadian-built Ross rifle like other troops, Pegahmagabow saw action during the Second Battle of Ypres where the German Army first used chlo-

▲ Francis "Peggy" Pegahmagabow became the most decorated Native-Canadian soldier for his feats of heroism in "no man's land" during WWI.

▲ A British sniper/scout team takes aim on a target during World War I using a Lee-Enfield rifle outfitted with a scope.

Name: Henry Norwest
Confirmed Kills: 115
Date: 1914–1918
Conflict: World War I

Not only was Canadian soldier Henry Norwest known as a crack shot, he was also recognized for his uncanny ability to blend into the landscape and his stealthy tactics. Norwest used a Ross rifle during his sniping in Europe. He was sent into no man's land to gather intelligence. On August 18, 1918, just three months before World War I ended, he was killed by the German sniper he was stalking.

Name: Simo Häyhä, a.k.a. "White Death"
Confirmed Kills: 542
Date: 1939–1940
Conflict: Winter War

The Winter War was a land grab by the Soviet Union to regain parts of Finland that the Soviet Union considered theirs. On November 30, 1939, three months after the outbreak of World War II, the Soviets attacked Finland with more than three times as many soldiers as the Finns and much more arms and equipment, but Stalin's purge of the officer ranks left the Soviet army weak. The Finns kept the

rine gas on the Western Front. He fought in the Battle of the Somme and was wounded. He acted a scout in no man's land and was nicknamed "Peggy" by fellow soldiers. The battle for the village of Passchendale had become a stalemate when 20,000 Canadian soldiers, Pegahmagabow among them, arrived. Pegahmagabow acted as a runner during the battle, delivering messages from the front lines to the rear to coordinate artillery bombardments. Pegahmagabow became the most decorated Native-Canadian soldier.

▲ Nicknamed "White Death" by the Soviets, Simo Häyhä racked up over 500 kills during the brief Winter War.

▲ Soviet sniper teams clothed in winter camo make their way to their hide through the ruins of a building.

Soviets at bay and Simo Häyhä was part of that effort. Born on a farm and an avid hunter at a young age, Häyhä also participated and excelled in shooting sports. When asked later in life how he had become such a good shot he had a simple, one-word answer: "Practice." The Red Army had planned to roll through Kollaa without much resistance, but the area had few roads and the snowy temperature hovered between -40°F and -4°F. The Finnish Army was maneuverable and fought on skis. Häyhä was able to hide in the snowy terrain clothed in white camouflage garments. Using a Finnish variant of the Mosin–Nagant rifle, the White Guard M/28 with iron sights and chambered in 7.62x54R, he was able to pick off an average of five Soviet soldiers a day. His confirmed total is 542 kills. If the total count is impressive so, too, is the effort. Häyhä accomplished this feat in less than 100 days. The Soviets nicknamed Häyhä "White Death" and unleashed counter-snipers. On March 6, 1940, shortly before peace was declared, Häyhä was shot in the lower left jaw. He recovered but was disfigured.

Name: Ivan Mikhaylovich Sidorenko
Confirmed Kills: 500
Date: 1939–1945
Conflict: World War II

Born a peasant, school dropout Ivan Sidorenko was conscripted into the Soviet Army and taught himself how to be a sniper. He used a Russian-manufactured Mosin–Nagant rifle with an optic and is credited with taking out an enemy tank using incendiary bullets. He was successful hunting enemy

▲ The Germany Army knew the value of deploying snipers in combat in WWII; a lesson they learned during WWI.

▲ A Soviet sharpshooter takes aim with a semiautomatic SVT-38 rifle equipped with a 3.5x PU telescopic sight.

▲ Some 400,000 Gewehr 43 semiautomatic rifles were built between 1943 and 1945, of those about 53 were sniper rifles fitted with ZF 4 4x power telescopic sights.

soldiers during the Battle of Moscow and his superiors assigned him to teach and train other soldiers in the art of sniping. Students were chosen for their eyesight, marksmanship, and endurance. Sidorenko had over 500 confirmed kills and taught over 250 snipers. Wounded while fighting Estonia, Sidorenko was awarded the Hero of the Soviet Union, which barred him from further combat but allowed him to continue training sniper recruits.

Name: Matthäus Hetzenauer
Confirmed Kills: 345
Date: 1939–1945
Conflict: World War II, Eastern Front

Matthäus Hetzenauer saw action against the Soviets on the Eastern Front in Slovakia, the Carpathians, and Hungary.

Hetzenauer is credited with 345 confirmed kills with the longest shot at some 1100 meters. He was an Austrian with the 3rd Mountain Division and received the Knight's Cross of the Iron Cross for bravery. The two rifles Hetzenauer used as a sniper were a Karabiner 98k sniper variant with 6x power telescopic sight and a Gewehr 43 with ZF4 4x power telescopic sight. He often worked with Josef Allerberger inflicting high Soviet body counts.

Name: Josef "Sepp" Allerberger
Confirmed Kills: 257
Date: 1939–1945
Conflict: World War II, Eastern Front

Josef Allerberger, like Matthäus Hetzenauer, was an Austrian and was assigned to II Battalion of the 144th Gebirgsjäger

▲ During World War II a German Army sniper maneuvers into a hide to stifle the Allied advance.

▲ A skilled sniper had an effective range of 1000 meters with the Karabiner 98k equipped with a Zeiss Zielvier telescopic sight.

▲ One of the original Mosin–Nagant 91/30 Sniper Rifles used by Vasily Zaytsev is exhibited in the Museum in Izhevsk, Russia.

▲ In a five-week period Vasily Zaytsev killed 225 German soldiers, including 11 enemy snipers during the Battle of Stalingrad.

Regiment of the 3rd Mountain Division. While recuperating from wounds suffered as a machine gunner, he began experimenting with a captured Soviet Mosin–Nagant M91/30 rifle with a 3.5x power PU telescopic sight. He was sent to sniper training school and was issued a sniper variant of the Karabiner 98k rifle with 4x telescopic sight. While on the Eastern Front, he and Matthäus Hetzenauer did exceeding well harassing the enemy.

Name: Vasily Grigoryevich Zaytsev
Confirmed Kills: 400
Date: 1939–1945
Conflict: World War II, Eastern Front

Vasily Zaytsev grew up in the Ural Mountains and was taught to hunt deer and wolves by his grandfather. He was twelve when he bagged his first trophy wolf. Zaytsev is probably the most well known Soviet sniper of World War II and was awarded Hero of the Soviet Union for his sniping activity during the Battle of Stalingrad. In a five-week period Zaytsev killed 225 German soldiers, including 11 enemy snipers, and was heralded in Soviet propaganda.

Propaganda Machine or Cover Up?

During the Battle of Stalingrad, a duel between a Soviet sniper, Vasily Zaytsev, and a German sniper, Erwin König, supposedly took place over a three-day period in the ruins of the city of Stalingrad. His hide betrayed by a glint from his scope, König was killed by Zaytsev—or so the story goes. The Soviets made Zaytsev into a hero helping Mother Russia defeat the German invaders. There is a scoped rifle in the Central Armed Forces Museum in Moscow that is said to have belonged to König, and Zaytsev specifically mentioned a German named König in his memoirs, yet there is no record of an Erwin König as a sniper in the *Wermacht* being sent to the Eastern Front. The German Army had a reputation for keeping impeccable records. Is this a case of the Soviet propaganda machine fabricating a story to boost morale? Or did the German Army destroy the record of Erwin König to save face? Numerous fictionalized books of the account, including *Enemy at the Gates* and *War of the Rats*, have been written about the duel, but perhaps the secret will remain an urban legend for eternity.

During the Battle of Stalingrad, Zaytsev faced off against a highly decorated German sniper, Erwin König. Zaytsev killed König after an intense game of cat and mouse and their story was memorialized in the book *Enemy At the Gates*, though some believe that the duel between Zaytsev and König never took place. Zaytsev used the standard-issue Mosin–Nagant rifle. One of his methods was to conceal himself, make a few kills, and then change position. Another of Zaytsev's tactics was to cover one large area from three positions, with two men—a sniper and a scout—at each point. The tactic became known as the "sixes" and is still used today.

Name: Lyudmila Mykhailivna Pavlichenko
Confirmed Kills: 309
Date: 1939–1945
Conflict: World War II, Eastern Front

▲ The Soviet Army trained some 2,000 female snipers during WWII since they found they were well suited for the role.

Lyudmila Pavlichenko is regarded as the most successful female sniper in history. As a teenager she joined a shooting club and later earned a master's degree in history, but when Germany invaded the Soviet Union she volunteered and was assigned to the 25th Rifle Division. Pavlichenko became one of 2,000 female snipers in the Soviet Army. She made her first two kills as a sniper near Belyayevka, using an SVT-40 semiautomatic rifle with 3.5x telescopic sight.

Name: Helmut Wirnsberger
Confirmed Kills: 64
Date: 1939–1945
Conflict: World War II, Eastern Front

Another user of the Gewehr 43 sniper variant was Helmut Wirnsberger. As a member of the 3rd Mountain Division on the Eastern Front, Wirnsberger is credited with 64 kills. After being wounded he trained snipers.

Name: John Fulcher
Confirmed Kills: Unknown
Date: 1939–1945
Conflict: World War II, Italy

John Fuller, whose mother was a Native American of the Cherokee nation and father was German-Irish, was a US Army Sergeant. As a recruit, when his drill sergeant asked if he knew how to shoot, Fulcher responded he could shoot an acorn out of the top of an oak tree with a .22.

▲ Soviet sniper Lyudmila Pavlichenko is regarded as the most successful female sniper in history with over 300 kills.

▲ Modern sniper/scout technique was developed during WWI and WWII; here a German team spots a potential Allied target.

That was enough for the sergeant to encourage Fulcher to volunteer for scout/sniper training, according to Charles Sasser and Craig Roberts in *One Shot–One Kill*. Fulcher was issued an M1D and by the end of training could easily hit a target at 500 yards. Landing in Italy with the 36th Division, Fulcher scouted and took out German targets as the Army moved forward. As a sniper squad leader, about half of his guys were Native Americans, two were full-blood Sioux. The group's sniper activity must have sent fear into the German ranks—word was the Germans would execute any US sniper caputred—as Fulcher and his patrol scalped nine German soldiers and neatly sat the dead enemy soldiers in a row with their hands folded on the side of a road.

Name: William E. Jones
Confirmed Kills: Unknown
Date: 1939–1945
Conflict: World War II, Normandy

William Jones referred to the Springfield M1903A4 he was issued as "the rifle." After landing on the beaches of Normandy the fight took to the countryside of France which in some areas was a maze of hedge groves, with walls of foliage separating farm fields like a wall. Jones's job as a US Army sniper was to help unplug the advance of the Allied forces when they became bogged down by German snipers or machine nests cleverly and strategically placed in the hedge groves. Though the M1 Garand was the grunts' rifle, Jones had "the rifle" that could reach out over long distances and help continue the advance inward.

▲ US Marines move across the rugged terrain during the Korean War.

Name: Clifford Shore
Confirmed Kills: Unknown
Date: 1939–1945
Conflict: World War II

Some soldiers shoot, some teach. William Shore was a British soldier who did both. After World War I the U.K. lacked any type of sniper training. All that was learned during World War I was quickly fading from memory. The need for snipers was great but many officers felt snipers gave a bad impression of the military. Shore helped change the minds of the military high ranks and trained snipers during World War II. He wrote the classic *With British Snipers To The Reich*, a how-to manual on sniper craft.

Name: Ian Roberson
Confirmed Kills: Unknown
Date: 1950–1953
Conflict: Korean War

In an interview well after the Korean War, former Australian sniper Ian Roberson recalled events during battle on Hill

614. Roberson had been firing on the hill for a week, "switching them off," as he said of the North Korean soldiers who were at the receiving end of Roberson's .303 British Enfield. After the Australian Army charged for the hill, Roberson determined he had killed 30 soldiers just that morning. "Just one morning," Roberson said. "And I'd been there all week. I got a feeling of horror. I never did the arithmetic. I still don't want to."

Name: Chet Hamilton
Confirmed Kills: Unknown
Date: 1950–1953
Conflict: Korean War

The Korean War was at times a battle for hills and many times the North Koreans outnumbered US forces 30 to 1. The enemy would launch attacks in which wave after wave of soldiers would attack. Chet Hamilton had no formal training but his commanding officer learned he was the only man in the company that had been on a rifle team and with any real experience with a rifle. Hamilton was issued an M1D, a sniper variant of the M1 Garand rifle, and told he was the company sniper. During a US assault on one of the hills near the infamous Pork Chop Hill, Hamilton noticed that the North Korean enemy defenders needed to lean out of the trenches to fire down at US troops. From Hamilton's vantage point it was about 400 yards to the enemy lines and as the Koreans exposed themselves to shoot, Hamilton fired. He recalls shooting enemy soldiers one after the other as if he was at a carnival shooting gallery popping steel crows on a revolving fence.

Name: Carlos Hathcock a.k.a. "White Feather"
Confirmed Kills: 93
Date: 1956–1975
Conflict: Vietnam War

USMC Gunnery Sergeant Carlos Hathcock is one of the most well known snipers of the Vietnam War. Hathcock's exploits are legendary. His most daring mission was behind enemy lines; the location was so top secret, even Hathcock did not know where he was going. The task was to kill a North Vietnamese general at his command center which was an old French plantation house with a perimeter of one kilometer with a wide open expanse surrounding it. It took Hathcock three nights and two days

▲ A sniper during the Vietnam War takes aim using an M14 equipped with a scope.

to creep and crawl through tall grass just to get within 700 yards of the house. So stealthy was Hathcock that he avoided numerous patrols that stepped within feet of his location and came nose to nose with a venomous green Burmese viper. He made the shot and it took him less than 10 minutes to hightail it out of the area. Hathcock used a modified .30-06 Winchester Model 70 with an 8x power Unertl scope. For 35 years, until 2002, Hathcock held the record for the longest recorded sniper kill at 2,500 yards. For the record shot a .50 caliber M2 Browning heavy machine gun with a telescopic sight was used. Like many US snipers during the Vietnam War, the North Vietnamese placed a bounty on his head. The Viet Cong nicknamed Hathcock "White Feather," because of the white feather he kept tucked in a band of his bush hat. Before the war, Hathcock was an accomplished competitive shooter who won numerous awards, including matches at Camp Perry and the Wimbledon Cup.

Name: Chuck Mawhinney
Confirmed Kills: 103
Date: 1956–1975
Conflict: Vietnam War

When sniper kills were totaled after the Vietnam War, USMC Sergeant Chuck Mawhinney had 103 confirmed kills with 216 probable kills. Mawhinney used both an M14 and an M40 while in country. The M40 was at the time the standard USMC sniper rifle built on a Remington 40X action, chambered in 7.62x51mm NATO and mounted with a Redfield variable power scope. The M14 Mawhinney used was mounted with what was then a high-tech scope, the MPS-9 Starlight scope. The M14 was fired in semiautomatic mode. The most famous of Mawhinney's missions took place on the side of a river during the monsoon season. He and his spotter set up on the river in a shallow area where Viet Cong soliders crossed. While waiting in ambush, sixteen Viet Cong showed up and Mawhinney picked them off, starting with the last enemy soldier and working his way forward. Sixteen shots, sixteen dead enemy. All head shots.

Name: Adelbert F. Waldron III
Confirmed Kills: 109
Date: 1956–1975
Conflict: Vietnam War

US Army Staff Sergeant Adelbert F. Waldron holds the record for the most confirmed kills by a US sniper during the Vietnam War. Waldron's sniper work was in the Mekong Delta where he used an M21. He is credited with making a 900-yard shot from a moving boat. Waldron was awarded a Silver Star, a Bronze Star, a Presidential Unit Citation, and two Distinguished Service Crosses.

Name: Gary Gordon and Randy Shughart
Confirmed Kills: Unknown
Date: October 3–4, 1993
Conflict: Somalia, Battle of Mogadishu

The heroism and fates of US Army Master Sergeant Gary Gordon and Sergeant First Class Randy Shughart became entwined during Operation Gothic Serpent in Somalia. They were Delta Force snipers who attempted to rescue

▲ This is an image taken of Super 64 on October 3, 1993, enroute to rescue the crew of the downed Black Hawk during the Battle of Mogadishu; it too was shot down.

the injured crew of a downed Black Hawk helicopter and downed rescue chopper, Super Six Four. Gordon and Shughart were providing sniper cover from the air but made numerous requests to be dropped into the crash site to help the crews from the crashed helicopters on the ground. Initial requests were denied but command eventually granted Gordon and Shughart permission. The two fought their way to the helicopters with Somali militia swarming the area. Gordon and Shughart were able to help the injured helicopter pilot and inflicted heavy casualties on the Somalis but, outnumbered and out of ammunition, they were killed by Somali gunfire. After the battle the Somali body count was twenty-five, with many more wounded. Both Gordon and Shughart were posthumously awarded the Medal of Honor.

Name: Chris Kyle, a.k.a. "The Devil of Rahmadi"
Confirmed Kills: 160
Date: 2003–2011
Conflict: Iraq War

US Navy Chief Chris Kyle of SEAL Team Three had four deployments to Iraq between 2003 and 2009. Kyle is considered to have the highest kill count of any US military sniper. During the Second Battle of Fallujah, Kyle killed forty insurgents, but he was most feared by enemy insurgents when he was deployed to Ramadi and nicknamed *"Al-Shaitan Ramad"* (the Devil of Rahmadi). In his auto-

▲ The wars in Iraq showed that the US Army M24 sniper rifle was highly effective and a reliable weapon. Courtesy of Remington Defense.

▲ This McMillan TAC-338 is similar to the rifle Chris Kyle used during his deployments in Iraq where he earned the nickname "the Devil of Rahmadi." Courtesy McMillan companies.

Top 3 Longest Confirmed Sniper Kills

#1) 2,707 yards: Corporal of Horse Craig Harrison of the U.K. Household Cavalry Life Guards, in 2009 during the War in Afghanistan. Harrison used an Accuracy International L115A3 chambered in .338 Lapua Magnum.

#2) 2,657 yards: Corporal Rob Furlong of Canada's 3rd Battalion, Princess Patricia's Canadian Light Infantry, in 2002 during the War in Afghanistan. Furlong used a McMillan Tac-50 chambered in .50 BMG using Hornady A-MAX ammo.

#3) 2,526 yards: Master Corporal Arron Perry of Canada's 3rd Battalion, Princess Patricia's Canadian Light Infantry, in 2002 during the War in Afghanistan. Perry used a McMillan Tac-50 chambered in .50 BMG using Hornady A-MAX ammo.

biography, *American Sniper*, Kyle tried to dismiss a misconception about snipers: ". . . contrary to what you're probably thinking, not all sniper shots, certainly not mine, take the bad guys in the head. Usually I went for center of mass . . . ." His longest confirmed kill was at 2,100 yards using a McMillan rifle chambered in .338 Lapua Magnum. "It was a straight-up luck shot," said Kyle in his autobiography of his longest kill shot taken in 2008 during fighting in Sadr City.

Name: Timothy L. Kellner
Confirmed Kills: 78
Date: 2003–2011
Conflict: Iraq War

Regarded as a top US Army sniper, Staff Sergeant Timothy L. Kellner's confirmed kills occurred during Operation Iraqi Freedom. Kellner used an M24, the standard US Army sniper rifle.

RIFLE TESTING & EVALUATION
4. Uberti 1874 Sharps Buffalo Hunter

Remake of America's First Long-range, Big-bore Cartridge Rifle.

Pick up the Uberti Sharps Model 1874 or any Sharps reproduction or original and you can tell by the heft that this rifle had its roots in black powder rifles. The Sharps is barrel heavy like a muzzle-loader. In fact Frank Sellers writes in *Sharps Firearms* that the barrel lengths and weights varied on the Sharps Sporting rifles. "Until 1877, a charge of $1 per pound over 12, and $1 per inch over 30 inches was standard." Twelve pounds back in the day was about the average weight of a sporting Model 1874 barrel by the pound and the inch.

Tales of the old west regale the power and accuracy of the Sharps in the hands of buffalo hunters. This is the "Buffalo Rifle" of lore: powerful, accurate, and capable of

▲ At the bench, the big rifle ejects an empty .45/70 case. Those cases seem to hold a handful of powder and when a fired case hits the cement deck, it sounds like an empty coffee can hitting the floor.

▲ The Uberti reproduction of a Sharps Model 1874 is a heavy rifle made to be fired from a rest, and with the Creedmoor tang sight has a range of up to 1,000 yards. Checkered walnut, a case-hardened frame and blued barrel create a beautiful nineteenth-century-style rifle.

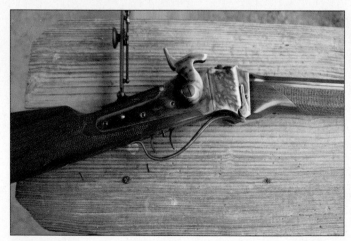

▲ The Uberti Sharps features double-set triggers. The rear trigger is pressed first to set the front trigger. When set, the front trigger can fire the gun with just light touch.

taking down a bison that could weigh up to 2,200 pounds. During the Indian and range wars the Sharps ended sieges. Mention Creedmoor and a modern day shooter conjures up an image of old-school shooters contorting with their Sharps in the prone or semi-prone shooting position, hitting bull's-eyes at 1,000 yards. It is important to understand where we have been to appreciate where we are when shooting long-range rifles.

Original Sharps were mostly custom guns. The Sharps factory would set up the rifle any way a buyer wanted it and was only limited by the buyer's budget. The Uberti Buffalo Hunter Sharps is a good example of what many buffalo hunters used back in the nineteenth century—if it was built by the Sharps Company it would be a Model 1874 Sporting Rifle. There were variations on the Sporting Rifles but in general they had straight stocks—pistol grip stocks were found more often on the Creedmoor and Long-Range Rifles—though the Sporting could be customized with a pistol grip stock if the buyer so wished. The Sporting Rifles generally had a full octagon barrel and are also classified by where they were manufactured as either a Hartford or Bridgeport model. The Sharps factory relocated from Hartford, Connecticut, to Bridgeport, Connecticut, in 1876 and those models are characterized by the contouring of barrel where it fits into the receiver. A Hartford rifle has a turned collar, while the barrel of a Bridgeport rifle flared out from the barrel flats to meet the receiver. The Uberti would be considered a

Bridgeport rifle. Sellers' book provides an excellent reference for deciphering variations of Sharps rifles.

The Uberti Sharps has a 32-inch octagon barrel with a slight taper. At the crowned muzzle the barrel diameter measures 7/8-inch from flat to flat. Total length of the rifle is 49 inches. Considering a Winchester Model 70 Sporter with a 24-inch barrel is about 44 inches in overall length, you soon realize the Uberti is a long rifle. The Uberti weighs over ten pounds without an optic, and the aforementioned Winchester Sporter weighs close to nine pounds with an optic, rings, and bases. The heft of the Uberti makes shooting the big bore .45/70 easy on the shoulder.

The barrel is deeply blued and has the Uberti rollmark on the top flat in a font reminiscent of a rifle from the nineteenth century. Under the barrel is a more modern marking indicating the model, caliber, and catalog number. There was no "Old Reliable" rollmarked on the Uberti like on some original Sharps. No confusing this reproduction with an original. The front sight is a thin silver blade on a steel base that is dovetailed into the barrel. It can be knocked left or right if adjustment is required. The rear sight is a ladder style sight that is dovetailed into the barrel. Folded in the down position, the rear sight has a notched shallow "V"; flip up the sight and the ladder with a second rear sight locks in place perpendicular to the barrel. The rear sight can then be adjusted up and down the ladder as elevation is needed. It is spring loaded and snaps into small notches to hold it in place during recoil. A screw at the top keeps the rear sight from accidentally coming off the ladder. The front of the ladder is labeled with graduations from 1 to 8 so the user can adjust to a certain height. Up to 100 yards I had no problems using this sight to get on target, though I needed the Creedmoor tang sight for longer ranges. This vernier rear sight is attached to the receiver tang via two screws. Creedmoor tang sights come in three heights depending on the range to be fired. The short-range sight—the lowest in height—is designed for up to 300 yards. The mid-range is effective to nearly 600 yards, and the long-range is for use at 1,200 yards and beyond. These sights use an eyedisc with a fine hole in it. The eyedisc is adjustable for elevation on the sight staff and can be locked in place. Viewing through the eyedisc, the shooter aligns the front sight on target (think of it as a precision peep sight). The Uberti uses a mid-range sight and the sight pivots forward and backward—toward muzzle or butt—depending on what is required. It also folds out of the way so a cleaning rod can be pushed through the bore.

▲ The Creedmoor sight mounts to the tang of the receiver. Uberti drills and taps holes for easy mounting. The eyedisc is adjusted for elevation by turning the adjustment screw.

▲ The rear sight is mounted on the barrel. It is a ladder type sight that flips up when shooting distance is required.

▲ The front sight is a thin silver blade attached to a steel base that is dovetailed into the barrel.

Legendary Shots from the Sharps

Tales from the old west are rife with deeds of shooters who made extraordinary shots with the Sharps. Native Americans on the plains came to respect the Sharps and, according to Sellers in *Sharps Firearms*, nicknamed them the "shoot today, kill tomorrow" rifle because of the weapon's extreme range and striking power. When Billy the Kid and his *compadres* were pinned down during one of the battles of the Lincoln County War, one of the Kid's pals, Fernando Herrera, used a heavy Sharps in .45 to snipe a pair of shooters who had them pinned down from about 900 yards away. Probably the most famous long shot from a Sharps came from buffalo hunter William "Billy" Dixon. Buffalo hunters at Adobe Walls, Texas, were trapped by Indians and Dixon fired a borrowed .50 2-½-inch Sharps at a group of Indians over 1,500 yards away, knocking one of the Indians off his horse. Dixon admitted it was a lucky shot but it convinced the Indians to vacate the area. The actual distance of Dixon's shot was 1,538 yards.

▲ Billy Dixon is one of only eight civilians to have received the US Medal of Honor. Dixon was awarded the medal after the Second Battle of Adobe Walls in June of 1874 where he fired what was then described as "The Shot of the Century."

The eyedisc is adjusted up and down via a screw adjustment and the disc itself can be screwed down to the staff so it does not move during recoil. A scale is on the left side of the staff from 1 inch to 2 inches with every ¼-inch increment indicated. The elevation slide wore no adjustment marks so I used the edge of the slide, and this allowed me to have a good idea of how high the sight should be adjusted for a specific distance. I assume that the Buffalo Rifles of lore had a similar setup and hunters were well aware of what elevation to set the eyedisc for a specific distance. The Creedmoor shooters of the day were excellent at adjusting the sight and compensating for wind. With some finely made Creedmoor sights 1 MOA adjustment is possible. Other Creedmoor sight allow windage adjustments, too.

The frame of the Uberti is finished in a frothy swirl of case-hardened colors—blue, gray, and a touch of violet. The hammer shares the case-hardened finish and is smartly checkered so you have a sure grip when thumbing back the hammer. The lever is also case-hardened and the edges are smoothed so working the lever is easy. Place the hammer on half cock and push the lever downward similar to a lever action rifle. As the lever is manipulated the breechblock falls or slides downward, exposing the chamber. The breechblock is blued. As the lever is fully rotated downward an extractor built into a notch in the breechblock and to the left of the

chamber kicks out the empty case or cartridge. The firing pin block is built into the right side of the breechblock. When the trigger is pressed to release the hammer, the hammer hits the firing pin block, which in turn slams the firing pin into the primer of the cartridge to fire the weapon.

As a nineteenth century design, the Sharps does not have a safety other than the half-cock notch for the hammer. Gun designers in the old days assumed shooters would be careful and cautious with their rifles.

Double-set triggers are featured on the Uberti. The curved rear trigger sets the front trigger so only a small amount of pressure is needed to fire the rifle. The front trigger can also be used without setting it with the rear trigger. The front trigger pull measured on average 11 pounds 2 ounces unset and 1 pound 9 ounces set. The front trigger has less curve to it compared to the rear. Set triggers tend to confuse modern day shooters until they become acclimated with its operation. Double-set triggers were common on muzzle-loading rifles and other rifles built in the nineteenth century. Today, set triggers are mostly found on bolt-action rifles built in the Czech Republic, Germany, and Austria.

The walnut forend is wrapped in a checkering that is neatly cut and has a rough texture that feels good in your hand while providing a good grip. The forend has a pewter cap that is nicely and neatly inlaid to the wood.

▲ With the lever pulled downward the breechblock falls or drops down, exposing the chamber so the rifle can be loaded or unloaded. Hence the name of this action is a falling block.

▲ With the breechblock lowered the chamber is open and ready for a cartridge to be loaded.

Two screws hold the forend to the barrel. The stock is also walnut with the wrist area checkered in the same pattern. The butt plate is crescent shaped and case-hardened like the action and some other parts. The workmanship on the Uberti was very good and the metal to wood fit was tight and clean; it is a well-made rifle.

To field strip the Model 1874, open the action and cock back the hammer to the half-cock position. Push in the tiny plunger pin on the right side of the frame where the frame and forend meet. With the plunger pin pushed in rotate the lever hinge pin next to the plunger pin about 180° from its original position. Flip the rifle so the lever and triggers face up then rotate the lever hinge pin back and forth while pulling it out of the frame. With the lever hinge pin

removed the lever and the breechblock can then be pulled out of the frame. Care should be taken when reassembling as the lever hinge pin may scratch the forend as you work it back in place. Uberti suggests the forend be removed to avoid marring the wood.

At the range I used Ultramax cowboy loads with a 405-grain RNFP (Round Nose Flat Point) lead bullet and current hunting load by Federal, a Power-Shok 300-grain Speer Hot-Core HP (Hollow Point) consisting of a lead core and copper jacket. Using a benchrest and the butt toe on a shooting bag, I sighted down the barrel at 100 yards with the rear ladder folded down. Just focusing on the front sight blade down that long barrel took some getting used to. I used the set trigger and when my breathing settled I touched the trigger—a touch was all it took—and

▲ At 100 yards that bull's-eye looked like a tiny red speck, but if I did my work with the trigger and sights the Uberti Sharps would too. This group was fired with Federal hunting ammunition.

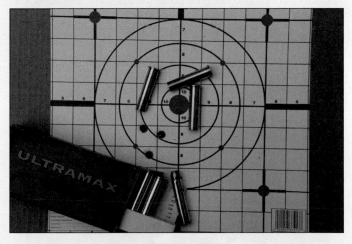

▲ With Ultramax cowboy ammunition the Uberti was able to consistently punch holes like these at 100 yards.

the Sharps barked. There was a slight delay before I heard the sound of the bullet punching through a layer of paper target and layer of cardboard. The 1-inch red bull's-eye looked like a red speck at that distance.

I used to competitively shoot rimfire pistols with an old timer who once hunted with these old calibers. His recommendation was to shoot and wait a bit before going after the deer. "You don't want to get hit in the back of the head with your own bullet," he'd laugh and slap his knee. It was his witty way of saying these old calibers have a slow velocity compared to modern cartridges. At slightly over 1800 fps (feet per second), the 400-grain is chugging along. A 400-grain bullet from a similar sized bullet from a modern caliber like the .416 Remington Magnum is in the range of 2300 to 2450 fps. This comparison shows the difference between a nineteenth century round compared to a twentieth century round.

The recoil from the Sharps was pleasant. If I had more ammunition I would have burned through it. The Uberti was pleasant to shoot but what really surprised me were the groups I was able to achieve with open sights at 100 yards. I looked through the Meopta spotting scope twice to make sure I wasn't imagining the hole in the center red bull's-eye. With the Ultramax I could achieve 1 MOA if I did my part and with the Federal my best group was 1.25 inches. I was pleasantly surprised. I also tried a few rounds sitting on the ground using a pair of shock cord shooting sticks. I didn't

wear my wide brimmed Stetson but I think I now know why Elmer Keith owned about 40 Sharps rifles at one time.

At 200 yards I used the Creedmoor tang rear sight and zeroed it for 100 yards. Looking at factory ballistics for the Federal load, the 300-grain bullet zeroed for 100 yards would drop about 12 inches at 200 yards. The BC (Ballistic Coefficient) is .289 for this bullet so I knew this bullet was not slipping through the air like a .223 Remington loaded with a Sierra MatchKing BTHP (Boat Tail Hollow Point) which has a BC of .301 and slices through air. I adjusted the eyedisc upward and tested the elevation adjusted at the 100 yard target. I needed to raise the eyedisc according the scale on the staff. Moving the target out to 200 yards and channeling my inner Creedmoor shooter, I touched off rounds. Using the Ultramax cartridges at 200 yards gave me 3-inch groups on average.

As Mike Venturio writes in *Shooting Buffalo Rifles of the Old West*, the .45/70 is the best caliber choice for starting out with Sharps rifles. I've done time behind muzzleloaders in the .45 to .54 caliber range and this Uberti has given me an itch that I need to scratch. My trigger time with the .45/70 consists of a Ruger No.1 and a Browning Model 1885 as well as a Winchester 1886 lever action, but I'm embarrassed I have not spent more time with a Sharps. That will change. I will be spending more time with this beautiful brute.

Ideal Tool: Reloading Like the Buffalo Hunters

Buffalo hunters of the 1870s bought lead and powder by the pound and many casted their own bullets. Reloading cases was a necessity due to the number of rounds expended in a day and the distance to any sort of town that might have your caliber in stock. I imagine the reloading process was done off the back of a wagon or on a buffalo hide in the hunter's down time. I don't suspect the quality control was the best and was only as good as the diligence of the reloader. Target shooters might have cringed at the process.

Modern factory loads worked well in the Uberti but I wanted to see what type of accuracy I could get reloading black powder cartridges like they did over a century ago. According to Venturio in *Shooting Buffalo Rifles of the Old West*, the US Army used bullets that weighed 400 or 405 grains depending on the source cited. The military eventually started loading 500-grain bullets in 1881. I used two lead bullet weights, a 500-

grain Round Nose from Montana Precision Swaging, and a 405-grain Flat Nose from Oregon Trail Bullet Company. Using a pair of Lyman 310 handles and Lyman dies I reloaded once-fired .45/70 brass.

Step 1: Neck Resizing and Decapping of the Case

In this first step the cartridge is lightly lubed. I use a slightly oily rag and rub the outside of the cases. (I imagine buffalo hunters might have used a lightly oiled piece of buffalo hide to do this. Of course, the brass was slightly different than what is used today.) If the cases aren't lubed they can get stuck in the dies. The case is then inserted into the die. As the handles are closed the used primer is punched out of the case's primer pocket and the case neck is resized back down to close to original dimensions.

Step 2: Inside Neck Expanding of the Case

After the neck diameter of the case is reduced by resizing—the process of firing the round expands the case and neck—it must be enlarged to a uniform diameter to accept the bullet. The Lyman die has a two-step expanding plug. As the handles are closed

the first step expands the case neck to just under bullet diameter, the second step expands the first 1/32 inch of the case neck to slightly more than the bullet diameter to allow the bullet to enter the case easily.

Step 3: Priming the Empty Case

A third die is used to seat the primer into the case. Insert the primer into the priming chamber and squeeze the tool handles together. The primer needs to be seated flush with the case head.

Step 4: Adding Powder and Seating the Bullet

The fourth die seats the bullet. Fill the case with the premeasured powder and place the bullet in the case neck. Insert the case into the die. Hold the handles so the bullet is pointing up; this will ensure the bullet will stay aligned and seated properly. Close the handles to seat the bullet. The tool allows the case to be crimped which holds the bullet in place. This is an important step in repeating weapons like revolvers and lever actions. Since numerous cartridges are loaded into the weapon the recoil from rounds can move the bullets out of the case. Crimping ensures the bullet stays in place.

Specifications	Uberti Buffalo Hunter Sharps
Caliber	.45/70
Barrel	32 in.
OA Length	48.9 in.
Weight (Unloaded)	10.25 lb.
Stock	A-grade walnut, checkered
Sights	adjustable tang-mounted Creedmoor and barrel-mounted ladder rear sights/flat blade front
Action	Falling block, single shot
Finish	blued barrel, case-hardened action
Msrp	$2,469
Performance	Uberti Buffalo Hunter Sharps

Load .45/70	Velocity	Best	Average
Federal Power-Shok 300 Speer Hot-Core HP	1828	1.25	2.125
Ultramax 405 RNFP	1219	1.0	1.312
Handload 405 FP Laser Cast	1097	0.7	1.4

Bullet weight measured in grains, velocity in feet per second 15 feet from the muzzle by a ProChrono digital chronograph, and accuracy in inches of three, three-shot groups at 100 yards.

5. Savage Arms Model 25 Lightweight Varminter-T

Varmint Evictor

The Savage Arms Model 25 Lightweight Varminter-T is interesting because it can easily shoot 100-yard, three-shot groups that can be covered with a coin. Some groups can be covered with a dime, some a quarter. I'm pretty sure Townsend Whelen would find the Model 25 interesting for that fact alone, but there are features that make the rifle even more interesting.

Like many Savage Arms rifles, the Model 25 is packaged with a test target. The target did not especially pique my interest with a three-shot group from Hornady V-Max 55-grain bullets that measured .6 inches. I was really interested in shooting inexpensive .223 ammo, like the type I train with in my AR. I also was interested in shooting "woodchuck evictors." (We call them woodchucks in my part of the country; you might call them prairie dogs or gophers.) Woodchuck evictors are lightweight bullets like the Speer TNT Green bullets loaded by Federal that load 43-grain bullets with a factory speed of 3600 fps. Hit a woodchuck and you will understand why some bullet and ammo brands call these types of fast-moving, fragmenting bullets grenades. From my perspective these bullets "evict" the critters from a farmer's pasture.

The Model 25 is one of those in-between rifles, larger than a rimfire rifle yet smaller than a typical centerfire varmint rifle. It's all barrel with an action scaled to fire small centerfire rounds in the range or .17 Hornet through to .223 Remington.

The 24-inch .223 barrel is heavy with a medium-heavy profile that measures at the crowned muzzle .625

inches. The blue is so deep I can almost shave in the reflection. It is free floated the entire length which no doubt contributes to the rifle's accuracy. The action is compact with a small right-hand ejection port that offers plenty of room to load rounds one at a time. A set of Weaver bases are attached to the Model 25 at the factory. The bolt cocks upon opening and is nicely jeweled with the Savage logo while the bolt bluing matches the barrel and action. It also sports three lugs which mean the bolt has a 60-degree lift. Most two-lug bolts have a 90-degree lift. The 60-degree bolt lift makes cycling the rifle faster and avoids jamming knuckles against the scope's eyepiece. I like the set up and was easily able to palm the bolt for fast follow-up shots. The safety, located on the right side of the action and behind the bolt, is made for right-hand shooters. Push it forward to fire the rifle. Push the safety back and it locks the sear but the bolt can still be manipulated. The Model 25 uses a polymer, four-round capacity box magazine that is detachable. Rounds are easily loaded into the magazine. I had to train myself to push the front of the magazine into the magazine well until the latch snapped closed. I also found that trying to insert a full magazine into the rifle while the bolt was closed needed some effort. I left the bolt open when inserting a full magazine. The thumbhole stock was made of a wood laminate with alternating dark and blonde stained wood with a satin finish. It fit my hand like a glove and is easy on the eyes. Three horizontal slots are cut through the forearm to help cooling. The forearm was also wide and flat so it was a

▲ The thumbhole stock comb comes straight out from the action and requires use of high scope mounts just like mounting a scope to an AR-style rifle.

bit steadier on the bench. Sling mounts are included as well as an extra mount on the forend to attach a bipod if desired. A thumbhole stock is similar to the stock on an AR style rifle. The Monte Carlo cheekpiece was plenty high. With thumbhole stocks, scope rings need to be higher than on a traditional style stock. I used high Leupold QRW rings to mount the scope. QRW rings are made of steel and allow the shooter to quickly and easily remove and replace the scope with a half minute of accuracy. The thumbhole stock is also similar to an AR's pistol grip as it is more vertical than the pistol grip from a more traditional stock. I like this set up because I sit when hunting coyotes and the pistol grip makes the rifle easy to manipulate and more comfortable to shoot when using shooting sticks. A well fitted, soft rubber butt is installed on the Model 25's aft end. The .223 is hardly a punishing round to shoot and the rubber pad makes recoil nil. The trigger is Savage's renowned AccuTrigger that is not only safe but crisp. A blade in the AccuTrigger acts as a safety and only until that blade is pressed fully rearward does the trigger release the firing pin. It also prevents the rifle form discharging if it should be accidentally dropped. The trigger is also adjustable after the barrel action is removed from the stock. The rifle's trigger pull averaged three pounds twelve ounces, which was perfect for my shooting needs. To adjust the trigger, remove the three bolts that hold the stock to the barreled action and use the small tool Savage provides. The pull weight ranges from about 2-½ to 4-½ pounds. The AccuTrigger is a great setup and frequently copied by Savage's competitors.

Small targets, like woodchucks, require specific optic requirements. Avoid scopes with front focal reticles, like many tactical scopes, since the reticle will enlarge as the scope magnification is dialed up. If shooting small targets, you could experience issues with the reticle enlarging enough to cover up parts of what you are shooting at. I mounted a Leupold VX-3 6.5-20x50mm Long Range Target with the VH reticle on the Model 25. The scope has a 30mm tube and I used high rings so my eye would align with the scope's eyepiece when my cheek was pressed to the Model 25's thumbhole stock. After tightening the rings to the bases and lifting the rifle to my shoulder for the first time, the rings, scope, and rifle fit me perfectly. The Leupold VX-3 magnification ranges starts at 6.5x and cranks up to 20x. At full magnification field of view is 5.5 feet. Eye relief is 3.7 inches which is plenty for such a mild recoiling rifle. The scope weighs over 20 ounces so the final setup of rifle rings and scope weighed slightly over 9.5 pounds, which is a nice heft to a varmint rifle. Varmint rifles should be heavy so they sit well on a rest. Lighter rifles can be greatly influenced by small movement and cause you to lose the target when at high magnification—even the beating of your heart when the rifle is shouldered can cause the reticle to pulsate with each beat. The VX-3 employs a Varmint Hunter reticle which uses what Leupold calls a Ballistic Aiming System. The reticle is a tricked out German #4 reticle—heavy duplex crosshairs at 3, 6, and 9 o'clock with everything above the horizontal reticle a fine vertical crosshair at 12 o'clock. Keeping the field of view clear above the

▲ It was a cold day at the range and my fingers were numb but I managed to do good work with the Model 25.

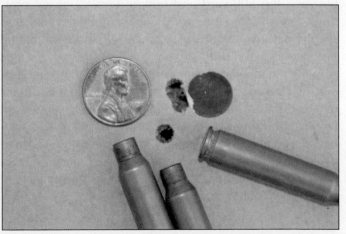

▲ This is a typical three-shot group using Hornady's Steel Match ammo. On average groups measured .75 inches.

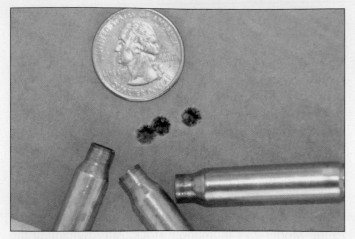

▲ Federal 43-grain Speer TNT Green bullets gave sub-MOA accuracy out of the Model 25.

holes in nice tight groups. Some rifles have a distinct character to them like the sound of the recoil spring in an AR rifle. With the Model 25 I could distinctly hear the spring of the AccuTrigger compress as I pressed the AccuTrigger blade into the trigger. The trigger itself was crisp and contributed to the outstanding accuracy.

The Savage Model 25 is interesting because of its accuracy, design, and performance.

Specifications	Savage Model 25 Lightweight Varminter-T
Caliber	.223 Rem.
Barrel	24 in.
OA Length	43.75 in.
Weight (Unloaded)	8.25 lb.
Stock	laminated wood
Sights	none/drilled and tapped for scope mounts
Action	3-lug, bolt
Finish	blued
Msrp	$754
Performance	Savage Model 25 Lightweight Varminter-T

horizontal allows the shooter an unobstructed view. The fine-lined German #4-style central aiming point is recommended to be sighted-in at 200 yards. It includes cross-wire hold points calibrated to 300, 400, and 500 yards for most cartridges. Leupold provides data on different cartridges and divides them into three groups. Just find your cartridge in one of the groups and that will tell you what magnification to set the scope to use the ballistic aiming points. These is a small and large triangle on the magnification ring and depending on your cartridge the magnification ring needs to be set on one of those triangles for the Ballistic Aiming System to work. There are 10 and 20 mph windage hold points at both the left and right ends of the 300, 400, and 500 yard cross-wire hold points. A prairie dog range estimator is between the 500-yard and bottom vertical heavy post. Once I spent some time with scope and reticle it became second nature and quite easy to use. No more estimating holdover or wind drift.

At the range is where things really started to get interesting. As I zeroed the rifle and moved target out to farther ranges, I had a hard time telling where the bullets were landing. The tiny .22s were grouping together as if they had a need to touch each other. At 100 yards I used a small black dot as an aiming point and whatever brand or quality of ammo I sent through the Model 25, it insisted on placing

Load .223 Rem.	Velocity	Best	Average
Federal V-Shock 43 Speer TNT Green	3600	0.625	0.75
American Eagle 55 FMJ	3068	0.5	0.75
Hornady Steel Match 55 HP	3009	0.5	0.75

Bullet weight measured in grains, velocity in feet per second 10' from the muzzle by a ProChrono digital chronograph, and accuracy in inches of three, five-shot groups at 100 yards.

6. Savage Arms Model 11/111 Long Range Hunter

A Beanfield Rifle Redefined for the 21st Century

▲ The Savage Arms Model 11/111 Long Range Hunter in 6.5 Creedmoor proved to be a capable Beanfield rifle in description—heavy and small caliber—and in performance—sub-MOA groups with 140-grain bullets.

▲ The AccuTrigger offers a high level of safety with delivering a clean, crisp trigger pull.

A learned gun scribe once called a custom Jarrett rifle a "Beanfield Rifle." Loosely defined by *Field and Stream* alums David E. Petzal and Phil Bourjaily, a Beanfield Rifle "is a heavy, small-caliber rifle with which you overlook a patch of oats, or corn, or a beanfield, and wait for a deer to materialize." The Savage Arms Model 11/111 Long Range Hunter in 6.5 Creedmoor can be considered a Beanfield Rifle because it can easily shoot sub-MOA three-shot groups at 100-yards. I've used the 6.5 Creedmoor on whitetails and it works just fine.

The Model 11/111 Long Range Hunter is based on Savage Arms Model 110 which was developed in the mid-1950s and offered commercially in 1958. This makes the Model 110 the oldest continuously manufactured bolt-action rifle in the United States. The rifle has a reputation as being accurate, reliable, and inexpensive. Many think Savage rifles skipped a meal when aesthetics were dished out but the rifle must have taken seconds when accuracy was served. The Model 110 was designed from the beginning for ease in manufacturing and assembly.

The Model 11/111 has five characteristics that make it and some of Savage's other rifles very accurate right out of box.

First is the button rifled barrels. For a barrel to be accurate it needs to be a perfect tube. The Model 11/111's barrel is button rifled in an effort to achieve the most consistency in rifling twist and bore diameter. The walls of the barrel are also consistent so there is less barrel walk, or shift of impact, as the barrel heats up during shooting. The barrel is also fully threaded into the action then locked in place via a barrel locknut. This helps better manage headspace tolerances and contributes to better accuracy. The barrel nut also gives Savage rifles a distinct look where the barrel and action mate up.

The second characteristic is the floating bolt head. It is unique, as most other rifle manufacturers use a solid bolt. As the bolt is closed, the two locking lugs—other bolt-action rifles may have three (Savage Model 25) or up to nine (Weatherby Mark V)—must bear evenly and equally in the recess of the receiver plus the bolt face needs to have full contact with the entire face of the cartridge. This ensures the cartridge is properly aligned in the chamber. The bolt head is made of two separate parts that allow for a slight amount of play or float to provide the best lug engagement in the recess of the receiver and lock the cartridge in the chamber. When you purchase a custom rifle, the builder spends time ensuring the bolt is tuned and squared up to the receiver.

The third is headspace. Headspace is the fit of the cartridge in a chamber. Depending on the type of cartridge—

rimmed, belted, or rimless—the headspace measurement is the distance from the breech face to the part of the chamber, which stops the forward movement of the case. On a rimmed cartridge like the .30-30 Winchester it stops on the rim, on a belted cartridge like the 7mm Remington Magnum it is the belt, and on a rimless cartridge like the .30-06 Springfield it is the case shoulder. Too much or too little headspace impacts accuracy and functioning of the rifle. Savage aggressively controls the headspace exactly to minimum with zero tolerance. They do this by placing a minimum headspace gauge in the barrel's chamber. The bolt is then closed and locked into the receiver and the barrel is threaded into the receiver until it stops. Finally the barrel nut locks the barrel and receiver in place.

The fourth characteristic is the bedding. As a round is fired the energy released travels along the length of the barrel creating harmonic waves. All highly accurate rifles free-float the barrel, meaning no part of the forearm comes in contact with the barrel. The other aspect is the action bedding. On some Savage rifles, the Model 11/111 included, Savage's AccuStock uses an aluminum rail system to secure the action to the stock in three directions. Keeping the action in place in the stock is paramount to achieving excellent accuracy.

The fifth feature for a truly accurate rifle is the trigger. A trigger that has creep or feels gritty as you press it and/or has a heavy pull weight is not conducive to accuracy since the effort and pressure applied with only a trigger finger can impact accuracy at long distance. The AccuTrigger by Savage is built into the Model 11/111 and other Savage rifles. It is designed with an integrated release—that's the thin blade in the center of the trigger—and it must be completely depressed to fire the rifle. This reduces liability for Savage yet gives the shooter a trigger that can be adjusted from six ounces to six pounds. It is crisp with no creep. It also provides a higher level of safety.

The Long Range Hunter is designed like a Beanfield rifle, chambered—this particular model anyway—in a small caliber, 6.5 Creedmoor. The rifle is long and heavy, a rifle made for sitting not stalking, though I have used it in both capacities. It is 46.5 inches in length and weighs 8.4 pounds unloaded and without a scope or mount and rings. That heft is due to a 26-inch barrel with a #2 contour. At the end is a muzzle brake which can be turned on or off. Dual knurled rings allow the operator to turn the muzzle brake. In the "on" position gases from a fired round can escape through the vent holes. I notice a marked difference in accuracy with the muzzle brake opened. With the

▲ The bolt easily cleared the eyepiece of the Leupold Mark 4 LR/T allowing easy cranking of the bolt. There was plenty of clearance to load cartridges.

▲ Press the floorplate release button and any rounds in the magazine spilled out.

▲ The three-position safety is located directly aft of the bolt. Left- or right-handed shooters can easily manipulate the serrated button.

muzzle brake closed my point of impact shifted slightly and my groups opened up.

Other than the jeweled bolt body, the Long Range Hunter is all business in matte black. The Savage logo is engraved into the bolt body and the bolt knob is standard size with the top half checkered. It has a 90° lift and was easy to manipulate. Cranking a follow-up round into the chamber proved to be fast and smooth. I could palm the bolt and crank it while the rifle was shouldered. There is a cocking indicator at the rear of the bolt that can be seen and felt.

The safety falls naturally under the thumb of a right- or left-handed shooter and has three positions. When slid all the way forward a red dot appears and the rifle is ready to fire. Slide it back to the middle position and part of the red dot is covered and the trigger is locked, but the bolt can be cranked. In the rearmost position the red dot is completely covered and both the trigger and bolt are locked into position. The safety is serrated and provides a good grip even with gloved hands. It is relatively silent when sliding forward to fire the rifle. Upon sliding it back to the rearmost position it makes an audible click; however, this wasn't an issue when on stand.

The trigger guard is metal and the bolt release button is built into the front of the trigger guard. This button must be pressed and the trigger pulled to remove the bolt from the receiver. Other Savage rifles have the bolt release on the right and rear side of the receiver. The rifle has a fixed magazine. The floorplate is metal and pressing the button built into the front of the floorplate will release the magazine

spring and follower, dumping out rounds. The AccuTrigger is a splendid trigger and this one broke clean on average of three pounds, four ounces.

The stock is made by Karsten and has an adjustable comb which is a U-shaped sleeve that slides over the stock comb. Twin knobs allow adjustment of the comb height. A thick and soft buttpad caps off the buttstock. The stock feels thin and slim in hand—a characteristic I like in a rifle. Since I hunt in cold temperatures I need to wear gloves; even with the gloves this rifle pistol grip and forearm feels lithe. The stock has checkering molded in the pistol grip area and the forearm and sling studs are built into the stock. The stock

▲ The comb of the Karsten stock is adjustable via two knobs and slots in the cheekpiece. The height can be used to fit most set ups.

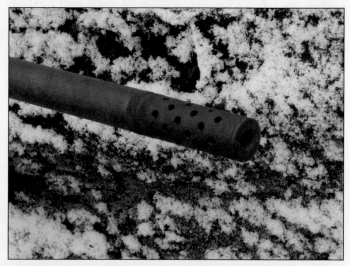

▲ This shows the muzzle brake in the open position. Twist to shut it.

to metal fit was nicely executed. The pistol grip cap was embossed with the Savage logo.

I mounted a Leupold Mark 4 4.5-14x50mm LR/T (Long Range/Tactical) rifle scope using the bases Savage included with the Model 11/111 and Warne Maxima series medium-height steel rings. The medium height allowed me the place the large 50mm objective of the Leupold as close to the barrel as possible. This Leupold was equipped with a TMR (Tactical Milling Reticle). In 1998 the Leupold Mark 4 LR/T M3 10x40 fixed-power was issued with the M24 SWS (Sniper Weapon System). This scope on the Long Range Hunter seemed well suited. I adjusted the comb until my eye was perfectly aligned and the scope came quickly to my eye when I shouldered the rifle. I bore-sighted the scope prior to going to the range.

Hornady is the only manufacturer of 6.5 Creedmoor ammunition, so for range work I chose Superformance and Match ammo. The Superformance is loaded with 120-grain GMX bullets. The GMAX bullets are constructed of a solid copper alloy with double cannelures to reduce fouling. A polymer tip protects the hollow point. The bullet provides good terminal performance at a wide range of velocities. Factory specs for the 6.5 Creedmoor out of a 24-inch barrel clock the 120-grain GMX at 3010 fps with 2099 ft-lbs. of muzzle energy at 100 yards. The Long Range Hunter with the 26-inch barrel eked out a bit more speed with 3061 fps. Factory data for the Match 140-grain A-MAX indicates a muzzle velocity of 2700 fps out of a 24-inch barrel. Again, the Savage with the longer barrel squeezed a bit more out of the round with a muzzle velocity of 2723 fps. The 140-grain boattail A-MAX features a copper jacket over a lead core with a polymer tip.

My routine for a newly mounted scope is to shoot at 50 yards with a target on a large piece of cardboard so I can see where the first few bullets hit. If there are no holes in the cardboard at 50 yards I know something is definitely off. With the Savage the first few rounds grouped close. I dialed in high at 50 yards then moved to the 100-yard range.

Using my range bag as a makeshift rest and my home-made toe bags—two former hiking socks filled with sand—I exhaled and pressed the trigger. The groups were tight. I adjusted the reticle as needed and in no time the Long Range Hunter was shooting the red out of the bull's-eye.

Opening and closing the muzzle brake I found that groups opened up and the impact slightly shifted.

The Savage preferred the 140-grain bullets. Sub-MOA groups were easy to make, but it was no slouch with the lighter 120-grain bullets either. With this load it shot an easy 1-MOA even if I wasn't paying attention. The manual says the Savage rifles prefer the 140-grain bullets.

Savage rifles and the Model 11/111 Long Range Hunter in particular offer outstanding accuracy at a fraction of the cost for a custom rifle. Call me frugal: I'll take the Savage.

Specifications	Savage Arms Model 11/111 Long Range Hunter
Caliber	6.5 Creedmoor
Barrel	26 in.
OA Length	46.5 in.
Weight (Unloaded)	8.4 lb.
Stock	Synthetic Karsten adjustable comb
Sights	none/drilled and tapped for scope mounts
Action	2-lug, bolt-action
Finish	matte black
Msrp	$1,020.00
Performance	Savage Arms Model 11/111 Long Range Hunter

Load 6.5 Creedmoor	Velocity	Best	Average
Hornady Superformance 120 GMX	3061	0.75	1.00
Hornady Match 140 A-MAX	2723	0.625	0.75

Bullet weight measured in grains, velocity in feet per second 15 feet from the muzzle by a ProChrono digital chronograph, and accuracy in inches of three, three-shot groups at 100 yards.

7. America's Last Bolt-Action Combat Rifle: M1903A3 Springfield

Destined for Greatness: The M1903 Springfield and the .30-06 Cartridge

▲ The M1903A3 is easy to identify by the rear aperture sight. Courtesy Springfield Armory National Historic Site.

*I*n 1898 it was brutally obvious to the US military that Spanish forces were better equipped. The Model 1898 Krag–Jørgensen rifle was no match for Model 1893 Mauser. More than fifteen thousand US troops attacked 1,270 entrenched Spanish forces at San Juan Hill and El Caney outside Santiago, Cuba, in the tropical heat of July. Over two hundred US soldiers were killed and nearly 1,200 wounded from the fire laid down by the Spanish with their Mausers. The US military needed a solution which would officially become known as the United States Rifle, Caliber .30-06, Model 1903.

The M1903 Springfield, as it is commonly called, would serve the US military from 1903 to 1974, participating in varying degrees in World War I, World War II, Korea, Vietnam, and other minor but no less lethal conflicts earning a reputation for reliability and accuracy. Part of the lore of these rifles is the numerous design variations and its chambering in the quintessential American cartridge, the .30-06. M1903 scholars and collectors read cartouches and markings like hieroglyphics to decipher each variation and debate the number of rifles built. The M1903A4 is a sniper variant of M1903 and the US Military's first attempt at a dedicated sniper rifle. Here's how it all began.

▲ The Krag–Jørgensen rifle was a liability during the Spanish-American War. Courtesy Springfield Armory National Historic Site.

▲ The M1903A4 sniper variation. Courtesy Springfield Armory National Historic Site.

After the brief Spanish-American War the US military wasted no time analyzing captured 1893 Spanish Mausers. They did not want to be caught flat footed again with outclassed equipment. The Mauser's edge was its ability to quickly reload via a stripper clip. The Krag rifle was loaded one round at a time. The .30-40 Krag caliber was outclassed, too. The 7x57mm had a farther effective range and was more accurate. In 1900 a design was finalized that borrowed many Mauser design features—fixed internal magazine, dual forward lug bolt, bolt-mounted safety, and magazine cut-off. An effort was made by the US Military to make the new design different than the Mauser with a two-piece firing pin and third safety lug, among other details. It also had a few Krag–Jørgensen rifle characteristics like the ladder-type rear sight. Production began in 1903—hence the name—at the federal armory in Springfield, Massachusetts. When Mauser became aware of the M1903 it filed a patent infringement suit in US courts and won. It is not clear if the US government made restitution, but

▲ Troops in the early 1900s with their Springfields. Courtesy Springfield Armory National Historic Site.

▲ The Springfield was not as widely fielded as the M1917 Enfield but still took part in WWI here in France. Courtesy Springfield Armory National Historic Site.

the United Kingdom and the decision was made not to retool factories for the M1903, but to use existing tooling and rechamber the Enfield in .30-06 and call it the M1917. But the story had yet another twist. The metallurgy of those early M1903s was questionable. Receivers were case-hardened and brittle and some did fail. These rifles can be identified by their serial number; Springfield guns

▲ US Marine Raiders on the Solomon Islands during WWII used Springfields along with M1 Carbines and M1 Garands. Courtesy National Archives.

when the United States entered World War I all bets were off as Germany was our enemy. But that's getting ahead of the tale.

The first M1903 featured a sliding rod-style bayonet under the barrel and weighed close to nine pounds with a 24-inch barrel. It was chambered for the .30-03 cartridge, which propelled a 220-grain round-nose bullet at a velocity of about 2300 fps. The .30-03 was only 100 fps faster than the .30-40 Krag round and no better ballistically than the .30-30 Winchester. In the meantime, French and German militaries were changing to spitzer-style or pointed bullets. From the start M1903 was nearly obsolete.

The rod bayonet was replaced with a flat blade bayonet called the M1905. While the Springfield Armory was retooling for the fix, the military decided to improve the sights and just as retooling was complete there were more changes: the M1903 was to be rechambered for the new Cartridge, Ball, Caliber .30, Model 1906 or .30-06. Rechambering also meant sights needed to be reworked again to match the new ammo's trajectory. Other minor design changes were still to come but by 1906 the M1903 Springfield was combat ready—and at an opportune time. In 1917 the US entered into World War I, which had been raging in Europe since 1914. About 840,000 M1903s were already built by Springfield Armory and Rock Island Arsenal in Illinois, but the US had an urgent need for more rifles. At this point the legend takes a turn. Remington and Winchester were producing Enfields for

▲ US troops in Fort Riley, Kansas, taking target practice with their Springfields. Courtesy Springfield Armory National Historic Site.

▲ Three quick shots at 50 yards stopped the zombie Nazi in his undead tracks.

▲ The M1903A3 employed a stamp steel floorplate.

▲ The M1903A3 still has teeth; this nice group was fired from a rest at 100 yards.

have a serial number under #800,000; Rock Island guns are below #285,507. Supposedly the military tested these low-numbered rifles and those that passed were re-issued while those that failed were taken out of service.

The M1903A1 was the first variation changing the straight grip to a pistol grip stock. Production was mothballed through the 1930s, resuming in September 1941 when the US military contracted with Remington. Germany was racing across Europe and just on the horizon in the Pacific was the "day of infamy" at Pearl Harbor on December 7, 1941, and World War II. Both Remington and Smith-Corona, a typewriter manufacturer, began production and offered

design changes that were adopted in the M1903A3 which was the last variation issued in large numbers.

The M1903A3 used stamped metal parts to replace machined parts, a different stock, a two-groove rifled barrel, aperture sight mounted on the receiver, and other changes to speed production and reduce cost. Soon after the next variation, a dedicated sniper rifle, M1903A4, replaced iron sights with a Weaver Model 330 scope on Redfield mounts. Since it used a 2-groove rifled barrel it was not especially accurate for a sniper rifle. A Bushmaster carbine with an 18-inch barrel was also produced but it saw no combat use. Other variants include the Hoffer-Thompson modified M1903 which fired .22 rimfire ammunition. A few national match rifles were also produced as well as .22 training rifles. Experimental models included the M1903 Mark I with the Pedersen device, which swapped the bolt for a mechanism that allowed semiautomatic fire. A 40-round detachable magazine used a .30 caliber pistol size cartridge. With trench warfare an M1903 was modified with a periscope so a soldier could fire the rifle while safely hidden in the trench.

After the wars the M1903 was sold off to military surplus liquidators. Some of them took on a new life as hunting rifles. Ernest Hemingway, Teddy Roosevelt, and countless other big game hunters used customized Springfields. Today a few military drill teams use the M1903 but these are inert weapons rendered in capable of firing or dummy rifles that look like an M1903.

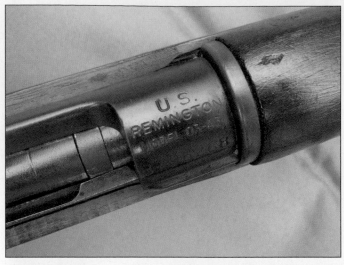

▲ Receiver markings denote this is a M1903A3 made by Remington.

bolt handle or by pulling the cocking piece rearward until it locks. The internal magazine has a cut-off switch that is clearly marked "ON" and "OFF." Flip the cut-off up in the "ON" position allowing the bolt to scrap a cartridge from the magazine and into the chamber. When in the "OFF" position, the bolt cannot be drawn fully rearward so cartridges are held under the bolt. The M1903A3—like all M1903s—is loaded via a five-round stripper clip. To charge the magazine the cut-off needs to be placed in the "ON" position, the bolt opened fully rearward, and either end of the stripper clip inserted in the slot in the receiver before pressing the cartridges down into the magazine. I

▲ Barrel markings decoding: "RA 5 43" means this A3 was made by Remington Arms (RA) in May 1943 (5 43).

▲ The M1903A3 like all M1903s employed a Mauser-style controlled-feed bolt.

The 1903A3 used for testing was built by Remington and bears a serial number and barrel markings that indicates it was produced in May 1943. The cartouche on the left side of the stock is worn but looks like the rifle was rebuilt at San Antonio Arsenal (SAA). The block letter "P" stamped in the wood behind the trigger guard indicates it was proof tested once and ready for acceptance by the military.

The Mauser design is evident from the controlled-feed claw or hook extractor and the two lugs on the bolt. There is a third safety lug located approximately in the middle of the bolt that cams against the rear shoulder of the receiver. The rifle is cocked by lifting or opening the

▲ A Gerber DMF folder points to the M1903A3's third safety lug.

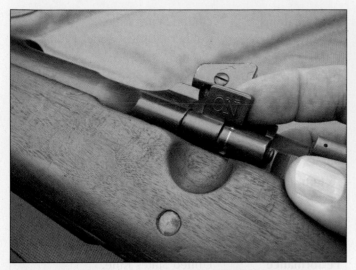

▲ The magazine cut-off allows a user to load a single round in the chamber while the magazine is full.

▲ The M1903A3 is a pleasant rifle to shoot and the peep sights make acquiring targets fast.

▲ The safety lever is also similar to a Mauser; "READY" means "FIRE."

purchased a handful of stripper clips from Numrich and found it was just as easy to load rounds singly into the magazine as it was to charge the magazine with a clip. Pushing the bolt forward after charging the cartridges ejects the stripper clip or it can simply be pulled free from the receiver slots. The safety lock—also similar to a Mauser—is a large lever clearly marked "READY" when rotated fully to the left, indicating the rifle is ready to be fired. Rotate the safety fully to the right and "SAFE" is indicated on the lever. The bolt and trigger are locked in place. The rear aperture or peep sight slides up and down a ramp locking in place

via detents to adjust elevation. Graduations are marked 1 to 8 for 100 to 800 yards. Windage is adjusted via a knob on the right side of the sight. At the base of the sight are graduations lines to indicate left/right adjustment.

My best guess is this 1903A3 was purchased at a Sears in the early 1960s. I had no idea when the rifle was last fired so I used a one-piece Dewey rod and plenty of solvent. On inspection the two grooves of the rifling were bright and sharp.

The front blade sight was bent either for someone with a bad stigmatism or from sloppy handling. Either way the blade was a weak spot. This was before protective wings were commonplace on front sights of combat rifles, but a pair of pliers corrected the blade. The bolt operated effortlessly and flawlessly, more so than many modern bolt-action rifles. I could easily palm it for fast follow-up shots. Of course, I have no idea what this particular 1903A3 did half a century ago. A minor gripe with the M1903A3 and other variations is the straight stock's recoil is directed back into the user's shoulder. An old-timer, a swabby, suggested I place a folded dish towel between my shirt and the Springfield's steel butt plate. You can feel the kick from modern juiced .30-06 cartridges but it was not particularly noticeable with mil-spec ammo. The rifle's heft eased the bite. Starting out at 50 yards, I was able to gut shoot a Zombies Industry Nazi target with a group no bigger than an iPhone without really trying. As I moved higher up on Dietric the Federal Eagles placed three rounds in the chest. Three rounds of the Federal Premium were all head shots. I was pleasantly intrigued this old war dog still had teeth.

At 100 yards a target with a white background was used to easier see the front blade. The rifle seemed to like the PPU ammo, hated the Federal Eagle, and absolutely loved the Federal Premium with 180-grain Nosler Partition bullets. Federal Eagle and PPU were loaded with 150-grain FMJ bullets similar to mil-spec cartridges. World War II spec ammo pushed a 150-grain FMJ bullet at a velocity of 2,700 fps.

As I became accustomed to the recoil and the two-stage trigger, which broke at five-pound, four-ounce trigger on average, the groups began to shrink. The barrel heated and the handguard sweated Cosmoline. The faster I cranked the bolt and fired rounds, the more the 1903A3 seemed to like the exercise. I now understand why so many servicemen liked the M1903A3. I was in the presence of a legend.

▲ The 5-round stripper clip made short work of loading the M1903A3.

Specifications	United States Rifle, Caliber .30-06, Model 1903A3
Caliber	.30-06
Barrel	24.0 inches
OA Length	43.9 inches
Weight (Unloaded)	8.67 pounds (unloaded)
Stock	wood
Sights	aperture rear, fixed ramp front
Action	bolt-action
Finish	light gray/green parkerized
Capacity	5-round fixed internal magazine
Performance	United States Rifle, Caliber .30-06, Model 1903A3

Load	Velocity	Average	Best
Federal Eagle 150 FMJ	2653	6	5
PPU 150 FMJ	2873	3.6	3
Federal Premium 180 Nosler Partition	2663	1.5	0.875

Bullet weight measured in grains, velocity in feet per second 10 feet from the muzzle by a ProChrono digital chronograph, and accuracy in inches of three, five-shot groups at 100 yards.

8. Mosin–Nagant M91/30 PU Sniper

The Greatest Generation's Sniper Rifle

In 1942 the US military modified the M1903A3 into a dedicated sniper rifle and called it the M1903A4. The M1903A3's iron sights were replaced with a Weaver 330C 2.5x scope on Redfield mounts, a pistol grip stock was swapped for the 03A3's stock, and the bolt handle was bent to clear the scope. There were other minor changes but it was the military's first try to standardize a sniper weapon. Some 28,000 M1903A4s were assembled and they are one of the rarer variants of the M1903 fetching prices in the range from $3,000 to $4,000. The scopes themselves are highly collectible.

The Gibbs Rifle Company calls its M1903-A4 a "Historical Remake" and collectors and shooters now have a fresh supply of pristine World War II-era sniper rifles. Gibbs is part of Navy Arms, which has been in the surplus and replica firearm business since the 1950s. In the 1990s they obtained a large quantity of original Remington-produced M1903A3 rifles and that is the platform on which their M1903-A4 is built. The actions and bolts are originals dating back to WWII. The barrels are new manufacture with four-groove rifling. Original 03A4s had quick-to-manufacture-in-wartime two-groove barrels. The stock is also new. Its walnut finished hardwood with inspector cartouches similar to those used during WWII. The receiver has the original military parkerized finish with parkerized stock furniture like originals. Also new is the M73B1 scope. Hi-Lux Optics manufactures the replica scope. The Gibbs rifle would be a dead ringer for originals but Gibbs was thoughtful and marked the rifle, scope, and rings so their 03-A4s would not be passed off as the real thing.

The Gibbs 03-A4 replica is made to be used. A fitting tribute to those sharpshooters a few generations ago who made the world safe.

▲ During WWII a GI in Italy looks over his 1903A4 sniper rifle. Courtesy National Archives.

▲ Old sniper rifles don't collect rust . . . they compete in Vintage Sniper matches. Courtesy CMP.

8. Mosin–Nagant M91/30 PU Sniper

Mother Russia's Sharpshooter

▲ The Mosin–Nagant Model 91/30 PU is an old bolt-action design that dates back to Imperial Russia and proved to be a precision shooter.

As much as the Mosin–Nagant Model 1891/30 is an old rifle design—it was adopted by the Imperial Russian Army before the Soviet Union ever existed—it is still used today in areas that were once under Soviet influence. The front page of *The New York Times* in the summer 2013 showed a photograph of a Syrian rebel firing a Model 91/30 with a long eye relief scope. The image is a reminder that some weapons have been manufactured in large amounts—some 45 million Model 91/30s have been built—and that some weapons have well-earned reputations. The Mosin–Nagant Model 1891/30 is a proven combat rifle. The Model 91/30 has been adopted by countries worldwide from Afghanistan, Latvia, and Ukraine to Russia, Turkey, Hungary, and China. The M44 Pattern made in Romania and the Type 53 produced in China are just two examples of the numerous licensed variants that have been manufactured in various parts of the world. In Russia and what was to become the Soviet Union, the most widespread variant of the Mosin–Nagant was the Model 1891/30. It was issued to all Soviet infantry soldiers from 1930 to 1945.

The Model 91/30 PU Sniper, however, is near and dear to Mother Russia. When other countries like Germany, England, and the United States forgot the lesson of World War I and the impact the lone rifleman or sniper had on the

battlefield, the Soviets built Mosin–Nagants equipped with low-power optics. The Soviets also trained both men and women in sharpshooting skills that they employed with efficiency. During World War II, when Germany needed precious oil to continue production of weapons and keep the German war machine rolling, the Germans attacked the Soviet Union in what would become the Eastern Front. The oil fields in southern Russia were the Germans' goal and Stalingrad stood between Germany and oil. At Stalingrad the German push ground to a stop as Soviet sharpshooters, both men and women, equipped with Model 91/30 PU Sniper rifles plied their skills on the *Wermacht*. The impact

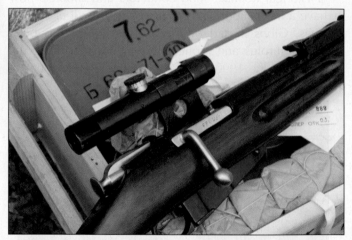

▲ The M91/30 PU is a combat rifle reconfigured for sniper service. The PU scope is simple, straight 30mm tube and windage and elevation turrets.

▲ The mount and scope are attached and secured via a screw to the left side of the rifle's receiver.

of precise shooting from small teams of snipers proved to be decisive in stopping the Germans.

Mitchell's Mausers has a stockpile of Model 91/30 PUs. The rifles come with all original accessories—oiler, maintenance tool, slings, cleaning rod, and ammo pouches—except for matching bayonets, presumably because these rifles were for police use and the police did not use bayonets. Beyond their normal safety and function checks, Mitchell's Mausers also checks scope alignment with a laser to confirm that the rifle zeros with the crosshairs reasonably in the center.

The 91/30 PUs are not pretty rifles. The one tested looked like it had hung over the fireplace mantle in a *dacha* then spent years encased in Cosmoline in a storehouse. But my experience with everything Russian taught me not to underestimate Russian engineering.

The Mosin–Nagant Model 1891/30 PU was built for hard, rough abuse. It is a push feed, bolt-action with two forward locking lugs and a spring loaded extractor that snaps over the base of the cartridge as the bolt is closed. At the rear of the bolt assembly is large knurled knob that is the rifle's safety. Pull it to the rear and rotate it to apply the safety. Since it works by compressing the firing pin mainspring, the knob takes muscle to operate. What is nice about the M 91/30 is it can be cocked by just pulling the knob straight back without having to rack the bolt handle.

The bolt handle on the M 1891/30 PU is bent to allow clearance to the PU scope. It has a 90° lift. I found that to fire the rifle with any speed a procedure different from a modern bolt-action was required. I achieved my fastest follow-up shots by pulling back the knurled knob to cock the weapon then cycling the bolt handle to eject and load. It uses a 5-round non-detachable magazine. Without the scope a stripper clip is used to recharge the weapon; with the scope in place each round is loaded individually. A button at the bottom of the magazine, if pressed, will release the follower and spring to quickly unload the rifle.

The full wood stock is similar to other combat rifles of the era. A deep groove is cut into the wood on the forend that allows a good grasp with or without gloves. The pistol grip is straight. There are sling slots in the butt and forend. A curved metal butt plate is screwed into the butt. A cleaning rod under the barrel can be unscrewed and used for maintenance. The iron sights consist of an adjustable ladder-style notched rear sight with graduations up to 2000 meters. The front is a fixed post under a hood. The hood has a hole in it to allow light through and shine on the post.

▲ The checkered button at the front of the trigger guard allows the user to quickly purge the magazine of cartridges.

▲ With the PU scope attached the operator still has access to the iron sights; the front post has a hood with hole to allow light in.

▲ The scope is set high from the bore's centerline but the rifle was not awkward to fire.

Our Man in Russia

The story behind the surplus M91/30s reads like a spy novel full of intrigue at a time when the Soviet Union was dissolving and the United Nations voted to destroyed stockpiles of surplus weapons.

According to Mitchell's Mausers' man in Russia, the Mosin–Nagant M91/30 rifles are original World War II sniper rifles not reconfigured rifles. In past years rebuilt snipers have come on the market with new bold handles and new Chinese-made scopes. The Mitchell's scopes were made in Ukraine.

Here is an email about the M91/30s I received obviously written by a person whose English was not their first language.

"... but now we have had the chance to by [sic] these totally original made WW.II snipers and by [sic] a time that the army warehouse are empty around the world. Many Governments as well the Russians decided by pressure of the United Nations not longer to sell the small arms, from know they have to destroy these. As well the Russians agreed on that and started already last year with the destroying of these arms. We worked very hard on it to get a few of these rifles out of Russia. It was really luck to find a way to get them. It was by a evening meeting with several Law & Enforcement Officers in Russia, we meet as well a Police General. And he told us that he just get for his collection a original WW.II Mosin Nagant sniper rifle. And he told us that he get it for free of out of a police arsenal. These was, stored for the Police as War-Reserve, but as well not many are left. Normally they were sold or destroyed as well, but they forgot this last warehouse ..."

It must be the Eastern European accent I can hear as I read the email. The condition of the Mosin–Nagant snipers is very good to excellent, with original mounts and scope, many of them with original matching numbers. These rifles are really a piece of history, but also usable high precision shooters.

From the proof marks on the barrel, the Soviet crest—sickle and hammer surrounded by a wreath—and "1943r" below it, this rifle was built by the arsenal in Izhevsk, Russia, in 1943. The receiver has a rounded top with stripper clip notches toward the rear. To the left side of the receiver are forward and rear notches that engage the optic mount. The mount is inserted into the forward recess, the mounted is pivoted into place, and then the rear screw is tightened to secure the mount to the rifle. It is hardly streamlined but suits the purpose. The PU scope is attached to the mount with a pair of rings that are secured with three slotted screws. The scope body is a straight tube with a 30mm diameter and has 3.5x magnification. Turrets adjust the reticle like a modern scope—one for elevation and one for windage. The reticle is a simple three-post design with thick crosshairs that can be used to range distance. It is a rudimentary reticle at best when compared to modern set ups. The scope is mounted high so the irons sights can be used for close range work. Looking through the scope was like looking through a greasy drinking glass. This is a relic from eons ago so I didn't want to make judgments. In the back of my mind though, I did not have high hopes.

The M 91/30 PU is chambered in 7.62x54mmR—also referred to as 7.62 Russian, 7.62 Mosin–Nagant, 7.62 Dragunov, Rimmed Russian—a round that was developed back when the Tsar ruled Russia in 1891. If the US has the .30-06, then Russia has the 7.62x54mmR. It is one of the oldest cartridges still being used in combat. The Dragunov and other sniper rifles like the bolt-action SV-98, as well as the PKM machine gun use the cartridge. It is a rimmed cartridge that uses a 147-grain bullet. Sniper rounds developed

▲ Notice how the bolt handle just clears the PU scope tube body; a revised cycling procedure is required to shoot the M 91/30 PU rapidly.

▲ This is a view of the inside of the PU scope; the over 70-year-old lens are murky and have a heavy 3-post reticle.

in 1999 use a 151-grain bullet with a hardened steel penetrator. The round has similar ballistics as the 7.62x51mm NATO/.308 Winchester rounds. A crate of 148-grain FMJ military surplus ammo of Russian manufacture was procured for testing. It is loaded in steel cases and Berdan primed.

At fifty yards, the scope was zeroed and I found the M 91/30 PU was pleasant to shoot. The weight of the rifle helped absorb the perceived recoil and though the scope was a bit fuzzy at the edges my interest started to be piqued. Moving a paper Zombies Industries target out to 100 yards, I settled behind the rifle using a rest on the bench. Racking the bolt back, I found the M 91/30 PU was easy to load and there was plenty of room between the bottom of the scope and the top of the action. The stock has a noticeable drop and it looked like the rifle would be awkward to shoot, but at the bench I found it comfortable with a trigger that broke on average at 5 pounds 1 ounce. The trigger was a two-stage military style with plenty of creep. I fired center of mass and then head shots on the zombie targets. I don't know if the Russian rifle channeled

Loading the M 91/30 PU was easy since there was plenty of room between the scope and action. ▶

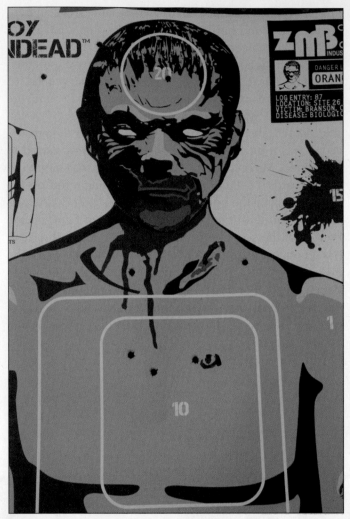

▲ At 200 yards the groups naturally opened but the M 91/30 PU was still deadly accurate.

▲ A Mosin–Nagant M 91/30 PU and crate of surplus ammo are ready to fill the freezer with deer meat.

my Eastern European ancestry, but at 100 yards I could easily shoot sub-MOA groups even with the murky scope and creepy trigger. I had to look twice through the spotting scope to confirm what I was seeing. This rifle was made in 1943, and I have no idea how much it was used. It performed well with the inexpensive surplus ammo. I was curious what I could do at 200 yards with the M 91/30 PU. The zombie head looked like a fuzzy grape in the scope and if I did my part, that zombie was dead. I could consistently place rounds at 200 yards into the head area of the target. I was amazed at how well the rifle performed. This ancient relic that looked like it had been dragged through the sewers during the Battle of Stalingrad shot better than some modern bolt-action rifles. Never judge a book by its cover, and never underestimate Russian technology.

Specifications	Mitchell's Mausers Mosin Sniper Rifle
Caliber	7.62x54mmR
Barrel	29 in.
OA Length	48.5 in.
Weight (Unloaded)	11 lb.
Stock	stained hardwood
Iron Sights	notch ladder adjustable rear/hooded fixed post front
Optics	3.5x PU rifle scope
Action	2-lug, bolt-action, 90° lift
Finish	blued
Msrp	$799.00–$999.00
Performance	Mitchell's Mausers Mosin Sniper Rifle

Surplus 7.62x54mmR (Russian manufacture)	Velocity	Best	Average
Military surplus 148 FMJ	2836	0.4	0.7

Bullet weight measured in grains, velocity in feet per second 15 feet from the muzzle by a ProChrono digital chronograph, and accuracy in inches of three, three-shot groups at 100 yards.

Reloading the Mosin–Nagant Circa 1954

In the manual published in 1945 by the Ministry of Defense of the USSR, a method of reloading the Mosin–Nagant sniper rifle equipped with the PU scope is detailed. The method describes a technique that allows the shooter to accelerate the rate of fire without lowering the rifle from the shooter's shoulder and while keeping the target in view through the scope. The Model 1891/30 is unique from modern bolt-action rifles as the hammer can be cocked without cycling the bolt. The Springfield M1903, Lee-Enfield, among other rifles also have a similar bolt systems.

STEP 1: Grasp the knurled knob of the hammer rearward until it cocks.

STEP 2: Place hand under bolt and raise bolt upward.

STEP 3: Grasp knurled knob and draw the bolt fully rearward to eject the empty cartridge case.

STEP 4: Push the knurled knob forward chambering a live round and push the bolt knob downward with the index and middle fingers.

At this point the rifle is ready to fire. A twenty-first century shooter may find this method awkward, but with practice and using a rest I was able to keep my eye on the target while reloading. The alternative method is to cycle the bolt handle, but the bent bolt handle has very little clearance between it and the scope. Sometimes old-fashioned ways are the best.

▲ Soviet instructive poster for the Mosin Nagant 1891/30, PE, PEM and PU Sniper Rifle Scopes and Mounts.
Courtesy Gunart.net

9. The Evolution of the USMC M40 Series Rifles

From Hunting Rifles to Long-range Sniper Tools

Out of the steaming jungles of Southeast Asia a sniper rifle began to take shape. The journey began in the early 1960s with a dire need for long-range precision rifles during the Vietnam War. The USMC had on hand civilian Winchester Model 70 rifles mounted with 8x Unertl scopes and chambered in .30-06. These rifles were used stateside for training and marksmanship competition, and were soon fielded and used in combat with newly formed sniper teams. Carlos Hathcock was issued a Winchester Model 70 during his first deployment to Vietnam. The Winchester Model 70 served well but had flaws. In the humid heat of the jungle the wood stocks swelled and warped. The scope was powerful and consistent but delicate. The Winchester proved to be a good start.

Doug Wicklund, Senior Curator at the NRA National Firearms Museum relates the story of the M40. Wicklund is a fourth generation NRA life member and happens to have an interest in sniper rifles. He has an extensive collection of military sniper rifles and talks freely about everything-from US-made rifles to Soviet-built Mosin–Nagants and Dragonovs, but we are here to talk about the M40.

In the late 1960s the Marines started to test rifles and the journey for a dedicated sniper rifle took a different path. The Winchester was battle tested, but the new Model 70—post 1964 models—were redesigned by Winchester to be manufactured more cost effectively. The new design had a weak extractor that required the chamber to be cleaned frequently or risk the possibility of breaking the extractor. Frequent cleaning can be a luxury in country, while breaking parts are not desirable. The Marines turned to Remington's Model 700 and 40X rifles and chose the 7.62x51mm NATO round known by civilians as the .308 Winchester.

Remington worked closely with the military and on April 7, 1966, the Marines adopted the M40, officially called: Rifle, 7.62mm Sniper, M40. The M40 was assembled by Remington's Custom Shop and consisted of a free-floated, medium weight barrel made of chrome-moly steel. It had a 1:10-inch twist rate. The actions were factory bedded in uncheckered wood stocks. The target rifle heritage of the M40 is evident with the stripper clip notches at rear of the receiver, a legacy of the Remington 40X target rifles. The slots were not used since the Redfield scope blocked access. The rifles had a matte Parkerized finish and were mounted with a 3-9x variable-power Redfield Accu-Range scope with a ranging feature out to 600 yards. The first scopes had a distinct green anodized finish and later were finished black. It was mounted with Redfield Junior bases and rings. The Corps ordered seven hundred rifles. The jungle was not easy on the M40. It, too, experienced swelling of the wood stock. Wicklund relates tales of operators shaving the swelled wood to refloat the barrel. The scope also succumbed to the rigor of battle and heat; at times the

▲ Three rifles that changed how Marines snipers shoot. The Winchester Model 70 with Unertl scope (top) evolved into the M40 (middle) based on the Remington Model 700 and 40X action and a Redfield optic and the M40A1 (bottom) what is considered a classic sniper rifle rebuilt from the M40 but with a McMillan fiberglass stock and U.S. Optics 10x scope an upgraded version of the Unertl 10x scope. Courtesy NRA National Firearms Museum.

▲ The M40 was a good interim rifle but the wood stock swelled in humidity and the Redfield reticle could melt in high heat. Courtesy NRA National Firearms Museum.

reticle melted in the sun. Hathcock was issued an M40 on his second deployment. Marine snipers viewed the M40 as the best sniper rifle at the time especially when match-grade ammo was used. By the early 1970s about 425 M40s survived and in 1977 the Marines decided the M40 needed an upgrade.

Three original M40s exist, says Wicklund, two of which are on display courtesy of the NRA. One is in the National Sporting Arms Museum at Bass Pro Shops in Springfield, Missouri, and one is displayed at the National Firearms Museum at NRA headquarters in Fairfax, Virginia.

The well-used and battered M40s were re-barreled, re-stocked, and modified by Marine armorers at Quantico. Atkinson stainless steel barrels were used as replacements with 1:12-inch twist rates. Green and earth-tone red camo McMillan fiberglass stocks with a Pachmayr brown rubber buttpad replaced the wood stocks. Additional alterations were made to the internal magazine and the Model 700 aluminum bottom metal—trigger guard and floorplate—was replaced with modified Winchester Model 70 bottom metal. The new rifles were designated M40A1. At twelve pounds, the M40A1 was almost three pounds heavier the M40. Redfield scopes originally were mounted on the M40A1s but around 1988 the Marines went back to Unertl and a 10x with a mil-dot reticle. The reticle was calibrated to M118 Lake City Match ammo. The Unertl scope was more robust. With the addition of the Unertl the M40A1 tipped the scales at 14.5 pounds. The extra weight makes for a robust rifle.

In 1996 many of the M40A1s in service had been rebuilt, some numerous times. The USMC started to look at upgrading their sniper rifle. Using extensive input from tactical rifle shooters and combat experience with the M40A1, the new M40A3 started to take shape. The rifles are all built

▲ Purpose-built using operator input and combat experience, the M40A1 replaced the wood stock for a fiberglass McMillan stock and is a hybrid of mostly Remington components but also some Winchester Model 70 parts. Courtesy NRA National Firearms Museum.

at the Marine's gunsmithing facility in Quantico, Virginia. The M40A3s are a combination of off-the-shelf parts and custom made. Again, the Remington Model 700 short-action was used as the platform with a 24-inch Schneider 610, heavy match grade barrel with 1:12-inch twist rate. The bottom metal is procured from DD Ross Company. The barreled action is bedded in a synthetic OD green McMillan A-4 stock. This is benchrest-style stock with a flat forend and modern ergonomics like a more vertical pistol grip. The length of pull is adjustable as well as the saddle-type cheekpiece. The barreled action is glass bedded into the stock using aluminum pillars. Under the forend there's a stud for attaching a bipod. The Schmidt and Bender Police Marksman II LP 3-12x50mm scope is mated to the M40A3. In military parlance the optic is called M8541 Scout Sniper Day Scope. It is mounted with Badger Ordnance USMC M40A3 34mm scope rings. The base is a DD Ross 30-MOA Picatinny rail. The set up weighs 16.6 pounds with the optic.

In 2009 the M40A3 was superseded by the M40A5 which had minor modifications. A straight taper barrel was used and it is threaded at the muzzle for suppressor and muzzle brake use. Surefire supplies the suppressor and muzzle brake. The bottom metal is made by Badger Ordnance and has a detachable 5-round box magazine. There is also a forward rail mount for attaching the AN/PVS-22 night vision optic.

The evolution of the M40 series continues and in 2015 a contract should be awarded for the M40A6. The newest M40 variant will include a foldable stock, a full-length rail to accommodate day and night optics, and must also be compatible with .338 Lapua Magnum actions.

Of all the USMC sniper rifles, the M40A1 is iconic with a legendary reputation among operators. Some custom gun makers like GA Precision and C&H Precision Weapons build mil-spec replicas of the M40A1 and M40A3. According to Wicklund the road to a USMC dedicated sniper rifle started with interim rifles that later helped write the spec on the current rifle.

As we ended our conversation, I asked Wicklund about Carlos Hathcock, a family friend of Wicklund's. I asked which rifle Hathcock preferred. Carlos Hathcock felt that either rifle was suitable and that more rests with the individual doing the shooting than the rifle, responded Wicklund.

10. SIG SSG 3000 Patrol

Built to Kill

▲ The SIG SSG 3000 is a well balanced and capable tactical rifle.

▲ The receiver is machined from one piece; rigid and stiff to aid accuracy.

The SIG Sauer SSG 3000 has a reputation for out-of-the-box precision and performance. It should, since it heritage can be traced back to wicked accurate Swiss-made rifles. Since 2000 the rifle has evolved, making it perform better and reducing the price. Expectations were high. "Made in Germany" was roll-marked on the barrel as well as SIG's Exeter, New Hampshire, location in the US. It reeks of hardcore precision.

The SSG 3000 uses a modular design that allows primary components like the trigger system, receiver, barrel, stock, and bolt to be easily and quickly swapped out or replaced. The rifle breaks down fast into four main components and a few screws.

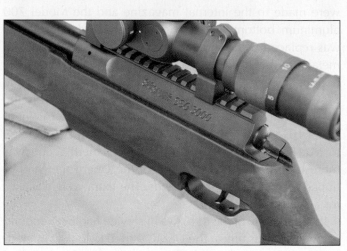

▲ The Picatinny rail and receiver are one piece.

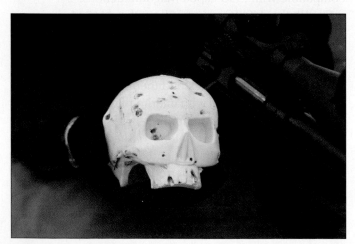

▲ Alas the SIG SSG 3000 grew to know poor Yorick well.

The trigger system is totally customizable. The take-up, let-off point, and pull weight can be adjusted by the operator using a hex wrench and without disassembling the rifle. Two clearance holes in the metal trigger guard give access to a wrench to the take-up and let-off screws. The pull weight is adjusted via the right side of the trigger; the factory set the trigger at 3.4 pounds. The trigger face is wide, smooth, and nearly flat with just a hint of curve.

The safety lock is simplicity itself—one button with a single function. Just aft of the bolt handle is the safety lock. It is a large tab that slides downward when pressed. With or without gloves the safety lock is easy to engage. With the safety engaged the bolt, trigger stop, firing pin shoe and

▲ The red cocking indicator is showing that the SIG is cocked and ready to fire.

trigger are locked. Within the trigger guard just forward of the trigger is a button to disengage the safety. This allows a shooter to keep their firing hand in position to flick the safety off. There is no need to break your grip or reposition your shooting hand to turn the safety off. The button is simply pushed up into the stock with the trigger finger. It's well protected from accidental manipulation and it's very tactile. The safety can also be disengaged by pulling up on the tab.

The bolt assembly is removed from the receiver by first lowering the cheekpiece. Release the safety and open the bolt and draw it partially backward, then engage the safety and pull the bolt assembly from the rear of the receiver.

A cocking indicator is located at the rear of the bolt assembly. A small red tab is visible when the rifle is

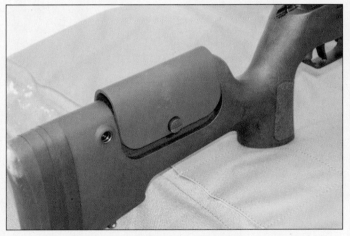

▲ SIG uses a McMillan stock adjustable for length of pull and comb height.

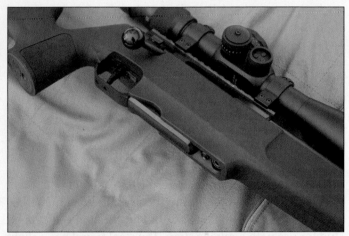

▲ The magazine well cut out at rear aids in pulling free a stuck magazine.

▲ The trigger allows multiple user adjustments without disassembling the rifle.

▲ The magazine release button is located in front of the magazine well; it is recessed so there's little chance of accidentally dumping the magazine.

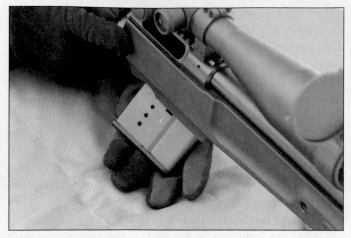

▲ Even with gloved hands the magazine was easy to access and change rapidly in the prone position.

▲ A Sinclair bipod proved durable and infinitely adjustable; an extra sling stud on the forend allowed attachment.

cocked. It can be felt with the thumb of an ungloved shooting hand. The bolt knob is smooth polymer that is easily palmed in the prone position or at the bench with or without gloved hands. The bolt cycles very smoothly like a hot framing nail sliding lengthwise in and out of a stick of margarine. The bolt is a short throw requiring only a 60° lift. It is fast and slick. Also, the short lift means there's more space between your hand and the scope when cycling the action. The bolt is a push-feed type and it uses six locking lugs.

Built into the receiver is a zero-MOA Picatinny rail that travels the entire length of the receiver. It offers numerous mounting location options. At the muzzle end is a capped stud for use with a mirage strap. The steel barrel has a slight taper and is rifled with four grooves and a 1:12 inch twist rate. The muzzle is threaded—5/8x24 TPI—and comes with a four-slot flash suppressor. The slots run from the nine o'clock position to the three o'clock position; no vents on the bottom side. The flash suppressor can be removed and other muzzle devices screwed on.

The short-action receiver has a small oblong ejection port that allows an operator to load rounds individually. It also provides plenty of room to eject spent round cases. The barrel is fitted into the receiver and secured with three set screws.

The stock is manufactured my McMillan, built from composite material and similar to McMillan A-3 stock. The barrel is free floated its entire length and it has aluminum bedding to secure the action to the stock. The length of pull is adjustable via a series of spacers. Use a screwdriver

▲ Recoil was mild with the heavy setup; the flash hider can be replaced with a suppressor if needed.

▲ The SIG performed perfectly in hot and cold weather; that's a Blackhawk drag bag/shooting mat.

▲ The bolt was easy to cycle and so, so smooth.

image resolution possible throughout the 5-25X power magnification range and at distances past 2,000 yards.

The front focal plane reticle is a Mil Scale GAP reticle that was designed in conjunction with George Gardner at GA Precision. It is a Mil-based reticle that offers full Mil and ½ Mil increments—nine Mil's from the center down the vertical axis and four Mil's left and right on the horizontal axis. It can be illuminated red with a press of a button and has twelve red illumination settings. The ER-25 also features an Erector Repositioning Elevation Knob (EREK) system that maximizes gross elevation travel adjustment

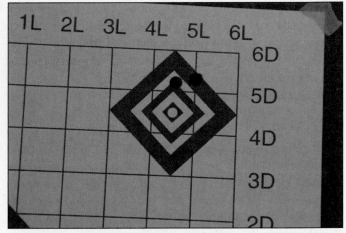

▲ This is a 3-shot group fired at 100 yards; two bullets went through the hole to the right.

to unscrew the buttpad screws and remove it, then add or remove spacers as required. The comb has an adjustable cheekpiece. Press the button to raise the comb to a desired height. Releasing the button locks the cheekpiece in place. The stock has a handy butt hook for use with a sand bag. The pistol grip is near vertical and has good ergonomics in most shooting positions. The texture on the sides is sandy and the front strap is serrated. A magazine well protects and encases the 5-round detachable magazine. The area forward the magazine well is relieved of material so the stock feels thin in hand. The bottom edge of the forend is flat for a better rest. Sling swivel studs are attached, plus there is an extra stud on the forend to attach a bipod. There are two attachment points for side rails along the sides of the forend.

Rounds are stored single-stack in the steel, detachable box magazine. Witness holes allow the user to keep track of rounds in the magazine. The follower and base pad are polymer. A small round serrated button just forward of the magazine well at the bottom of the stock releases the magazine. The magazine falls free loaded and unloaded and the magazine release button is inset into the stock so it can't be accidentally pressed. I could operate the button with or without gloves with no problems. A small cutout to the rear of the magazine well allows a user to pull the magazine from the stock if it should get stuck.

Using Warne 34mm rings, a U.S. Optics ER-25 5-25x58mm scope was mounted to the SSG 3000. The 58mm objective lens sits in front of a Turret Parallax Adjustment Locater (TPAL) system that ensures the sharpest

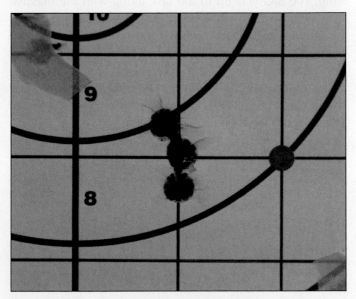

▲ At 200 yards these are the typical groups the SSG 3000 produced.

for maximum elevation adjustment. This is a true 2,000 yard scope. I figured the ER-25 would help squeeze out the accuracy of the SIG.

I scrounged for ammo, assembling a mix that ranged from premium match ammo to dirt cheap, steel case FMJ. Before setting up on the bench, a Sinclair tactical bipod was attached to the forend stud. The SSG 3000 was ready to roll.

I fired the rifle at fifty yards to see where it was printing and adjusted the big scope about an inch high. Moving the target out to 100 yards I zeroed the Sig in with the 168-grain Norma ammo. The first few rounds after zeroing were good. The rifle had my interest, but as the barrel broke in I saw groups shrink. I cleaned the bore and began to shoot groups again. It didn't really matter what brand of ammo I fed the SSG 3000, it was shooting sub-MOA groups without me trying that hard. The inexpensive ammo, like PMC and Bear, gave slightly over 1-MOA at 100 yards. At 200 yards the Sig was in a zone. Again I could easily fire sub-MOA groups. I think the Sig and the U.S. Optics scope were getting acquainted. The rifle was simple to adjust to my average stature. The trigger was crisp and it was easy to break cleanly.

Paper at distance is one test, but life is more dynamic. At 100 yards I dropped a Do All Targets Impact Seal Bonehead skull I called Yorick. The skull bounced upon impact and the idea was to hit it again as fast as possible. The SIG was up to the task along with the massive U.S. Optics scope and I bounced the skull well past 100 yards. Viewing a target through the scope, we anticipate the outcome but in reality we need to be prepared for the unexpected.

The cost of the SSG 3000 is much less than many other sniper class rifles. It will put a grin on your face. A grin that takes days to wear off.

Specifications	SIG Sauer SSG 3000 Patrol 24
Caliber	7.62x51mm NATO/.308 Win.
Barrel	23.5 in.
OA Length	45 in.
Weight (Unloaded)	12 lb.
Stock	matte black composite
Iron Sights	n/a
Optics Rail	zero MOA M1913 Picatinny Rail
Action	6-lug, push-feed, bolt-action, 60° lift
Finish	matte black
Msrp	$1,499.00

.308 Winchester	Velocity	Average	Best
PMC 147 FMJ-BT	2640	0.65	1.1
Hornady Match 168 A-Max	2789	0.45	0.6
SSA (7.62x51mm) 150 FMJ	2588	0.41	0.53
Hornady TAP 155 TAP FPD	2693	0.15	0.35
Norma 168 Sierra HPBT	2380	0.15	0.35
Brown Bear 145 Bimetal FMJ	2749	0.9	1.4

Bullet weight measured in grains, velocity in feet per second 15 feet from the muzzle by a ProChrono digital chronograph, and accuracy in inches of three, three-shot groups at 100 yards.

11. Accurate-Mag's Multi-Caliber Rifle Chassis System

Scenario Adaptive for Precision or Suppression Mission Requirements

As precision rifles have evolved the concept of a modular chassis system has been developed. These systems offer flexibility to customize the stock, forend, optics, and other components for a specific mission. The process is quick and has little to no change on point of impact. In the approach taken by BML Tool, the modular chassis system allows caliber changes from short to long bolt-actions and semiautomatic actions, as well as the ability for less lethal situations and other classified scenarios.

▲ The feed lips of Accurate-Mag magazines allow the bolt to chamber a round closer to the centerline of the chamber and help spit the cartridge out from the magazine.

▲ Accurate-Mag's Multi-Caliber Rifle Chassis System gives operators a wide range of capabilities from precision to suppression fire.

▲ Two barreled and very different actions that drop into the chassis system.

Back in 1968, BML Tool opened up shop out of a two-car garage. Now over fifty-five years later, BML is a 38,000 square foot facility nestled in the hills of western Connecticut. BML's roots are deep into tool and die making. Walking through the facility, tool bits buzz in a wet slurry of cutting fluid as CNC machines reveal a familiar shape from aluminum forgings. Metal stamping machines the size of small buildings pound steel into magazine components. BML Tool is a precision metal craft vendor that makes critical parts for the military and commercial markets. They are also involved with small weapons research and development with an eye on a modular weapon system. Parts manufactured by BML are used in aircraft, medical devices, and small arms.

If you are a shooter of ARs and precision tactical rifles you may have used a weapon with a component manufactured

▲ An aluminum forging is CNC machined to create the receiver section of the chassis system.

by BML. Accurate-Mag is one of BML's product lines. To say Accurate-Mag magazines are the Cadillac of rifle magazines is an understatement. Accurate-Mag magazines are single-stack, metal, centerfire rifle cartridge magazines that meet all Mil-Spec and NATO Stanag requirements. These magazines fit all M24 and M40 type service rifles as well as MK13 and NATO variants. OEM rifle manufacturers like Colt, Savage, Ruger, McMillan, Remington, and others use Accurate-Mag magazines. You'll note the Accurate-Mag cartouche on the magazines for Ruger's Gunsite Scout rifle. Accurate-Mag is also the proprietary manufacturer of magazines for the US Military's XM2010 sniper system.

The magazines are built from steel, heat-treated, and coated with Teflon. On long-action box magazines the feed lip configuration allows the bolt to chamber the round closer to the centerline of the chamber. The feed lips also have a spring action that helps to spit the cartridge out from the magazine and into the chamber as the bolt is pushed forward into battery. This results in the fastest round release time for a center feed cartridge delivery system. It is patented under US8,322,063. BML Tool holds sixteen other patents too.

In addition, Accurate-Mag manufactures bottom metal kits for short- and long-actions. The kits include a magazine and bottom metal of 6061-T6 aluminum that fits OEM rifles manufactured by Remington, Savage, Badger, and AICS among others. They allow an internal magazine to be replaced with a high-capacity, detachable box magazine.

That familiar form taking shape in the CNC machines is the Multi-Caliber Rifle Chassis System. And that piece in the CNC is the center section of Accurate-Mag's three-piece chassis system. The center section is built in short- and long-action configurations. The other two components of the chassis system are the buttstock and forend. This system has been developed from military requirements.

Since 1988 the US military has fielded the M24 SWS (Sniper Weapon System), a version of the Remington Model 700 action chambered in 7.62x51mm NATO (.308 Winchester) mated to a H-S Precision stock topped with a Leupold Ultra M3A 10x42mm fixed power optic. This is an excellent weapon but as it has been fielded with more frequency it has shown limitations. Military spec calls for the barrel to maintain .35 MOA accuracy for up to 10,000 rounds. Between training and in-field use, there are times when the rifle needs to be repaired requiring

▲ The Savage M100 action is modified with a full Picatinny rail allowing plenty of options for mounting the Leupold scope.

▲ Accurate-Mag magazines are used with the system and the extended magazine release allows quick reloads even when wearing gloves.

▲ The buttstock is totally customizable to the operator. This is an experimental version with adjustable butt spike.

the weapon to be pulled out of service and shipped to an armorer. Modular chassis systems can keep a weapon in field indefinitely as modular systems can be maintained in the field by the shooter. In September of 2010 the US Army awarded Remington a contract for the M24E1 ESR (Enhanced Sniper Rifle) which has since been renamed the XM2010. The XM2010 differs from the M24 in a number of characteristics, mainly a caliber change to .300 Winchester Magnum, a detachable five-round magazine, a fully adjustable chassis to fit any user, a suppressor and muzzle brake, and others. As much as the XM2010 has done to advance sniper rifles, the current XM2010 still needs to be maintained by an armorer. Accurate-Mag's Multi-Caliber Rifle Chassis is designed for the next evolution of the XM2010.

Accurate-Mag's system can be maintained by the shooter in the field with a minimum of down time. Their innovative inserts attach to a barreled action, like Savage or Remington bolt-action, allowing the user to change out a barreled action in mere minutes. Accurate-Mag refers to them as "insert rifles." Insert rifles employ a dedicated action block that is bolted to the action receiver and barrel. These action blocks are designed to fit like a glove on either a Savage, Remington, or M14 action. Other action blocks for the .50 BMG, non-lethal, and high tech weapons like a user-guided grenade are in development. Each action block is unique to a manufacturer's barreled action. What they all share in common are a trunion track on the left and right side of the action block. These trunion tracks of the action block mate to the trunion pins in the chassis.

On a cold day in January we traveled to an old and private club in Chappaqua, New York, to put the Multi-Caliber Rifle Chassis through its paces. Accurate-Mag 10-round magazines were loaded with Black Hills .308 cartridges with 175-grain Match Hollow Point bullets. Factory speed is 2600 fps. The chassis held a Savage M10 action with an experimental 17-¾ inch barrel.

The stock is completely ambidextrous with the length of pull (LOP) adjusted able from 13-½ to 15 inches. The check piece has a two-inch adjustment range. It can also be folded. Some models can fold to the left side of the chassis or in this case to the right side which secures the bolt handle.

At a bench and using a Harris bipod, I centered the reticle of the Leupold Mark 4 ER/T 6.5-20x50mm dead

▲ This is an R&D setup using a Remington action tricked out by Rob Snyder that uses a 17.75-inch barrel. The barrel length allows for a full burn of the .308 Winchester cartridge.

▲ With the short-barreled .308 Winchester setup I could bang the gong at 100 yards all day long—or as long as the Black Hills ammo held out.

▲ Going from the mild .308 Winchester round to the wild .338 Norma Mag. round was simple, quick, and easy.

▲ We did not adjust the zero of the Leupold for me, but these groups show the consistency I could get in sub-zero weather with the rifles.

center on the target at 200 yards. Savage Accu Triggers are sweet and I hit black with the first round. I did not zero the scope nor was I able to test for muzzle velocity or accuracy, but the subsequent nine rounds clustered between 5 and 6 o'clock. Some bullets shared the hole of a previous bullet.

We then tried a magazine in another .308 barreled action tuned by RW Snyder Gunsmithing. It was based on the Remington design and again 10 rounds, 10 holes. As before, I didn't adjust the big Leupold to my dope but kept shooting to a spot. This time I saw hits at 1 o'clock. Even though it was cold enough to hear pond water freeze, I was pleased. I liked the V-shaped notch in the stock. With

my non-shooting hand I was able to push the stock using the notch into my shoulder while pushing forward with my shooting hand on the pistol grip to lock the rifle in place. I varied the pressure and the groups on the target show that, as I found the right balance. I ran an additional magazine through each action again and consistently hit a metal plate at 200 yards even though the tip of my nose was numb. Bang a gong. Get it on.

The ballistics to the .338 Norma are mighty different from the .308—the .338 Norma pushes a Sierra 300-grain hollow point boat tail with a muzzle velocity of 2660 fps—and I aimed for a spot and Vin Battaglia, VP Operations & Principal of BML Tool & Mfg. Corp., called the shot while looking through a Kowa spotting scope. I adjusted my aim and steel sung from being hit by the .338 Norma.

Back at the BML Tool's facility, Vin swapped actions out of the chassis with an M14 barreled action. Within minutes the rifle that was set up for long-range precision use now had an M14 insert set up for suppression fire. There is no need to check head space nor any mechanical checks required to get the rifle on line. This does mean a shooter will need an entire barreled action with insert block at his disposal, but when you think about the time a more traditional tactical weapon would be out of service—weeks or months—while it is being rebarreled with an armorer, Accurate-Mag's system allows a shooter to be back on line in minutes. And when a shooter knows the zero for his optic for different rounds there is no need to sight-in the weapon. The tactical rifle has evolved.

Multi-Caliber Chassis System Changeover

Vin Battaglia, the VP of Operations & Principal at BML Tool, demonstrated how easy it is to swap out the barreled actions of the Multi-Caliber Rifle Chassis System. It takes more time to describe how to swap barreled actions than it takes to actually do it.

▲ Step 1: Vin pulled the bolt from the action and removed the scope. He pressed the detent pin in the chassis with a bullet tip and pulled back on the pistol grip.

▲ Step 2: Remove the upper forend rail.

◀ Step 3: Placing the rifle on its butt and pointing the muzzle skyward, he unscrewed the handscrew with a wrench.

◀ Step 4: The Savage barreled action is then pivoted on the trunion pins and pulled out of the chassis.

◀ Step 5: Vin replaced the Savage M10 barreled action with a Savage M110 in .338 Norma Magnum in the same chassis and reassembled the components.

▲ Step 6: A Gemtech suppressor was added to help tame the .338 Norma Magnum and we were good to go.

12. PTR91KC and Surplus Hensoldt Scope

Ersatz HK G3A3ZF Variant

▲ The PTR91 rifle recreates the renowned HK G3A3ZF sniper variant.

▲ The newly manufactured PTR91KC by PTR Industries is a civilian version of the famed battle rifle. I wanted to see what type of results I would find when I mounted a surplus Hensoldt scope from the 1970s.

There was a time when battle rifles were not considered particularly accurate weapons, but militaries since World War I have mounted optics on them for long-range work. Not the best solutions for true, long-range, precision work but some were quite capable.

The M1 Garand is an example of an excellent battle rifle reconfigured as a sniper rifle. Equipped with either a 2.5x power M82 or 2.2x power M84 scope the M1 was designated the M1C or M1D sniper variation, respectively. The M1Cs used a Griffin & Howe mount; M1Ds a Springfield Armory mount. The rifle was widely used during the Korean War and was found to have good accuracy out to 600 yards. M14s were also made into sniper rifles by using M14 National Match rifles modified with a Redfield/Leatherwood 3-9x power ART (Automatic Ranging Scope) optic and designated the M21 and have been in US service since 1969.

The German military was following a similar course during the 1950s and 1960s. The military mounted optics on the FN FAL and designated it the FN FAL G1 Sniper. When FN refused to allow German production of the FAL, Germany developed the Heckler & Koch (HK) G3 battle rifle and mounted optics on some for sniper use. The G3A3ZF variant was a G3A3 with a Hensoldt 4x power scope. With the G3SG/1variant, G3A3s were hand-selected for their accuracy at the factory then equipped with an improved trigger, a cheekpiece on the buttstock, and a Zeiss 1.5-6x power optic.

Back in 1950s West Germany, the arms manufacturing firm of HK was asked by the Spanish arms manufacturer Centro de Estudios Técnicos de Materiales Especiales (CETME) to help tweak the Stg-45, a design for an assault rifle prototype that had been on the drawing boards since late World War II, following on the heels of the first assault rifle, the Stg-44. By the late 1950s the redesign resulted in the HK G3. CETME manufactured the rifles and simply called the rifle the CETME. These rifles were adopted by nearly fifty countries including West Germany, Sweden, Pakistan, Greece, Iran, Portugal, and Turkey, as well as numerous African nations and countries in South America. Many of these nations still use a derivative of the HK G3/CETME. The G3 was made under license in numerous countries including Portugal where it was designated the FMP m/961. Under the same

▲ The PTR91 has a reputation as being one of the best-built HK clones. It has a cult-like following; the online forums buzz with shooters enamored and impressed with the PTR91's performance.

▲ In the hands of an operator, the HK PSG1A1 can provide precision firepower.

▲ The G3 is known for really flinging empties. The used brass from a G3 or PTR91 typically is a bit mangled (left), making it difficult or next to impossible to reload the cases.

license the G3A3 was known as the FMP m/963. In 2002, the tooling from a manufacturing facility in Portugal was purchased and shipped to Farmington, Connecticut, where PTR Industries was established. The equipment is original HK machinery built to German mil-specs. PTR Industries has since moved their production facilities to South Carolina.

It is easy to see the World War II German DNA of the Stg-44 in the PTR91 as it makes use of steel stampings, pistol grip, high-capacity magazine, and cocking lever located on the left side of the receiver. There is minimal machining needed to build the G3 and the PTR91 since most parts are of stamped out steel. This reduces costs as well as eases manufacture—one reason why so many countries adopted the HK G3. The G3 rifles have an outstanding reputation in the field. It is known as a reliable design and in some configurations provides precision accuracy. It also works in any type of environment it could encounter.

The PTR91 is semiautomatic, and like the HK, employs a roller-delayed blowback system which is simplicity itself. ArmaLite AR-10 and FN FAL rifles by contrast use a gas operating system where gas from a fired round is vented off the barrel to work the action. The FN FAL uses a short stroke piston; the AR-10 a gas impingement system. The AR-10 and FAL were contemporaries to the G3 and all of these rifles were chambered in 7.62x51mm NATO. The operating system of the AR-10 and FAL offer minimal recoil but subjects the actions to burning power debris and high heat that dries lubricant. Maintenance with these rifles is more frequent. A roller-delayed blowback operating system on the G3 and PTR91 consists of a bolt assembly made up of a bolt head and bolt carrier. The bolt is held in battery by two sliding cylindrical rollers that fit into recesses in the

barrel extension, also called a trunnion or mounting block. The breech is opened when both rollers are compressed inward against the camming surfaces and driven by the rearward pressure of a fired round. As recoil energy is transferred to the locking piece and bolt carrier, the rollers move inward while the bolt head moves rearward. As the bolt carrier clears the rollers, pressure in the bore drops and the bolt head is held by the bolt carrier and moves to the rear together. This system distributes slightly more recoil to the shooter but the rifle is easier to maintain and parts last longer. All burning powders are expelled through the bore. No residue from burning gases gets in the operating system. This operating system requires less maintenance. The barrel chamber is fluted to aid case extraction.

The PTR91, like the G3, is a modular weapon, meaning the butt, handguard, and pistol grip/fire control assembly can be swapped and changed out by an operator.

The PTR91KC model has a welded muzzle flash suppressor. PTR Industries makes rifles as close to the original HK as you can get with numerous configurations offered from classic versions with wood or OD green polymer furniture to models with free-floated barrels set up for precision work. The PTR91KC has a 16-inch match grade, bull barrel chambered in .308 Win./7.62 NATO with a twist rate of 1:12. It is not free floated. A barrel extension on the

KC model is welded in place. PTR Industries outsources barrel manufacturing to Green Mountain and Thomson Center. The handguard surrounding the barrel is a tube of machined aluminum with oblong cooling vents. It gives the PTR a solid feel and the fine grooved serrations along the length give a non-slip grip. The handguard is also drilled and tapped on the sides and bottom for mounting accessories. Above the barrel and handguard is the cocking lever housing, basically a tube the holds the cocking lever in place. The 1.75-inch bolt handle folds out for use and has a rubber boot for ease of use. It is a non-reciprocating bolt handle, meaning as the weapon is fired the bolt handle does not move, unlike a bolt handle on an M14 or M1 Garand. The bolt handle is positioned on the left side of

▲ The front sight is hooded post. The iron sights on the PTR91KC were easy to use and fast to acquire the target.

the weapon and folds so it will not snag on gear or the environment in which you are working.

The cocking lever housing is part of the receiver. The front sight is hooded post. The rear sight uses a rotary drum that adjusts for windage and elevation. To adjust elevation the drum is turned to one of four positions. The notch is for up to the 100 meters and three apertures are calibrated for 200, 300, and 400 meters, indicated on the drum as 1, 2, 3 and 4, respectively. The sights are calibrated for 7.62 NATO ammo. The top, outer edge of the drum is knurled so it is easy to rotate. Windage is adjusted by loosening a set screw with a Philips screwdriver then rotating the

▲ The cocking handle is positioned on the left side of the weapon and provides good leverage to cock the weapon. The right-handed user can keep their shooting hand on the pistol grip while manipulating the cocking lever.

▲ The bolt does not lock back after the last round is fired. Here, the bolt handle was manually locked back.

▲ Shooters with small to average size hands will have a difficult time pressing the magazine release button while still gripping the pistol grip.

▲ The safety is more conveniently located and easily manipulated by a right-handed shooter's thumb.

▲ The lens covers are turned inside out and they position themselves along the side of the scope. Turn them back and they automatically cover the lens.

knurled windage adjustment knob. One full turn of the knob will move bullet impact 5.14 inches at 100 yards. The PTR91KC requires a claw mount for optic use. The magazine release is located on the right side of the weapon, slightly above and forward of the trigger guard.

The safety is located on the left side of the weapon and perfectly positioned to be manipulated with a right-handed shooter's thumb. Flick it up and it blocks the trigger; in the down position the weapon is ready to fire. An "S" and "F" for "safe" and "fire," respectively, are molded and filled with paint to indicate what condition the rifle is in. It flicked on and off easily and confidently. The pistol grip is similar to the naval-version of the HK G3 with extra fine textured polymer grip and trigger guard. Original HK trigger assemblies are not compatible with PTR91 rifles. The black polymer stock with a hard plastic recoil pad has a retro-Teutonic look. The butt pad is ridged so it is less likely to slip when shouldered. The sling attachment is built into the left side of the stock. A small ring for sling attachment is located toward the muzzle end just below the front sight. The stock has a slight drop so you can use low scope rings when mounting optics, unlike an AR style stock that comes straight out and require high rings.

Along with the hardcase, the PTR91KC came with a 10-round magazine. At one time there was a glut of surplus 30-round magazines. The aluminum magazines were so inexpensive I purchased a PTR91 to go along with them.

To build my G3A3ZF variant, I mounted the PTR91KC with a German military surplus Hensoldt Z24 with a STANAG claw mount. The entire scope/mount setup came

▲ The reticle is a modified German #1 style with a scale along the horizontal axis.

in a hard case with a tool kit and lens cleaning supplies. My guess is it was manufactured in the late 1960s or sometime in the 1970s. This 4x power scope is small and compact. It has windage and elevation knobs and a simple scope. The lens covers are very simplistic yet ingenious. They are made of pliable rubber and silent in use.

The scale allows a user to estimate range to target. If an average adult man is 18 inches wide at the shoulders, then the vertical hashmarks along the horizontal wire can determine distance. If the target fits between two of the hashmarks then the target is 100 meters away. If the target fits in the space between three of the hashmarks it is 50 meters away. If it fits half way between two marks it is 200 meters away. The Hensoldt required I brush up on my high school German: The elevation adjustment knob is marked T (*Tiefe*) and H (*Höhe*) which roughly translates to Down and Up, respectively. The windage knob is marked L (*Links*) for Left and R (*Rechts*) for Right.

The scope screws onto the STANAG claw mount via two slotted screws. The STANAG mount is smartly engineered. The center brace is hollow allowing use of the iron sights. The mount uses two pairs of claws that grasp a groove in the receiver. It is simple and secure, and can be quickly removed in seconds and installed just as quickly.

Military surplus ammo can be used in these rifles. You should not feed this pedigree cheap ammunition, but if you do—and I have—be aware the sealants on military surplus ammo will require the rifle to be cleaned more often.

PTR claims the barrels are capable of groups of a little over two inches at 200 yards. At the range, a supply of PMC Bronze 147-grain FMJ-BT, Norma 168-grain Sierra HPBT, and SSA 150-grain FMJs were used. I bore-sighted the PTR91 and at 100 yards I zeroed the Hensoldt. I did not expect bolt-action accuracy out of PTR; after all, it is a battle rifle. The temperature was about 45°F with a slight three mph breeze. Since the heritage of this rifle is combat, I used Zombie Industries paper targets that are life size. I called the 100 yard testing the "Precision Undead" routine. In 1968, George Romero directed the cult classic *Night of the Living Dead*, so we all know only a head shot kills zombies, and on the agenda were zombie head shots at 100 yards.

Recoil with the PTR91 is slightly more pronounced but the weight of the weapons helps mitigate felt recoil. The reticle of the Hensoldt was quick to acquire the target and the two-stage trigger averaged nine pounds, four ounces. Not exactly a target trigger pull but the results had me grinning; the zombies not so much. I was easily able with all the ammo brands to produce three-shot groups that averaged a little over three inches. In fact I always seemed to have a flier in the three-shot groups. The other two holes were always sub-MOA, their hairy edges almost touching. I could not complain about the accuracy.

I've used hunting rounds in the PTR for coyote and deer. In the dead of winter when it is still, bitter, and cold and the coyotes roam for food, I wait sitting in snow wearing winter camo almost rendered invisible. With a pair of shooting sticks, PTR-91 is ready to sting.

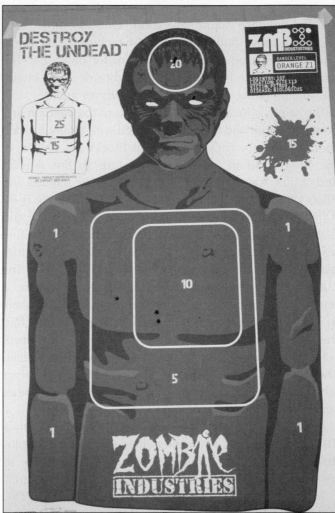

▲ At 100 yards the PTR91 rung out some nice groups with an assortment of FMJ ammunition.

▲ The sting of the scorpion indicated by Gerber's DMF folder.

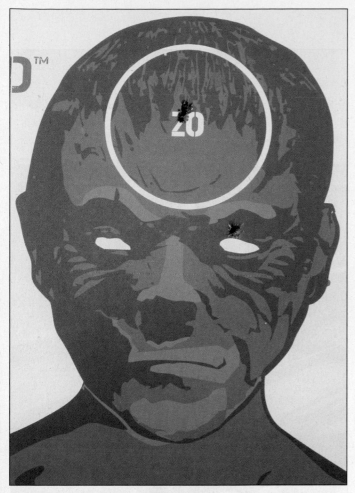

Specifications	PTR-91 PTR91KC
Caliber	.308 Win. / 7.62x51mm NATO
Barrel	16 in.
OA Length	38.75 in.
Weight (Unloaded)	9 lbs.
Stock	Polymer stock and pistol grip/ anodized aluminum handguard
Sights	Front hooded post/Rear: adjustable rotary drum
Action	Recoil operated, delayed roller-lock, semiautomatic
Capacity	5-, 10-, 20-round magazine
Finish	Matte black
Msrp	$1,245
Performance	PTR-91 PTR91KC

Load .308 Win. / 7.62x51mm NATO	Velocity	Best	Average
PMC Bronze 147 FMJ-BT	2437	0.25	1.725
SSA 150 FMJ	2422	1.187	1.875
Norma 168 Sierra HPBT	2231	0.625	1.937

▲ Those first two bullets also share the same hole. At 100 yards the PTR91 can hold its own with many precision rifles and do it faster with fewer magazine reloads.

Bullet weight measured in grains, velocity in feet per second 15 feet from the muzzle by a ProChrono digital chronograph, and accuracy in inches of three, three-shot groups at 100 yards.

13. The Scout Rifle

Jeff Cooper's General Purpose Rifle

"The general-purpose rifle will do equally well for all but specialized hunting, as well as for fighting; thus it must be powerful enough to kill any living target of reasonable size."

— Colonel Jeff Cooper, *The Art of the Rifle*

In the early 1980s Jeff Cooper developed the concept of a Scout Rifle. Cooper believed there was a place for a general purpose rifle that could span both hunting and tactical situations as needed. Cooper was a lifelong student of the gun, originator of the

▲ Cooper poses with two things precious to him, his wife Janelle and the Steyr Scout Rifle. Courtesy Gunsite Academy.

▲ Jeff Cooper was the consummate student of the rifle and is shown here in perfect form with a big bore African rifle. Courtesy Gunsite Academy.

▲ Shown here with an early prototype of the Scout Rifle, Cooper wrings the short rifle through its paces. Courtesy Gunsite Academy.

Modern Technique in pistol shooting, creator of the Cooper Color Code for the combat mindset, and founder of the American Pistol Institute (API) which later became Gunsite Training Center. He drew inspiration for the Scout Rifle from short and maneuverable rifles with characteristics such as lightweight, compact length, ability for fast follow-up shots, and chambered-in cartridges that are powerful enough to kill a living target of reasonable size. Reasonable size in Cooper's mind was 1,000 pounds.

Many bolt-action carbines chambered in .308 Winchester fit Cooper's criteria for the Scout Rifle. Some of the more defining characteristics include:

Though several firearm manufacturers have built their version of the Scout Rifle, the benchmark in Cooper's estimation is the Steyr Mannlicher Scout which most closely met his definition of the Scout Rifle. Compared to traditional hunting and military rifles of the day the Steyr looked different but it met the specs.

An unusual characteristic of the Scout Rifle is the optic mounted forward of the receiver instead of on top of the receiver. Mounting the scope forward of the receiver allows the user easy access to the action for reloading an internal box magazine plus it aids in clearing jams. The forward mounted scope also gives the user faster target acquisition since the user can keep both eyes open and on the target as well as the scope's reticle. The balance of the rifle is slightly changed, putting weight more forward on the non-shooting hand. Today Scout Rifles are more common and what was once an odd set-up of scope and rifle is now seen as a good combination.

The Steyr Scout features an integral bipod, as well as storage for a spare, loaded magazine. The rifle is also designed to allow either single-shot, manually loaded fire or normal magazine feeding. This is accomplished by a second notch in the magazine catch, which permits the magazine to ride in the weapon slightly too low for the bolt to engage the top cartridge. The shooter may immediately switch to magazine feeding by driving the magazine all

▲ The concept of a Scout Rifle was not new; here, members of the Wermacht sport a K98k with forward-mounted ZF-41 scope during WWII.

- An overall length of less than 1 meter (39.3 inches)
- Weight of less than 3 kilograms (6.6 pounds)
- Both iron and optical sights. Typically a ghost ring rear sight with a square post front sight with a 2-3x power, long eye relief scope mounted forward of the action to allow easy access to the action for rapid reloading. If the scope is damaged it can easily be removed and the iron sights employed.
- A sling to use as a shooting aid and for carrying the rifle
- 2 MOA accuracy consisting of a three-shot group at 200 yards
- The ideal caliber is .308 Winchester/7.62x51mm NATO, with 7mm-08 and .243 Winchester as alternate chamberings.
- A synthetic stock for better durability and no negative impact on the barrel.
- Other optional features include a bipod, detachable magazine, butt magazine, and accessory rail for accessories.

▲ Steyr built what was in Cooper's mind the best example of the Scout Rifle.

▲ A student at Gunsite Academy with a Steyr Scout Rifle during training. Courtesy Gunsite Academy.

The Scout Rifle • **89**

▲ A variant of the original, the Ruger Gunsite Scout Rifle is employed by a student at Gunsite Academy. Courtesy Gunsite Academy.

▲ Late in Cooper's life he was presented an anniversary edition of the Steyr Scout Rifle by Steyr's then CEO. Courtesy Gunsite Academy.

the way into the well. Single-round feeding is aided by the mounting position of the scope.

The length of the buttstock on the Steyr Scout is easily adjusted through the use of detachable sections, though Cooper promotes the practice of removing all of the sections to allow the shooter to bring the rifle to the shoulder faster.

The Steyr Scout features a lightweight, freefloated 19-inch barrel, and sythentic stock. Overall length is 38.6 inches and weight unloaded is 6.6 pounds. The rifle is compact, manuverable and capable of excellent accuracy. Caliber choices include .223 Rem., .243 Rem., 7 mm-08 Rem., and .308 Win.

In addition to Steyr, Savage and Ruger among other firearms manufacturers produce bolt-action Scout Rifles that

are close to Cooper's specifications. Ruger has introduced various Scout Rifle models over the years; the Model 77 Mark II Frontier debuted in 2005 and more recently in 2010 the Gunsite Scouting Rifle. The Gunsite Training Rifle was developed in conjunction with Gunsite. The Gunsite Scout Rifle is a credible rendition of Cooper's Scout Rifle. It is chambered in .308 Winchester with a 16.5-inch cold-hammer forged alloy steel barrel with a 5/8-24 threaded muzzle. Other Scout Rifle features include a forward mounted Picatinny rail, detachable box magazine in 3-, 5- or 10-round configurations, and adjustable ghost-ring rear iron sight. It sports ablack laminate wood stock with spacers to adjust the length-of-pull. Total weight without optics is seven pounds and an overall length of about forty-one inches, depending on how many butt spacers are used.

The Model 10FCM Scout from Savage Arms offers a Scout-type rifle chambered in .308 Winchester or 7.62x39mm. Both sport a 20-inch free-floated barrel, synthetic checkered AccuStock with aluminum bedding, detachable 4-round magazine, barrel mounted scope mount, and ghost ring sights. The 10FCM also employs Savage's excellent AccuTrigger that has a pull weight adjustable between 2.5 and 6 pounds. It also has an over-sized bolt knob. They are lightweight at 6.6 pounds without optics and are 39.7 inches in length.

Though not true to Cooper's spec, Springfield Armory's semiautomatic Scout rifles follow the spirit Cooper envisioned. The rifles from Springfield Armory differ from a true Scout Rifle in that they are semiautomatic actions not manual bolt-actions. Based on the M1A, Springfield Armory's civilian version of the US military M14, the Scout Squad, SOCOM 16 and SOCOM II are relatively lightweight, short-barreled rifles—18 inches and 16.2 inches, respectively—chambered in .308 Winchester with a forward scope mount. All three models have detachable 10-round magazines, post front sight with Tritium insert, and a rear sight that is an enlarged military aperture, a ghost ring in so many words. The SOCOM and SOCOM II weigh ten pounds, slightly more than Cooper envisioned, and are 37.2 inches long. All three sport synthetic stocks and the Squad is also offered in wood.

Fulton Armory also produces an M14-style Scout Rifle called the M14 Service 16 with a sixteen-inch barrel. It has a walnut, GI contour stock and fiberglass handguard. The Scout is a concept destined to evolve and change form but stay true to Jeff Cooper's idea for a general purpose rifle.

14. Mauser 98k-ZF 41 Replica

Remake of a Sniper Rifle That Really Wasn't

We tend think that optics are a relatively new feature to the modern combat rifle. US military M4s with an ACOG or other low-power

▲ The 98k-ZF 41 was fielded in great quantities during World War II and saw use by all branches of the German *Wehrmacht*.

magnification sight are common. A few generations ago the Mauser Karabiner 98k, also referred to as K98, Kar98k or K98k, was the consummate bolt-action battle rifle and standard issue service rifle for the German army. Over fourteen million were produced and I am sure there are still numerous examples of these Mausers still being used to protect homes or inciting revolution with rebels. A variant of the 98k was suggested by the Army Ordnance Office in 1939 to fill a need for better sharpshooting equipment. They requested 4x power magnification. What they received was 1.5x power scope on the 98k and it was designated the 98k-ZF 41. Nearly 90,000 98k-ZF 41s were sent to the field and served as a sharpshooter's weapon, not a true sniper weapon. The optic did give the operator an edge just like the Tijicon and Eclan optics, as well as others, do today. Mitchell's Mausers offers a reproduction of the 98k-ZF 41.

Mitchell's Mausers sourced these rifles behind the Iron Curtain—when there was an Iron Curtain—and imported them to the US. To ensure fit, function, and aesthetics the rifles were disassembled and cleaned then reassembled to what Mitchell's calls a military-new condition. All major parts—receiver, bolt, stock, floorplate—have original matching serial numbers. The rifle from the box looks like a new Mauser circa 1943 or so. Any patina of war or storage was scrubbed clean. The manufacturing code stamped

on the top of the receiver is "ar" above "42" which indicates the rifles was manufactured by Mauser Werke A.G., Berlin-Borsigwalde in 1942. These rifles are collectable because they can actually be used and fired without the chance of ruining a rare specimen. Included with the rifle is bore cleaning tools, an oiler, bolt take-down tool, sling, a few stripper clips, and two reproduction ammo pouches. A refurbished rifle is a shooter and any shooter's bucket list should include time behind a 98k.

Based on the Mauser M98 rifle, the K98k is a shorter, carbine variant. The K98k uses a control feed bolt-action with three locking lugs that has a 90° bolt lift. The bolt cocks on

▲ The German *Wehrmacht* never considered the 98k-ZF 41 a true sniper rifle, it was generally considered a sharpshooter's weapon.

▲ The bolt handle of the K98k is turned down which made it more effective in rapid fire than the straight bolt Gewehr 98.

A classic in every respect, the Mauser signature control feed extractor grasps the rim of the cartridge to chamber the round.

opening. The bolt knob is large and the wood stock is inlet to allow quick access. The three-position safety is classic Mauser. The lever when viewed from the rear clearly indicates to the operator the state of the weapon. Full left and weapon is ready to fire. Vertical blocks the sights and tells the user the rifle is on safe but the bolt is unlocked and can be operated to reload the rifle. To the right the rifle is on safe and the bolt is locked and cannot be operated. To remove the bolt put the safety lever in the vertical position and open the bolt and pull it back. On the left side and to the rear of the receiver is the bolt stop release lever. It is hinged, swinging from the front to rear, and is spring loaded. Pull the forward section of the bolt stop away from the receiver and hold it outward, then remove the bolt from the receiver.

The floorplate is removed by using a small punch (or the tip of a cartridge in a pinch) to depress the plunger. Depress the plunger and slide the floorplate rearward about an eighth of an inch. The floorplate will release but use caution as the floorplate is under spring tension from the follower spring. The floorplate, follower spring, and follower can then be removed from the bottom of the stock.

The K98k has an internal box magazine that is loaded via a five-round stripper clip. Open the bolt fully to the rear and insert the end of the clip in the rear notches of

Safety lever to full left means the rifle is ready to fire (left). In the vertical position the rifle is on safe but the bolt can be opened (middle). Safety lever to full right engages the safety and locks the bolt (right).

Pull the bolt stop away from the receiver and withdraw the bolt to begin field stripping the K98k.

A stripper clip is used to quickly load the Mauser or cartridges can be loaded one at a time.

▲ A small punch or tip of a cartridge is required to remove the floorplate.

▲ At the muzzle end of the K98k is a cleaning rod stored under the barrel; the sight is protected by a hood.

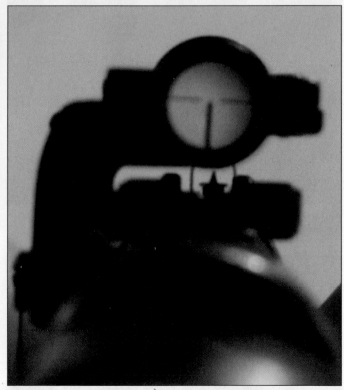

▲ A rear view of the K98k shows how the sights look to the operator. Note the iron sights can be used as well as the optic.

the receiver then push down on the cartridges using your thumb. Make sure the rounds are fully seated in the magazine. The stripper clip can then be removed by hand or it will be pushed out of the rifle as the bolt is closed and round is chambered.

At the muzzle end there's a short length of cleaning rod under the barrel. The rod is unscrewed to remove it. In the field, three rods could be attached together to clean the bore. The front sight post is protected by a hood. The rear sight is a V-notch on a ladder style setup with graduations that indicate distances from 100 to 2000 meters. The effective range of the K98k is 500 meters (550 yards) with iron sights and, depending on the optic, about 1,000 meters (1,090 yards). The K98k is mounted with a ZF-41 scope.

Original scopes were made by numerous manufacturers with Zeiss being the most well known. The "41" indicates the year the optic was adopted. The Mitchell's Mauser 1.5x power ZF-41 optic is a reproduction and closely matches an original in construction and operation. The optic is mounted forward of the action in similar fashion as a modern Scout Rifle. The long eye relief of the ZF-41 allows the user to keep both eyes open when aiming. It also provides a wide field of view which can be diminished by high magnification settings on optics.

The K98k uses a side mount that allows the scope/mount assembly to slide with two rollers and click into place. The optic is easily and quickly removed and attached. The Mitchell's replica comes with an extended cover that fits over the objective to block sun, rain, and protect the lens from dust. The outside diameter of the objective is 28mm and the eyepiece opening is about .75 inches. Total length without the sunshade is six inches. The reticle is a three-post crosshair and comes with a factory zero at 300 yards.

▲ The serrated ring is how the elevation is adjusted on the ZF-41's three-post reticle.

▲ The ZF-41 scope attaches to the removable mount via four screws, and the serrated tab at the front allows easy removal.

▲ With the sunshade attached the optics can be used in bright sunlight. The shade also protects the lens from rain.

I set up a target at fifty yards and used a rest to see how the K98k grouped. The two-stage trigger pull averaged six pounds, 7.5 ounces, which is typical for a military style weapon but not conducive to accurate shooting. The heft of the rifle helped absorb the felt recoil of the 8mm rounds. The actions cycled perfectly, like a new rifle. The bolt was a bit loose, not tight and glass smooth like some sporting rifles. With only one type of ammo I was able to get two-inch groups at fifty yards. The ZF-41 scope was easy to use with both eyes open and for fast snap shooting, like this rifle was intended for, it proved more than adequate in performance and accuracy. The length made it quick to point.

▲ The K98k comes up easy to the shoulder and was a natural pointer; the optic allowed for aiming with two eyes.

▲ The ability to use either the iron sights or the low-power optic gives the K98k versatility.

Specifications	Mitchell's Mausers German ZF-41 Sniper Rifle
Caliber	7.92x57mm, also known as 8mm Mauser or 8x57mm
Barrel	24.2 in.
OA Length	43.7 in.
Weight (Unloaded)	8.2 lb.
Stock	oil-resistant laminated wood
Iron Sights	V-notch rear/inverted V
Optics	1.5x ZF-41 long eye relief rifle scope
Action	3-lug, bolt-action
Finish	blued
Msrp	$1,399.00
Performance	Mitchell's Mausers German ZF-41 Sniper Rifle

Surplus 8mm (Portuguese manufacture)	Velocity	Average	Best
Military surplus 198 FMJ	2393	3.0	2.0

Bullet weight measured in grains, velocity in feet per second 15 feet from the muzzle by a ProChrono digital chronograph, and accuracy in inches of three, three-shot groups at 50 yards.

MAINTENANCE
15. Precision Rifle Maintenance

Strip It Down and Scrub It Out

The inside of your barrel is most important. Without cleaning, residue from copper jacket bullets and lead can build up and adversely affect accuracy. A poorly maintained barrel can also lead to rust and pitting. The bolt should also be cleaned after every range session. The internals need only be cleaned once a year or more frequently depending the use and/or the environment the weapon is used in. Rain, snow, saltwater, heat, and dust can all contribute to rifle inaccuracy at the least or in worst case a malfunction.

For cleaning high-power rifles, the list of required tools is simple:

Powder Solvent: Hoppe's No. 9, Shooter's Choice, KG-1, and other products dissolve powder residue and fouling. Solvents come in liquid, aerosol sprays, gels, and paste. Avoid getting cleaning solvents and oils on optics. If the lenses are dirty or become contaminated with oil or solvents, spray the lens with a lens cleaner and use a lens cleaning cloth. Wipe the cleaner with the cloth in a circular motion. Never clean an optic lens that is dry since you may scratch the surface coating on the lens.

Copper Solvent: These solvents usually contain about 5 percent ammonia which is effective in breaking down and dissolving the copper residue from shooting copper jacketed bullets. Ammonia-based solvents attract moisture so be sure to completely remove the solvent and lightly oil the barrel afterward. Sweets, Butch's Bore Shine, Montana X-treme, and others will remove copper from bores. FrogLube CLP is an environmentally friendly CLP (Clean Lubricate Protect). CLP-type products are fast and easy to use.

Lubricant: Less is more when it comes to lubricant. Rem. Oil, Break-Free, Birchwood Casey, and others make excellent lubricating products that keep mechanisms functioning as well as protected from rust.

Rods: There are rods you push through a bore, like Dewey Rods, and rods you pull through a bore, like the cable rods from Otis Industries. These rods are coated with a polymer so they won't scratch the bore or wear out the chamber area or muzzle. At one end of the rod should be a handle or grip and at the other a female tip that will accept a variety of patch pullers, mops, and brushes. Otis Industries and Dewey rods offer one long straight piece of rod which is better than the sectioned rods which flex and rub inside the bore.

Bore Guide: This device guides a rod through the chamber end of the barrel and ensures the rod is properly centered. A chamber that is worn even by a thousandth of an inch can adversely impact accuracy.

Brushes, Jags and Mops: Bronze and nylon brushes are softer than steel so will not scratch the bore or cause excessive wear of the chamber. When using copper removing bore cleaners with ammonia, use a nylon brush. Bronze is made with copper and if copper-removing solvents are left on bronze bore brushes the brush bristles will erode. Jags and patch loops are made of soft brass or polymer and allow a variety of patches to be used. Mops will coat the bore with solvent prior to using a brush.

Patches: Only use 100 percent cotton patches. They absorb and hold solvents and grime better than synthetic fabric patches.

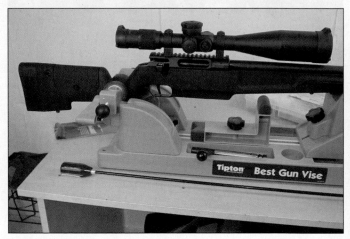

▲ A gun vise like this one from Tipton holds the rifle in place making it easier to work on a rifle.

Periodic Maintenance Process

Frequency: After Every Range Session

Step 1: Confirm the weapon is unloaded. A support like a Tipton gun vise makes cleaning easier. Place the rifle in the cradle of the vise and remove the bolt. Only field stripping is necessary. Insert a bore guide into the action. It works like a hollowed out bolt allowing the cleaning rod to align with the bore so it does not rub in the chamber.

▲ Insert a bore guide into the receiver just as if it was the bolt assembly; it ensures the cleaning rod is centered in the bore.

Step 2: Always clean the bore from breech to muzzle. Attach a jag or patch loop to the end of the cleaning rod and attach a patch to the jag. Soak the patch with solvent and run the patch by pulling or pushing it from the breech to muzzle. Remove the patch while the rod is still in the bore, then pull the rod from the bore. Let the solvent work for a few minutes. With heavier gunk buildup, allow the solvent to work longer. While I wait for the solvent to work I wipe down the bolt and scrub the extractor with a tooth brush and solvent as needed.

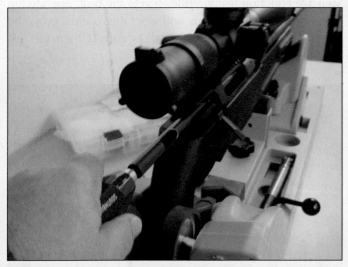

▲ With a solvent-soaked patch attached to a jag or patch loop push it through the bore.

Step 3: Replace the jag or patch loop with a bore brush of the correct caliber. Soak the brush in solvent and insert it via the bore guide into the barrel and push it through. Dirt particles will be expelled out the muzzle. Pull the brush

back through the barrel. You may need to repeat this step depending on how fouled the weapon is. Be extra cautious at the muzzle; poor cleaning practices can wear the muzzle and adversely impact accuracy.

Step 4: Replace the brush with the patch loop or jag and run a clean, dry patch through. Repeat this process until the patch comes out clean. If fouling is persistent, then repeat Step 2 through Step 4. A clean patch at Step 4 indicates a clean bore.

Step 5: Replace the patch with a clean one, add some lubricant to it, and run it through the bore. Do not use a lot of oil. A little goes a long way.

Step 6: Wipe down the exterior metal surfaces of the weapon with a lightly oiled, clean cotton cloth. Use a

▲ Notice the progression of the patches from filthy to clean; the last patch should be clean.

▲ Spray the muzzle device—flash hider or brake—with a solvent to clear vent holes from fouling residue.

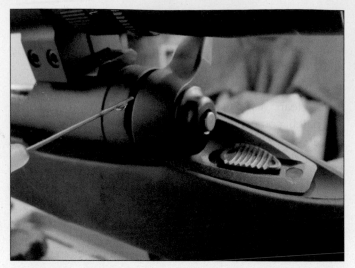
▲ A little goes a long way when it comes to oil; a drop between the bolt handle and rear of the receiver will make the action cycle smoothly.

gentle spray cleaner to remove built up gunk on the stock. Reassemble the weapon.

Yearly Maintenance Process

Frequency: After extreme extended use, use in adverse climates, or once a year. Follow Steps 1 through 5 above.

Step 7: Complete disassembly of the rifle is required so make sure you have the correctly sized screwdrivers or Torx wrenches—whatever is specific to your weapon. Remove the barreled action from the stock per manufacturer's procedure.

Step 8: Depending on the amount of gunk, soak a soft bristle brush, like an old tooth brush, in solvent and use it to remove debris. Canned air is extremely helpful. A blast of air helps dislodge crud from the trigger mechanism and magazine area. Use the canned air to blow the gunk out of the action, not into it. An aerosol solvent like Shooter's Choice, Break-Free, Gunslick, and others makes short work of the procedure. Dental picks are helpful to clean out hard to reach areas inside a weapon's frame. Give the solvent time to work, then wipe it clean with a soft clean cloth. Make sure the floorplate operates and the magazine follower is clean. For rifles with detachable magazines, disassemble the magazine and run a cloth through the magazine body. Wipe the interior with a very lightly oiled cloth. Oil and ammo hate each other.

Step 9: Field strip the bolt and remove the firing pin assembly. A CLP product works great form this step. Too much lubricating oil during reassembly of the bolt can lead to misfires. Too much oil attracts dust which can hinder operation, and in cold climates oil can thicken, also hindering operation. Ensure the extractor is operating. Use a small dental pick or toothpick to clean the recesses. Function

test the extractor to ensure the spring works and nothing is causing it to stick or not operate. Use a fired case of the correct caliber and hook the rim of the case under the extractor to compress the ejector spring.

Step 10: Blow out the trigger mechanism with canned air being sure to blow debris out of the trigger, not into it. Too much oil gunks up triggers attracting dust and gumming up in cold weather, less is better.

Step 11: Clean the exterior and wipe out the interior of the stock using a solvent recommended by the manufacturer. Polymer stocks can be cleaned with mild spray cleaners and a clean, soft cloth. If equipped with an adjustable LOP and cheek riser make sure the turn knobs operate smoothly.

Step 12: Reassemble the bolt. Reassemble the barreled action to the stock and torque it to manufacturer's specs. Place a drop of oil or tiny bit of grease on the bolt assembly lugs. The lugs mate with recesses in the receiver; it's a tight metal-against-metal fit. Insert the bolt into the action and make sure it cycles smoothly. Judicious use of oil—not too much—on wear points per manufacturer's specs. With the weapon reassembled wipe down the exterior metal surfaces of the weapon with a lightly oiled, clean cotton cloth.

Step 13: Inspect the scope mount and rings. If a screw is loose, place a drop of LocTite on the threads and tighten it. Clean optic lens if needed per manufacturer's recommendations. Cleaning lenses too often can remove lens coatings.

Step 14: Function test the rifle—cycle the bolt, operate the safety, load dummy rounds and eject the rounds, press the trigger with dummy rounds. If all is correct then fire test the rifle to see if the zero is off.

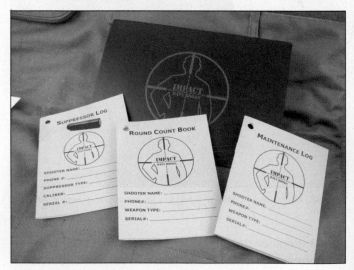
▲ Log books are a good idea to track maintenance and rounds fired; these log books are from Impact Data Books.

16. Optic Maintenance

Most optics require little maintenance, but because they are used in messy environments like deserts and alpine forest as well as being exposed to rain and sun, optics can become dirty. The most sensitive part of an optic is the coating on the lens. It can be easily scratched if the wrong cleaning procedure is performed. Better quality lenses have coatings that repel dirt and smudges from fingers. Here's the correct procedure to clean dirty lens on scopes, binoculars, spotting, and rangefinders.

STEP 1: Blow off any dirt. If dirt is still present, use a soft brush like the brush in the Lens Pen. Use the brush to sweep away particles.

STEP 2: Breathe onto the lens to create a bit of condensation. With a dry lens cleaning cloth use a circular motion to clean the lens. Only use lens cleaning cloths, as a shirt tail or rag will only transfer dirt to lens and will scratch the lens coating. A Lens Pen with a cleaning tip can help remove a stubborn smudge.

STEP 3: For the outside surfaces of the optics such as the body, use a soft clean cloth and try to avoid getting the debris in the lens.

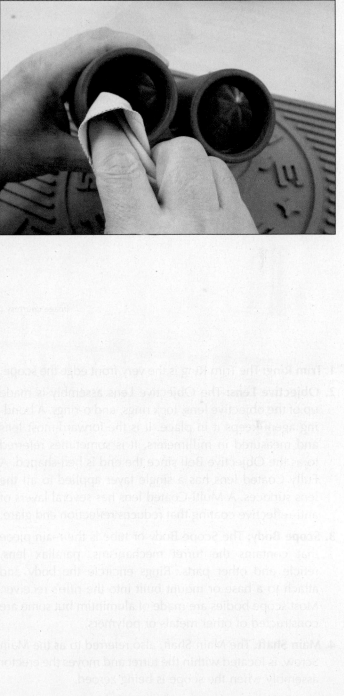

OPTICS
17. Anatomy of a Rifle Scope

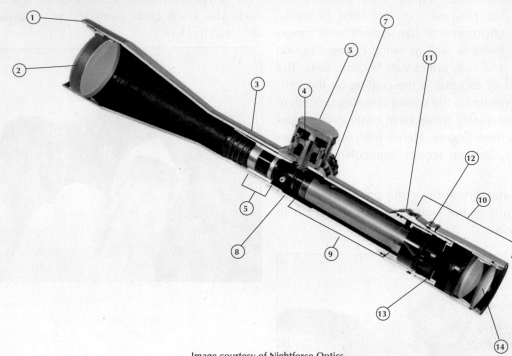

Image courtesy of Nightforce Optics.

1. **Trim Ring:** The Trim Ring is the very front edge the scope.

2. **Objective Lens:** The Objective Lens assembly is made up of the objective lens, lock rings, and o-rings. A bonding agent keeps it in place. It is the forward-most lens and measured in millimeters. It is sometimes referred to as the Objective Bell since the end is bell-shaped. A Fully Coated lens has a single layer applied to all the lens surfaces. A Multi-Coated lens has several layers of anti-reflective coating that reduces reflection and glare.

3. **Scope Body:** The Scope Body or tube is the main piece that contains the turret mechanisms, parallax lens, reticle and other parts. Rings encircle the body and attach to a base or mount built into the rifle's receiver. Most scope bodies are made of aluminum but some are constructed of other metals or polymers.

4. **Main Shaft:** The Main Shaft, also referred to as the Main Screw, is located within the turret and moves the erector assembly when the scope is being zeroed.

5. **Parallax Lens:** In a scope, parallax is the apparent movement of the reticle in relationship to the target when the shooter moves his head up/down or left/right which can cause a shift in aim and a missed shot. If a shooter views straight through the scope, parallax will have little effect. High end scopes with high magnification have a Parallax Lens that helps reduce parallax.

6. **Elevation Turret:** This is the top knob on the scope that adjusts the reticle point of impact for elevation (up and down). Elevation adjustments are made in increments, also referred to as clicks. The amount of movement per click is specific to each scope. For example on some scopes one click equals ¼ MOA.

7. **Windage Turret:** The knob on the right side of the scope that adjusts the reticle point of impact for windage (left and right). Windage adjustments, like elevation adjustments, are made in increments, also referred to as clicks. The amount of movement per click is specific

to each scope. For example on some scopes one click equals ¼ MOA.

8. First Focal Plane: The First Focal Plane (FFP) is located in front of the erector assembly. This is where some reticles are located within the scope. If the reticle is located in the FFP then the reticle will increase in size as the magnification is increased. Many military/LE scopes use a FFP reticle. The Reticle is also referred to as crosshairs and can take a variety of configurations. Most reticles are constructed of wires. Etched reticles are engraved onto a glass plate. Leupold's Mark 8 series, Vortex Razor HD Gen II series, and other brands use FFP reticles.

9. Erector Assembly: The Erector Assembly has lenses that move closer together and farther apart to change magnification. The best assemblies correctly index all lenses so there is no POI (Point Of Aim) shift when changing magnification. The erector lens is located between the objective lens and the ocular lens and inverts the image. Wiring in the erector is used to power illuminated reticles.

10. Eyepiece: The Eyepiece is adjustable for magnification and on high end scopes has a feature to set the diopter adjustment. Diopter is a measure of the focusing power of a lens.

11. Magnification Ring: The Magnification Ring is how the magnification power adjusts higher or lower making the target appear larger or smaller, respectively. On the outside of the magnification ring are graduations indicating magnification power. A Fixed Power scope does not have a magnification ring and is fixed at a specific magnification. Field Of View (FOV) is the amount of observable area as seen through the scope. As magnification increases the FOV is reduced.

12. Diopter Lock Ring: This locks down the diopter once it has been focused for a specific user's eye.

13. Second Focal Plane: The Second Focal Plane (SFP) reticle is located behind the erector assembly. As the magnification is increased, the reticle stays the same size. Most hunting scopes use a SFP setup.

14. Ocular Lens: The Ocular Lens is located within the eyepiece of the scope and this is the lens the user sights through. The ocular lens is what the user looks views through. Eye Relief is the distance from the shooter's eye and the ocular lens that provides a full view through the scope. It is measured in inches and typically a scope has a given eye relief range to accommodate the different stature of shooters.

18. Ballistic Reticle Rifle Scopes

Taking the Guesswork Out of Long-range Shooting

Beasts usually like to keep as much woodlot, coulee, or cornfield between us and them as possible, and that may mean shooting our rifles farther than the sighted-in distance. Essentially we use old-fashioned Kentucky elevation and take our best guess at crosshair holdover. Combine a good sense of distance with shooting experience and you could fill out your tag; if not, you'll kick up dirt below two sets of hooves, whiz a round over their back, or sadly wound an animal.

A rifle scope with a reticle like the Bushnell DOA 600, Leupold Boone & Crockett, Nikon BDC and others can help take the guesswork out of long-distance shooting by combining a typical crosshair with additional aiming points at set distances. These are not as sophisticated as some tactical scopes, but offer hunters an edge. The ballistic reticles are calibrated to popular hunting cartridges with muzzle velocities in the range of 2,800 to 3,000 fps or more. The usual suspects fall into that range—.243, 6mm, .25-06, .270, .308, .30-06, 7mm Rem. Mag., .300 Win. Mag., including a slew of others. Since the aiming points are not calibrated to a specific load they offer general approximations, which means you will need to shoot your rifle with the cartridge you are going to hunt with to understand how the reticle will work with your specific rifle/cartridge combination. These reticles are chockfull of aiming points and seem cluttered compared to a typical duplex reticle found in many hunting scopes, but they are quite easy to master. I make a cheat sheet on an index card or a piece of masking tape and fix it to the stock or the top of the eyepiece so I can remember what aiming points are for what distances with what load. These reticles remove some of the guesswork but you will still need to know the distance to the target, and some scopes offer a way to estimate range.

At first glance the Bushnell DOA (Dead On Accurate) 600 reticle looked like a cross between a wiring schematic and totem pole. Luckily the manual helped quickly decipher it. The DOA 600 reticle consists of a main duplex-style crosshairs and five additional aiming points. Four additional aiming points combine MOA dots with shorter horizontal crosshairs and finally a short duplex in the six-

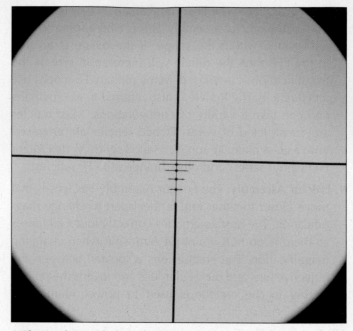

▲ The view from inside the Bushnell Elite 3200 shows the DOA 600 reticle. Those small vertical hashmarks on the horizontal crosshairs help determine range.

o'clock position. Per the manual, the main crosshair was zeroed to 100 yards thus calibrating the four MOA dot/crosshair combinations to 200, 300, 400 and 500 yards, and the bottom post at 600 yards. To use the additional aiming points, hunters must remember to set the power ring of the scope to maximum magnification. What is nice about the DOA 600 is you can place the black dots on the target and that's where the bullet would hit. The horizontal crosshairs also help to get back on target if the black dot was lost on a dark target. The manual lists many calibers and bullet weights that are matched to the reticle. The Bushnell website offers a comprehensive list of compatible ammo. Calibers are listed by cartridge brand and by bullet brands for handloaders.

Built into the DOA 600 is a distance estimator called the Rack Bracket System that consists of vertical hash marks on the horizontal crosshairs of the MOA dots. The hash marks are set at 17 in. and 24 in., which are the average width of a mature whitetail's and mule deer's ears, respectively. To use this feature the deer must be facing or looking directly away from the hunter. Bushnell claims that if the ears fit into the bracket you have an accurate estimation of range.

The Rack Bracket was on the 200, 300, 400, and 500 MOA dot/crosshair combinations. It is wishful thinking that a deer with keep its ears still, but the range estimator is better than a bad guess.

The Boone & Crockett (B&C) is Leupold's proprietary name for its ballistic reticle. The main crosshair is zeroed to 200 or 300 yards depending on cartridge used. Four additional aiming points include two CPC-style taper crosshairs at 300 and 400 yards, a bar for 450 yards, and the lower duplex post for 500 yards. Per the manual, calibers are categorized into one of three groups: A, B or C. The groups cluster calibers' muzzle velocity, bullet weight, and bullet drop at 500 yards. For group B calibers the manual specifies that the main crosshairs be zeroed at 200 yards and to dial in the small triangle on the power ring to use the additional aiming points. Two triangles, a small one for calibers in group B, and a larger one for calibers in group A and C, were easy to distinguish on the scope's magnification ring.

The ability to estimate range on the animal's body size, seems precise. Adjust the power ring while placing the horizontal crosshair on the animal's back and bottom duplex post to the animal's brisket then read the number on the power ring to determine approximate distance. But the extra time and movement could reveal your location to wary game.

The Nikon BDC (Bullet Drop Compensation) reticle does not use a caliber chart. Nikon is transparent in their manual stating the reticle was built ". . . to offer 'generic' hold-over points that will accommodate most centerfire rifle cartridges . . . ." If your ammo has a muzzle velocity of 2800 fps, sight-in at 100 yards. For calibers with muzzle velocities of 3000 fps or higher, sight-in at 200 yards. If sighted in for 100 yards you have four additional aiming points—200, 300, 400, and 500 yards—that consist of open circles along the vertical main crosshair. The power

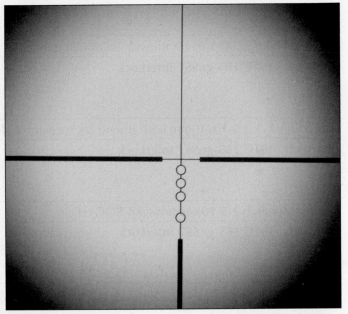

▲ The BDC reticle in the Nikon Monarch uses circles as aiming points. At long distances the target is not obscured by the circles.

▲ A T/C Icon Classic in .30TC was the odd ball—but loved—caliber used to test the scopes from Nikon, Bushnell, and Leupold that incorporate a ballistic reticle.

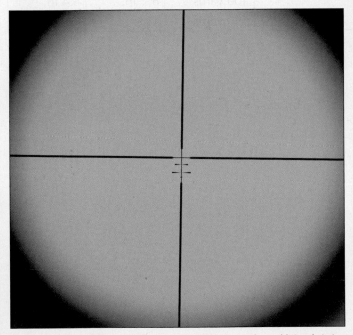

▲ The Boone & Crockett reticle in the Leupold VX-3 uses four additional aiming points and includes two CPC-style taper crosshairs.

ring must be turned to maximum magnification to use the aiming points. The open circles are easy to use and do not cover up the target. The intersection of the vertical crosshair and the circles provide additional aiming points for fine tuning to a specific load.

Not-so-popular calibers that fall into the muzzle velocity range, like the proprietary cartridges from Weatherby, would work with these scopes. To be fair these cartridges should be referred to as more uncommon than unpopular. The .30TC is just one of these cartridges. It debuted in 2007 with the then new T/C Icon rifle and is only loaded by Hornady. With less recoil than a .308 or .30-06 it achieves a higher velocity using the same weight bullet. I tested an Icon Classic in .30TC with the three reticles using Hornady 165-grain SST InterLock bullets. The scopes were mounted to the Icon Classic via Warne Picatinny rings. Using a rest and firing at a range of 100 yards, I found that it did not so much matter the caliber or popularity of the round, but the muzzle velocity and bullet weight. All reticles performed within the calculated range.

	Range	Path*	Actual
Bushnell Elite 3200 3-9x40mm with DOA 600 reticle			
Hornady .30TC 165-gr.SST InterLock	300 yards	4.8 in.	4.6 in.
	400 yards	8.2 in.	7.8 in.
	500 yards	12.2 in.	10.9 in.
Leupold VX-3 3.5-10x40mm with Boone & Crockett reticle			
Hornady .30TC 165-gr.SST InterLock	300 yards	4.8 in.	5.8 in.
	400 yards	8.2 in.	7.5 in.
	450 yards	9.2 in.	9.4 in.
Nikon Monarch 2.5-10x42mm with BDC reticle			
Hornady .30TC 165-gr.SST InterLock	300 yards	4.8 in.	3.8 in.
	400 yards	8.2 in.	6.4 in.
	500 yards	12.2 in.	10.8 in.

*Trajectory path calculated using online ballistic calculator with 100-yard zero.

19. Leupold Mark 4 LR/T 4.5-14x50mm

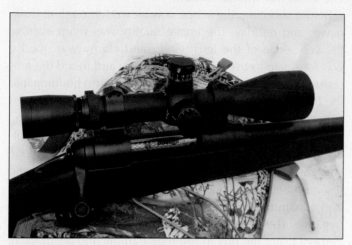

▲ The windage and elevation turret knobs are standard style.

Workhorse Military-Grade Optic

The Leupold Mark 4 series of scopes have been in production for over thirty years. The US Marine Corps uses a Mark 4 optic on the USMC DMR, which is an accurized M14 rifle. A Mark 4 is also part of the US Army's M24 SWS. It is a proven performer in combat; the type of optic you expect can take abuse and still be dead on.

The Mark 4 series is built on a one-piece 30mm tube made of aircraft grade aluminum. It sports an all-business matte black finish. Numerous reticle configurations are available in illuminated and non-illuminated versions. I opted for the M1 TMR (Tactical Milling Reticle) reticle SFP (Second Focal Plane). The 4.5-14x50mm LR/T (Long Range/Tactical) model has a 50mm objective that sucks in light. It is large and required medium height rings to mount on the Savage Model 11/111 Long Range Hunter platform. I used a set of Warne Maxima series medium height steel rings. The eye relief is 3.5 to 4.5 inches which is plenty for the mild recoiling 6.5 Creedmoor and well suited to recoil-generating calibers like the .300 Win. Mag. The objective allows use of a sunshade.

The Mark 4 uses what Leupold calls the Xtended Twilight lens system which uses index matched glass with wavelength specific coatings to optimize light transmission. The lens also have a DiamondCoat 2 coating which is an ion-assist coating that is abrasion resistant and exceeds military standards for hardness and durability. Argon/Krypton gas is pumped inside the scope to reduce variations in temperature that put many scopes into "shock" by fogging.

The blackened lens edge is one of those details only appreciated when the scope is viewed through. It reduces unwanted glare and diffusion through the lens to provide better resolution and improved contrast.

The eyepiece is lockable via a serrated ring. It turned with the just the right amount of effort. The zoom is 3:1 so you can get on target quickly. A knob projects out from the magnification ring and it allows the user to get a good grasp. Magnification settings are located around the ring and are easy to see even when the weapon is shouldered.

The guts on the Leupold uses a twin bias spring erector system so zeroed rifles stay zeroed and the click values are precise and consistent. Turrets knobs are the same size and each have .25 MOA per click. They are finger adjustable. The turrets are standard style that need to be unloosened by setting a screw to be zeroed. The gnarly turrets provide a good

▲ The side focus knob rotated smoothly and easily.

▲ The 50mm objective lens required the use of medium height rings.

grip with or without gloves. The turret body is marked with windage (R with an arrow) and elevation (U with an arrow) directions. These indicators can be seen when the rifle is shouldered. There are 60 MOA of adjustment in elevation and 30 MOA in windage. The side focus knob adjusts parallax. The knob is larger than the turret knobs and less gnarly.

The reticle is located in the second focal plane, so it stays one size even as the magnification power is increased. To use the mil-dot ranging features the scope must be set to the highest magnification. With first focal plane reticles

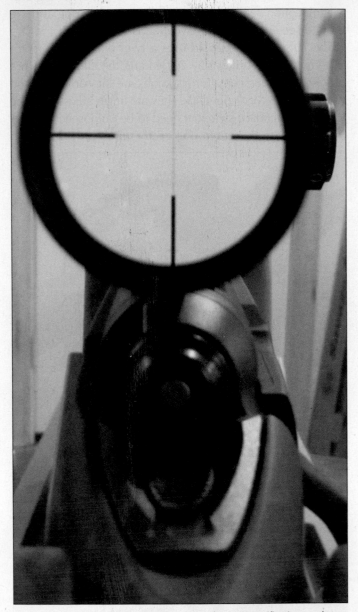

▲ The reticle is an M1 TMR; to use the ranging feature magnification needs to be on the highest setting.

ranging can be performed on any magnification setting. The knob was smooth to turn.

Before shooting, the scope was viewed through at dusk, dawn, and midday. The image quality was sharp even to the very edge of the lens. Color and clarity was good. I was fortunate to use the scope in snow and found the lens resisted water. Taking the scope out of a warm building into the less than 32°F outdoors caused slight fogging, which I expected, but the Leupold cleared within a few minutes.

With the Leupold mounted to the Savage and boresighted, range worked starting at the 50 yard line. The scope was zeroed at 50 then brought to the 100 yard range and the zero tweaked. I then fired at 100 yards on minimum and maximum magnification to see if the zero changed—negative. The Leupold was spot on. Satisfied the rifle was zeroed, I shot the box to test repeatability and accuracy of the adjustments. Three shots were fired at the same corner of the box with elevation and windage cranked out the same number of clicks. The fifth and last three-shot group landed in the exact space spot as the first three-shot group. Taking my shooting ability into account the Leupold was dead on. I also cranked the windage 20 MOA to the right, fired three rounds, then cranked it back to zero and the left another 20 MOA. I then measured the groups to evaluate the clicks. The measurement was very close and like the expression goes: Good enough for government work. The Mark 4 LR/T scopes are combat-proven scopes and a benchmark for all other tactical scopes.

Specifications	Mark 4 LR/T 8.5-25x50mm
Magnification	8.5-25x
Objective Lens	50 mm
Reticle	M1
Finish	Matte black
Field of View	11.2 ft (low)/4.4 ft (high) @ 100 yds
Exit Pupil	5.9 mm (low)/2 mm (high)
Click Value	¼ MOA
Adjustment Range	70 MOA
Eye Relief	3.7-5.3 in
Tube Diameter	30 mm
Length	14.4 in
Weight	22.5 oz
MSRP	$1,749.99

20. U.S. Optics ER-25 5-25xT

Big Glass

▲ The U.S. Optics ER-25 5-25xT is an optic purpose built for long range shooting.

The size of the U.S. Optics ER-25 5-25xT is massive. The tube diameter is 34mm and the 58mm objective funnels in light. It is 18 inches long and weighs over 2 pounds. There's nothing small about the ER-25. It is a big scope and provides big performance. The ER-25 is built for extreme long-range shooting, out to and beyond 2,000 yards.

The glass in the ER-25 provides sharp image quality and good color and contrast. It made dusk seem like noon the way it collects light. It was easy to read the local newspaper headlines from many yards away.

The body is made with 6061-T6 aircraft aluminum and then coated with a matte black type III hard anodizing. The eyepiece focus ring was nicely knurled around the edge and has the right amount of resistance. So, too, did the magnification ring. A large section of this ring is knurled so it is easy to get a good grip. Magnification power is indicated on the ring and if the rifle is shouldered you just need to raise your head to read the power setting. The markings and graduations are all gray. It takes about ¾ of a turn to go from 5x to 25x magnification power.

The ER-25 has U.S. Optics trademark box turret housing. On top is the EREK (Erector Repositioning Elevation Knob), which provides plenty of elevation per revolution.

▲ The right side of the scope housed the reticle illumination controls just forward of the windage turret.

▲ The massive 58mm objective funnels light.

▲ The large yet low profile knob is the EREK elevation

The knob is low profile. Two set screws hold the EREK turret cap down. They need to be removed to zero the turret indicators. The windage turret uses a U.S. Optics #3 knob that is smaller with grippy knurling and easy to read graduation marks. Dual elevation and windage rebound springs help insure reliability and accurate adjustments. All clicks felt positive and sure.

In front of the windage turret are the reticle illumination controls. The three buttons each perform a role: one turns the reticle on, one increases illumination, and one decreases illumination. The red reticle has twelve illumination settings. The rubber buttons are easily operated even with gloves. A Turret Parallax Adjustment Locater (TPAL) system is used to adjust parallax. The knob is large with knurling around the edge. It reads from seventy-five yards to infinity.

▲ The SIG/U.S. Optics setup was smokin' at whatever distance tested.

The reticle is located in the first focal plane and increases in size as the magnification is turned up. A Mil Scale GAP retile was installed, though there are many options. This reticle was designed with input from GA Precision rifles. The reticle was uncluttered and simple to use.

The ER-25 was bolted onto to a SIG SSG 3000 using Warne rings. The rifle/optic setup made for a hefty rig. After zeroing in 100 yards, the reticle was easy to keep on target—the weight of the setup helped. Shooting the box and cranking over left or right produced no issues with click values. Dead on. At 200 yards the results were the same—good clarity, sharpness, and resolution—and with a pounding from the .308 Winchester bullets the SSG 3000 was spitting out, there is little doubt about the quality of the ER-25. The ER-25 can take on bigger calibers with ease.

▲ The TPAL knob on the left side of the scope adjusts parallax.

▲ The Mil Scale GAP reticle was cleanly laid out and simple to master.

Specifications	U.S. Optics Scope ER-25 5-25xT
Magnification	5–25x
Objective Lens	58 mm
Reticle	Mil Scale GAP
Finish	Matte black
Field of View	16.6 ft (low)/5.3 ft (high) @ 100 yds
Click Value	1/10 Mil
Adjustment Range	100 MOA
Eye Relief	3.5 in
Tube Diameter	34 mm
Length	18 in
Weight	2.5 lb
MSRP	$2,976.00

21. Unertl Target Scope

Old School Optic

▲ The Unertl was mounted to a Remington Model 37.

To look at a Unertl target scope is to look at a legend. To look through it can be an epiphany. I had a chance to use an original Unertl on a classic rimfire rifle, a Remington Model 37 Rangemaster.

The Unertl scope looks odd compared to a modern scope. Think of a Unertl as a modern scope turned inside out. The body of the scope lies between two mounts. The rear mount also serves to adjust windage and elevation using a precise micrometer type setup. At the forward mount is a recoil spring assemble which absorbs recoil

from heavier calibers. The objective on this model is 1.5 inches and the tube body has a diameter on .75 inches. Length is about twenty-five inches and it weighs close to two pounds.

Sighting through the Unertl, the image was crystal clear even for a scope that was manufactured in the mid-twentieth century. The Model 37 and the Unertl played nice together. At fifty yards, I shot the box cranking the windage and elevation controls at a set number of clicks. This old scope was on.

▲ This image shows the recoil spring that reduces the punishment that a large caliber can give scopes.

◄ Splitting playing cards took minimal luck with the Model 37 setup with Unertl.

▲ Here the rear mount of the Unertl is shown with its micrometer type windage and elevation knobs.

22. Anatomy of a Binocular

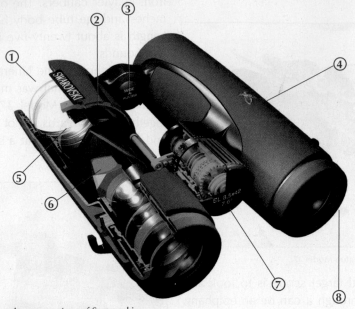

Image courtesy of Swarvoski.

1. Objective Lens: The Objective Lens assembly is the front lens and is measured in millimeters. Lenses have coating than perform different functions like reducing reflection and glare. The Objective Lens gathers the image and sends it through the body of the binocular to the Prism which turns the image right side up and is seen through the Ocular Lens by the user.

2. Focus Housing: The Focus Housing holds the Focusing Lens and is mechanically moved forward and backward by the user manipulating the Focus Knob to focus the view within the binocular.

3. Hinge: The Hinge attaches the two tubes of the binocular. There are two types of binoculars: Roof Prism and Porro Prism. Roof Prism binoculars use a prism that is shaped like a roof, hence the name; these binoculars are constructed with two straight tubes. Swarovski EL series, Leupold Cascades, and Bushnell Elite 8 binocular are examples of a roof prism binocular. A Porro Prism binocular uses two prisms that are positioned in a z-shaped configuration making this type of binocular wider and shorter than Roof

Prism binoculars. An example of a porro prism binocular are Steiner military and police series.

4. Housing: The Housing makes up the two tubes that hold the lenses and mechanisms. A modern binocular housing is constructed of polymer or a light weight metal, then given a textured coating.

5. Focusing Lens: Located in the focus housing between the objective lens and the ocular lens, the Focusing Lens is user adjusted to sharpen the view through the binocular.

6. Prism: The Prism inverts the image between the objective and ocular lenses.

7. Focusing Wheel: The Focusing Wheel is rotated by the user to sharpen the view through the binocular. As the knob is rotated the mechanism either moves the focusing lens forward or rearward depending on the user's eyesight.

8. Eyecup: The Eyecup is the rubber ring around the ocular lens and can be adjusted for users who wear eyeglasses.

23. Rangefinder Binocular

Combining a Rangefinder with a Binocular

▲ Four examples of range-finding binocular are the Swarovski EL Range 10x42 (bottom left) , Bushnell Fusion 1600 ARC 10x42 (top left), Steiner Military 10x50 LRF (bottom right), and Zeiss Victory RF 8x45 T* (top right). All emit a pulsing laser beam that bounces off a target and uses a known variable—the speed of light—to calculate the unknown variable—the distance to the target.

Adding a rangefinder to binoculars seems like a logical combination of technologies. Not only does it mean carrying less equipment, there's less fumbling between binocs and rangefinder when a target comes into view. All things equal, the only downside is a heavier binocular. On average the combined technologies adds 11 ounces to the binocular, compared a Swarovski EL 10x42 non-range finding binocular which weighs 29.6 ounces. Here are four examples of combined technology.

The Bushnell, Zeiss, and Swarovski are roof prism designs that use two tubes to house the lens. Roof prism designs are usually lighter and more compact than porro prism design binoculars. Porro prism models use an S-shaped setup that makes the binoculars wider than roof prism models. The Steiner is a porro prism type.

Ergonomics play a major factor. The ability of a binocular to be used for extended periods without user fatigue is mandatory. The roof prism models are narrow and easy to grasp and the laser operating buttons naturally fall under the operator's finger tips when the binocs are grasped. The porro prism model is wider and fatter. All felt good in hand and all perform the same during extended glassing sessions.

Two buttons not normally found on a binocular are built into the Swarovski, Bushnell, Steiner, and Zeiss. One button activates a rangefinder while the other allows the user to change the display from meters to yards.

When testing optics I follow a set process that includes water and fog resistance, shock resistance, resolution, brightness, image and color clarity, range testing, and finally ergonomics. All four models slipped a few bubbles out of the hinge in the water test. The rangefinder could be used immediately after taking the binocs out of the water. No moisture was detected inside any of the binocs. The four were then placed in a freezer and removed from the -4° F environment and brought outside to a 90°F environment. All lenses fogged and the bodies sweated like an ice cold bottle of *cerveza* in a Texas heat wave. The Swarovski, Zeiss, and Bushnell did not fog as much as the Steiner. The rangefinder on Swarovski, even with the fogged lens, worked on a test tree. But the other three took fifteen minutes for the lens to clear and allow use of the rangefinder. The drop test left all four models unscathed after a fall from a height of three feet onto a sheet of plywood.

The brightness of the Steiner, Swarovski, and Zeiss were near equal. The Bushnell was slightly darker and I attribute this to the slight green tint in the lens used to project the readout display. I tested with a grid pattern and a section of a local newspaper. The Swarovski and Zeiss tied in this respect. The glass in these two binoculars was excellent and the Steiner and Bushnell were very close behind. I could read headlines and distinguish made-made and natural colors. A doe appeared during testing and I named her Seven Ticks as I could easily count seven engorged ticks on her back with all four models. The color with the Bushnell was slight muddy compared to the others and again I attribute it to the green tint. Viewing the grid pattern, the Swarovski and Zeiss easily bested the other two. I was able to discern the finest grid pattern with these two models. Testing was conducted at dawn/dusk light conditions and in bright noontime sun.

On a test tree, which measured 35 yards from the test position, all four models gave a slightly different measurement: Steiner 32 yards, Bushnell 35 yards, Zeiss 33 yards, and Swarovski 35 yards. Measurements were all within the manufacturer's specifications. I also used the rangefinder during a rain storm, through leafy trees, and off many surface types from vehicles to deer fur. I ranged distances at known distances at a pistol range with three set distances—12, 25, and 50 yards—and a rifle range with two set distances—100 and 200 yards. I also tested past 200 yards. The Swarovski and Bushnell consistently provided the same range distance. How well the rangefinder will work depends on the reflectivity of the target. Hard reflective surfaces, like a vehicle, are very reflective while soft targets, like the fur of an animal, are less reflective. When a target, say a buck, is partially obscured by bushes, tall grass, or leaves the pulsating beam of the laser helps identify the target versus the clump of grass or leafy bush. All did a very good job of distinguishing an obscured target. The Bushnell even had a brush mode that allows brush and branches to be ignored by the laser. Rain and snow can cause false readings and I was fortunate to be able to have moderate rain during testing and all rangefinders ranged our test tree the same as if it was sunny.

The Swarovski EL Range 10x42 reticle intensity levels could adjust to five different settings or you could set it on automatic and the reticle brightness would automatically adjust the display brightness. At first it was difficult to see the reticle and the display in the Swarovski, Steiner, and the Zeiss compared to the Bushnell but it was only a matter a becoming acclimated to this characteristic. The reticle was a light color on these models compared to the Bushnell which was dark and thick. The EL's left tube held the display output and the right tube held the reticle.

The display could be customized to show the angle to the target. Under the distance display an angle icon appears indicating whether the target is above or below your line of sight in degrees. Or the display can indicate

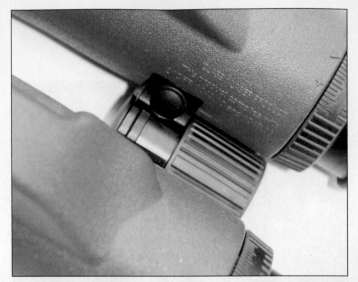

▲ The small button under the Swarovski EL Range 10x42 is used to change modes.

the corrected shooting distance under the actual shooting distance. Swarovski calls it SWARO-AIM which means the rangefinder uses the angle to target and distance to target to determine the trajectory of the bullet.

The Zeiss Victory RF 8x45 T* display was housed in the right tube. Intensity could not to be adjusted manually; the display automatically adjusted to the brightness of the surrounding. The optics and ergonomics were again superb. The distance was instantly displayed and in the scan mode—holding down the rangefinder button—the display distance changed as it panned across targets. It includes a ballistic calculator called BIS (Ballistic Information System) which has six ballistic curve settings that match most car-

▲ The Zeiss Victory RF 8x45 T* has two buttons located on the top side of the binocular; the large button fires the laser, the smaller changes settings.

tridge ballistics curves. Once set, press the rangefinder button and the distance is displayed, and about one second later a correction value is displayed with either an "H" or "L," so a display of "H 2" means a shooter should aim two inches high to hit the target. I checked the ballistic calculator built into the Swarovski, Zeiss, and Bushnell using a .30-06 load zeroed for 100 yards and found all three models provided proper holdover information.

Where the Swarovski and Zeiss displays are minimal, the Bushnell Fusion 1600 ARC 10x42 provides a display that rivals an HUD. The Fusion 1600 has three targeting modes: scan, Bullseye, and Brush. While on scan the rangefinder works like the others. On Bullseye a target icon appears in the display and allows the user to acquire distances of smaller targets. A crosshair appears around the target icon indicating the distance of the closer object has been ranged. In Brush mode the rangefinder ignores brush and tree branches so only the distance to the target beyond the brush is displayed. A circle appears on the brush icon when the farthest object is acquired. This worked well when objects were targeted through branches; think of a shooting lane from a tree stand or an antlered beast standing behind a juniper or sage.

The Bushnell rangefinder includes their proprietary ARC (Angle Range Compensating) which has two modes, either bow or rifle. There was one setting for the bow mode and eight caliber-specific settings for the rifle mode. While in rifle mode you could also choose the sight-in distance. Bushnell calls this VSI (Variable Sight-In) from 100, 200,

300, and 400 yards, plus you can choose bullet hold-over and drop in inches or MOA. If you choose meters, drop/hold-over only appears in centimeters.

When ranging at distance some binocs had easier to operate buttons, but the Bushnell range finding button on the top side of the right tube was small and took a bit more effort to operate. The mode setting button was on the top side of the left tube. Both buttons were the same size and there was some ramp up time needed to distinguish which button did what. This might not seem like a big issue but when you are ranging on a same target at distance the slightest movement can throw the reticle off target.

The Steiner Military 10x50 LRF was all business without the ballistic calculator feature of the other models. The brightness and clarity of the optics is excellent. The rangefinder display appears in the right side tube and the laser had its own dedicated optic unlike the other three which fired the laser out of one of the viewing tubes. The lens cap lanyards blocked the laser optic unless they were out of the way. The Steiner seemed to be the best suited unit to take the most abuse.

Combined technologies is beneficial in all binoculars tested allowing users to find a target and range a target with speed.

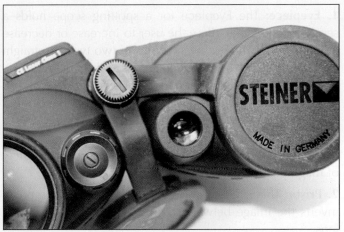

▲ Unlike the other models reviewed, the Steiner Military 10x50 LRF had a separate lens from where the laser was emitted.

▲ The battery compartment on the Bushnell Fusion 1600 ARC 10x42 is integrated into the hinge; the battery is easily found at a gas station or convenience store.

24. Anatomy of a Spotting Scope

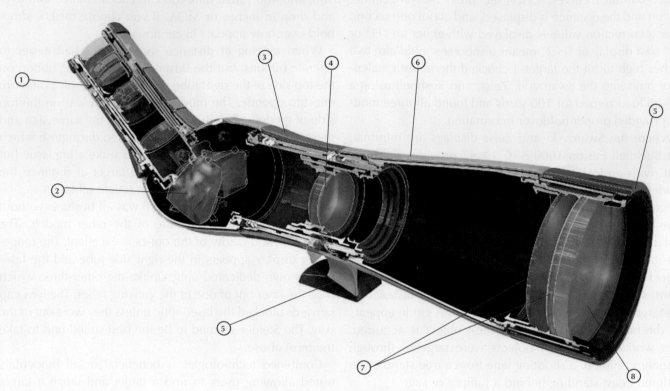

Image courtesy of Meopta.

1. Eyepiece: The Eyepiece for a spotting scope holds a series of lenses that allow the user to increase or decrease magnification. The eyepiece comes in two types, a straight eyepiece that has the same center axis as the spotting scope body, or an angled eyepiece which is set at a 45° angle from the body. The choice in eyepiece type depends on a user's method of viewing. An angled eyepiece requires a user to be above the scope, a straight eyepiece requires a user to be directly behind. Eyepieces also come in a variety of magnification powers.

2. Prism: This is an example of a porro prism. The prism inverts the image between the objective lens and ocular lens.

3. Focus Wheel: The focusing lens is housed in an assembly that moves forward and backward as a user adjusts the focusing wheel.

4. Focusing Lens: This lens is positioned between the objective lens and ocular lens within the body of the scope and adjusted via the focusing knob or wheel to focus the image.

5. Tripod Mount: Large spotting scopes require a sturdy tripod; the Tripod Mount is the point where the spotting scope attaches to the tripod.

6. Body: The Body of the spotting scope houses the objective lens, focusing lens and prism. It is typically constructed of a polymer or light weight metal then covered with a protective, pliable coating. The body is sealed and nitrogen filled in many spotting scopes.

7. Fluorite Lenses: In some spotting scopes like the Meopta MeoStar S2 82 HD there are two fluorite lens elements for clarity and sharpness of images.

8. Objective Lens: Spotting scopes are usually referred to by the size of the Objective Lens which is measured in millimeters. The objective lens is made of fluorite glass and is coated for clarity, sharpness, and antireflection.

9. Sun Shade: The outer edge of the spotting scope should accommodate a sun shade which allows use of the scope in bright sunlight without the sunlight shining in the user's eye.

25. Leica APO-Televid 82

Distinguished Optical Characteristics, Bar None

▲ The Leica APO-Televid 82 is a brilliant spotter allowing a user to easily find targets.

The Leica brand is iconic. Leica has a reputation for building high quality glass. This spotter is all business in its black finish—a serious scope for serious work be it competitive shooting or hunting. Never mind the birders who bow at the altar of Leica.

The APO-Televid features fluorite lenses that deliver an image with excellent color fidelity and sharpness with maximum contrast. The HDC multicoating helps create the vivid images. Magnesium-alloy chassis has rubber armoring.

The eyepiece is a 25-50x power zoom which attached to the body with ease. The focusing system of the Lecia utilizes a dual wheel focus system. These focus knobs each have a different focusing ratio. The smaller knob is the fine focus and the larger knob is the coarse focus.

A lens hood slides out to block the sun when required. Tripod attachment was in the spot it should be and offered good balance when repositioning the scope.

Rugged, reliable, and refined, the Leica is a near perfect spotting scope.

▲ Extended viewing sessions were effortless and comfortable with the Leica.

▲ Shown here are the dual focus knobs—one fine, one coarse—and the eyepiece.

Specifications	APO-Televid 82
Magnification	25-50x
Objective Lens	82mm
Field of View	123 ft (low)/84 ft (high) @ 1000 yds
Focus	9.5 ft (low)
Length	12.3in
Weight	51.8 oz
Finish	Black
MSRP	$2,999.00 (straight or angled body) + $900.00 (25-50x eyepiece)

26. Meopta MeoStar S2 82 HD Angled

Czech Made Since 1933

There are some things we take for granted and a good spotting scope is on my list. The Meopta MeoStar S2 82 HD Angled spotting scope is one of the better, more durable and precise viewing instruments I have used, and I am not easy on equipment.

The MeoStar has an 82mm objective that provides excellent resolution, great contrast, and vivid colors. Try finding .223 Remington bullet holes at 100 yards. Through the varmint scope I was using I thought I had missed. Looking through the MeoStar revealed the three shots were touching

▲ It's all about seeing downrange and Meopta performs.

each other. The MeoStar has uncovered truths unseen from a distance.

I opted for the 20-70x power magnification eyepiece. It easily twists into the body and locks. The chassis is constructed of magnesium and aluminum alloy and is very lightweight for such a big scope. The outside of the chassis is covered in a rubber armor that can take a bump—or a few bumps, especially in the back of my truck.

The proprietary MeoBright lens coating helps eliminate glare and reflection. The MeoShield coating resists scratching or abrasion and meets military specifications of durability and surface hardness. To repel water a MeoDrop coating is used. It also resists oil and grease. The coating-HD lens elements work well together. Imagery is excellent.

At the center of the body is an oversized focus control. It's a rubberized wheel that's easy to adjust with or without gloves. There is also an integrated sunshade built in.

Attaching the scope to a tripod was simple thanks to a lever lock.

What is cool is the MeoPix iScoping adaptor that slips over the eyepiece and holds an iPhone. It was satisfying to see an excellent group and snap a picture of it, then send the image to my pals. Instant bragging rights.

Specifications	MeoStar S2 82 HD Angled
Magnification	20-70x
Objective Lens	82 mm
Eye Relief	18 mm
Focus	5.5 ft (low)
Length	13.4 in
Weight	55.4 oz
Finish	Black/green
MSRP	$2,199.99

27. Laser Rangefinders

There's an old expression: "Close only counts in horseshoes."

▲ A rangefinder like the Nikon ProStaff 3 (left), Simmons LSF 600 (center), and Redfield Raider (right) can help you to be a better marksman since understanding the amount of space between you and a target is a critical part of the equation when shooting at long distances.

 laser rangefinder is basically a monocular that sends out a pulsating laser beam. That beam bounces off a target back to the unit to provide an instantaneous readout in yards or meters. The laser is similar technology as used in auto focus cameras. The design of laser rangefinders differs slightly. On the Nikon, the top objective lens is where a user views a target and where the laser is emitted. Under the objective lens is the laser detector aperture where the "bounce back" of the laser is captured by the unit. The Redfield and Simmons uses a setup with three lens: an objective lens for viewing the target, a lens to emit the laser, and one to detect the laser bounce back. On the Simmons the lens are stacked vertically. The Redfield tucked the laser lens between and to the left of the objective and detector aperture.

The price of rangefinders is directly attributed to the quality of electronics of the rangefinder. More expensive rangefinders have lasers with less beam divergence, which is when the laser beam diameter begins to spread out over distance. Instead of a tight narrow beam the beam becomes wider like a cone at the target end of the beam. The more beam divergence, the less accurate the distance reading. Those more expensive rangefinders also have more added features like a ballistic calculator, modes for use in rain or snow, different reticle choices, and can range at farther distances, to name just a few.

The Nikon ProStaff 3, Simmons LSF 600, and Redfield Raider 550 are bare-bones models that only provide distance readings out to 550 or 600 yards. However, that distance capability depends on the target's reflectivity.

The target's reflectivity determines how well the rangefinder will work. Hard reflective surfaces, like a rock or vehicle, are very reflective while soft targets, like the fur of an animal, is less reflective. Manuals state the best results on highly reflective targets are targets that are orientated perpendicular or at 90 degrees. Laser rangefinders can also provide false readings from ground scatter or beam interference. Some rangefinders can become confused when a target is partially obscured by terrain features. The pulsating laser beam may distance the brush instead of the deer standing behind it. False readings can also be caused by heavy rain and snow.

All the units needed to be turned on prior to ranging. Press the power button once, then aim the reticle at the target and while holding the reticle on target press the button again for the distance to be displayed. Many rangefinders use a black LCD display.

Measurements can vary on average +/- one yard, which is well within the manufacturers' specifications and not much of an issue when targets are close, say less than 200 yards, but it is something to keep in mind as you

▲ The reticle for the Nikon is a traditional crosshair; when the laser is activated an "X" appears with the center open so the target is not obscured. If the unit is unable to range a distance, three dash marks appear in the distance display.

▲ On the top of the Nikon ProStaff 3 are two buttons: one to range distance and the other to change distance measurement from meters or yards.

▲ The Redfield Raider 550 uses a simple reticle. The distance measured is displayed above the reticle; in scan mode the user could continuously measure distances as long as the button is pressed.

push the limit of the rangefinder and your ability to shoot accurately at distance. A white-tailed deer at 200 yards is a small target and to place the rangefinder's reticle on the target and activate the rangefinder can be tricky. As you depress the activation button the rangefinder must be kept steady or you might accidently jar the unit by pressing the button and accidently range the clump of grass in front of that deer. Taking multiple readings is best practice to ensure you are truly ranging on the intended target. This may sound time consuming especially with an itchy buck ready to bolt, but rangefinders operate instantaneously. At greater distances targets like deer are smaller and more difficult to range.

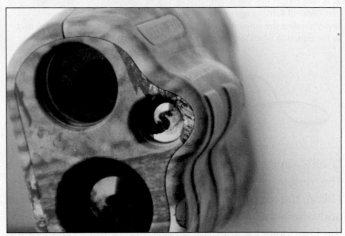

▲ The smaller lens on the Redfield is where the laser beam is projected.

▲ For the Simmons the target is located inside the rectangle of reticle; at the four corners of the rectangle the legs of an "X" appear with the distance measurement under the reticule.

Ammunition
28. Anatomy of a Cartridge

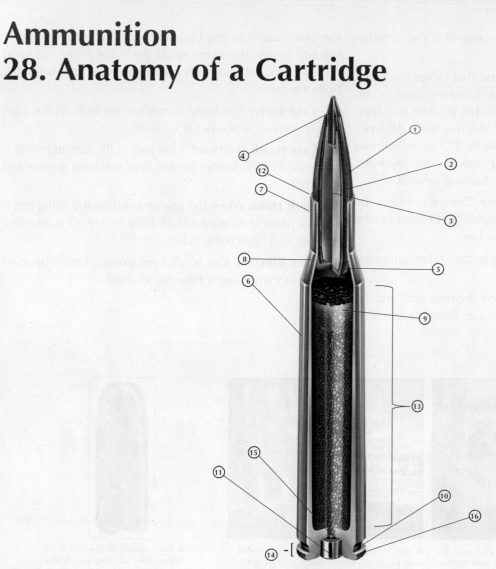

Image courtesy of Hornady.

1. Bullet: This is the projectile. Accurate bullets have a center of gravity that is concentric with its core. A bullet is made up of the following: base, heel, core, jacket, shoulder, ogive, meplat, point cannelure, bearing surface, and head height.

2. Bullet Jacket: Outside casing of bullet typically constructed of copper but also of silver, nickel, or brass.

3. Bullet Core: The center section of the bullet, typically made of lead. Steel core bullets have a steel core and are mainly used for military applications.

4. Bullet Point: The very tip of the bullet. Shown is a Hornady SST bullet with a red polymer flex tip that helps provide rapid expansion.

5. Bullet Base: In this example the bullet had a boat tail which provides better long-range accuracy due to less air drag.

6. Case: The case holds all the components of a cartridge in a water tight package. Typically cases are made from brass or steel. Some cases are partially made of polymer. PCP Ammunition is constructed with a polymer case body and a metal shoulder/neck and base.

7. Case Neck: The Neck is the portion of the case that holds the bullet in place and ensures the bullet will align with the barrel bore.

8. Case Shoulder: The Shoulder is where the case body tapers down to hold the bullet. On cartridges such as the .308 Win./7.62x51mm NATO, .30-06, and others, the cartridge headspaces on the cartridge shoulder. A Belted Cartridge, like the 7mm Rem. Mag. and others, headspaces on a belt around the base of the case; a Rimmed Cartridge, like the .30-30, headspaces on the rim of the cartridge; and a Rebated Rim Like that on the .284 Win. cartridge has a rim smaller than the diameter of the case body. Headspace is the measurement of a cartridge fit in a barrel chamber from the breech face to the part of the chamber that stops the forward movement of the cartridge in the chamber.

9. Powder: Powder is the propellant that drives the bullet through the bore and to the target. Powders come in two types, extruded and spherical. Extruded powder is shaped like tiny rods, Spherical is shaped like tiny balls. All types of powder are classified by burn rate. A .223 Rem./5.56mm cartridge will use a fast burning powder, for example, while the .30-30 Win. uses a slow burning powder.

10. Extractor Groove: The Extractor Groove is where the weapon's extractor grasps the cartridge to remove the round or empty case from the chamber.

11. Primer: When hit by the firing pin the Primer ignites the powder in the body of the case.

12. Case Mouth: The Mouth is where the case ends and the tip of the bullet extends from the case. Some cases crimp the case mouth to the bullet's cannelure, or groove in a modern bullet. The crimp holds the bullet in the case and avoids the bullet accidently moving forward and extending from the case.

13. Case Body: The Body comprises the bulk of the case and is where the powder is located.

14. Case Head: The Head is the part of the cartridge that is comprised of the primer pocket, rim, extractor groove and flash hole.

15. Flash Hole: When the primer is hit by the firing pin it sends a flame through the Flash Hole to ignite the awaiting powder and launch the bullet.

16. Case Rim: The Rim is what the extractor pulls back on the case to withdraw it from the chamber.

Bullet Types

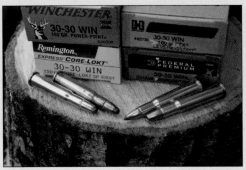

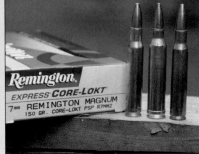

▲ Old-school .30-30 Win. cartridges have a rimmed case and use round nose bullets. Round and flat nose bullets are required for use in rifles with tubular magazines like the Winchester Model 94 and Marlin Model 336.

▲ This 7mm Rem. Mag. cartridge (middle) is an example of a belted cartridge; the .30-06 (right) and .270 Win. (left) on either side of the 7mm are rimless cartridges and headspace on the case shoulder.

▲ The Hornady DGS bullet is designed for the deep penetration in dangerous game. It is constructed of a copper clad steel jacket that will penetrate and not deform.

▲ The Remington Core-Lot bullet is shown at various expansion diameters when hitting a soft target at a variety of distances. From left to right shows the progression of expansion on a close to far target.

◄ The BTHP (Boat Tail Hollow Point) bullet is known as a match bullet used for precision shooting where accuracy is the goal.

◄ The Hornady GMX bullet is an example of a leadless bullet. This bullet is made of copper.

▲ The Interlock bullet from Hornady is designed with interlock rings that lock the core and the jacket together. These bullets are used for hunting.

29. 6.5 Creedmoor

Bred for Match Competition

The 6.5 Creedmoor was initially developed as a factory-loaded cartridge for match competition shooters. As the story goes, the idea of a new target round started during a conversation between Dave Emary, senior ballistics scientist at Hornady, and Dennis DeMille, a two-time NRA High Power Rifle Champion and general manager of Creedmoor Sports. They came up with a list of characteristics that a cartridge needed to possess to make it a great high-power target round. Characteristics included match-grade accuracy; a bullet with a high ballistic coefficient (BC), meaning the bullet has good air resistance in flight, allowing it to retain velocity and shoot flat. Low recoil and the ability for it to be used in a short-action rifle would both be pluses. Long barrel life and ease in reloading rounded out the list.

Emary's team at Hornady started with their 6.5mm 140-grain A-MAX bullet with a 0.585 BC. Target shooters have long known that 6mm bullets resist the wind and offer good accuracy without the recoil of typical match calibers like the .308 Winchester. Some of the 6mm calibers used by long-range paper punches are the 6x47 mm, 6mm PPC, 6.5x47 Lapua, 6.5-284 Winchester and .260 Remington.

Hornady then necked down the .30 TC case to accept the 6.5mm bullet. The .30 TC case itself was based on the .308 Win but with slight differences. The case is slightly shorter, has less taper, and the shoulder angle is a sharp 30°. This means when a bullet is seated to the 2.88 inch overall length (OL) the bullet takes up less room in the case. With other cartridges, seating the bullet to the proper OL begins to displace powder. We all know that less powder equals less speed.

In 2008 Hornady debut the new cartridge naming it the 6.5 Creedmoor. The name is apt, having a patina of tradition. Creedmoor harkens back to 1872 when a shooting range opened at the Creed Farm on Long Island in New York State and was the site for long-range rifle matches.

The new cartridge was offered in two initial loads using a 120- or 140-grain A-MAX bullet. Out of a 24-inch barrel, the 120-grain clocked 2910 FPS, the 140-grain at 2710 fps. The round is moderately fast. And it has won matches. At the 2011 Sniper's Hide Cup in Texas, which pits shooters

◀ Three 6.5 Creedmoor cartridges from left to right: 120-gr. GMX, 129-gr. SST and 140-gr. A-MAX

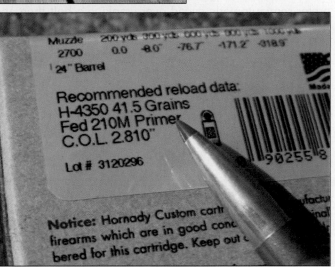

▲ Hornady includes the load data on the box for the 140-gr. A-MAX Match ammo—powder type, powder charge, and primer type.

in various tactical scenarios with shooting out to 1,000 yards, the 6.5 Creedmoor was used by four of the top ten finishers. What's impressive is the top two finishers used the round.

Since its debut Hornady has released other loads under their Superformance product line including a 120-grain GMX bullet and two 129-grain bullets, an Interbond, and SST. Not surprisingly, it has been used in the field. Not only do 6.5mm bullets have a good BC they also have a good sectional density, or ratio of bullet weight to its diameter. Because it retains velocity and energy downrange, it offers good penetration. It has been used on whitetails, mule deer, and even on plains game in Africa.

I contacted Dave Emary about the accuracy of the round and he told me from his own personal experience in a TC ICON with the 129-grain SST SPF loads he is able to shoot consistent 3-shot groups at 200 yards under 1.00 inch. "I have done it five times in a row," he explained. "The first four groups came in at .75 inch and the last opened up to 1.00 inch." He joked saying it was pretty ridiculous when you're disappointed with a 1.00 inch group at 200 yards from a lightweight barreled hunting rifle. That's how accurate the round is. It's a consistent performer.

Since the overall length (OL) of the 6.5 Creedmoor is close to the OL of .308 Winchester that means the 6.5 Creedmoor can be used in short-action rifles. It also means the 6.5 Creedmoor will fit in the AR-10 platform. So if you prefer semiautomatic speed over cranking a bolt then any AR-10 will work with an upper barreled in 6.5 Creedmoor.

▲ The rifle was assembled from a Remington R-10 lower receiver and a Fulton Armory upper receiver. The upper was designed for competition shooting.

▲ The AR-10 was mounted with a Konus M30 4.5-16x 40mm illuminated mil-dot reticle scope using Weaver 30mm Tactical 4-Hole Skeleton rings.

▲ Typical groups achieved at 100 yards with 120-gr SST cartridges were .75 to 1 inches. The largest was 1.5 inches.

Standard AR-10 .308 Winchester magazines will work with the 6.5 Creedmoor, too.

My first experience with the 6.5 Creedmoor took form in an AR-10 platform I assembled using a Remington R-25 lower and a heavy Fulton Armory upper courtesy of Clint McGee. The barrel was stout at 26 inches with four grooves that twisted bullets at a ratio of 1:8. The muzzle diameter was .920 inches with a full target crown and a gas block diameter was .936 inches. Unlike most AR-10s, the Fulton Armory upper used a side cocking lever and no forward assist. Clint mentioned that the uppers were getting groups of .5 MOA or better with the upper. Though it was designed for competitive shooting it should easily prove itself in a 20-acre clear cut. I mounted a Konus M30 4.5-16x 40mm illuminated mil-the 6.5 Creedmoor and .308 Win, it was obvious the 6.5 Creedmoor was a softer recoiling round with comparable bullet weight and velocity, though felt recoil is different for each shooter.

The setup was just below the lip of the bowl. I had a shooting lane out to 300 yards into the basin, a distance the 6.5 Creedmoor could easily handle. At 200 yards the 6.5 Creedmoor was silly accurate for a hunting cartridge. The deer never showed during the day but creeping back home up the steep path before dusk I saw movement and antlers. I slowly dropped to my knees, resting on my heels. Some sixty-plus yards downhill from the buck. I pulled the heavy AR-10 into my shoulder. Through the Konus the buck was broadside. I released the 6.5 Creedmoor and he stumbled then took off. I lost sight of him but heard the distinct crunching of leaves as he ran. Then silence. The buck was lying on his side, a small sapling held his body from sliding any deeper into the bowl. His rack held five nice points, I thanked him for the fine hunt and knelt at his belly to start the knife work. The 6.5 Creedmoor had entered his left rib cage, disconnected his heart, and exited out the right side.

▲ Getting to know the 6.5 Creedmoor, I was pleasantly surprised at the combination of low recoil, flat trajectory, and accuracy.

dot reticle scope. Weaver 30mm Tactical 4-Hole Skeleton Picatinny-style rings secured the optic to the upper.

At the range I was consistently able to group three shots in under one inch at 100 yards. With more time and ammo I am sure I could easily decrease group size, but 10°F temperatures have an effect on powder burn and trigger fingers. Recoil was nil and the rifle weight contributed to that. Doing some quick math to compare recoil energy between

▲ The 5-point buck was taken with one 120-grain SST bullet.

30. .300 Norma Magnum and .338 Norma Magnum

Efficient Burn with More Downrange Energy

ccurate-Mag and Norma along with Black Hills have skin in the game to build an accurate—out to 1200 yards—rifle that would be reliable and consistent, and chambered in cartridges that provide excellent down range ballistics.

Accurate-Mag's Special Service Rifle is designed to have the ability to be customized for any scenario and be adjustable to fit any shooter. The .300 Norma Magnum has 6 percent better burn than the .300 Winchester Magnum because the case is slightly larger in diameter. What this means is downrange the Norma round has more energy than the Winchester. The .338 Norma Magnum rivals the .338 Lapua Magnum. Again, the Norma round has a better burn rate and is smaller in size than the Lapua. At distance it offers more energy. The .338 Norma Magnum is a shortened .338 Lapua Magnum. The shoulder angle is the same but the body has less taper. The rounds are loaded with 300-grain Sierra MK bullets. Barrel twist is relatively quick at 1:9-¼ inches.

▲ Accurate-Mag's Special Service Rifles chambered in the new Norma rounds.

▲ The two sample Special Service Rifles are long, heavy brutes that help tame the new Norma magnums.

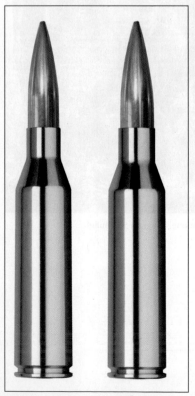

◄ The .300 Norma Magnum (left) and the .338 Norma Magnum (right) rival and surpass more well established calibers.

The military has shown interest in the cartridge and General Dynamics has built a light machine gun based on the cartridges. Black Hills factory specs on the .338 Norma Magnum are 2725 fps and 4946 ft-lbs. of muzzle energy. These are all very good indications that the round works. The .300 Norma Magnum is a necked-down .338 Norma Magnum. Berger 215-grain bullets were used in the load. The twist rate is 1:9 inches.

Black Hills loads the Norma rounds here in the US and they use Norma 217 powder. It is a slow burning powder made for large magnum cartridges like the .338 Lapua Magnum, .338 Norma Magnum, and 30-378 Weatherby. It is also a good powder for loading large overbore magnums like 7mm Remington Magnum and Ultra Mags. This powder-like URP contains a lot of energy and is less sensitive to changes in temperature and moisture compared to other powders.

The new Norma rounds have been approved by CIP in Europe, which is basically the same as SAAMI (Sporting Arms and Ammunition Manufacturers' Institute) here in the United States. The cartridge is currently with SAAMI for approval.

The Special Service rifle chassis is built from forged 7075 aluminum that is machined out to accept either a Remington or Savage short- or long-action. The chassis is made with three components: the stock section, the bedding section, and forend. The stock is completely customizable for any shooter stature. The length of pull and cheekpiece can be adjusted. The bedding section holds the barreled action via the two action bolts, but Accurate-Mag ensures the barrel action is rock solid and snugs it up with a set screw in the forward end of the bedding section. While the action screws hold the barreled action to the chassis, the set screw pushes it into the chassis. When I disassembled the rifle I could see the action was making full contact with the chassis. The workmanship was excellent. The magazine well has a steel insert which is different than most aluminum chassis rifles. The steel insert reduces wear that would normally occur on the aluminum chassis and is also what the magazine stops against when fully seated. This small feature could go a long way in the maintenance of the rifle and lessen the wear on the aluminum. Finally, the forend section is a vented piece of aluminum that

▲ I do not doubt that the Precision Armament muzzle brake helped tame the recoil in the .338 Norma Magnum.

▲ At about $6 per round, I did not want to waste ammo on chrono testing—I was getting more satisfaction shooting one tight, hairy hole at distance—but I did run a few rounds through the chrono.

▲ The .338 Norma Magnum was sweet to shoot and provided superb accuracy.

▲ Chrono results for the .300 Norma Magnum were slightly higher than factory data.

▲ The .338 Norma Magnum stayed true to factory specs.

▲ This group is typical of what the Accurate-Mag Special Service Rifle and Norma calibers can produce.

◄ After the barrel warming shot, the groups began to cluster with ease at 100 yards.

allows the barrel to free float. A Harris bipod was attached to the two sample rifles.

The two samples rifles sported Savage Model 110 barreled actions. The actions were stock from the factory and employ their sweet AccuTrigger. A 20 MOA Picatinny rail was mounted on each rifle. The 26-inch barrel has a contour that is somewhere between a varmint contour and USMC-type contour, offering a good combination of weight and rigidity. A Precision Armament muzzle brake was attached to the muzzles of each rifle. With the 26-inch barrels the length is 49 inches and the total weight is 13 pounds.

Leupold MKIV 6.5-20x50mm scopes with H58 reticles were used on both rifles. The H58 is a milliradian-based grid system for fast ranging and holdovers. It also features markers to adjust lead on moving targets. Eye relief is close to four inches which is plenty for this recoiling rifle.

At the range on a spring day with no wind and a temperature in the mid fifties, I tested two rifles, one chambered in .300 Norma Magnum and the other .338 Norma Magnum. I opted to cut my teeth on the smaller of the new Norma rounds and extended the bipod leg of .300 Norma Mag and got comfortable behind it.

I have fired .300 Winchester Magnums in light hunting rifles and the recoil can be something to reckon with, but the weight of the Special Service Rifle and the ergonomics made the felt recoil similar to a .308 Winchester. It was as if I had been shooting the Special Service and the Norma rounds for years. Velocity numbers were actually better than factory specifications. By the second magazine I was shooting groups that were ¼-inch MOA. You can't ignore that type of accuracy.

Moving to the .338 Norma Magnum, I was anticipating a lot of felt recoil as I loaded the single stack magazine. On the bench or in the prone position, the magazine fell free from the chassis, and the gaping magazine well afforded quick reloads. I especially liked the large magazine release lever which allows the user to keep their shooting hand on the pistol grip and operate the magazine release while replacing the magazine with the non-shooting hand.

Touching off the .338 Norma Magnum was enjoyable and it proved to be just as accurate as its .300 sibling. By the second magazine I was again shooting sub-MOA

groups. I liked the Accurate-Mag Special Service Rifle's combination of weight, ergonomics, and customization. The rifle and caliber is a great matchup.

Specifications	Accurate-Mag Special Service Rifle
Caliber	.300 Norma Magnum or .338 Norma Magnum
Barrel	26 in.
OA Length	49 in.
Weight (Unloaded)	13 lb.
Stock	aluminum chassis
Sights	20 MOA Picatinny
Action	Savage Model 110, bolt
Finish	matte black barreled action/ desert tan, forest green or matte black chassis
MSRP	$4100.00
Performance	Accurate Mag Special Service Rifle

◀ A few boxes of the Norma magnums were only a tease.

	Velocity	Best	Average
.300 Norma Magnum			
Black Hills Berger Match Hybrid 215	3149	0.25	0.5
.338 Norma Magnum			
Black Hills Sierra Match King 300	2739	0.5	0.625

Bullet weight measured in grains, velocity in feet per second 15 feet from the muzzle by a ProChrono digital chronograph, and accuracy in inches of three, five-shot groups at 100 yards.

SHOOTING TECHNIQUE
31. Anatomy of a Sling

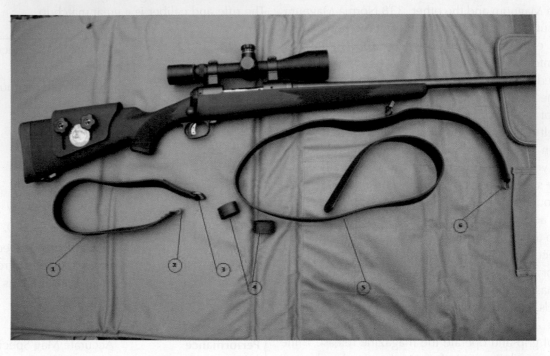

1. Rear or Short Strap
2. Lower Hook
3. D-Ring
4: Keepers
5. Front or Long Strap
6: Upper Hook

How to Attach a Rifle Sling

STEP 1: Place both Keepers on the Front or Long Strap then slip the end of the Front or Long Strap through the D-Ring

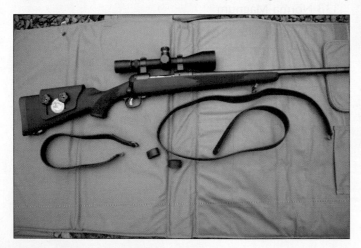

of the Rear or Short Strap making sure both Hooks point the same way.

STEP 2: Put the end of the Front or Long Strap back through the Keepers. This is how the sling should look when it is not attached to the rifle.

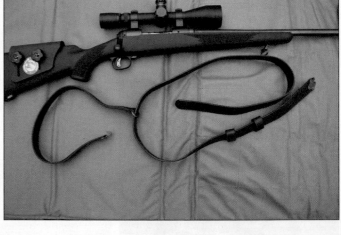

STEP 3: Attach the sling on the rifle by placing the end of the Front or Long Strap through the front sling swivel, from the front to the back, and insert the Hook into holes #9 or

#8. This is a good starting point to then adjust sling for the standing position.

How to Adjust a Sling

STEP 1: In a standing or sitting position place the butt of the rifle on your hip and the rifle cradled in the crook of your right arm, then loosen the sling by unhooking the Lower Hook and rehooking it down near the butt swivel.

STEP 2: Next, unhook the Upper Hook and rehook it four to six holes from the end of the Front or Long Strap. You may need to go back and forth with the exact holes. Use the Upper Hook to make these adjustments. The loop formed between the D-Ring and the Lower Keeper is the loop you place your arm through.

STEP 3: Make sure the sling lies flat, then rotate it to the left. Insert your left arm (for a right-handed shooter) through the loop until the loop is high on your upper arm, above

your bicep. You may want to experiment with the position of the loop on your arm. Tighten the loop by pulling the lower portion of the front loop in front of the keepers to tighten the strap.

STEP 4: With the sling now adjusted to your stature, grasp the rifle with your left hand so the sling lies flat against the back of your left hand then place the butt to your shoulder. The sling should not be loose but provide a solid steady hold. With a properly adjusted sling for a right hand shooter, the rifle should feel like it is welded to your left (non-shooting) hand and to your right shoulder. Do the just the opposite for left hand shooters.

If all the military/competition hook and loops seem overly complicated—it's not, once you have adjusted the sling a few times—there are other slings that make sling adjustment easy, simple, and fast. The Latigo sling from Brownells is good example of a fast and simple adjustable sling. With the Latigo a shooter can quickly go from a shoulder carry to a rock solid shooting position. This is how I transition from a shoulder carry to solid standing shooting position.

STEP 1: Pull down on the two straps immediately below the keeper to fully extend the sling.

STEP 2: Insert your left arm (for a right hand shooter) between the sling and the rifle.

STEP 3: Wrap your arm around the sling, grasp the rifle, and shoulder the rifle.

This procedure can be accomplished very quickly. Practice the routine until you know exactly how loose to make the sling.

32. Shooting Positions

Perfecting Form

"Perfect Practice Makes Perfect" is an expression used to describe shooter training. Your practice needs to be disciplined for maximum effect. A few well-placed shots can have a better impact on your overall shooting than spending hours at the range burning up ammo. Take the shots with the mindset that it is your last round and you only have one shot to succeed. Train with a specific task in mind, like standing at fifty yards to shoot and placing the entire magazine in a circle the size of a paper plate. Don't try to accomplish too much in one session. No matter how you decide to approach your practice sessions, basic marksmanship skills are the foundation.

Read and re-read Jeff Cooper's *The Art of the Rifle*; it provides excellent advice based on Cooper's years of experience behind a rifle. Cooper defines the shooter's body as the gun mount, and that couldn't be more true when it comes to the basic firing/shooting positions. What follows are the basic shooting positions, from least stable to most stable. You may need to modify these positions to suit your individual needs.

Standing Position

The Standing Position is the least stable firing position because the shooter's center of gravity—think your belly button—is high off the ground. The proper standing position form is displayed by competitive shooters where the shooter supports their off hand elbow on the hip and supports the rifle with their hand beneath the trigger guard. They lean their shoulders slightly rearward from the waist.

Off Hand Position

A hunter has little time to get into a proper standing position but they can quickly get into the Off Hand Position. In this position, you have the option of using a sling or not. When I practiced Seido karate one of the basic stances was called *Sanchin-dachi*. In this stance the feet are wider than the shoulder width, with one foot moved forward until the toes of the rear foot are on the same horizontal line as the heel of the front foot. This is a powerful stance used in the multitude of *katas*. Many advanced breathing techniques are exercised in this stance. I use a similar stance to shoot

▲ Off Hand Right Side View: The shooter's feet are widely spaced; note how the shooter slightly leans into the rifle and knees are slightly bent.

▲ Off Hand Left Side View: The shooter's knees are slightly bent and weight is on the balls of the feet, not the heels.

▲ Off Hand Front View: The sling provides a solid weld point, making the shooter more stable.

off hand as it gives me a solid base and I slightly lean into the rifle. After the shot, I am still on the balls of my feet and not knocked back from the recoil. I can get back on target faster for a follow-up shot.

Kneeling Position

In the Kneeling Position the shooter is lowering his center of gravity closer to the ground. One knee is placed on the ground while the other is used as a rest for the non-shooting arm.

▲ Kneeling Right Side View: The right hand shooter's right knee is placed so the shin makes full contact with the ground.

▲ Kneeling Front View: The shooter can create a solid mount and use this position if there is an obstruction that does not allow a position closer to the ground.

Sitting Position

The Sitting Position has two variations that I use regularly: open leg or cross ankle. This position is quick to assume and provides the second best stable platform to fire a rifle. A modification of this position is to use a short seat. When turkey hunting I use a short gardener's seat or cushion, which helps me to reposition more quickly for a shot.

▲ Kneeling Right Left View: The right hand shooter's left knee is used to support the elbow of the non-shooting arm. Note how the shooter's butt rests on the heel of the right leg.

▲ Sitting Cross Ankle Right Side View: With ankles crossed, the shooter's elbows rest directly on the knees.

▲ Sitting Cross Ankle Left Side View: Note how the shooter is leaning into the rifle. This helps to absorb recoil better.

▲ Sitting Open Leg Left Side View: The shooter's elbows are firmly resting on the knees and, by bending knees more or less, the shooter can adjust height.

▲ Sitting Cross Ankle Front View: The forearms create a human bipod, with elbows welded to the knees.

▲ Sitting Open Leg Front View: The shooter's heels dig into the ground for better stability.

Prone Position

The most stable position is the Prone Position, as all the shooter's body weight is supported by the ground and the shooter's center of gravity is at its lowest point. There are two main prone positions: military prone and Olympic prone. Try each and use the position that feels best for you. I prefer the Olympic prone position.

▲ Sitting Open Leg Right Side View: Notice how the shooter's body is slightly turned toward the target, with legs spread wide.

▲ Military Prone Right side View: The body is flat to the ground with the torso slightly raised at the shoulders, elbows on the ground.

▲ Military Prone Front View: The shooter's elbows are firmly on the ground and spread widely enough to support the weight of the rifle.

▲ Military Prone Rear View: The significant characteristics of the military prone position are the spread legs and the sides of the feet flat to the ground.

▲ Olympic Prone Right Side View: The shooter's torso is slightly rolled to the left and off the ground.

▲ Olympic Prone Rear View: The Olympic prone position can be more comfortable for shooters.

Improvised Positions

I have had very few deer wait until I was into a proper shooting position. At best, I was 100 yards or more away and was able to get into a sitting or kneeling position. At worst, I am crossing a stone wall or wind-fallen tree and the buck decided to make his exist post haste. In the real world, unlike a competitive shooting match, there is very little time to get into position. A compendium could be assembled of all the improvised shooting positions. The bottom line is it needs to be steady and solid so you can do your work.

Rice Paddy Position

The Rice Paddy position, also referred to as the military squat, is a fast technique that allows a shooter to get into a

▲ Rice Paddy Position: The shooter squats down with both feet shoulder wide and rests his arms just above the elbows on his knees.

relatively stable position quickly, fire the rifle, and quickly move on.

Improvised Kneeling

This position, like the Rice Paddy position, allows a shooter to quickly get into a stable position. Similar to the Rice Paddy position, the Improvised Kneeling position is quick to get into position but it takes more time for the shooter to stand and move quickly. I have used this position numerous times to shoot up an incline.

▲ Tree position: Grasp the tree with your non-shooting hand and place the rifle on your hand when you are standing.

▲ Improved Kneeling Position: Notice how the shooter kneels on both knees and sits back on his heels.

Using Natural Rests

Most hardwood forests are full of rifle rests. Grab the nearest oak or maple and use it to steady a standing position. Rocks—and, I have been told, ant hills—also make excellent improved rest when shooting sticks are unavailable. I prefer to lay my hand flat on the rest while some like to create a fist and place their fist between the rifle and the rest.

▲ Rock position: Place your hand between the rifle and in this situation the rock.

33. Shooting Technique

The Years of the Rodents

I learned about long-range shooting from wood-chucks and a .22 Long Rifle Marlin-Glenfield bolt-action rifle. Growing up in the country next to a dairy farm had advantages like acres and acres of hay fields which made for some excellent shooting lessons with woodchucks and squirrels. The pastures were separated by stands of hardwood with white oak and hickory. Those early lessons taught me how to stalk, to understand the limitations of equipment, the importance of getting within range to ensure a perfect shot, and how trajectory plays a part in long-range shooting. I also learned what happens if you miss (farmers hate unwanted holes in their barns), how to estimate range, and how to choose my target (it's not the woodchuck or the squirrel, but the squirrel's eye or the woodchuck's nose or below his ear). My shooting buddies, unbeknownst to me, were in fact rudimentary spotters. We swapped on and off until our boxes of cartridges were depleted or the woodchucks had enough. Mostly it allowed me to shoot often and shoot with a definite goal.

tra-jec-to-ry [truh-jek-tuh-ree], noun.

Part of long-range shooting is being able to solve complex equations in your head while under pressure. When we are taught about trajectory in high school geometry class, the definition is something like a curve or surface that cuts all the curves or surfaces of a given system at a constant angle. Are your eyes glazed over yet? If my teachers had described trajectory as the curve described by a projectile in flight, they would have had my attention. I learned to love math.

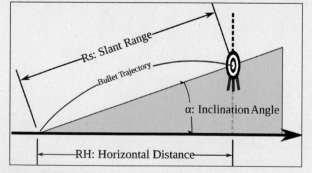

▲ Drawn out this is what a projectile's trajectory looks like.

A Minute of Angle (MOA) is an angular measurement, 1/60th of a degree, or 1.047 inches at 100 yards. It is typically used as a measure of group size or shot dispersion at various ranges. At 100 yards it spans 1.047 inches, but just call it an inch. Since it is an angular measurement, its value increases with distance. At 200 yards, a 1 MOA group spans 2.094 inches. At 300 yards, 3 inches, and so on. Since we are rounding the measurement it is important to know that at 1,000 yards, a MOA is not 10 inches but actually 10 ½ inches. Those fractional amounts rounded down add up over distance.

The MOA of a rifle is important at longer distances, typically at 300 yards and farther. If your rifle is zeroed for 200 yards all shots under 200 yards require no sighting compensation. Aim dead on. At 300 yards and more, the kill zone of, say, a deer is 8 inches, the size of an inexpensive paper plate. At longer distances, wind has more of an effect on a bullet's trajectory. An inaccurate rifle may mean the difference between a freezer full of venison or fish sticks.

Here's some quick math to determine MOA increments. Divide the distance in yards to target by 100 to determine MOA.

$$150 \text{ yards} \div 100 = 1.5 \text{ MOA}$$

You can use this to determine the number of clicks for your scope's elevation turret. Many manufacturers build their scopes with ¼ MOA clicks. That means 4 clicks equal one MOA. The more you practice this the easier it is, just like your high school geometry teacher said.

A mil, also known as an angular mil, is a unit of angle. One mil equals 1/6400th of a circle or 1 yard at 1,000 yards. Knowing this many tactical scopes use mil-dot reticles which serve to estimate range and correct trajectory. The dots on a mil-dot reticle are placed along the crosshairs at set dimensions. The reticle can be used to determine distance to a target of a known size or the size of a target at a known distance. Here's some more math on how to calculate distance to a target of known size:

Distance = 1000 x (object size in yards) ÷ (the number of mils the object measures in the reticle)

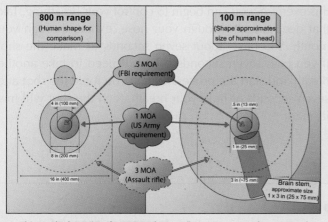

▲ This is why knowing the MOA of your rifle is important; the greater the MOA the less accurate the rifle is at long range.

Doping Wind

Wind blowing directly in your face or directly behind you will have little effect on your shot. Wind blowing at you perpendicularly or at an angle will affect the bullet. How much effect depends on the bullet speed, type of bullet, and wind speed. Yes, more math. If the wind direction is perpendicular to the path of the bullet, wind drift is calculated like this:

Wind Drift in yards = (Wind Speed in yards per second) x (Time in seconds of bullet to target)

If all the math is making your head spin, don't panic. There are other ways to make calculations. Apps can be downloaded to an iPhone or android device. There are many that offer fast solutions to your targeting problems. But what happens when the batteries die? My old engineering professor was quick to offer up his calculator if your calculator's battery died. He'd smile and pull a slide rule from his pocket protector.

Mildot Master is an analog calculator, similar to a slide rule, which provides rapid and simple calculation of range to target, amount of sight correction needed to compensate for bullet drop or wind drift, and angle of fire up or down hill.

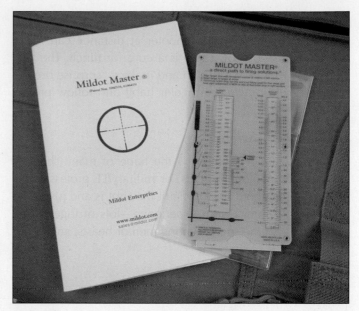

▲ The Mildot Master should be part of every long-range shooter's kit. It is even weatherproof.

Another simple solution is a cheat sheet like the Ballisticards produced by Schwiebert Precision. Lou Schwiebert originally created the system for military and law enforcement sniper use. In 1997 Lou offered the cards to civilians. The laminated cards are customized to an operator's specific rifle and cartridge. The cards provide the following information: horizontal trajectory to 500 yards (1,000 yards for military models), uphill/downhill trajectory for various angles, scope clicks for changing zero, wind deflection at 5 mph and 10 mph, and moving target speed.

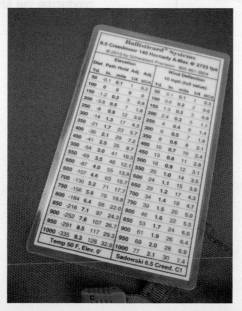

◀ This is the Ballisticard customized for my Savage 11/111 Long Range Hunter chambered in 6.5 Creedmoor for Hornady 140-grain A-MAX bullets which leave the Savage at 2723 fps.

Flinch Fix

An error on the part of a shooter at distance can mean a bad or missed shot. There is a cure for flinch. The best method is to trick your brain and make a "surprise break." Make dry fire practice a regular habit and follow prefect form.

Performance Anxiety

Performing under pressure is the bane of many shooters be they competitors, hunters, or military/LE professionals. Stop thinking about how difficult the shot is and just do it. Just doing it comes from experience—lots of trigger time on the range, time spent hunting men or beasts, and confidence in your equipment.

Breathe Right

Many times a situation will have your heartbeat jacked, and you can see the reticle bounce from your heartbeat. I practice a drill where I jog back from the 100 yard or 200 yard line after stapling up a target. I time myself to shoot under five seconds and hit an 8-inch diameter target. With this exercise, you can begin to control your breathing. Take that deep breath through your nose, exhale through your mouth. You have about seven seconds to make the shot. If you pass seven seconds, you will need to take another breath and start the process over. If you force the shot after seven seconds or hold your breath, then the shot will miss its mark.

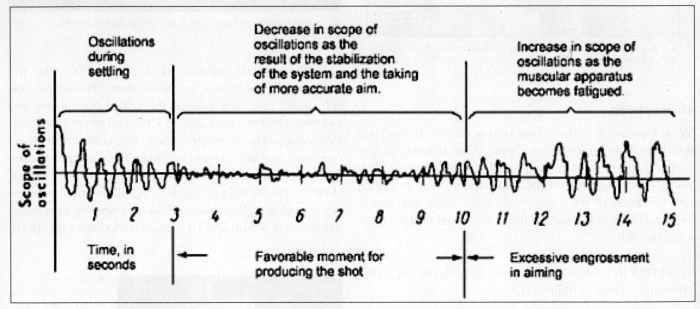

▲ This is what a breath looks like when charted out.

34. Shooting Drills

Get Down and Gimme Five Down Range, Now!

Training should be perfect, so the drills you perform should build your skill level and confidence. It is also a way to measure your progress as a shooter. Shoot and take notes.

▲ Kings should tell no lies; what is the aiming point on a one-eye jack or the deuce of clubs?

When I asked Eduardo Abril de Fontcuberta, author of *100+ Sniper Exercises*, about a drill for hunters, he suggested the following exercises and goals.

Fontcuberta suggested starting with a SHORT RANGE (10–300 yards) exercise on moving targets from sitting, kneeling, and standing positions. This is the range most hunters will encounter a beast. You might want to try to place a piece of cardboard in the center of a car tire and then roll the tire down an incline. Make sure the backstop is safe. The next step would be a MID RANGE (300–700 yards) exercise shooting prone at static targets. The animal most likely will not see you at that distance so you will be able to shoot while it is still.

In regards to accuracy, Fontcuberta said not to focus on extreme 1 MOA accuracy, but work on quick follow-up shots into a target around 10-inches in diameter with the goal of hitting the target all the time.

Tony Gimmellie at Impact Data Books is a former military sniper who now teaches long-range shooting and produces shooting data books. As for drills, Gimmellie does a lot of 100-yard and 200-yard hard precision slow fire drills

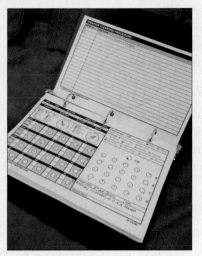

◀ Your data book should be accurate and complete so you can measure your progress.

with a focus on slow fire and shooting small groups on sub MOA size targets.

Here are two drills recommended by Gimmellie.

5-Shot Rapid Bolt Drill

Objective: Fire all five shots into your intended targets. This drill will help strengthen your multiple target engagement or allow you to get back to your initial target for a follow-up shot if needed.

Target: 8x11 inch sheet with 5 ½-diameter dots (D-RBD5D target/data card)

Distance: 100 yards

▲ This is the target for the 5-Shot Rapid Bolt Drill; it can be downloaded off the Impact Data Books website.

Shooting Position: Prone

Course of Fire: Five rounds max. Initially there is no time limit, but as you successfully engage the targets start to put a time limit in place. Start with one minute for five shots. Once you can do that in the allotted time, start reducing the time in fifteen-second increments. If you get to under twenty seconds for five rounds, you're smoking.

10-Shot Rapid Bolt Drill

Objective: Once you have mastered the 5-shot drill it is time to up your game with the 10-shot drill. This drill will again help strengthen your multiple target engagement or allow you to get back to your initial target for a follow-up shot if needed.

Target: 8x11 inch sheet with 5 ½-diameter dots (D-RBD10D target/data card)

Distance: 100 yards

Shooting Position: Prone

Course of Fire: Ten rounds max. Your initial goal should be to get all ten shots into your intended targets. If you can successfully do this then you should start putting a time limit to fire all ten shots. One minute and thirty seconds for ten shots is a good starting point. Once you can do that in the allotted time then you can start reducing the time in ten-second increments. Try to get yourself down under forty seconds for ten rounds and you will have accomplished some serious bolt speed and follow through.

After firing the drills, record your hits in a data book. When collecting data in your data book you want to keep complete and accurate information so that it can be used at a later date. What you did on your last shooting session is important and useful for the future target engagements. Having this information, and being able to properly analyze it, becomes the starting point to base future shots.

I also like to have some fun when I'm training and non-paper targets like those from Do All Outdoors add another dimension to shooting. Varmint hunters hunt varmints and the Impact Seal 3D Prairie Dog can be staked into the ground and shot over 1,000 times. It is fixed to a spring so once it is hit it moves back and forth. I try rapid fire on the orange beast at 100 yards. Metal wobblers or spinners are also fun when trying to shoot for time. Try cycling the action and getting back on target before it stops spinning. Yorick is my latest favorite; an Impact Seal Bonehead looks like a human skull. It is challenging to skip it along the range at 100 yards or more.

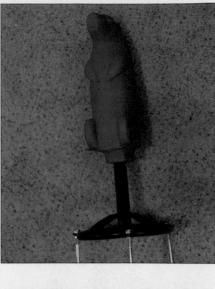

◀ This orange prairie dog from Do All Outdoors can take a beating—over 1,000 rounds—and it is a challenge at varmint hunting ranges.

◀ Impact Seal Bonehead, Dancing Ball, and Hot Box bounce erratically when hit.

◀ Do All Outdoors' Wobbler Kit is made of steel and can take the abuse of rifles chambered in calibers up to the .30-06.

RIFLES, OPTICS, AMMUNITION & ACCESSORIES
35. Custom Precision Rifles

Accurate Ordnance (accurateordnance.com)

Located in Winder, Georgia, Accurate Ordnance make custom rifles to order. Dave Walker, Thomas Woods, and Jason Nixon make up the gunsmithing team. Woody Satayabut and Mark Kuczka round out the rest of the team.

.308 Win, TAC30AW, Rock Creek, AX

Caliber: .308 Win.
Action: Stiller TAC30AW action with Stiller TAC knob
Barrel: 22 in. Rock Creek Sendero contour barrel; threaded 5/8x24 with a knurled thread protector
Rifling Twist: RH 1:11.27 in.
Muzzle Device: None
Action/Barrel Finish: Cerakote FDE
Stock: Accuracy International AX chassis with folding buttstock
Stock Finish: FDE
Trigger: Jewel trigger, set at 1 lb. 2 oz.
Optics Mount: Stiller 20 MOA base
Magazine: 5-round AW magazine
Overall Length: 41.5 in. (stock extended)
Weight: 12.4 lb. (without optics or bi-pod)
Features: The chassis includes a modular rail piece with a flush cup for easy sling use, a second modular rail for mounting other accessories such as lights and/or lasers, and a bipod stud.
MSRP: $3,665.00

TMR

Caliber: .260 Rem., 6.5 Creedmoor, 6mm Creedmoor, .308 Win.
Action: Stiller TAC30AW action with Stiller TAC knob
Barrel: 24 in. (.308 Win.), 26 in. (other calibers); Brux Accurate Ordnance Varmint contour barrel; threaded 5/8x24 with a knurled thread protector
Muzzle Device: None
Action/Barrel Finish: Cerakote Spider Monkey OD
Stock: Manners model MCS-T4A stock with an adjustable cheekpiece
Stock Finish: Molded gel coat in Accurate Ordnance Dark Forest camouflage pattern
Trigger: Timney set at 2.25 lb.
Optics Mount: Stiller 20 MOA base
Magazine: Manners mini chassis, 10-round AW magazine
Overall Length: dependent on barrel length/contour
Weight: dependent on barrel length/contour
Features: TMR (Tactical Match Rifle) was designed specifically with tactical match competitions as the primary intended purpose.
MSRP: $3,950.00

CPR

Caliber: .308 Win.
Action: Stiller TAC30AW action with Stiller TAC knob
Barrel: 18 in. Bartlein Remington Varmint contour barrel; threaded 5/8x24 with a knurled thread protector
Muzzle Device: None
Action/Barrel Finish: Cerakote tungsten
Stock: Accuracy International 2.0 side-fold stock with an adjustable cheekpiece and length of pull
Stock Finish: Black
Trigger: Timneythin shoe trigger, set at 2.25 lb.
Optics Mount: Stiller 20 MOA base
Magazine: 10-round AW magazine
Overall Length: 37.5 in. (stock extended)
Weight: 10.8 lb.
Features: The Compact Precision Rifle (CPR) was designed to be a handy, easily transported, lighter-weight, multi-purpose rifle that is suppressor ready. Ideal for target shooting, hunting, and most tactical competitions. Left hand variant available. Also available in FDE finish.
MSRP: $3,365.00

.308 Win, TAC30AW, Bartlein, T4

Caliber: .308 Win.
Action: Stiller TAC30AW action with Stiller TAC knob
Barrel: 22 in. Bartlein Remington Varmint contour barrel; threaded 5/8x24 with a knurled thread protector
Rifling Twist: RH 1:11 in.
Muzzle Device: None
Action/Barrel Finish: Cerakote FDE
Stock: Manners T4
Stock Finish: Med. Tan, ,and Light Tan
Trigger: Timney thin shoe trigger, set at 2.5 lb.
Optics Mount: Stiller 20 MOA base
Magazine: 5-round AW magazine
Bottom Metal: Badger M5 bottom metal setup for 10-round AI AW magazines
Overall Length: 41.5 in. (stock extended)
Weight: 10 lb. (without optics or bi-pod)
Features: Tricked out hunter or tactical competition setup.
MSRP: $3,455.00

.308 Win, TAC30AW, Rock Creek, TF3
Caliber: .308 Win.
Action: Stiller TAC30AW action with Stiller TAC knob
Barrel: 22 in. Rock Creek Sendero contour barrel; threaded 5/8x24 with a knurled thread protector
Rifling Twist: RH 1:11.27 in.
Muzzle Device: None
Action/Barrel Finish: Cerakote Spider Monkey OD
Stock: Manners TF3 side-fold buttstock, pillar bedded

Stock Finish: GAP camo
Trigger: Jewell trigger, set at 1 lb. 8 oz.
Optics Mount: Stiller 20 MOA base
Magazine: 5-round AW magazine
Bottom Metal: Badger M5 bottom metal setup for 10-round AI AW magazines
Overall Length: 41.75 in. (stock extended)
Weight: 12.2 lb. (without optics or bi-pod)
Features: Custom rifle with tactical setup.
MSRP: $3,885.00

American Precision Arms (americanprecisionarms.com)

APA (American Precision Arms) is located in Jefferson, Georgia, and provides a host of rifle services from general action tuning and threading a muzzle for a suppressor to complete rifle builds for hunting and tactical applications.

Paragon
Caliber: .223 Rem. and .308 Win. Mag. (standard calibers)
Action: APA Genesis tactical action
Barrel: 22 in. Broughton #6 5C stainless steel match grade barrel (.308 Win.), 20 in. Broughton #5.75 5C stainless steel match grade barrel (.223 Rem.)
Rifling Twist: 1:11 in. (.308 Win.), 1:8 in. (.223 Rem.)
Muzzle Device: None
Action/Barrel Finish: Cerakote corrosion resistant finish
Stock: Manners composite TF1 folding-stock
Stock Finish: Black gray tiger stripe camo
Trigger: Huber Two-stage, set at 2.5 lb.

Optics Mount: APA 30 MOA rail
Magazine: Detachable box, 10-round AW magazine
Bottom Metal: APA RTG trigger guard
Overall Length: depending on caliber/barrel choice
Weight: depending on caliber/barrel choice
Accuracy: ¼ MOA with match grade ammunition
Features: Designed for the harsh environment that our Military and Police personnel deal with on a daily basis. Boasts a ¼ MOA guarantee with factory match grade ammunition. Each rifle is broken in and shipped with three certification targets.
MSRP: $6,640.00

The Do It All APR

Caliber: .308 Win. Mag.
Action: APA Genesis tactical action, APA tactical bolt knob
Barrel: 22 in. Broughton custom #5.8 contour, 5/8x24 muzzle thread with knurled thread cap
Rifling Twist: 1:11 in.
Muzzle Device: None
Action/Barrel Finish: Cerakote corrosion resistant finish
Stock: McMillan HTG
Stock Finish: Dark tan, OD and medium tan tiger stripe camo
Trigger: Timney, set at 2.5 lb.

Optics Mount: APA 30 MOA rail
Magazine: Detachable box, 10-round AW magazine
Bottom Metal: APA RTG trigger guard
Weight: 9.25 lb.
Accuracy: ⅓ MOA with Copper Creek custom loaded ammo and ½ MOA with match grade or premium grade ammunition
Features: Designed from the ground up to be the perfect choice for the shooter looking for one precision rifle to use for hunting, competition, training classes, fun plinking and relaxing, long distance target shooting.
MSRP: $4,950.00

The Critter Get'r

Caliber: .300 Win. Mag. (standard caliber)
Action: APA Genesis hunting action, fluted bolt
Barrel: 24 in. Broughton #3 contour 5C match grade stainless
Muzzle Device: None
Action/Barrel Finish: Cerakote corrosion resistant finish
Stock: Holland sporter bedded with pillars
Stock Finish: Black gray tiger stripe camo
Trigger: Timney trigger, set at 2.5 lb.
Optics Mount: 20 MOA base
Magazine: Internal box
Bottom Metal: Williams steel trigger guard

Overall Length: depending on caliber/barrel choice
Weight: depending on caliber/barrel choice
Accuracy: ⅓ MOA with Copper Creek custom loaded ammo and ½ MOA with match grade or premium grade ammunition
Features: Designed by experienced hunters, this rifle will work well for 95 percent of hunters' needs. The perfect balance between weight, function, and accuracy. It's designed to be functional in a deer stand or hiking up the mountain on a sheep hunt, and work inside 400 yards, but can easily be extended for longer shots.
MSRP: $5,160.00

The Meat Stick

Caliber: .300 Win. Mag. (standard caliber)
Action: APA Genesis hunting action, fluted bolt
Barrel: 24 in. Broughton Sendero contour 5C match grade stainless
Rifling Twist: RH 1:11 in.
Muzzle Device: APA Little Jimmy muzzle brake
Action/Barrel Finish: Cerakote corrosion resistant finish
Stock: McMillan HTG with adjustable cheekpiece
Stock Finish: Black green tiger stripe camo
Trigger: Timney trigger, set at 2.5 lb.

Optics Mount: 20 MOA base
Magazine: Internal box
Bottom Metal: Williams steel trigger guard
Overall Length: depending on caliber/barrel choice
Weight: 11 lb. (on average)
Accuracy: ⅓ MOA with Copper Creek custom loaded ammo and ½ MOA with match grade or premium grade ammunition
Features: Hunting rifle designed to take extended 500 yard plus shots on a regular basis.
MSRP: $5,615.00

Beanland Custom Rifles (beanlandrifles.com)

Beanland Custom Rifles builds precision rifles capable of sub .5 MOA accuracy and specialize in tactical and hunting rifles. Rifles are built by Jon Beanland with over 17 years experience as a gunsmith and as a competitive benchrest shooter. All rifles built per customer request.

Rifle 1 (recent build)

Caliber: 7mm Rem. Mag.
Action: Sturgeon DBM, fluted bolt
Barrel: Krieger match grade
Rifling Twist: RH 1:8.75 in.
Muzzle Device: Kampfeld muzzle brake
Action/Barrel Finish: Cerakote graphite black

Stock: McMillan HTG with adjustable cheekpiece
Stock Finish: Black green tiger stripe camo
Trigger: Jewell
Optics Mount: Picatinny style base
Magazine: Detachable box
Bottom Metal: Williams steel trigger guard
Features: One-off design for long-range hunting.
MSRP: . . . . .Call for pricing

Bergara Custom Rifles (bergarausa.com)

Bergara's custom-rifle services started in early 2012, offering various configurations of precision bolt-action rifles, all built around the famous Bergara barrel.

BCR12 Mountain Rifle

Caliber:.243 Win., 7mm-08,.308 Win., .270 Win., .30-06, .300 Win. Mag.
Action: Custom Bergara action
Barrel: 20 in., Bergara barrel stainless steel, #2 contour
Muzzle Device: none
Action/Barrel Finish: Nitride black
Stock: Lightweight fiberglass, pillar bedded with Marine Tex steel filled epoxy
Stock Finish: Paint gray
Trigger: Timney
Optics Mount: Two-piece base
Magazine: Internal box
Bottom Metal: Machined "Oberndorf" style trigger guard
Overall Length: 40.5 in.
Weight: 5.6 lb.
Features: Lightweight hunting rifle, optional KDF muzzle brake.

BCR15 Long Range Hunter

Caliber:.300 Win. Mag., .300 RUM
Action: Custom Bergara action
Barrel: 24 in., Bergara barrel stainless steel, #5 contour
Muzzle Device: none
Action/Barrel Finish: Nitride black
Stock: McMillan A3 sporter
Stock Finish: Olive background with tan and black marble
Trigger: Timney or Shilen
Optics Mount: Bergara Custom 20 MOA Picatinny rail
Magazine: Internal box
Bottom Metal: Badger M4
Overall Length: 43.5 in.
Weight: 8.5 lb.
Features: Long range hunting rifle, optional KDF muzzle brake.

BCR18 Medium Tactical

Caliber: .308 Win.
Action: Custom Bergara action
Barrel: 22 in., Bergara barrel stainless steel, #6 contour
Muzzle Device: none
Action/Barrel Finish: Nitride black
Stock: APO Sporter modular chassis

Stock Finish: Matte black
Trigger: Timney
Optics Mount: Bergara Custom 20 MOA Picatinny rail
Magazine: Detachable box, 5-round
Overall Length: 43.5 in.
Weight: 10.5 lb.
Features: Medium weight tactical rifle; optional "Little Bastard" muzzle brake, folding stock, mono pod.

BCR20 Heavy Tactical

Caliber: .308 Win.
Action: Custom Bergara action
Barrel: 24 in., Bergara barrel stainless steel, #6 contour
Muzzle Device: none
Action/Barrel Finish: Nitride black
Stock: APO Mod-1 chassis with folding stock, adjustable cheekpiece

Stock Finish: Matte black
Trigger: Timney
Optics Mount: Full length 20 MOA Picatinny rail
Magazine: Detachable box, 10-round
Overall Length: 45.5 in.
Weight: 10.5 lb.
Features: Heavy weight tactical rifle; optional "Little Bastard" muzzle brake, folding stock, mono pod; other calibers available.

BCR13 Sport Hunter

Caliber: .270 Win., .308 Win., .30-06
Action: Custom Bergara action
Barrel: 22 in., Bergara barrel stainless steel, #3 contour
Muzzle Device: none
Action/Barrel Finish: Nitride black
Stock: McMillan Hunter
Stock Finish: Olive background with tan and black marble

Trigger: Timney
Optics Mount: Two-piece base
Magazine: Internal box
Overall Length: 43.5 in.
Weight: 7.3 lb.
Features: The BCR13 is designed for hunting; optional KDF muzzle brake; other calibers available.

BCR17 Medium Tactical

Caliber:.308 Win.
Action: Custom Bergara action
Barrel: 22 in., Bergara barrel stainless steel, #5 contour
Muzzle Device: none
Action/Barrel Finish: Nitride black
Stock: McMillan A1-3, pillar bedded with Marine Tex steel filled epoxy

Stock Finish: Olive background with tan and black marble
Trigger: Timney or Shilen
Optics Mount: Bergara Custom 20 MOA Picatinny rail
Magazine: Detachable box
Bottom Metal: Badger M4
Overall Length: 41.5 in.
Weight: 9.9 lb.
Features: The BCR17 is designed for tactical scenarios or competition; numerous options available.

BCR19 Heavy Tactical
Caliber: .308 Win., .300 Win. Mag.
Action: Custom Bergara action
Barrel: 24 in., Bergara barrel stainless steel, #7 contour
Muzzle Device: none
Action/Barrel Finish: Nitride black
Stock: McMillan A-4, USMC spec, pillar bedded with Marine Tex steel filled epoxy, adjustable length of pull and cheekpiece

Stock Finish: Molded in OD Green
Trigger: Timney or Shilen
Optics Mount: Bergara Custom 20 MOA Picatinny rail
Magazine: Detachable box, 5-round
Bottom Metal: Badger M4
Overall Length: 43.5 in.
Weight: 12.5 lb.
Features: The BCR19 is designed for heavy duty tactical use or sniper competition;numerous options available.

Black Ops Precision (blackopsprecision.com)
Shop in Columbia Falls, Montana, that builds tactical bolt-action rifles.

Perseus
Caliber: .308 Win.
Action: BlackOps Precision Model 911 long-action
Barrel: 19–22 in. Krieger 5R barrel, PERSEUS contour
Muzzle Device: Surefire muzzle brake/suppressor adaptor
Action/Barrel Finish: Custom Cerakote
Stock: BlackOps/Manners MCS-T4A
Stock Finish: Black

Trigger: Timney
Optics Mount: 20 MOA Picatinny rail
Magazine: Detachable box
Bottom Metal: BlackOps enhanced Heavy Duty DBM (accepts AICS and AW magazines)
Accuracy: ¼ MOA or better guarantee (average of five, five-shot groups)
Features: The Perseus is a precision duty rifle.
MSRP: $5,725.00

Jaeger

Caliber: .300 Win. Mag., .338 Lapua Mag.
Action: BlackOps Precision Model 911 long-action
Barrel: 20-26 in. Krieger 5R barrel (.300 Win. Mag.), 27.5 in. Krieger 5R barrel (.338 Lapua Mag.)
Muzzle Device: Surefire muzzle brake/suppressor adaptor
Action/Barrel Finish: Custom Cerakote
Stock: BlackOps/Manners MCS-T4A
Stock Finish: Black
Trigger: Timney
Optics Mount: 20 MOA Picatinny rail
Magazine: Detachable box
Bottom Metal: BlackOps enhanced Heavy Duty DBM (accepts AICS magazines)
Accuracy: ¼ MOA or better guarantee (average of five, five-shot groups)
Features: The Jaeger is a precision duty rifle with long-range capability.
MSRP: $5,995.00

Specter-Babr

Caliber: .308 Win.
Action: BlackOps Precision Model 911 action (feeds from AICS and AW Magazines interchangeably)
Barrel: 18 in. (standard) Krieger Tight Bore 5R Barrel, KUKRI contour
Muzzle Device: Surefire muzzle brake/suppressor adaptor
Action/Barrel Finish: Custom Cerakote
Stock: BlackOps/Manners special application stock
Stock Finish: Black
Trigger: Timney
Optics Mount: 20 MOA Mil-Std 1913 rail
Magazine: Detachable box
Bottom Metal: BlackOps enhanced Heavy Duty DBM
Weight: 10 lb (with optics and bipod)
Accuracy: ¼ MOA or better guarantee (average of five, five-shot groups)
Features: The Specter-Babr is light, fast, and versatile and perfectly adept in the close urban environment or from expedient or static field positions. Includes BlackOps Precision integral BUIS system. Also available in .223 Rem.
MSRP: $6,625.00

Infidel

Caliber: .223 Rem., .260 Rem., .308 Win., .300 Win. Mag., .338 Lapua Mag.
Action: Remington Model 700, carbon steel or stainless
Barrel: Krieger Perseus contour 5R Barrel; cut, crowned; length depending on caliber
Muzzle Device: none
Action/Barrel Finish: Custom Cerakote
Stock: Accuracy International chassis system
Stock Finish: Black, OD green, Desert Tan
Trigger: Remington X-Mark Pro
Optics Mount: 20 MOA Mil-Std 1913 rail
Magazine: Detachable box
Accuracy: 3/8 MOA or better guarantee with match quality ammunition
Features: The Infidel rifle uses tuned and accurized Remington action and trigger in a variety of caliber options.
MSRP: $3,725.00

Ranch

Caliber: .308 Win.
Action: BlackOps Precision Model 911 action (feeds from AICS and AW Magazines interchangeably)
Barrel: 18 in. (standard) Bartlein stainless steel 5R barrel
Muzzle Device: none
Action/Barrel Finish: Custom Cerakote
Stock: BlackOps fiberglass with aluminum bedding
Stock Finish: Custom color in Catalyzed Polyurethane Enamel
Trigger: Timney set to 3 lb.
Optics Mount: 20 MOA Mil-Std 1913 rail
Magazine: Detachable box
Bottom Metal: BlackOps enhanced Heavy Duty DBM
Accuracy: 3/8 MOA or better guarantee with match quality ammunition
Features: The Ranch rifle is a meticulously manufactured shooting platform designed specifically for the "field" environment; intended to function within harsh environments and offer the utmost in reliability when used in locations where debris, ice, water, and other particulate contaminants are likely to be encountered.
MSRP: $4,725.00

Brown Precision (brownprecision.com)

Chet Brown pioneered a fiberglass stock in 1965. The stock concepts and precise action machining techniques started by Brown Precision are used by numerous companies today. Brown Precision has also been at the forefront of many industry innovations, including the use of various stock materials, stainless steel barrels, specialized rust proof metal finishes, and numerous other materials and techniques in the manufacturing of custom and production rifles.

Tactical Elite

Caliber: .223 Rem., .308 Win., .300 Win. Mag., others on special order
Action: Bolt, Remington 700 or 40-X short- or long-action, 2 lug
Barrel: Length and contour to order, Shilen Select Match Grade stainless
Muzzle Device: None
Stock: Fiberglass/Kevlar/Graphite composite target-style stock with high roll-over comb/cheekpiece, vertical pistol grip and palms well, 3-way adjustable butt plate
Stock Finish: Black, camo, to order
Trigger: Remington custom trigger others on special order
Optics Mount: Talley TNT
Magazine: Hinged floorplate, 3- or 5-round
Action/Barrel Finish: Non-reflective Custom Black Teflon for smooth operation, 100 percent weatherproofing
Overall Length: dependent on barrel length/contour
Weight: 9 lb. on average, dependent on barrel length/contour
Features: Designed for LE and military applications, optional muzzle brakes.
MSRP: . . .$4,995.00, $3,995.00 (built on customer supplied action)

Pro Varminter

Caliber: Any standard or wildcat cartridge
Action: Bolt, Remington 700 or 40-X short- or long-action, 2 lug
Barrel: Length and contour to order, Shilen Select Match Grade stainless
Muzzle Device: None
Stock: Fiberglass, Kevlar or Graphite stock in Varmint Special, Hunter Bench or Remington 40X Benchrest configuration
Stock Finish: Black, camo, to order
Trigger: Tuned per customer request
Optics Mount: Talley TNT Quick Detachable
Magazine: Hinged floorplate; single-, 3- or 5-round
Action/Barrel Finish: Non-reflective Custom Black Teflon for smooth operation, 100 percent weatherproofing
Overall Length: Dependent on barrel length/contour
Weight: Dependent on barrel length/contour
Effective Range: 500 yd.
Features: Built for varmint hunting and rooted in benchrest rifle design.
MSRP: . . $4,195.00, $3,195.00 (built on customer supplied action)

Light Varminter

Caliber: Any standard or wildcat cartridge
Action: Bolt, Remington 700 or 40-X short- or long-action, 2 lug
Barrel: Length and contour to order, Shilen Select Match Grade stainless
Muzzle Device: None
Stock: Fiberglass, Kevlar or Graphite stock in Varmint Special, Hunter Bench or Remington 40X Benchrest configuration
Stock Finish: Black, camo, to order

Trigger: Tuned per customer request
Optics Mount: Talley TNT Quick Detachable
Magazine: Hinged floorplate; single-, 3- or 5-round
Action/Barrel Finish: Non-reflective Custom Black Teflon for smooth operation, 100 percent weatherproofing
Overall Length: Dependent on barrel length/contour
Weight: Dependent on barrel length/contour
Effective Range: 500 yd.
Features: Similar to Pro Varminter but built with a lighter overall weight for carrying.
MSRP: . . $4,195.00, $3,195.00 (built on customer supplied action)

CheyTac (cheytac.com)

The company is known for their proprietary long-range calibers—.375 CheyTac and .408 CheyTac—which compete with the .338 Lapua Magnum and .50 BMG rounds in long-range accuracy and power.

408 M300 Intervention

Caliber: .408 CheyTac
Action: CheyTac long-action
Barrel: 29 in.
Rifling Twist: RH 1:13 in.
Muzzle Device: ported brake
Action/Barrel Finish: Non-reflective gray
Stock: CheyTac carbon fiber chassis, adjustable length of pull and cheekpiece

Stock Finish: Black
Trigger: adjustable match
Optics Mount: Built-in 40 MOA base
Magazine: Detachable box; 7-round
Weight: 21 lb.
Effective Range: 2,500 m
Features: Designed for long-range shooting.

Colt Competition (coltcompetitionrifle.com)

Colt Competition rifles are licensed products of New Colt Holding Corp., and are manufactured under License by Bold Ideas Texas. Made in USA.

CRL-20

Caliber: .308 Win./7.62x51mm NATO
Action: semiautomatic, gas impingement
Barrel: 20 in., heavy weight, match grade, air-gauged, 416 stainless steel
Rifling Twist: RH 1:10 in.
Muzzle Device: Colt Competition Triple Port
Action/Barrel Finish: Matte black
Stock: Magpul PRS adjustable for length of pull and comb height, Magpul MOE grip with extended backstrap, Magpul enlarged trigger guard, 15-in. JDM float tube handguard
Stock Finish: Black
Trigger: Geissele two-stage Match, factory set at 3.5 lb.
Optic Mount: Picatinny Rail on upper receiver
Magazine: Detachable box, 20-round
Overall Length: 41.25 in. to 42.25 in. depending on stock position
Weight: 11.04 lb.
Features: Colt Competition charging handle with extended tactical latch, low profile finger-adjustable gas block, rifle-length gas block location, two 3-in. accessory rails.
MSRP: $2,979.00

CRG-20

Caliber: 6.5 Grendal
Action: semiautomatic, gas impingement
Barrel: 20 in., heavy weight, match grade, air-gauged 4140 chrome-moly steel
Rifling Twist: RH 1:9 in.
Muzzle Device: Colt Competition Triple Port
Action/Barrel Finish: Matte black
Stock: Magpul CRT 6-position adjustable, Magpul MOE grip with extended backstrap, Magpul enlarged trigger guard, Colt Competition 15-in. modular free floated handguard
Stock Finish: Black
Trigger: Colt Competition Match
Optic Mount: Picatinny Rail on upper receiver
Magazine: Detachable box, 30-round
Overall Length: 37.5 in. to 40.75 in. depending on stock position
Weight: 8.478 lb.
Features: Colt Competition charging handle with extended tactical latch, low profile finger-adjustable gas block, rifle-length gas block location, two 3-in. accessory rails.
MSRP: $1,649.00

Cooper Firearms of Montana (cooperfirearms.com)

Cooper Firearms was started by a few former employees of Kimber of Oregon back in 1990. Their purpose was to build the finest production rifles and they now create rifles that have a reputation for craftsmanship and accuracy.

Model 52
Caliber: .25-06, 6.5x284, 6.5-06, .270 Win., .280, .30-06, .338-06, .35 Whelen
Action: Cooper bolt, long, 3 lugs
Barrel: 22 in.
Rifling Twist: RH 1:8 in. (6.5x284, 6.5-06), RH 1:9 in. (.338-06), RH 1:10 in. (25-06, .270 Win., .280, .30-06, .35 Whelen)
Muzzle Device: None
Action/Barrel Finish: Matte black, stainless, per customer request
Stock: Walnut or synthetic

Stock Finish: Per customer request
Trigger: Adjustable, single-stage
Optic Mount: Drilled and tapped
Magazine: Per customer request
Overall Length: 44 in. depending on barrel length
Weight: 6 lb. -6.5 lb. depending on barrel length and contour
Accuracy: Guarantee ½ MOA 3-shot group at 100 yd.
Features: Model can be built in numerous styles—Classic, Custom Classic, Western Classic, Mannlicher, Jackson Game, Jackson Hunter, Schnabel, Excalibur; numerous options available.
MSRP: . . . . Starting at $1,755.00

Model 54
Caliber: .22-250 Rem., .220 Swift, .243 Win., 6mm Rem., .250 Savage, .257 Roberts, .260 Rem., 6.5 Creedmoor, 6.5x47 Lapua, 7mm-08, .308 Win.
Action: Cooper bolt, long, 3 lugs
Barrel: 22 in.-26 in.
Rifling Twist: RH 1:8 in. (6.5 Creedmoor, 6.5x47 Lapua, .260 Rem.), RH 1:9 in. (7mm-08), RH 1:10 in. (.243 Win., 6mm Rem., .250 Savage, .257 Roberts, .308 Win.), RH 1:12 in. (.22-250 Rem., .220 Swift)
Muzzle Device: None
Action/Barrel Finish: Matte black, stainless, per customer request
Stock: Walnut or synthetic

Stock Finish: Per customer request
Trigger: Adjustable, single-stage
Optic Mount: Drilled and tapped
Magazine: Hinged floorplate or detachable box, depending on style choice
Overall Length: 44 in. depending on barrel length
Weight: 6.5 lb. depending on barrel length and contour
Accuracy: Guarantee ½ MOA 3-shot group at 100 yd.
Features: Model can be built in numerous styles—Classic, Custom Classic, Western Classic, Mannlicher, Varminter, Varminter Laminate, Montana Varminter, Varmint Extreme, Jackson Game, Schnabel, Excalibur, Phoenix; numerous options available.
MSRP: . . . . Starting at $1,855.00

Dakota Arms (dakotaarms.com)

Owned by the Freedom Group, Dakota Arms builds exquisite hunting rifles like the Model 76 in the classic tradition—Mauser-style bolt-action with checkered wood and blued steel. They also produce a line of proprietary cartridges.

Model 97 Long Range

Caliber: from .22-250 Rem. up to .375 RUM
Action: Mauser-style bolt, short or long, 2 lugs
Barrel: 22 in. or 25 in. depending on caliber
Muzzle Device: None
Action/Barrel Finish: Matte black
Stock: Synthetic
Stock Finish: Matte black
Trigger: Model 70 style
Optic Mount: Drilled and tapped

Magazine: Blind box
Overall Length: 44 in. depending on barrel length
Weight: 7 lb. -7.5 lb. depending on barrel length and contour
Features: A lighter, round body configuration than the Model 76. It includes all the best pre-64 Model 70 and Mauser features, plus a match-grade barrel and adjustable Model 76 trigger.
MSRP: . . . .$3,295.00-$4,310.00

Varminter

Caliber: from 17 Rem. to 6.5 SPC
Action: Nesika bolt, short
Barrel: 24 in., recessed 11° target crown
Muzzle Device: None
Action/Barrel Finish: Matte stainless
Stock: Walnut or synthetic, beavertail forend
Stock Finish: Matte
Trigger: Adjustable

Optic Mount: Drilled and tapped
Magazine: None, single-shot
Overall Length: 44 in. depending on barrel length
Weight: 8.25 lb.
Features: Built with benchrest tolerances for use with small caliber cartridges; Deluxe model with better wood stock, Heavy Varminter with heavy contour barrel, Heavy Varmint All Weather model with synthetic stock.
MSRP: . . . . $2,840.00–$3,390.00

Desert Tactical Arms (deserttacticalarms.com)

In 2007 the SRS (Stealth Recon Scout) rifle system debuted; a bullpup design with the magazine positioned behind the trigger. This makes the rifle nearly 12 inches shorter than conventional sniper rifles while still maintaining the same barrel length as a conventional rifle. The system also allows the user to change the weapon's caliber and length.

DTA SRS-A1 Rifle

Caliber: .243 Win, .308 Win., .260 Rem., 6.5x47 Lapua, 7mm WSM, .300 Win. Mag., .338 Norma Mag., .338 Lapua Mag.

Action: Bolt, short or long, 60° lift, push feed, 6 lug

Barrel: Match grade, fluted, free floated, crowned, 22 in. (.308 Win.) or 26 in. (.243 Win., .260 Rem., 6.5x47 Lapua, 7mm WSM, .300 Win. Mag., .338 Norma Mag., .338 Lapua Mag.)

Rifling Twist: 1:7.5 in. (.243 Win.), 1:9 in. (7mm WSM), 1:8.5 in. (.260 Rem., 6.5x47 Lapua), 1:10 in. (.300 Win. Mag., .338 Norma Mag.), 1:11 in. (.308 Win.)

Muzzle Device: muzzle brake, .75x24 threads

Stock: Polymer stock panels, adjustable length of pull, optimized cheek weld, contoured pistol grip, raised recoil pad, adjustable monopod

Stock Finish: Flat dark earth, Black, OD green, Black/Flat dark earth, Black/OD green

Trigger: Match grade, adjustable, set at 3 lb.

Optics Mount: Picatinny rail

Magazine: Detachable box, 5-round (7mm WSM, .300 Win. Mag., .338 Lapua Mag.) or 6-round (.243 Win, .308 Win., .260 Rem., 6.5x47 Lapua)

Action/Barrel Finish: Black

Overall Length: 31.5 in. (.308 WIN), 35.5 in. (.300 Win. Mag.), 37.5 in. (.338 Lapua Mag.)

Weight: 11 lb. (.308 WIN), 12 lb. (.300 Win. Mag.), 12.4 lb. (.338 Lapua Mag.)

Accuracy: Guarantee ½ MOA 3-shot group at 100 yd.

Maximum Range: 1640 yd. (1500 m)

Features: Caliber conversion between .308 Win., 300 Win. Mag., 338 Lapua Mag. takes less than 60 seconds, ambidextrous controls, 14 flush-mount sling attachments, two-position safety.

MSRP: . . . .$4,531.50 (.308 Win., .260 Rem., 6.5x47 Lapua), $4,694.25 (7mm WSM, .300 Win. Mag.), $4,899.00 (.338 Norma Mag., .338 Lapua Mag.)

DTA SRS-A1 Covert Rifle

Caliber: .308 Win., .300 Win. Mag., .338 Lapua Mag.

Action: Bolt, short or long, 60° lift, push feed, 6 lug

Barrel: Match grade, fluted, free floated, crowned, 16 in. (.308 Win.) or 18 in. (.300 Win. Mag., .338 Lapua Mag.)

Rifling Twist: 1:8 in. (.308 Win.), 1:9 in. (.338 Lapua Mag.), 1:10 in. (.300 Win. Mag.)

Muzzle Device: none, .75x24 threads

Stock: Polymer stock panels, adjustable length of pull, optimized cheek weld, contoured pistol grip, raised recoil pad, adjustable monopod

Stock Finish: Flat dark earth, Black, OD green, Black/Flat dark earth, Black/OD green

Trigger: Match grade, adjustable, set at 3 lb.

Optics Mount: Picatinny rail

Magazine: Detachable box, 5-round (.300 Win. Mag., .338 Lapua Mag.) or 6-round (.308 Win.)

Action/Barrel Finish: Black

Overall Length: 27.5 in. (.308 WIN), 29.5 in. (.300 Win. Mag., .338 Lapua Mag.)

Weight: 10 lb. (.308 WIN), 11.2 lb. (.300 Win. Mag., .338 Lapua Mag.)

Accuracy: Guarantee ½ MOA 3-shot group at 100 yd.

Maximum Range: 1640 yd. (1500 m)

Features: Caliber conversion between .308 Win., 300 Win. Mag., 338 Lapua Mag. takes less than 60 seconds, ambidextrous controls, 14 flush-mount sling attachments, two-position safety, optimize accuracy for both subsonic and full-power ammunition.

MSRP: . . . . $4,531.50 (.308 Win.), $4,694.25 (.300 win. Mag.), $4,899.00 (.338 Lapua Mag.)

DTA HTI Rifle

Caliber: .375 CheyTac, .408 CheyTac, .416 Barrett, .50 BMG
Action: Bolt, long, 60° lift, push feed, 6 lug
Barrel: Match grade, fluted, free floated, crowned, 29 in., 22x1.5 6G threaded muzzle
Rifling Twist: 1:10.5 in. (.375 CheyTac), 1:12 in. (.416 Barrett), 1:13 in. (.408 CheyTac), 1:15 in. (.50 BMG)
Muzzle Device: Muzzle brake, 6 ports
Stock: Polymer stock panels, adjustable length of pull, optimized cheek weld, contoured pistol grip, raised recoil pad, adjustable monopod
Stock Finish: Flat dark earth
Trigger: Match grade, adjustable 1 lb.–6 lb.

Optics Mount: Picatinny rail
Magazine: Detachable box, 5-round
Action/Barrel Finish: Black
Overall Length: 44.3 in. (.375 CheyTac, .408 CheyTac), 45.3 in. (.416 Barrett, .50 BMG)
Weight: 20 lb. (.375 CheyTac), 20.2 lb. (.408 CheyTac, .416 Barrett, .50 BMG)
Accuracy: Guarantee ½ MOA 3-shot group at 100 yd.
Maximum Range: +2000 yd.
Features: Quick caliber conversion, ambidextrous controls, 14 flush-mount sling attachments, two-position safety, repeatable return-to-zero barrel mounting system.
MSRP: . . . $7,135.25 (.375 CheyTac), $7,239.25 (.50 BMG), TBD (.408 CheyTac, .416 Barrett)

E.R. Shaw Rifles (ershawbarrels.com)

E.R. Shaw has been making rifle barrels in Pennsylvania for over 100 years. Their barrels are renowned for accuracy and are used by some of the biggest and well-known factory firearms manufacturers in the world. Shaw builds complete rifles using Remington, Savage, and Winchester actions.

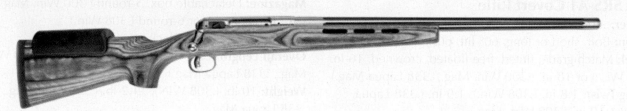

Mk. VII VS

Caliber: from 17 Rem. to .35 Whelen Ack
Action: Single shot and repeater configurations, chrome-moly or stainless steel
Barrel: 3.5 barrel contour, stainless, or chrome-moly, available with fluting and/or bluing for the barrel, multiple barrel lengths
Muzzle Device: None

Action/Barrel Finish: Matte or polished stainless, matte or blued chrome-moly
Stock: Laminate stock with a adjustable length of pull and cheekpiece
Stock Finish: Satin green/gray
Features: Customer choice on options: caliber, barrel, action, finish, and stock. Repeater models available.
MSRP: . . . . .starting at $740.00

Forbes Rifle (forbesriflellc.com)

Melvin Forbes of Granville, West Virginia, has manufactured a hunting rifle that is known for its light weight, superior workmanship, and precise accuracy. Forbes has teamed up with Titan Machine in Westbrook, Maine, to form Forbes Rifle LLC to produce a production model of his award-winning design.

M24B

Caliber: .26-06 Rem., .270 Win., 6.5x55mm Swed., .280 Rem., .30-06, .35 Whelen
Action: Bolt, 2-lug
Barrel: 24 in., sporter crown, button rifled, Forbes Custom #2 profile (.26-06 Rem., .270 Win., 6.5x55mm Swed., .280 Rem., .30-06), Forbes Custom #2 ½ profile (.35 Whelen)
Rifling Twist: 1:14 in. (.35 Whelen), 1:10 in. (.26-06 Rem., .270 Win., .280 Rem., .30-06), 1:8 in. (6.5x55mm Swed.,)
Muzzle Device: None
Action/Barrel Finish: Matte, non-reflecting, Mil-Spec phosphate or stainless steel

Stock: Straight comb, American-sporter type, hand laid carbon fiber Kevlar
Stock Finish: Hunter Green, Coyote Brown, Charcoal Gray, or 10 camo options
Trigger: Timney adjustable for weight and over travel
Optic Mount: Drilled and tapped
Magazine: internal blind box, 3-round capacity
Overall Length: 44.5 in.
Weight: 5.5 lb.
Features: Ultra light hunting rifle with extreme accuracy. Left hand models available.
MSRP: . . . . $1,499.00 (alloy steel); $1,567.00 (stainless); $1,584.00-$1,684.00 (left hand models)

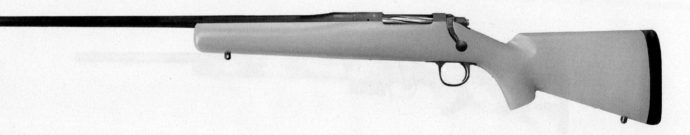

M20B

Caliber: .243 Win., 7mm-08 Rem., .308 Win.
Action: Bolt, 2-lug
Barrel: 21 in., sporter crown, button rifled, Forbes Custom #1 profile
Rifling Twist: 1:10 in. (.308 Win., .243 Win.), 1:9.5 in. (7mm-08 Rem.).
Muzzle Device: None
Action/Barrel Finish: Matte, non-reflecting, Mil-Spec phosphate or stainless steel
Stock: Straight comb, American-sporter type, hand laid carbon fiber Kevlar

Stock Finish: Hunter Green, Coyote Brown, Charcoal Gray, or 10 camo options
Trigger: Timney adjustable for weight and over travel
Optic Mount: Drilled and tapped
Magazine: internal blind box, 3-round capacity
Overall Length: 41.5 in.
Weight: 4.8 lb.
Features: Extreme ultra light hunting rifle with extreme accuracy. Left hand models available.
MSRP: . . . . $1,499.00 (alloy steel); $1,567.00 (stainless); $1,584.00-$1,684.00 (left hand models)

G. A. Precision (gaprecision.net)

G.A. Precision was founded by George Gardner in 1999 and currently builds rifles for many LE agencies, including: FBI SWAT, FBI HRT Team Quantico, ATF SRT, Chicago P.D. SWAT, as well as other municipal and state agencies. They also specialize in providing rifles to the rapidly growing community of tactical long-range rifle shooters.

Base Custom Rifle
Caliber: Choice of caliber
Action: Remington short or long bolt, 2-lug
Barrel: 20-26 in., Bartlein stainless steel with 5R rifling
Muzzle Device: None
Action/Barrel Finish: Matte black Cerakote
Stock: McMillan M40A-1 HTG, Pachmayr Decelerator recoil pad
Stock Finish: OD Green
Trigger: Remington X-Mark trigger set to 2.5 lb.

Optic Mount: Picatinny rail
Magazine: internal box
Bottom Metal: Pacific Tool and Gauge custom steel BDL type
Overall Length: Dependent of caliber and barrel length
Weight: Dependent of caliber and barrel length
Accuracy: ½ MOA with factory match grade ammo
Features: Built around a brand new factory fresh Remington 700 BDL action.
MSRP: $3,200.00

The Thunder Ranch Rifle
Caliber: .308 Win.
Action: GA Precision Templar Short-action, oversized tactical bolt knob
Barrel: 22 in., Bartlein stainless steel with 5R rifling GAP #6 contour
Rifling Twist: 1:11.25 in.
Muzzle Device: None
Action/Barrel Finish: Mil-Spec OD Cerakote
Stock: Manners MCS T yr Decelerator recoil pad

Stock Finish: molded-in field grade GAP camo
Trigger: Set to 2.5 lb.
Optic Mount: 20 MOA Picatinny rail
Magazine: Detachable box
Bottom Metal: Manners Mini Chassis
Weight: 10 lb.
Accuracy: 3/8 MOA guarantee with factory match grade ammo
Features: Built to Clint Smith's specs with Thunder Ranch logo.
MSRP: $3,870.00

FBI HRT Rifle

Caliber: .308 Win.
Action: GA Precision Templar Short-action, oversized tactical bolt knob
Barrel: 22 in., Bartlein stainless steel with 5R rifling GAP #7 contour
Rifling Twist: 1:11.25 in.
Muzzle Device: SureFire 7.62 SSAL suppressor adapter/muzzle brake
Action/Barrel Finish: Mil-Spec OD Matte Cerakote
Stock: McMillan A3-5 adjustable length of pull and cheekpiece
Stock Finish: OD green
Trigger: Set to 2.5 lb.
Optic Mount: 20 MOA Picatinny rail
Magazine: Detachable box, 5-round
Bottom Metal: Badger M5 DBM
Weight: 11.5 lb.
Accuracy: 3/8 MOA guarantee with factory match grade ammo
Features: As built for FBI HRT Unit, Badger Ordnance EFR rail installed (ANPVS 22/27 ready).
MSRP: $4,600.00

Gladius

Caliber: .308 Win.
Action: Remington Model 700 short-action, oversized tactical bolt knob
Barrel: 18 in., Bartlein stainless steel with 5R rifling GAP #6 contour
Rifling Twist: 1:10 in.
Muzzle Device: SureFire suppressor adapter/muzzle brake
Action/Barrel Finish: Matte black Cerakote
Stock: Manners T-2A adjustable length of pull and cheekpiece
Stock Finish: Multicam camo pattern
Trigger: Set to 2.5 lb.
Optic Mount: 20 MOA Picatinny rail
Magazine: Detachable box, 5-round
Bottom Metal: Badger M5 DBM
Weight: 10 lb.
Accuracy: ½ MOA guarantee with factory match grade ammo
Features: Nicknamed "Short Sword" by Snipers Hide founder, Frank Galli.
MSRP: $4,100.00

The Crusader

Caliber: .308 Win.
Action: GA Precision Templar Short-action, oversized tactical bolt knob
Barrel: 18 in., Bartlein stainless steel with 5R rifling GAP #7 contour
Rifling Twist: 1:11.25 in.
Muzzle Device: none
Action/Barrel Finish: Mil-Spec OD Cerakote
Stock: McMillan A5

Stock Finish: GAP camo
Trigger: Set to 2.5 lb.
Optic Mount: 20 MOA Picatinny rail
Magazine: Detachable box, 5-round
Bottom Metal: Badger M5 DBM
Weight: 11 lb.
Accuracy: 3/8 MOA guarantee with factory match grade ammo
Features: Field tested performer.
MSRP: $3,990.00

Rock

Caliber: Choice of caliber
Action: Remington short or long bolt, 2-lug, oversized Badger bolt knob
Barrel: 22 in., Bartlein stainless steel with 5R rifling, fluted
Muzzle Device: None
Action/Barrel Finish: Matte Cerakote
Stock: McMillan M40A1

Stock Finish: Numerous camo finish options
Trigger: Set to 2.5 lb.
Optic Mount: 20 MOA Picatinny rail
Magazine: internal box
Bottom Metal: Badger Ordnance steel M4
Weight: 10 lb.
Features: Built around a brand new factory fresh Remington 700 BDL action; multi-purpose rifle; numerous upgrades available.
MSRP: $3,495.00

GAP-10

Caliber: .308 Win.
Action: GA Precision GAP-10 upper/lower
Barrel: 16.5-22 in., Bartlein stainless steel 5R
Muzzle Device: Surefire 762 SSAL/RE muzzle brake
Action/Barrel Finish: Matte black
Stock: Magpul PRS buttstock and MOE pistol grip, free-floated aluminum handguard
Stock Finish: Black
Trigger: Single stage, match trigger, tuned to 4.5 lb.
Optic Mount: GAP 20 MOA base
Magazine: detachable box, 20-round, Magpul LR-20
Features: Long range capable AR-platform rifle, numerous barrel and caliber options.
MSRP: $3,215.00

Hospitaller

Caliber: .308 Win.
Action: Templar V2 integral short-action, oversized tactical bolt knob
Barrel: 24 in., Bartlein stainless steel with 5R rifling
Rifling Twist: 1:11.25 in.
Muzzle Device: none
Action/Barrel Finish: Matte Cerakote
Stock: Manners T4 adjustable cheekpiece
Stock Finish: OD
Trigger: Set to 2.5 lb.
Optic Mount: 20 MOA Picatinny rail
Magazine: Detachable box, 5-round
Bottom Metal: Badger M5 DBM
Weight: 12.5 lb.
Accuracy: 3/8 MOA guarantee with factory match grade ammo
Features: Rock-solid reliability for long-range precision shooting, other caliber options available.
MSRP: $4,500.00

USMC M40A1

Caliber: .308 Win./7.62 NATO
Action: Remington Model 700 short-action
Barrel: 25 in., stainless steel, USMC contour, 6 groove
Rifling Twist: 1:12 in.
Muzzle Device: none
Action/Barrel Finish: Matte black
Stock: McMillan M40A1-HTG
Stock Finish: Forest Camo
Trigger: Old style Remington set to 2.5 lb.
Optic Mount: 20 MOA Picatinny rail

Magazine: Internal box, 5-round
Bottom Metal: USMC spec Winchester Model 70 steel floorplate/trigger guard
Weight: 12.5 lb.
Accuracy: ½ MOA guarantee with factory match grade ammo
Features: Mil-Spec rifle built to the USMC, Quantico-RTE/Precision Weapon Shop build procedure. The USMC stopped building M40A1 Rifles in 1999, but G.A. Precision still builds them to the same specs the PWS 2112 Armours did from 1980 to 1999.
MSRP: $3,700.00

USMC M40A3

Caliber: .308 Win./7.62 NATO
Action: Remington Model 700 short-action
Barrel: 25 in., stainless steel, USMC contour, 6 groove
Rifling Twist: 1:12 in.
Muzzle Device: none
Action/Barrel Finish: Matte black
Stock: McMillan A4, adjustable saddle cheek and length of pull
Stock Finish: OD Green

Trigger: Remington set to 2.5 lb.
Optic Mount: 20 MOA Picatinny rail
Magazine: Detachable box, 5-round
Bottom Metal: Badger Ordnance M5 trigger guard
Weight: 16.5 lb.
Accuracy: ½ MOA guarantee with factory match grade ammo
Features: Mil-Spec rifle built to the USMC, Quantico, PWS build procedures.
MSRP: $3,970.00

USMC M40A5

Caliber: .308 Win./7.62 NATO
Action: Remington Model 700 short-action
Barrel: 25 in., stainless steel, USMC contour, 6 groove
Rifling Twist: 1:12 in.
Muzzle Device: Surefire Comp/Suppressor Adapter
Action/Barrel Finish: Matte black
Stock: McMillan A4, adjustable saddle cheek and length of pull
Stock Finish: OD Green
Trigger: Remington PTR trigger
Optic Mount: 20 MOA Picatinny rail
Magazine: Detachable box, 5-round
Bottom Metal: Badger Ordnance M5 trigger guard
Accuracy: ½ MOA guarantee with factory match grade ammo
Features: Mil-Spec copy of the most current USMC sniper rifle.
MSRP: $4,490.00

US Army M-24

Caliber: .308 Win./7.62 NATO
Action: Remington Model 700 long-action
Barrel: 24 in., stainless steel, 5R
Rifling Twist: 1:11.25 in.
Muzzle Device: none
Action/Barrel Finish: Matte black
Stock: HS Precision M-24, adjustable length of pull
Stock Finish: Matte black
Trigger: Remington trigger set to 2.5 lb.
Optic Mount: Drilled and tapped for base
Magazine: Internal box, 5-round
Bottom Metal: Steel M-24 trigger guard
Accuracy: ½ MOA guarantee with factory match grade ammo
Features: Mil-Spec copy of the US Army sniper rifle.
MSRP: $3,670.00

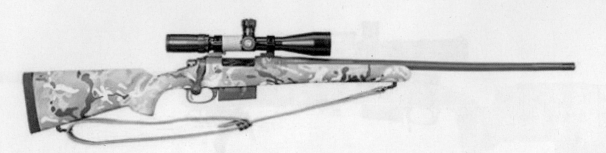

Xtreme Hunter

Caliber: 6.5 SAUM 4S (GAP version of the RSAUM)
Action: Templar short-action hunter
Barrel: 24 in., Bartlein stainless steel, 5R, #3 contour, fluted
Rifling Twist: 1:8.75 in.
Muzzle Device: Vais muzzle brake
Action/Barrel Finish: Choice of Cerakote color
Stock: Manners SL, 90 percent carbon fiber
Stock Finish: Choice of color dip or paint

Trigger: Remington X-Mark Pro trigger set to 2.5 lb.
Optic Mount: Drilled and tapped for base
Magazine: Detachable box, 5-round
Bottom Metal: APA RTG/SA trigger guard
Accuracy: ½ MOA guarantee with factory match grade ammo
Features: Flatter trajectory, light weight, minimal wind correction, light recoil, barrel life 2,500+ rounds, cartridge component life 8+ reloads
MSRP: $4,370.00

Gradous Rifles (gradousrifles.com)

Small shop in Hephzibah, Georgia, that specializes in building hunting and tactical rifles on Surgeon actions.

Tactical Short-action

Caliber: .308 Win., .260 Rem., 6.5 or 6 Creedmoor, 6.5 X 47, 6 X 47, 6 XC, .243 Win., .223 Rem.
Action: Surgeon 591 short-action repeater
Barrel: up to 28 in., match grade barrels are selected based upon availability from Bartlein, Broughton, and Krieger; choice of contours
Muzzle Device: none
Action/Barrel Finish: Choice of Cerakote color

Stock: McMillan A5 or M40A1 adjustable
Stock Finish: Choice of color
Trigger: Jewel HVR
Optic Mount: Drilled and tapped for base
Magazine: Detachable box, 5-round, accuracy International magazine
Bottom Metal: Surgeon
Accuracy: ½ MOA
Features: Long and XL action lengths available.
MSRP: $4,450.00

Premium Hunting Rifle

Caliber: Most caliber choices available
Action: Surgeon 591 short-action repeater or 1086 depending on caliber choice
Barrel: up to 28 in., match grade barrels are selected based upon availability from Bartlein, Broughton, and Krieger; choice of contours
Muzzle Device: none
Action/Barrel Finish: Choice of Cerakote H-series
Stock: Choice of McMillanor Manners
Stock Finish: Choice of color
Trigger: Jewel HVR
Optic Mount: Drilled and tapped for base
Bottom Metal: Choice of H-S Precision, Remington ADL or BDL, Sunny Hill or Surgeon DBM
Accuracy: ½ MOA or better
Features: Rifles are based on the Surgeon integral actions and carefullyselected premium components are used throughout. Paired with obsessive attention to fit and finish.
MSRP: . . $4,350.00 (short-actions); $4,450.00 (long-actions)

H-S Precision Rifles (hsprecision.com)

With originality, quality, and accuracy, H-S Precision provides civilians and military/LE personnel with innovative products and services, using world class manufacturing techniques and proprietary technology.

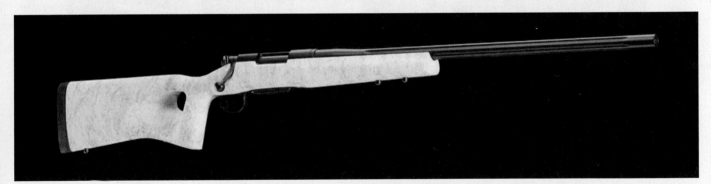

VAR

Caliber: .223 Rem., .22-250 Rem., .220 Swift
Action: Pro-Series 2000 stainless steel action, long or short, RH or LH
Barrel: 20in. or 20 in., Pro-Series 10X match grade stainless steel
Muzzle Device: none
Action/Barrel Finish: Matte black Teflon
Stock: Pro-Series 2000 straight stock, Kevlar/fiberglass/carbon fiber construction, wide forend, full length aluminum bedding
Stock Finish: Tri-Color Desert Camo, Black/Olive, Green Camo, Gray/Black, Tan/Black, Black/Tan Camo, Green/ Tan Camo, Black/Red, Grassland Camo, Desert Camo, Woodland Camo, Prairie Grass Camo, Sand
Optic Mount: Drilled and tapped for base
Magazine: detachable box, 4-round
Bottom Metal: Pro-Series
Accuracy: ½ MOA or better
Features: VAR medium weight rifles are designed for serious varmint hunters. All actions available as single shot or stainless steel floorplate with detachable magazine.Numerous caliber, barrel and stocks options available. Six-month build time.
MSRP: $3,395.00

PHL

Caliber: Most caliber choices available
Action: Pro-Series 2000 stainless steel action, long or short, RH or LH
Barrel: up to 28 in., Pro-Series 10X match grade stainless steel
Muzzle Device: none
Action/Barrel Finish: Choice of Cerakote H-series
Stock: Pro-Series 2000 straight stock, Kevlar/fiberglass/carbon fiber construction, wide forend, full length aluminum bedding

Stock Finish: Tri-Color Desert Camo, Black/Olive, Green Camo, Gray/Black, Tan/Black, Black/Tan Camo, Green/Tan Camo, Black/Red, Grassland Camo, Desert Camo, Woodland Camo, Prairie Grass Camo, Sand
Optic Mount: Drilled and tapped for base
Bottom Metal: Pro-Series
Accuracy: ½ MOA or better
Features: The Pro-Series 2000 PHL rifle is built with the high altitude hunter in mind. Numerous caliber, barrel, and stocks options available. Six month build time.
MSRP: $3,705.00

HTR

Caliber: Available in any standard SAAMI Calibers
Action: Pro-Series 2000 stainless steel action, long or short, RH or LH
Barrel: up to 28 in., Pro-Series 10X match grade stainless steel
Muzzle Device: none
Action/Barrel Finish: Choice of Cerakote H-series
Stock: Pro-Series 2000 straight stock, Kevlar/fiberglass/carbon fiber construction, wide forend, full length aluminum bedding, models with adjustable length of pull and cheek riser available

Stock Finish: Tri-Color Desert Camo, Black/Olive, Green Camo, Gray/Black, Tan/Black, Black/Tan Camo, Green/Tan Camo, Black/Red, Grassland Camo, Desert Camo, Woodland Camo, Prairie Grass Camo, Sand
Optic Mount: Drilled and tapped for base
Bottom Metal: Pro-Series
Accuracy: ½ MOA or better
Features: The Pro-Series 2000 HTR (Heavy Tactical Rifle) comes standard with a fully adjustable stock and heavy fluted barrel. Used by FBI, BATF, and IDF as their precision long-range weapon of choice. Numerous caliber, barrel, and stocks options available. Six month build time.
MSRP: $3,600.00

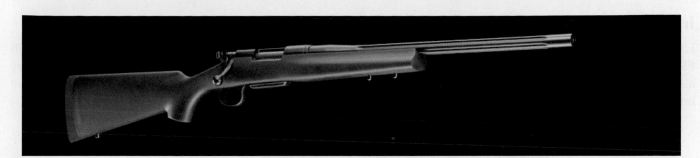

RDR

Caliber: Available in any standard SAAMI Calibers
Action: Pro-Series 2000 stainless steel action, long or short, RH or LH
Barrel: up to 28 in., Pro-Series 10X match grade stainless steel
Muzzle Device: none
Action/Barrel Finish: Choice of Cerakote H-series
Stock: Pro-Series 2000 straight stock, Kevlar/fiberglass/carbon fiber construction, wide forend, full length aluminum bedding, models with adjustable length of pull and cheek riser available

Stock Finish: Tri-Color Desert Camo, Black/Olive, Green Camo, Gray/Black, Tan/Black, Black/Tan Camo, Green/Tan Camo, Black/Red, Grassland Camo, Desert Camo, Woodland Camo, Prairie Grass Camo, Sand
Optic Mount: Drilled and tapped for base
Bottom Metal: Pro-Series
Accuracy: ½ MOA or better
Features: The RDR (Rapid Deployment Rifle) have all the features of the HTR, but with a shorter barrel and smaller stock. The lighter weight makes the RDR easier and quicker to handle. Pro-Series 2000 Stainless steel action, short-action only. Numerous caliber, barrel and stocks options available. Six month delivery schedule.
MSRP: $3,395.00

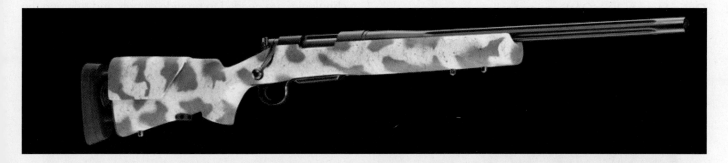

STR

Caliber: Available in any standard SAAMI Calibers
Action: Pro-Series 2000 stainless steel action, short, RH or LH
Barrel: 20 in., Pro-Series 10X match grade stainless steel, fluted
Muzzle Device: none
Action/Barrel Finish: Choice of Cerakote H-series
Stock: Pro-Series 2000 straight stock, Kevlar/fiberglass/carbon fiber construction, wide forend, full-length aluminum bedding, adjustable length of pull and cheek riser

Stock Finish: Tri-Color Desert Camo, Black/Olive, Green Camo, Gray/Black, Tan/Black, Black/Tan Camo, Green/Tan Camo, Black/Red, Grassland Camo, Desert Camo, Woodland Camo, Prairie Grass Camo, Sand
Optic Mount: Drilled and tapped for base
Bottom Metal: Pro-Series
Accuracy: ½ MOA or better
Features: The STR (Short Tactical Rifle) combines the lighter weight of the RDR with the hardware and adjustability of the HTR.
MSRP: $3,600.00

Iron Brigade Armory (deathfromafar.com)

Law Enforcement departments across the nation rely on Iron Brigade Armory (IBA) for accurized, tougher than nails PSS Remington sniper rifles that hold zero virtually forever under the most adverse of conditions. Iron Brigade Armory also produces the toughest and most reliable scope mounts ever devised. Their Badger/Chandler steel trigger guards are unmatched, and their heavy-duty recoil lugs are found on the best of accurate rifles.

XM-3

Caliber: .308 Win./7.62 NATO
Action: Bolt, Remington Model 700 short-action, clip slotted, IBA combat bolt handle
Barrel: 18.5 in., Hart 416R stainless steel
Rifling Twist: 1:10 in. RH
Muzzle Device: none
Action/Barrel Finish: Matte black
Stock: McMillan A-6, adjustable length of pull
Stock Finish: OD Green
Trigger: Remington
Optic Mount: 20 MOA Picatinny rail
Magazine: Internal/welded, 5-round
Bottom Metal: IBA steel trigger guard

Overall Length: 40.5 in. (without suppressor)
Weight: 16 lb.
Effective Range: 1,000 yds
Features: IBA, under contract to the Defense Advanced Research Projects Agency (DARPA), developed and built the XM-3 to incorporate the best available technology into a sniper weapon system that addresses current operational concerns on size, weight, target detection, sound suppression, accuracy, range, day/night operations, and the use of titanium. The XM-3 has established the baseline from which DARPA will identify investment areas where new technologies are needed to provide snipers and riflemen the greatest possible advantage on tomorrow's battlefield.
MSRP: $8,295.00

Standard Grade

Caliber: .308 Win./7.62 NATO (other calibers available)
Action: Bolt, Remington Model 700 short-action
Barrel: 20 or 26 in., Hart 416R stainless steel, PSS taper, USMC crown
Rifling Twist: 1:12 in. RH
Muzzle Device: none
Action/Barrel Finish: Polymer resin-based Manowar
Stock: Bell and Carlson BCS1000 with aluminum bedding
Stock Finish: Black or OD Green
Trigger: Remington

Optic Mount: IBA one-piece mount
Magazine: Internal box, 5-round
Accuracy: sub MOA @ 600 yds
Effective Range: 600 yds
Features: The Standard Grade is a combination of the Tactical Precision Rifle integrated with features used on the Chandler Sniper Rifle to enhance overall performance. By using the HS Precision Stock and modifying the bedding block, IBA is able to offer a very accurate rifle at an affordable price.
MSRP: . . . . . $2,295.00; $2,850.00 (Super Grade model, upgraded trigger guard and barrel)

Chandler Sniper Rifle M40

Caliber: .308 Win./7.62 NATO (other calibers available)
Action: Bolt, Remington Model 700 short-action, clip slotted
Barrel: 18.5, 20 or 26 in., Hart 416R stainless steel, Heavy #7 contour, USMC muzzle crown
Rifling Twist: 1:10 in. RH (18.5 in. barrel, 175-gr. Match ammunition); 1:12 in. RH (20 or 26 in. barrel, 168-gr. Match ammunition)
Muzzle Device: none
Action/Barrel Finish: Matte black
Stock: McMillan A1
Stock Finish: USMC Camo
Trigger: Remington
Optic Mount: 20 MOA Picatinny rail
Magazine: Internal/welded, 5-round
Bottom Metal: M4 Chandler style one piece steel trigger guard and floorplate
Accuracy: sub MOA @ 1,000 yds
Effective Range: 1,000 yds
Features: Starting with a Remington 700 Action, the Chandler Rifle also incorporates a McMillan stock, Hart barrel, high quality Leupold tactical scope with mil-dot reticle, Iron Brigade Armory one-piece scope mount, Badger Ordnance M4 steel one-piece steel trigger guard, and all required accessories. The Chandler Sniper Rifle is chambered as a standard in .308 Winchester for the Sierra 168 or 175-grain Matchking bullet. These rounds are available through Black Hills and Remington. Twelve month delivery schedule.
MSRP: $5,995.00

Jarrett Custom Rifles (jarrettrifles.com)

Jarrett Rifles holds sixteen World Records in bench rest shooting. From the outset, Kenny Jarrett established the absolute highest performance and accuracy standards for his rifles and then met them by designing and manufacturing all major parts to assure their unsurpassed quality. Jarrett's passion for performance means this: total control of quality and performance by using flawless Jarrett Tri-Lock receivers, his own hand lapped Jarrett barrels, his premium quality Jarrett stocks and the finest components, like Talley rings and bases and excellent triggers.

Wind Walker

Caliber: Any long-action, standard or magnum up to .338
Action: Jarrett Tri-Lock, left or right hand
Barrel: 26 in. Jarrett hand lapped with 1/10th deviation standard, full length, crowned at 24", mandatory muzzle brake adds 2 in.
Muzzle Device: muzzle brake
Action/Barrel Finish: Choice of colors
Stock: Jarrett ADL Fiberglass for weight reduction
Stock Finish: Choice of colors
Trigger: Shilen
Optic Mount: Drilled and tapped for bases
Magazine: Internal box, 5-round
Weight: 7 lb.
Accuracy: ½ MOA
Features: Lighter gun for strenuous high mountain hunts, specially devised barrel taper that features Jarrett's 1/10th deviation standard, full length. Muzzle brake to counter recoil and unwanted muzzle rise.
MSRP: $7,380.00

Long Ranger

Caliber: .30
Action: Jarrett Tri-Lock, left or right hand, single shot
Barrel: 26 in. Jarrett 3 taper
Muzzle Device: muzzle brake
Action/Barrel Finish: Choice of colors
Stock: Jarrett ADL Fiberglass for weight reduction
Stock Finish: Choice of colors
Trigger: Jewell set at 6 oz.
Optic Mount: Drilled and tapped for bases
Magazine: n/a
Weight: 7.8 lb.
Accuracy: ½ MOA
Features: For long distance shots, Jarrett's Long Ranger produces a 4-inch three-shot group at 800 yards. Usesa single shot Tri-Lock and Jarrett's .30 caliber barrel with Jarrett's 190-gr. to 240-gr. bullets for co-efficiency advantage and energy level. Available in competition and hunting models.
MSRP: $7,640.00

KMW (kmwlrs.com)

KMW is a small specialty shop in Forest Hill, Louisiana, that focuses on bolt-action rifles for LE and tactical competition shooters. Owner and riflesmith Terry Cross personally does all machining, bedding, coating, and assembly of each rifle.

Sentinel S.W.S.

Caliber: .308 Win., .260 Rem., .243 Win., 6mmXC, 6.5 Creedmoor, 6.5x47 Lapua
Action: Bolt, Surgeon Model 591 short-action, KMW Gen II Tactical bolt handle
Barrel: Krieger match grade, custom lengths available
Muzzle Device: muzzle brake
Action/Barrel Finish: Cerakote H series ceramic hybrid coating, choice of color
Stock: KMW design built by McMillan, ambidextrous thumbhole grip, adjustable cheekpiece and length of pull, Pachmayr D550 recoil pad
Stock Finish: Marble and camo patterns molded into the Gel Coat outer layer
Trigger: Remington
Optic Mount: Integral 20 MOA Picatinny 1913 Mil-Spec base
Magazine: Detachable box, Accuracy International, 5-round
Bottom Metal: KMW
Accuracy: Guaranteed to group ½ MOA or better @ 100 yards including cold bore shot with Match quality ammunition.
Features: The SENTINEL S.W.S. (Sniper Weapon System) is KMW's benchmark for state of the art precision call out weapons.

Les Baer Rifles (lesbaer.com)

For almost three decades, Les Baer Custom (LBC) in LeClaire, Iowa, has been building 1911 pistols and AR style rifles that are a standard of excellence against which all other semiautomatic firearms are judged.

.308 Semi-Auto Sniper

Caliber: .308 Win.
Action: semiautomatic, gas impingement
Barrel: 24 in., LBC Bench Rest 416R stainless steel
Rifling Twist: RH 1:10 in.
Muzzle Device: Enforcer muzzle brake
Action/Barrel Finish: DuPont S coating
Stock: Magpul PRS buttstock, LBC custom pistol grip with extra material under trigger guard, LBC precision machined free-float handguard

Stock Finish: Black
Trigger: Geissele two-stage trigger group
Optic Mount: Picatinny style flat top rail
Magazine: detachable box
Accuracy: Guaranteed to shoot ½ MOA
Features: Upper and lower machined from 7075-T6-51 billet, no forward assist, muzzle brake reduces recoil to just slightly more than .223 Rem. level, Harris bipod included.
MSRP: ...... $3,490.00; $3,222.00 (Match Rifle model)

.308 Semi-Auto SWAT

Caliber: .308 Win.
Action: semiautomatic, gas impingement
Barrel: 18 or 24 in., LBC Bench Rest 416R stainless steel
Rifling Twist: RH 1:10 in.
Muzzle Device: none
Action/Barrel Finish: DuPont S coating
Stock: Magpul PRS buttstock, LBC custom pistol grip with extra material under trigger guard, railed handguard

Stock Finish: Black
Trigger: Geissele two stage trigger group
Optic Mount: Picatinny style flat top rail
Magazine: detachable box, 20-round Magpul
Accuracy: Guaranteed to shoot ½ MOA
Features: Upper and lower machined from 7075-T6-51 billet, no forward assist, monolithic upper.
MSRP: $3,940.00

LBC AR .223 Super Match
Caliber: .308 Win.
Action: semiautomatic, gas impingement
Barrel: 18 or 24 in., LBC Bench Rest 416R stainless steel
Rifling Twist: RH 1:10 in.
Muzzle Device: none
Action/Barrel Finish: DuPont S coating
Stock: Magpul PRS buttstock, LBC custom pistol grip with extra material under trigger guard, railed handguard

Stock Finish: Black
Trigger: Geissele two stage trigger group
Optic Mount: Picatinny style flat top rail
Magazine: detachable box, 20-round Magpul
Accuracy: Guaranteed to shoot ½ MOA
Features: Upper and lower machined from 7075-T6-51 billet, no forward assist, monolithic upper.
MSRP: $2,390.00

AR .223 Super Varmint
Caliber: .223 Rem.
Action: semiautomatic, gas impingement
Barrel: 18 in., LBC Bench Rest 416R stainless steel
Rifling Twist: RH 1:9 in.
Muzzle Device: none
Action/Barrel Finish: DuPont S coating
Stock: A2 style buttstock, LBC custom pistol grip with extra material under trigger guard, LBC precision machined adjustable free float handguard

Stock Finish: Black
Trigger: Geissele two stage trigger group
Optic Mount: Picatinny style flat top rail
Magazine: detachable box, 20-round Magpul
Accuracy: Guaranteed to shoot ½ MOA
Features: Flagship model of Les Baer's AR rifle line is built to be accurate enough to be a trusted companion on any excursion for prairie dogs, woodchucks, or coyotes at long range. 18-, 22-, and 24-inch barrel lengths and 1:12, 1:8, 1:7 inch twist rates available.
MSRP: $2,390.00

LBC AR .223 IPSC

Caliber: .223 Rem.
Action: semiautomatic, gas impingement
Barrel: 20 in., LBC Bench Rest 416R stainless steel
Rifling Twist: RH 1:9 in.
Muzzle Device: LBC muzzle brake
Action/Barrel Finish: DuPont S coating
Stock: A2 style buttstock, LBC custom pistol grip with extra material under trigger guard, LBC precision machined adjustable free-float tube handguard
Stock Finish: Black

Trigger: Geissele two stage trigger group
Optic Mount: Picatinny style flat top rail
Magazine: detachable box, 20-round Magpul
Accuracy: Guaranteed to shoot ½ MOA
Features: IPSC Action Model is designed for competition with features like a unique integral compensator which totally eliminates the unattractive, permanently mounted muzzle brakes used by most other companies; it is also effective, almost completely eliminating recoil and muzzle rise.
MSRP: $2,540.00

McMillan Tactical Products, LLC (mcmfamily.com)

McMillan companies began producing stocks in 1973 to gain a competitive edge in benchrest match competition. They are known for producing custom stocks for competition, benchrest, hunting and tactical applications. They also produce custom rifles for hunting—ultra-light weight for mountain hunting, safari-ready big bores, and long-range hunting. Their competition rifles are renowned and their tactical rifles are designed for professional operators. McMillan offers it own proprietary action, the G30 in both push-feed and control-feed as well as an action for the .50 BMG.

TAC-308

Caliber: 6.5 Creedmoor, .308 Win.
Action: Bolt, G30, short, push or control feed, 2 lug
Barrel: 20 in. (.308 Win. only) or 24 in., match grade stainless steel, medium-heavy contour, free floated, threaded muzzle
Rifling Twist: 1:8 in. (6.5 Creedmoor) or 1:11 in. (.308 Win.), polygon rifling
Muzzle Device: None
Stock: McMillan A3-5, fiberglass construction, adjustable length of pull and comb
Stock Finish: Black, olive, gray, tan or dark earth
Maximum Length of Pull: 13.5 in.

Trigger: Single-stage, adjustable from 2.5-4.5 lb., set at 3 lb.
Optics Mount: Drilled and tapped for 8x40 base screws
Bottom Metal: Detachable box magazine (5- or 10-round) or hinged floorplate (5-round)
Action/Barrel Finish: NP3 electroless nickel with Teflon or black oxidized on bolt assembly, Dura-coat black, olive, gray, tan or dark earth on barrel to match stock
Overall Length: 41 in. (20-in. barrel), 45 in. (24-in. barrel)
Weight: 9.5 lb.
Accuracy: ½ MOA with match grade ammunition
Features: Designed for urban tactical scenarios, two-position safety, tight benchrest tolerances, action is pillar bedded, accepts night-visions optics.
MSRP: $6,495.50

TAC-338

Caliber: .338 Lapua Mag., .338 Norma Mag.
Action: Bolt, G30, long, push or control feed, 2 lug
Barrel: 26.5 in., match grade, medium-heavy contour, free floated, threaded muzzle
Rifling Twist: RH 1:10 in., polygon rifling, 6 grooves
Muzzle Device: Muzzle brake
Stock: McMillan A3-5, fiberglass construction, adjustable length of pull and comb
Stock Finish: Black, olive, gray, tan or dark earth
Maximum Length of Pull: 14 in.
Trigger: Single-stage, adjustable from 2.5-4.5 lb., set at 3 lb.
Optics Mount: Drilled and tapped for 8x40 base screws
Bottom Metal: Detachable box magazine (5-round) or hinged floorplate (5-round)
Action/Barrel Finish: NP3 electroless nickel with Teflon or black oxidized on bolt assembly, Dura-coat black, olive, gray, tan or dark earth on barrel to match stock
Overall Length: 48 in.
Weight: 11 lb.
Accuracy: ½ MOA with match grade ammunition
Features: Designed for a sniper in combat or internal security operations, two-position safety, tight benchrest tolerances, action is pillar bedded, accepts night-vision optics.
MSRP: $6,895.00

TAC-50 A1

Caliber: .50 BMG
Action: Bolt, McMillan 50, long, push feed
Barrel: 29 in. heavy contour, fluted, match grade, free floated, threaded muzzle
Rifling Twist: RH 1:15 in., 6 grooves
Muzzle Device: McMillan muzzle brake
Stock: McMillan TAC-50 A1 take-down, fiberglass construction, adjustable saddle, pistol grip
Stock Finish: Black, olive, gray, tan or dark earth
Maximum Length of Pull: 14 in.
Trigger: Single-stage, adjustable from 3.5-4.5 lb., set at 3.5 lb.
Optics Mount: Drilled and tapped for 8x40 base screws
Bottom Metal: Detachable box magazine, 5-round
Action/Barrel Finish: NP3 electroless nickel with Teflon or black oxidized on bolt assembly, Dura-coat black, olive, gray, tan or dark earth on barrel to match stock
Overall Length: 57 in.
Weight: 26 lb.
Accuracy: ½ MOA with match grade ammunition
Maximum Range: 2000 m
Features: Designed for long-range sniper operations, two-position safety, tight benchrest tolerances, action is pillar bedded, steel bipod, 5 in. longer than TAC-50 stock, monopod.
MSRP: $9,990.00

TAC-50 A1-R2

Caliber: .50 BMG
Action: Bolt, McMillan 50, long, push feed
Barrel: 29 in. heavy contour, fluted, match grade, free floated, threaded muzzle
Rifling Twist: RH 1:15 in., 6 grooves
Muzzle Device: McMillan muzzle brake
Stock: McMillan TAC-50 A1-R2 take-down, fiberglass construction, adjustable saddle, pistol grip, hydraulic recoil mitigation system reduces peak recoil by 90 percent
Stock Finish: Black, olive, gray, tan or dark earth
Maximum Length of Pull: 14 in.
Trigger: Single-stage, adjustable from 3.5-4.5 lb., set at 3.5 lb.

Optics Mount: Drilled and tapped for 8x40 base screws
Bottom Metal: Detachable box magazine, 5-round
Action/Barrel Finish: NP3 electroless nickel with Teflon or black oxidized on bolt assembly, Dura-coat black, olive, gray, tan or dark earth on barrel to match stock
Overall Length: 57 in.
Weight: 26 lb.
Accuracy: ½ MOA with match grade ammunition
Maximum Range: 2000 m
Features: Designed for long-range sniper operations, two-position safety, tight benchrest tolerances, action is pillar bedded, steel bipod, 5 in. longer than TAC-50 stock, monopod.
MSRP: $11,990.00

ALIAS CS5 "Stubby"

Caliber: .308 Win.
Action: Bolt, McMillan ALIAS, short, push feed, 75° bolt lift
Barrel: 12.5 in., match grade stainless steel, free floated, threaded muzzle
Rifling Twist: 1:8 in.
Muzzle Device: Muzzle brake, Elite Iron Brigade suppressor
Stock: Quick-detachable; adjustable length of pull, height, cant and cheekpiece; AR tube-style or quad-style forend; pistol grip
Stock Finish: Matte black
Trigger: Anschutz two-stage; adjustable pull weight, length and shoe angle

Optics Mount: 20 MOA rail
Magazine: SR-25 type, detachable box, 10- or 20-round
Action/Barrel Finish: Hard anodized matte black
Overall Length: 38 in.
Folded Overall Length: 23.5 in.
Weight: 10.6 lb., 12.2 lb. with suppressor
Accuracy: .5 MOA with McMillan's 200-gr. Subsonic ammunition or with supersonic/full power match grade ammunition
Features: Subsonic/supersonic sniper system designed to be concealable, uses McMillan's ALIAS interchangeable component customization system, accessory rails, comes with carry case.
MSRP: $5,000.00

ALIAS Star

Caliber: 6.5 Creedmoor, 6.5x47 Lapua, .308 Win.
Action: Bolt, McMillan ALIAS, short, push feed, 75° bolt lift
Barrel: 18.5-24 in., match grade stainless steel, free floated, threaded muzzle
Rifling Twist: 1:8 in. (6.5 Creedmoor, 6.5x47 Lapua), 1:11 in. (.308 Win.)
Muzzle Device: None
Stock: Quick-detachable; adjustable length of pull, height, cant and cheekpiece; AR tube-style or quad-style forend; pistol grip
Stock Finish: Matte black

Trigger: Anschutz two-stage; adjustable pull weight, length and shoe angle
Optics Mount: 20 MOA rail
Magazine: Detachable box, 10-round
Action/Barrel Finish: Hard anodized matte black
Overall Length: 44 in. (18.5-in. barrel)
Folded Overall Length: 29.5 in. (18.5-in. barrel)
Weight: 11.6 lb. (18.5-in. barrel)
Accuracy: Sub-MOA
Features: Sniper system designed for concealment, uses McMillan's ALIAS interchangeable multi-caliber component system, accessory rails, comes with carry case.
MSRP: $5,000.00

Dynasty

Caliber: 7mm Rem. Ultra Mag., .300 Rem. Ultra Mag., 30-378 WBY Mag.
Action: Bolt, G30, long-action, push or control feed, 2 lug
Barrel: 28 in., match grade stainless steel, #4 contour, fluted
Rifling Twist: 1:10 in. (7mm Rem. Ultra Mag.) or 1:12 in. (.300 Rem. Ultra Mag., .30-378 WBY Mag.)
Muzzle Device: Vias muzzle brake
Action/Barrel Finish: Matte black NP3 electroless nickel with Teflon or black oxidized on bolt assembly,

Stock: McMillan Dynasty, free floated barrel, Pachmayr Decelerator recoil pad
Stock Finish: Black texture
Maximum Length of Pull: 13.5 in.
Trigger: Jewell
Optics Mount: Drilled and tapped for bases
Magazine: Internal box, 5-round
Bottom Metal: Aluminum hinged floorplate
Features: Ultra-high velocity, long-range rifle design for hunting.
MSRP: $6,450.50

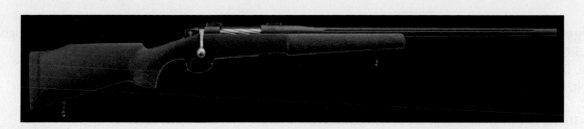

Tactical Hunter

Caliber: .243 Win., 7mm Rem. Mag., .308 Win., .300 Win. Mag.

Action: Bolt, G30, short or long-action, push or control feed, 2 lug

Barrel: 22 in. (.243 Win.) or 24 in. (7mm Rem. Mag., .308 Win., .300 Win. Mag.), match grade stainless steel, target crown, fluted, #5 taper

Rifling Twist: 1:10 in. (.243 Win., 7mm Rem. Mag.) or 1:12 in. (.308 Win., .300 Win. Mag.)

Muzzle Device: none

Action/Barrel Finish: Matte black NP3 electroless nickel with Teflon or black oxidized on bolt assembly

Stock: McMillan Tactical Hunter with EDGE ultra light graphite technology, pillar glass bedding, free floated barrel, Pachmayr Decelerator recoil pad

Stock Finish: Black texture

Maximum Length of Pull: 13.5 in.

Trigger: Jewell

Optics Mount: Drilled and tapped for bases

Magazine: Internal box, 5-round

Bottom Metal: Aluminum hinged floorplate

Weight: 7 lb. to 7 lb. 4 oz. (depending on caliber)

Features: Blends classic rifle contours with modern tactical rifle ergonomics.

MSRP: $6,415.50

ELO Mountain Extreme Alpine

Caliber: 6.5x284 Norma

Action: Bolt, G30, long-action, push or control feed, 2 lug

Barrel: 26 in., match grade stainless steel, #4 contour, fluted

Rifling Twist: 1:8 in.

Muzzle Device: Vias muzzle brake

Action/Barrel Finish: Matte black NP3 electroless nickel with Teflon or black oxidized on bolt assembly,

Stock: McMillanTactical Hunter with EDGE ultra light graphite technology, pillar glass bedding, free floated barrel, Pachmayr Decelerator recoil pad

Stock Finish: Khaki base with gray/brown specks

Maximum Length of Pull: 13.5 in.

Trigger: Jewell

Optics Mount: Drilled and tapped for bases

Magazine: Internal box, 5-round

Bottom Metal: Hinged floorplate

Weight: 7 lb. 4 oz.

Features: The EOL (Extreme Outer Limit) Mountain Extreme rifle line is optimized for ultra-long-range hunting. They are built for the EOL Mag series of cartridges which utilizes a standard Ultra Mag parent case, but with very long, high-VLD bullets that are seated out longer than usual to free up additional powder capacity inside the case. The result is higher velocity and less bullet drop at extreme ranges. The rifles feature long-actions, ejection ports, and magazine boxes that can accommodate .338 Lapua and other similar length cartridges. Throats are specifically cut for the EOL Mag cartridge series. Consequently, EOL Mountain Extreme rifles will deliver extreme performance with EOL Mag ammunition, but can also fire factory Remington Ultra Mag ammunition when desired. The ELO Mountain Extreme Denali model uses an A3-5 stock, and the ELO Mountain Extreme Yukon model is chambered in long magnum calibers.

MSRP: $6,775.00

Alias Target

Caliber: 6.5 Creedmoor, 6.5x47 Lapua, .308 Win., 6XC, .308 Palma, .206 Rem.

Action: Bolt, McMillan ALIAS, short, push feed, 75° bolt lift

Barrel: 24-30 in., match grade stainless steel, free floated, threaded muzzle

Rifling Twist: 1:7.5 in. (6XC), 1:8 in. (6.5 Creedmoor, 6.5x47 Lapua, .206 Rem.), 1:10/1:11/1:12in. (.308 Win.), 1:13in. (.308 Palma)

Muzzle Device: None

Action/Barrel Finish: Hard anodized matte black

Stock: Quick-detachable; adjustable length of pull, height, cant and cheekpiece; AR tube-style or quad-style forend; pistol grip

Stock Finish: Matte black

Trigger: Anschutz two-stage; adjustable pull weight, length and shoe angle

Optics Mount: 20 MOA rail

Magazine: Detachable box, 10-round

Overall Length: 48 in. (24-in. barrel)

Weight: 12 lb. (24-in. barrel)

Accuracy: Sub-MOA

Features: Developed with input from world champion high-power shooters, the design evolved into a cutting edge rifle to meet the demands of literally the best competitive shooters in the world. Buttstock, cheekpiece, forend, sight position, trigger—almost every component of this rifle is fully adjustable so that a shooter can hold exactly the right position across the course of fire. The components are also indexed so the adjustments can be quickly repeated during a match.

Noreen Firearms (onlylongrange.com)

Peter Noreen out of Belgrade, Montana, has been a gunsmithing legend for the last quarter century. He made his mark custom-building scaled-up Pre-64 Model 70 Winchester actions for use in heavy calibers for hunting dangerous game. He works with his son Phil to design and build Noreen Ultra Long Range rifles and AR platforms chambered in .30-06, .270 Winchester, and .25-06 Winchester.

ULR

Caliber: .50 BMG, .416 Barrett, .408 Chey Tac, .338 Lapua Mag.

Action: Bolt, single shot

Barrel: 32 in. (416 Barrett, .408 Chey Tac, .338 Lapua Mag.), 34 in. (.50 BMG); free floated

Rifling Twist: 1:15 in. (.50 BMG), 1:12 in. (.416 Barrett), 1:13 in. (.408 Chey Tac), 1:10 in. (.338 Lapua Mag.)

Muzzle Device: Noreen muzzle brake

Action/Barrel Finish: Black or camo

Stock: Noreen collapsible buttstock with recoil pad, A2 style pistol grip

Stock Finish: Black or camo

Trigger: Timney adjustable

Optics Mount: Integral rail

Magazine: n/a

Overall Length: 34 in.

Weight: 32 lb.

Features: The ULR (Ultra Long Range) rifle is a single shot built to handle the most powerful long-range cartridges available.

MSRP: . . . $2,599.00 (.50 BMG); $2,899.00 (.416 Barrett, .408 Chey Tac, .338 Lapua Mag.)

Bad News

Caliber: .300 Win. Mag., .338 Lapua Mag., .338 Norma Mag.
Action: Semiauto, piston driven system
Barrel: 26 in.
Rifling Twist: 1:10 in.
Muzzle Device: Noreen muzzle brake
Action/Barrel Finish: Black

Stock: Magpul PSR adjustable buttstock, A2 style pistol grip
Stock Finish: Black
Trigger: Timney Match trigger
Optics Mount: Integral rail
Magazine: detachable box, 5- or 10-round
Weight: 13 lb.
Features: AR style rifle with piston system that uses magnum length cartridges.
MSRP: $5,995.00

BN36

Caliber: .25-06 Win., .270 Win., .30-06
Action: Semiauto, direct gas impingement system
Barrel: 22 in.
Rifling Twist: 1:11 in.
Muzzle Device: Noreen muzzle brake
Action/Barrel Finish: Black
Stock: A2 style buttstock and pistol grip

Stock Finish: Black
Trigger: Mil-spec
Optics Mount: Integral rail
Magazine: detachable box, 5-, 10- or 20-round
Weight: 8 lb.
Features: AR style rifle with direct gas impingement system that uses standard length cartridges.
MSRP: $1,999.00

PROOF Research (proofresearch.com)

Located in Northwest Montana, PROOF Research is a science-based company that produces carbon fiber barrels and complete rifle systems that are light, durable, and accurate.

Tactical II

Caliber: from .243 Win. to .338 Lapua Mag. available
Action: Bolt, PROOFT6 action
Barrel: 16-28 in. (depending on caliber), PROOF carbon fiber wrapped
Muzzle Device: 3-port Vais muzzle brake
Action/Barrel Finish: Cerakote, numerous color options
Stock: PROOF Tactical II, free-floated barrel, adjustable length of pull and cheekpiece
Stock Finish: Numerous color options
Trigger: Jewell or Timney
Optics Mount: Seekins or Badger
Magazine: Detachable box, 10-round
Bottom Metal: Badger
Weight: 8.8 lb. (with optics and 28-in. barrel)
Features: The TAC II is a light weight, long-range rifle designed from the ground up to be a versatile and lightweight tactical system for the serious shooter.
MSRP: . . . . starting at $6,850.00

The Terminus

Caliber: from .204 Ruger to .338 Lapua Mag. available
Action: Bolt, PROOF H6 action
Barrel: 16-28 in. (depending on caliber), PROOF carbon fiber wrapped
Muzzle Device: 3-port Vais muzzle brake
Action/Barrel Finish: Cerakote, numerous color options
Stock: PROOF Monte Carlo, free-floated barrel
Stock Finish: Numerous color options
Trigger: Jewell or Timney
Optics Mount: Seekins or Talley
Magazine: Internal box, 5-round
Bottom Metal: ADL/BDL style
Weight: Depending on caliber
Features: The Terminus uses PROOF's Monte Carlo stock with raised cheekpiece.
MSRP: . . . . starting at $5,690.00

Summit

Caliber: from .204 Ruger to .338 Lapua Mag. available
Action: Bolt,PROOF H6 action
Barrel: 16-28 in. (depending on caliber), PROOF carbon fiber wrapped
Muzzle Device: 3-port Vais muzzle brake
Action/Barrel Finish: Cerakote, numerous color options
Stock: PROOF Summit, free-floated barrel
Stock Finish: Numerous color options

Trigger: Jewell or Timney
Optics Mount: Seekins or Talley
Magazine: Internal box, 5-round
Bottom Metal: ADL/BDL style
Weight: Depending on caliber
Features: The Summit uses PROOF's Summit stock with straight cheekpiece.The Summit YL model uses Summit CFB stock.
MSRP: . . . . starting at $5,540.00

RW Snyder Gunsmithing (rwsgunsmithing.com)

Established in 2002, RW Snyder Gunsmithing in Manning, Iowa, offers a full line of gunsmithing services and custom built rifles for long-range, hunting and tactical scenarios.

RWS Custom Tube

Caliber: from .223 Rem. to .300 WSM available
Action: Bolt,RWS receiver
Barrel: 16-30 in. (depending on caliber), Brux stainless steel, fluted (helical, straight or interrupt)
Muzzle Device: none
Action/Barrel Finish: Cerakote black, sniper gray, OD green or FDE
Stock: Fully adjustable buttstock, free-floated barrel

Stock Finish: Cerakote black, sniper gray, OD green or FDE
Trigger: Jewell trigger with bottom safety
Optics Mount: Integral 20 MOA Mil-Spec 1913 rail
Magazine: Detachable box, 5-round
Features: Tube rifles are some of the most high-tech and accurate rifles in competition. RWS offers numerous caliber and barrel options. Base rifle details shown.
MSRP: . . . . starting at $3,300.00

RWS Premier Tactical

Caliber: from .22-250 Rem., .243 Win., 6.5 Creedmoor, 6mm Creedmoor, .260 Rem., .308 Win.
Action: Bolt,blueprinted Remington Model 700 action
Barrel: 16.5-26 in. (depending on caliber), Brux or Kreiger stainless steel, Remington varmint or mtu/m24 contour, 11° target crown
Muzzle Device: none

Action/Barrel Finish: Cerakote black, sniper gray, OD green, brunt bronze or FDE
Stock: Numerous stock options, free-floated barrel
Stock Finish: Numerous color options
Trigger: Tuned Remington
Optics Mount: 20 MOA Mil-Spec 1913 rail
Magazine: Internal box, 5-round
Features: Numerous caliber, barrel, action, stock options. Base rifle details shown.
MSRP: . . . . from $1,400.00

RWS Base Custom

Caliber: from .22-250 Rem., .243 Win., 6.5 Creedmoor, 6mm Creedmoor, .260 Rem., .308 Win.
Action: Bolt, blueprinted Remington Model 700 action
Barrel: 16.5-26 in. (depending on caliber), Brux or Kreiger stainless steel, Remington varmint or mtu/m24 contour, 11° target crown
Muzzle Device: none
Action/Barrel Finish: Cerakote black, sniper gray, OD green, brunt bronze or FDE

Stock: Numerous stock options, free-floated barrel
Stock Finish: Numerous color options
Trigger: Tuned Remington
Optics Mount: 20 MOA Mil-Spec 1913 rail
Magazine: Internal box, 5-round
Features: Numerous caliber, barrel, action, stock options. Base rifle details shown.
MSRP: . . . . from $1,400.00

RWS Long Range Tactical

Caliber: .300 Norma Mag., .338 Norma Mag., .338 Lapua Mag.

Action: Bolt, RWS receiver, one-piece spiral fluted bolt

Barrel: 30 in. (depending on caliber), Brux stainless steel, fluted (helical or straight)

Muzzle Device: RWS muzzle brake

Action/Barrel Finish: Cerakote black, sniper gray, OD green or FDE

Stock: Accuracy International AX folding buttstock, free floated barrel

Stock Finish: Cerakote black, sniper gray, OD green or FDE

Trigger: Rifle Basix

Optics Mount: 30 MOA rail

Magazine: Detachable box, 5-round

Features: Designed for long-range shooting. RWS offers numerous options.

MSRP: . . . . starting at $4,000.00

RWS Extreme Long Range Tactical

Caliber: .338 Snipetac, .375 CheyTac, .408 CheyTac, .50 BMG

Action: Bolt, Stiller TAC408, fluted bolt

Barrel: 29 in., Benchmark stainless steel

Muzzle Device: RWS muzzle brake

Action/Barrel Finish: Cerakote black, sniper gray, OD green or FDE

Stock: PDC folding buttstock, free-floated barrel

Stock Finish: Cerakote black, sniper gray, OD green or FDE

Trigger: Jewell trigger with bottom safety

Optics Mount: Picatinny style rail

Magazine: Detachable box, 7-round

Features: Designed for extreme long-range shooting. RWS offers numerous options.

MSRP: . . . . starting at $4,500.00

Sisk Rifles (siskguns.com)

Charlie Sisk of Sisk Rifles LLC builds custom hunting and tactical rifles out of Dayton, Texas.

STAR

Caliber: Short-action calibers
Action: Bolt, Remington 700 short-action
Barrel: Numerous options
Muzzle Device: Numerous options
Action/Barrel Finish: Cerakote, numerous color options
Stock: STAR folding and fully adjustable buttstock, aluminum construction, free-floated barrel
Stock Finish: Cerakote, numerous color options

Trigger: Numerous options
Optics Mount: Picatinny style rail
Magazine: Detachable box
Features: The Sisk Tactical Adaptive Rifle (STAR) offers shooters a take-down rifle with near-infinite adaptability featuring adjustment points at the butt, comb, and wrist for customizable, ergonomic performance in any shooting situation or position.
MSRP: . . . . starting at $6,495.00

Surgeon Rifles (surgeonrifles.com)

Pritchett Machining started out just southwest of Prague, Oklahoma, in January 2001. Preston Pritchett, a longtime machinist and gun guru, had visions of a small machine shop where he could work close to home and set his own hours. Little did he know it would turn into a large high-tech manufacturing facility, housing multiple CNC machining centers and Surgeon Rifles, Inc. Surgeon Rifles manufactures a variety of rifles, actions, and other accessories for custom hunting and tactical rifle enthusiasts.

Short-action Scalpel

Caliber: .223 Rem., 6XC, .206 Rem., 6.5 Creedmoor, .308 Win.
Action: Bolt, Surgeon 591/R action with SR bolt knob
Barrel: Numerous options
Muzzle Device: Numerous options
Action/Barrel Finish: Cerakote
Stock: Accuracy International 1.5

Stock Finish: Numerous options
Trigger: Remington 700 trigger
Optics Mount: 20 MOA rail
Magazine: Detachable box, 5-round
Features: Surgeon actions and bolts are renowned as the most accurate and strongest actions available. Numerous upgrades are available for the Scalpel.
MSRP: . . . . . . $4,355.00; $4.489.00 (long-action Scalpel; 6.5x284, .284 Win., .300 Win. Mag.)

Remedy

Caliber: .223 Rem., 6XC, .206 Rem., 6.5 Creedmoor, .308 Win.
Action: Bolt, Surgeon 591/R action with SR bolt knob
Barrel: Numerous options
Muzzle Device: Numerous options
Action/Barrel Finish: Cerakote
Stock: Accuracy International 1.5

Stock Finish: Numerous options
Trigger: Remington 700 trigger
Optics Mount: 20 MOA rail
Magazine: Detachable box, 5-round
Features: Surgeon actions and bolts are renowned as the most accurate and strongest actions available. Numerous upgrades are available.
MSRP: $5,600.00

Tactical Operations (tacticaloperations.com)

Tactical Operations Inc. (Tac-Ops) has never advertised and until recently has never been exposed to the general public. Most clients of Tac-Ops are law enforcement agencies at local, state, and federal levels, as well as the military and individual operators. Their sales have always been based on reputation and word of mouth.

Alpha

Caliber: .308 Win., .300 Win. Mag.
Action: Bolt, accurized Remington Model 700, blueprinted to Tac Ops specifications, custom tactical bolt knob
Barrel: 20 to 24 in. (.308 Win.) or 22 to 26 in.(.300 Win. Mag.), Tac Ops proprietary chrome-moly or stainless steel Krieger, muzzle with a class 3A thread for optional sound suppressor
Muzzle Device: none

Action/Barrel Finish: Walter Birdsong's proprietary Green-T and Black-T finish
Stock: McMillan Baker Special, sniper fill with custom-fitted Anschutz rail
Stock Finish: Black and green epoxy finish
Trigger: Standard Remington, set to 2.25-2.5 lb.
Optics Mount: Picatinny style rail
Magazine: Internal box, 5-round
Features: Alpha rifles come standard with an aluminum three-way adjustable butt plate to allow just about any size person to have a truly custom fit rifle. Barrel and action cryogenically treated.

Delta

Caliber:.308 Win., .300 Win. Mag.
Action: Bolt, accurized Remington Model 700, blueprinted to Tac Ops specifications, custom tactical bolt knob
Barrel: 20 to 24 in., Tac Ops proprietary chrome-moly or stainless steel Krieger, muzzle with a class 3A thread for optional sound suppressor
Muzzle Device: none
Action/Barrel Finish: Walter Birdsong's proprietary Green-T and Black-T finish

Stock: McMillan A3, sniper fill with custom-fitted Anschutz rail
Stock Finish: Black and green epoxy finish.
Trigger: Standard Remington, set to 2.25-2.5 lb.
Optics Mount: Picatinny style rail
Magazine: Internal box, 5-round
Features: The Delta series of rifles has a three-way adjustable aluminum butt plate, with a fully adjustable comb, making it ideal for night vision optics. Barrel and action cryogenically treated.

Echo

Caliber:.308 Win.
Action: Bolt, accurized Remington Model 700, blueprinted to Tac Ops specifications, custom tactical bolt knob
Barrel: 18 to 20 in., Tac Ops proprietary chrome-moly or stainless steel Krieger, muzzle with a class 3A thread for optional sound suppressor
Muzzle Device: none

Action/Barrel Finish: Walter Birdsong's proprietary Green-T and Black-T finish
Stock: McMillan A-2, sniper fill with custom-fitted Anschutz rail, 3-way LOP or spacer system
Stock Finish: Black and green epoxy finish.
Trigger: Standard Remington, set to 2.25-2.5 lb.
Optics Mount: Picatinny style rail
Magazine: Internal box, 5-round
Features: The Echo Series of rifles was designed with one purpose in mind, to be the premier tactical engagement rifle.

Lima

Caliber: .308 Win.
Action: Bolt, accurized Remington Model 700, blueprinted to Tac Ops specifications, custom tactical bolt knob
Barrel: 18 to 20 in., Tac Ops proprietary chrome-moly or stainless steel Krieger, muzzle with a class 3A thread for optional sound suppressor
Muzzle Device: none

Action/Barrel Finish: Walter Birdsong's proprietary Green-T and Black-T finish
Stock: McMillan A4, sniper fill with custom-fitted Anschutz rail
Stock Finish: Black and green epoxy finish
Trigger: Standard Remington, set to 2.25-2.5 lb.
Optics Mount: Picatinny style rail
Magazine: Internal box, 5-round
Features: The Lima series is thought to be the ultimate in tactical precision rifles.

Sierra

Caliber: .308 Win.
Action: Bolt, accurized Remington Model 700, blueprinted to Tac Ops specifications, custom tactical bolt knob
Barrel: 20 to 24 in., Tac Ops proprietary chrome-moly or stainless steel Krieger, muzzle with a class 3A thread for optional sound suppressor
Muzzle Device: none
Action/Barrel Finish: Walter Birdsong's proprietary Green-T and Black-T finish

Stock: McMillan A1, sniper fill with custom-fitted Anschutz rail
Stock Finish: Black and green epoxy finish
Trigger: Standard Remington, set to 2.25-2.5 lb.
Optics Mount: Picatinny style rail
Magazine: Internal box, 5-round
Features: Tac Ops takes the M40A1 one step further with the introduction of the Sierra series of rifles. Utilizing state-of-the-art manufacturing techniques, the Sierra series takes the basic M40A1 design to accuracy levels that could only be dreamed of with the standard issue M40A1.

Tango

Caliber: .308 Win.
Action: Bolt, accurized Remington Model 700, blueprinted to Tac Ops specifications, custom tactical bolt knob
Barrel: 18 to 20 in., Tac Ops proprietary chrome-moly or stainless steel Krieger, muzzle with a class 3A thread for optional sound suppressor
Muzzle Device: none
Action/Barrel Finish: Walter Birdsong's proprietary Green-T and Black-T finish

Stock: McMillan Sako varminter, sniper fill with custom-fitted Anschutz rail
Stock Finish: Black and green epoxy finish
Trigger: Standard Remington, set to 2.25-2.5 lb.
Optics Mount: Picatinny style rail
Magazine: Internal box, 5-round
Features: The Tango series is the flagship of Tac Ops rifles and was designed from the ground up to be the ultimate tactical precision rifle. All of the metal is finished in an extremely durable, self-lubricating finish that can withstand the harshest operational environments.

X-Ray

Caliber: .308 Win., .300 Win. Mag.
Action: Bolt, accurized Remington Model 700, blueprinted to Tac Ops specifications, custom tactical bolt knob
Barrel: 20 to 24 in. (.308 Win.) or 22 to 26 in.(.300 Win. Mag.), Tac Ops proprietary chrome-moly or stainless steel Krieger, muzzle with a class 3A thread for optional sound suppressor
Muzzle Device: none

Action/Barrel Finish: Walter Birdsong's proprietary Green-T and Black-T finish
Stock: McMillan A-5, sniper fill with custom-fitted Anschutz rail
Stock Finish: Black and green epoxy finish
Trigger: Standard Remington, set to 2.25-2.5 lb.
Optics Mount: Picatinny style rail
Magazine: Internal box, 5-round
Features: Similar to Alpha rifles but with a McMillan A-5 stock.

36. Factory Precision Rifles

Accuracy International (accuracyinternational.com)

Accuracy International (AI) Ltd. was established in 1978 by a two-time Olympic Gold Medalist, and four other international and national target shooters. Their goal was to incorporate performance features from Olympic and international target rifles into a rifle platform built for military use. In some 60 countries worldwide these rifles are used by military and police units.

AE MkIII

Caliber: .308 Win.
Action: Bolt, short, 60° bolt lift
Barrel: 20 in. or 24 in., match grade
Rifling Twist: 1:12
Muzzle Device: none
Stock: Aluminum chassis with polymer stocksides, adjustable cheekpiece, fixed butt pad
Stock Finish: Black, green, or dark earth

Trigger: Two-stage, adjustable 3.3 - 4.4 lb.
Optic Mount: none, Picatinny rail
Magazine: Detachable steel box, 5-round, flush fit
Action/Barrel Finish: Black
Overall Length: 40 in. (20-in. barrel), 44.5 in. (24-in. barrel)
Weight: 12.1 lb. (20-in. barrel), 12.8 lb. (24-in. barrel)
Features: LOP adjustable via spacers, three-position safety, bipod adaptor, four sling fixing points.
MSRP: $3,810.00

AW series

Caliber: .243 Win., .308 Win., .300 Win. Mag., .338 Lapua Mag.
Action: Bolt, short or long, 60° bolt lift, flat bottom
Barrel: Match grade; 16 in. and 20 in. (.308 Win.), 24 in. (.243 Win., .308 Win.), 26 in. (.300 Win. Mag.), 27 in. (.338 Lapua Mag.)
Rifling Twist: 1:9 in. (16-in barrel, .308 Win. suppressed), 1:10 in. (.243 Win.), 1:12 in. (.308 Win.), 1:11 in (.300 Win. Mag., .338 Lapua Mag.)
Muzzle Device: Muzzle brake (.308 Win., .300 Win. Mag., .338 Lapua Mag. models)
Stock: Aluminum chassis with polymer stocksides, thumbhole, adjustable cheekpiece, fixed butt pad
Stock Finish: Black, green, or dark earth
Trigger: Two-stage, adjustable 3.3–4.4 lb.

Optics Mount: Optional Picatinny rail
Magazine: Detachable steel box, 10-round (.243 Win., .308 Win.) or 5-round (.300 Win. Mag., .338 Lapua Mag.)
Action/Barrel Finish: Black
Overall Length: 40 in. (20-in. barrel), 44 in. (24-in. barrel), 46 in. (26-in. barrel, 27-in. barrel in .300 Win. Mag.), 48.5 in. (16-in. in .308 Win. Suppressed, .338 Lapua Mag.)
Weight: 13.5 lb. (20-in. barrel), 14.5 lb. (24-in. barrel in .243 Win., .308 Win.), 14.3 lb. (.300 Win. Mag.), 15.1 lb. (.338 Lapua Mag.), 16 lb. (.308 Win. Suppressed)
Features: Flat bottom action permanently bonded and bolted to full-length aluminum chassis, LOP adjustable via spacers, three-position safety, trigger easily removes from chassis, bipod adaptor, four sling fixing points.
MSRP: . . . . $6,268.00-$7,940.00 (depending on caliber)

AX series

Caliber: .338 Lapua Mag.
Action: Bolt, long, 60° bolt lift, flat bottom
Barrel: Stainless steel match grade; 27 in.
Rifling Twist: 1:11 in.
Muzzle Device: Muzzle brake
Stock: Aluminum chassis with polymer stocksides, folding buttstock, adjustable cheekpiece, fixed butt pad, adjustable rear support leg, pistol grip
Stock Finish: Black, green or dark earth
Trigger: Two-stage, adjustable 3.3–4.4 lb.

Optics Mount: Full-length Picatinny rail in flat, 20 MOA or 30 MOA cants
Magazine: Detachable steel box, 10-round
Action/Barrel Finish: Black
Overall Length: 49.2 in.
Weight: 17.6 lb.
Features: Flat bottom action permanently bonded and bolted to full-length aluminum chassis, LOP adjustable via spacers, three-position safety, trigger assemble is easily removed, accessory rails, bipod adaptor, four sling fixing points, optional barrel lengths, and adjustable butt pad.
MSRP: . . $6,290.00; $5,850.00–$7,080.00 (other calibers)

AX50

Caliber: .50 BMG
Action: Bolt, long, 60° bolt lift, flat bottom
Barrel: Match grade, fluted, free floated, 27 in.
Rifling Twist: 1:9 in.
Muzzle Device: Double chamber muzzle brake
Stock: Folding aluminum chassis, adjustable cheekpiece, fixed butt pad, polymer pistol grip
Stock Finish: Black, green or dark earth
Trigger: Two-stage, adjustable 3.3 - 4.4 lb.

Optics Mount: Picatinny rail
Magazine: Detachable steel box, 5-round
Action/Barrel Finish: Black
Overall Length: 53.9 in.
Folded Length: 43.9 in.
Weight: 27.5 lb.
Features: Flat bottom action bolted to full-length aluminum chassis, LOP adjustable via 10mm spacers, two-position safety, forend rail system, bipod adaptor, three sling fixing points.
MSRP: $10,609.99

ArmaLite Inc. (ArmaLite.com)

Back in the 1950s, ArmaLite was organized to produce small weapon designs. They are perhaps best known for designing the AR-10 rifle, which was adopted by military organizations in a few countries. Many features of the AR-10 were used by ArmaLite to design the AR-15, which was adopted by the US military in 1963 and is still in use, albeit with numerous design changes. Currently ArmaLite produces AR-15 and AR-10 rifles as well as .50 BMG rifles and Semiautomatic pistols.

AR-30A1

Model: 30A1B300
Caliber: .300 Win. Mag.
Action: Bolt, long
Barrel: 24 in., Chrome-moly
Rifling Twist: 1:10
Muzzle Device: Muzzle Brake
Action/Barrel Finish: Military grade anodizing and phosphating
Stock: Black synthetic, fixed
Length of Pull: 13.5 in.
Trigger: Shilen standard single-stage trigger
Optic Mount: none, 20-minute angles top rail
Magazine: Detachable steel box, 5-round
Overall Length: 46 in.
Weight: 12 lb.
Accuracy: ¼ to ¾ MOA at 300 Yards
Features: bolt-mounted safety mechanism locks firing pin to rear; integral cleaning rod guides in cheekpiece; multiple sling mount locations; v-block bedding; threaded muzzle (5/8x24) compatible with sound suppressors; magazine well; Hard Case; Sling; Owner's Manual
MSRP: $3,264.00

AR-30A1

Model: 30A1B338
Caliber: .338 Lapua
Action: Bolt, long
Barrel: 26 in., Chrome-moly
Rifling Twist: 1:10
Muzzle Device: Muzzle Brake
Action/Barrel Finish: Military grade anodizing and phosphating
Stock: Black synthetic, fixed
Length of Pull: 13.5 in.
Trigger: Shilen standard single-stage trigger
Optic Mount: none, 20-minute angles top rail
Magazine: Detachable steel box, 5-round
Overall Length: 48 in.
Weight: 13.4 lb.
Accuracy: ¼ to ¾ MOA at 300 Yards
Features: bolt-mounted safety mechanism locks firing pin to rear; integral cleaning rod guides in cheekpiece; multiple sling mount locations; v-block bedding; threaded muzzle (¾x24) compatible with sound suppressors; magazine well; Hard Case; Sling; Owner's Manual.
MSRP: $3,404.00

AR-30A1

Model: 30A1BT300
Caliber: .300 Win. Mag.
Action: Bolt, long
Barrel: 24 in., Chrome-moly
Rifling Twist: 1:10
Muzzle Device: Muzzle Brake
Action/Barrel Finish: Military grade anodizing and phosphating
Stock: Black synthetic, adjustable cheek (height) and buttstock (length)
Length of Pull: 13.6 - 15.6 in.

Trigger: Shilen standard single-stage trigger
Optic Mount: none, 20-minute rail
Magazine: Detachable steel box, 5-round
Overall Length: 46.1 - 48.1 in.
Weight: 14.5 lb.
Accuracy: ¼ to ¾ MOA at 300 Yards
Features: bolt-mounted safety mechanism locks firing pin to rear; integral cleaning rod guides in cheekpiece; multiple sling mount locations; v-block bedding; threaded muzzle (5/8x24) compatible with sound suppressors; magazine well; Hard Case; Sling; Owner's Manual.
MSRP: $3,460.00

AR-50A1

Model: 50A1B
Caliber: .50 BMG
Action: Bolt, extended triple front locking lugs
Barrel: 33 in., Chrome-moly, 8 groove
Rifling Twist: RH 1:15
Muzzle Device: Muzzle Brake
Action/Barrel Finish: Military grade anodizing and phosphating, black
Stock: 3 sections (extruded forend, machines grip frame, forged/machines removable buttstock), adjustable cheekpiece

Length of Pull: 14.7 in.
Trigger: Shilen standard single-stage
Optic Mount: none, 15-minute top rail
Magazine: none, single shot
Overall Length: 61.5 in.
Weight: 33.6 lb.
Accuracy: 7–8 in. @ 1000 yds.
Features: v-block bedding; threaded muzzle (1x14).
MSRP: $3,359.00

AR-50A1

Model: 50A1B-416
Caliber: .416 Barrett
Action: Bolt, extended triple front locking lugs
Barrel: 30 in., Chrome-moly, 8 groove
Rifling Twist: RH 1:12
Muzzle Device: Muzzle Brake
Action/Barrel Finish: Military grade anodizing and phosphating, black
Stock: 3 section (extruded forend, machines grip frame, forged/machines removable buttstock), adjustable cheekpiece

Length of Pull: 14.7 in.
Trigger: Shilen standard single-stage
Optic Mount: none, 15-minute top rail
Magazine: none, single shot
Overall Length: 58.5 in.
Weight: 34.7 lb.
Accuracy: not specified
Features: v-block bedding; threaded muzzle (1x14)
MSRP: $3,359.00

AR-10 Super S.A.S.S.

Model: 10SBF
Caliber: .308 Win./7.62x51mm NATO
Action: Semiautomatic, gas impingement
Barrel: 20" Triple lapped, Ceramic Coated AISI 416R Stainless Steel Match, Threaded 5/8x24
Rifling Twist: RH 1:10" 150–175-grain bullets (168-grain recommended)
Muzzle Device: Flash Suppressor
Action/Barrel Finish: Military spec anodizing and phosphating, black
Stock: Magpul PRS Precision-Adjustable Stock (comb/length)
Length of Pull: 13.8–14.8 in.

Trigger: National Match two stage: 1st stage 2.5 lbs , 2nd stage 4.5–5 lbs
Optic Mount: Picatinny Rail on handguard and upper receiver
Magazine: detachable box
Overall Length: 41–42 in.
Weight: 11.84 lb.
Accuracy: 1 MOA
Features: forged upper and lower receivers, free-floated barrel, adjustable gas system to optimize rifle function with suppressor, floating rail system with rail covers, one 10-round magazine, one 20-round magazine, USMC quick adjustable sling, sling swivel mount, black hard case.
MSRP: $3,100.00

Ashbury Precision Ordnance (ashburyprecisionordnance.com)

Founded in 1995, Ashbury International Group, Inc. leverages their government security and defense industry experience with organic engineering competencies and technology-driven products for government and non-governmental organizations in the US and allied foreign nations.

ASW308

Caliber: .308 Win.
Action: Bolt, Surgeon 591-II Repeater, short
Barrel: 20 in. Pinnacle Series 416R SS, 5R rifling, 11° crown
Rifling Twist: 1:10 in.
Muzzle Device: AAC Blackout muzzle brake
Stock: Folding SABER PBA-H (Push Button Adjustable Hybrid) adjustments for length of pull, cheekpiece height, and vertical recoil pad placement; aluminum and polymer; Magpul M1AD pistol grip
Stock Finish: Black, OD green, Nordic Gray or Flat dark earth

Trigger: Huber Staged Break Tactical two stage, approx. 3.5 lb.
Optics Mount: 20 MOA MIL-STD 1913 rail
Magazine: Detachable steel box, 10-round
Action/Barrel Finish: MIL-STD 810G corrosion resistant, dull and non-reflective tan or black
Weight: 12.4 lb.
Accuracy: sub-MOA, 5-shot group with match grade ammunition
Features: Suppressor ready, accessory rails, ambidextrous paddle lever magazine release.
MSRP: $7,700.00

ASW300

Caliber: .300 Win. Mag.
Action: Bolt, Surgeon 1086-II Repeater, long
Barrel: 24 in. Pinnacle Series 416R SS, 5R rifling, 11° crown, hand lapped
Rifling Twist: 1:10 in.
Muzzle Device: AAC Blackout muzzle brake (suppressor ready)
Stock: Folding SABER PBA-H (Push Button Adjustable Hybrid) adjustments for length of pull, cheekpiece height, and vertical recoil pad placement, aluminum and polymer, SABER SLA-A1A or SLA-A2 MOD-1 chassis, Quattro carbon fiber forend, Magpul M1AD pistol grip

Stock Finish: Black, OD green, Nordic Gray or Flat dark earth
Trigger: Huber Staged Break Tactical two stage, approx. 3.5 lb.
Optics Mount: 30 MOA MIL-STD 1913 rail
Magazine: Detachable steel box, 5- or 10-round
Action/Barrel Finish: MIL-STD 810G corrosion resistant, dull and non-reflective tan or black
Weight: 13.5 lb.
Accuracy: sub-MOA, 5-shot group with match grade ammunition
Features: Suppressor ready, accessory rails, ambidextrous paddle lever magazine release, two-position safety.
MSRP: $8,550.00

ASW338LM

Caliber: .338 Lapua Mag.
Action: Bolt, Surgeon 1581 XL-II Repeater, long
Barrel: 20 in. or 27 in., Premium Rock Creek Pinnacle Series hand lapped, 5R rifling w/11 degree crown
Rifling Twist: 1:9.4 in.
Muzzle Device: AAC Blackout muzzle brake (suppressor ready)
Stock: Folding SABER PBA-H (Push Button Adjustable Hybrid) adjustments for length of pull, cheekpiece height, and vertical recoil pad placement, aluminum and polymer; SABER SLA-A1A or SLA-A2 MOD-1 chassis, Quattro carbon fiber forend, Magpul M1AD pistol grip
Stock Finish: Black, OD green, Nordic Gray or Flat dark earth

Trigger: Huber Staged Break Tactical two stage, approx. 3.5 lb.
Optics Mount: 30 MOA MIL-STD 1913 monolithic top rail
Magazine: Detachable steel box, 5-round (A1 configuration) or 10-round (A2 configuration)
Action/Barrel Finish: MIL-STD 810G corrosion resistant, dull and non-reflective tan or black
Weight: 15 lb. (20-in. barrel), 17 lb. (27-in. barrel)
Accuracy: sub-MOA, 5-shot group with match grade ammunition
Features: Accepts thermal imaging and night vision devices, accessory rails.
MSRP: $8,550.00

ASW50

Caliber: .50 BMG
Action: Bolt, long, 60° bolt lift, flat bottom
Barrel: Match grade, fluted, free floated, 27 in.
Muzzle Device: Double chamber muzzle brake
Stock: Folding aluminum chassis, adjustable cheekpiece, fixed butt pad, polymer pistol grip
Stock Finish: Black, green or dark earth
Trigger: Two-stage, adjustable 3.3–4.4 lb.
Optics Mount: Picatinny rail
Magazine: Detachable steel box, 5-round

Action/Barrel Finish: Black
Overall Length: 53.9 in.
Folded Length: 43.9 in.
Weight: 27.5 lb.
Accuracy: sub MOA 5-shot groups with match grade ammunition
Features: Flat bottom action bolted to full-length aluminum chassis, LOP adjustable via 10mm spacers, two-position safety, forend rail system, bipod adaptor, three sling fixing points.
MSRP: $12,575.00

TCR Short-action Series

Caliber: .223 Rem., 6.5 Creedmoor, .260 Rem., .308 Win.

Action: Bolt, Surgeon RSR Repeater, short

Barrel: 20 in. (.308 Win.), 22 in. (.223 Rem.), 24 in. (.260 Rem., 6.5 Creedmoor), Rock Creek Pinnacle Series 416R SS, 5R rifling, 11° crown

Rifling Twist: 1:8 in. (.223 Rem., 6.5 Creedmoor), 1:9 in. (.260 Rem.), 1:10 in. (.308 Win.)

Muzzle Device: none

Stock: Fixed SABER HTA adjusts for length of pull, cheekpiece height, and vertical recoil pad placement, aluminum and polymer construction, SABER SSA-A3 chassis, Magpul M1AD modular pistol grip

Stock Finish: Black, OD green, Nordic Gray or Flat dark earth

Trigger: Huber Tactical two stage, approx. 3.5 lb.

Optics Mount: 20 MOA MIL-STD 1913 rail

Magazine: Detachable steel box, 10-round

Action/Barrel Finish: MIL-STD 810G corrosion resistant, dull and non-reflective tan or black

Weight: 11 lb. (.223 Rem.), 12 lb. (6.5 Creedmoor, .260 Rem., .308 Win.)

Accuracy: sub-MOA, 5-shot group with match grade ammunition

Features: Designed for tactical competition, accepts thermal imaging and night vision devices, accessory rails.

MSRP: $6,325.00

TCR Magnum Caliber

Caliber: .300 Win. Mag., .338 Lapua Mag.

Action: Bolt, Surgeon 1581 XL-II Repeater, long

Barrel: 24 in. (.300 Win. Mag.) or 27 in. (.338 Lapua Mag.), Premium Rock Creek Pinnacle Series 416R SS, 5R rifling, 11° crown

Rifling Twist: 1:10 in. (.300 Win. Mag.), 1:9.4 in. (.338 Lapua Mag.)

Muzzle Device: Badger FTE muzzle brake

Stock: Fixed SABER HTA adjusts for length of pull, cheekpiece height, and vertical recoil pad placement; aluminum and polymer construction, SABER SLA-A1A or SLA-A2 MOD-1 chassis, Magpul M1AD modular pistol grip

Stock Finish: Black, OD green, Nordic Gray or Flat dark earth

Trigger: Huber Tactical two stage, approx. 3.5 lb.

Optics Mount: 20 MOA MIL-STD 1913 rail

Magazine: Detachable steel box, 5-round

Action/Barrel Finish: MIL-STD 810G corrosion resistant, dull and non-reflective tan or black

Weight: 13 lb. (24-in. barrel), 15 lb. (27-in. barrel)

Accuracy: sub-MOA, 5-shot group with match grade ammunition

Features: Designed for tactical competition, accepts thermal imaging and night vision devices, accessory rails.

MSRP: $7,295.00

Barrett (barrett.net)

Barrett Firearms Manufacturing's sole purpose in 1980 was to build Semiautomatic rifles chambered in .50 BMG; by 1982 Barrett had produced the M82. Since then the Barrett has become an iconic long-range tactical rifle renowned worldwide.

Model 82A1

Caliber: .416 Barrett, .50 BMG
Action: Semiautomatic, recoil-operated, rotating bolt
Barrel: 20 in. (.50 BMG) or 29 in., fluted, match grade
Rifling Twist: RH 1:15 in. (.50 BMG), RH 1:12 in. (.416 Barrett)
Muzzle Device: Muzzle brake, 2-port (.50 BMG), 3-port (.416 Barrett)
Action/Barrel Finish: Tan or black parkerized
Stock: steel with Sorbothane recoil pad
Optic Mount: 18-in, 27 MOA rail

Magazine: detachable box, 10-round
Overall Length: 57 in. (29-in. barrel), 48 in. (20-in. barrel)
Weight: 31.4 lb. (20-in. barrel), 32.7 lb. (29-in. barrel)
Accuracy: Sub-MOA with match ammo
Effective Range: 1,969 yd.
Features: Muzzle brake absorbs up to 70 percent recoil, free-floated barrel, battle-grade trigger, rotating AR-rifle style safety, chrome line chamber and bore, accessory rails, steel receiver, flip up iron sights, detachable folding/adjustable bipod, carry handle, sling attach points, Pelican hard case.
MSRP: $8,900.00

Model 99

Caliber: .416 Barrett, .50 BMG
Action: bolt, 15 lug
Barrel: Match grade 32 in. heavy or 29 in. fluted (.50 BMG)
Rifling Twist: RH 1:15 in. (.50 BMG), RH 1:12 in. (.416 Barrett)
Muzzle Device: Muzzle brake, 3-port, fanned
Action/Barrel Finish: Tan Cerakote or black anodized
Stock: Aluminum with Sorbothane recoil pad
Trigger: Match quality

Optic Mount: 13.7-in, 27 MOA rail
Magazine: none, single shot
Overall Length: 50 in. (32-in. barrel), 47 in. (29-in. barrel)
Weight: 25 lb. (32-in. barrel), 23 lb. (29-in. barrel)
Features: One-piece aluminum extrusion receiver, battle-grade trigger, rotating AR-rifle style safety, detachable folding/adjustable bipod, sling attach points, Pelican hard case.
MSRP: . . . . . . $3,849.00 (32-in. barrel, black finish, .416 Barrett), $3,949.00 (32-in. barrel, tan finish, .416 Barrett), $3,999 (29-in. barrel, black finish, .50 BMG), $4,099 (29-in. barrel, tan finish, .50 BMG)

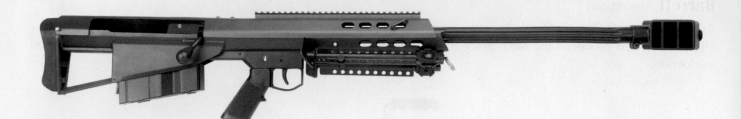

Model 95
Caliber: .50 BMG
Action: bolt, 15 lug
Barrel: Match grade 29 in. fluted
Rifling Twist: RH 1:15 in.
Muzzle Device: Muzzle brake, 3-port, fanned
Action/Barrel Finish: Black parkerized
Stock: Aluminum with Sorbothane recoil pad, accepts monopod

Trigger: Match quality
Optic Mount: 11.7-in. 27 MOA rail
Magazine: detachable, steel, 5-round
Overall Length: 45 in.
Weight: 23.5 lb.
Features: Bullpup design, one-piece aluminum extrusion receiver, lightweight and portable, rotating AR-rifle style safety, detachable folding/adjustable bipod, sling attach points, Pelican hard case.
MSRP: $6,500.00

Model 98B
Caliber: .338 Lapua Mag.
Action: bolt, 9 lug
Barrel: Match grade, 20 in. heavy or 26 in. fluted
Muzzle Device: Muzzle brake
Action/Barrel Finish: Mil-Spec Type 3, Class 2 Hardcoat anodized, black
Stock: Fixed aluminum with Sorbothane recoil pad, adjustable cheekpiece, accepts monopod
Trigger: Adjustable, 2–3.5 lb.; match grade

Optic Mount: Integral 18-in. 30 MOA rail
Magazine: detachable, polymer, 10-round
Overall Length: 43 in. (20-in. barrel), 49.9 in. (26-in. barrel)
Weight: 12.4 lb. (20-in. barrel), 13.5 lb. (26-in. barrel)
Accuracy: Sub-MOA
Features: Aluminum upper receiver, ambidextrous magazine release, thumb-operated safety; accessory rails, accepts most standard M4/M16 pistol grips, sling attach points, Harris bipod, Pelican hard case.
MSRP: . $4,849.00 (fluted barrel), $4,699.00 (heavy barrel)

M107A1

Caliber: .50 BMG
Action: Semiautomatic, recoil-operated, rotating bolt
Barrel: 20 in. or 29 in. fluted
Rifling Twist: RH 1:15 in.
Muzzle Device: Muzzle brake, 4-port designed to work withBarrett QDL suppressor
Action/Barrel Finish: Tan or black Cerakote
Stock: steel with Sorbothane recoil pad and thermal cheek guard

Optic Mount: 18-in. 27 MOA rail
Magazine: detachable box, 10-round, witness holes
Overall Length: 57 in. (29-in. barrel), 48 in. (20-in. barrel)
Weight: 27.4 lb. (20-in. barrel), 28.7 lb. (29-in. barrel)
Effective Range: 1,969 yd. (1,800 m)
Features: Muzzle brake designed to work with Barrett QDL suppressor, adjustable monopod, free-floated barrel, battle-grade trigger, rotating AR-rifle style safety, chrome-lined chamber and bore, steel receiver, flip up iron sights, detachable folding/adjustable bipod, Pelican hard case.
MSRP: $12,000.00

MRAD

Caliber: .338 Lapua Mag.
Action: bolt, 9 lug
Barrel: Match grade; heavy or fluted; 20 in., 24 in. or 26 in.
Rifling Twist: RH 1:9.35 in.
Muzzle Device: Muzzle brake
Action/Barrel Finish: Multi-Role Brown (MRB) or black anodized
Stock: Folding aluminum with Sorbothane recoil pad, adjustable length of pull and cheekpiece
Trigger: Adjustable, modular
Optic Mount: Integral21.7-in, 30 MOA rail
Magazine: detachable, polymer, 10-round
Overall Length: 42.4 in. (20-in. barrel), 46.9 in. (24-in. barrel) , 49.4 in. (26-in. barrel)
Folded Length: 35.4 in. (20-in. barrel), 39.9 in. (24-in. barrel) , 42.4 in. (26-in. barrel)

Weight: 13.56 lb. (20-in. barrel, fluted), 14.28 lb. (24-in. barrel, fluted), 14.72 lb. (26-in. barrel, fluted), 13.24 lb. (20-in. barrel, heavy), 14.04 lb. (24-in. barrel, heavy), 14.50 lb. (26-in. barrel, heavy)
Features: MRAD (Multi-Role Adaptive Design) features user-changeable free-float barrel system and trigger module; multi-caliber system for use with .338 Lapua Mag., .300 Win. Mag. or 7.62x51mm (.308 Win.); aluminum upper receiver; polymer bolt guides acts as dust cover and provide smooth bolt cycling; ambidextrous magazine release; magazine well; ambidextrous thumb-operated safety; accessory rails; stock folds onto bolt handle; oversized trigger guard; accepts most standard M4/M16 pistol grips; sling attach points; Pelican hard case.
MSRP: . . $6,000.00 (fluted barrel), $5,850.00 (heavy barrel)

Bushmaster (bushmaster.com)

Bushmaster Firearms International started in 1973 and is the leading supplier of AR-15 type rifles in the United States, manufacturing both aluminum and advanced carbon-fiber AR-15 type rifles. Bushmaster firearms are used by hundreds of police departments and law enforcement organizations nationwide, by the militaries of more than 50 countries worldwide, in private security applications, and by civilians for hunting, recreation, competition, and home defense.

308 Hunter

Caliber: .308 Win.
Action: Semiautomatic, gas impingement
Barrel: 20 in., fluted, 4150 chrome-moly-vanadium, crowned muzzle
Rifling Twist: RH 1:10 in.
Muzzle Device: None
Action/Barrel Finish: Matte black
Stock: Magpul MOE, Hogue pistol grip, free-floated aluminum handguard
Stock Finish: Black

Trigger: Standard AR-style
Optic Mount: Picatinny Rail on upper receiver with two 1.25 -in. risers
Magazine: detachable box, 5-round
Overall Length: 35 in.
Weight: 8.2 lb.
Features: Designed for big game hunting, mid-length gas system for smoother recoil, MOE trigger guard for use with gloved hands.
MSRP: $1,685.00

Varminter Stainless

Caliber: 5.56 NATO/223 Rem.
Action: Semiautomatic, gas impingement
Barrel: 24 in., non-fluted, stainless steel, non-chrome lined, competition muzzle crown
Rifling Twist: RH 1:8 in.
Muzzle Device: None
Action/Barrel Finish: Matte black
Stock: Hogue pistol grip, free-floated aluminum handguard

Stock Finish: Black
Trigger: Standard AR-style
Optic Mount: Picatinny Rail on upper receiver with two 1.25 -in. risers
Magazine: detachable box, 5-round
Overall Length: 42.2 in.
Weight: 8.4 lb.
Features: Designed for varmint hunting, mid-length gas system for smoother recoil.
MSRP: . $1,392.80; $1,392.80 (fluted, chrome-moly steel barrel); $1,572.87 (A-TACS Varminter)

A-TACS Predator

Caliber: 5.56 NATO/223 Rem.
Action: Semiautomatic, gas impingement
Barrel: 20 in., fluted, chrome-moly, non-chrome lined, crowned
Rifling Twist: RH 1:8 in.
Muzzle Device: None
Action/Barrel Finish: Camo
Stock: Hogue pistol grip, free-floated aluminum handguard

Stock Finish: Camo
Trigger: Standard AR-style
Optic Mount: Picatinny Rail on upper receiver with two 1.25 -in. risers
Magazine: detachable box, 5-round
Overall Length: 38.2 in.
Weight: 8 lb.
Features: Designed for varmint hunting, mid-length gas system for smoother recoil.
MSRP: . . . .$1,556.94; $1,377.66 (20 in barrel)

CC International (ccintnl.com)

CC International specializes in building rifles for Extreme Long Range and Hard Target Interdiction. They offer a "power through precision" system that is purpose-built for use in any part of the world and under any conditions. They offer bolt-action rifles built with Spartan receivers by Truvelo Manufacturers in South Africa.

Alpha

Caliber: 6.5 Creedmoor, .260 Rem. 7.62x51 NATO
Action: Bolt, Spartan, short-action, 2 lug, 90° bolt lift
Barrel: 26 in., cold-forged, match-grade, fluted, free floated
Muzzle Device: None

Stock: Folding aluminum and polymer construction, pistol grip, choice of chassis or stock systems
Stock Finish: Black
Optics Mount: Picatinny-style rail
Action/Barrel Finish: Matte black
Overall Length: 46 in.
Folded Overall Length: 36 in.
Weight: 13 lb.

Bravo

Caliber: .338 Norma Mag., .338 Lapua Mag.
Action: Bolt, Spartan, long-action, 4 lug, 45° bolt lift
Barrel: 26 in., cold-forged, match-grade, fluted, free floated
Muzzle Device: Muzzle brake
Stock: Folding aluminum and polymer construction, pistol grip, choice of chassis or stock systems
Stock Finish: Black
Optics Mount: Picatinny-style rail
Action/Barrel Finish: Matte black
Overall Length: 47 in.
Folded Overall Length: 38 in.
Weight: 13 lb.

Charlie

Caliber: .375 CheyTac, .408 CheyTac
Action: Bolt, Spartan, long-action, 4 lug, 45° bolt lift
Barrel: 28 in., cold-forged, match-grade, fluted, free floated
Muzzle Device: Muzzle brake
Stock: Folding aluminum and polymer construction, pistol grip, choice of chassis or stock systems
Stock Finish: Black
Optics Mount: Picatinny-style rail
Magazine: Detachable steel box, 5-round
Action/Barrel Finish: Matte black
Overall Length: 55 in.
Folded Overall Length: 47 in.
Weight: 28 lb.

Delta

Caliber: .375 VM, .416 Barrett, .460 Steyr, .50 BMG, .510 DTC
Action: Bolt, Spartan, long-action, 4 lug, 45° bolt lift
Barrel: 28 in., cold-forged, match-grade, fluted, free floated
Muzzle Device: Muzzle brake
Stock: Folding aluminum and polymer construction, pistol grip, choice of chassis or stock systems

Stock Finish: Black
Optics Mount: Picatinny-style rail
Magazine: Detachable steel box, 5-round
Action/Barrel Finish: Matte black
Overall Length: 55 in.
Folded Overall Length: 47 in.
Weight: 28 lb.

Echo

Caliber: 14.5x114mm
Action: Bolt, Spartan, long-action, 4 lug, 45° bolt lift
Barrel: 39 in., cold-forged, match-grade, fluted, free floated
Muzzle Device: Muzzle brake
Stock: Folding aluminum and polymer construction, pistol grip, choice of chassis or stock systems

Stock Finish: Black
Optics Mount: Picatinny-style rail
Magazine: Detachable steel box, 5-round
Action/Barrel Finish: Matte black
Overall Length: 71 in.
Weight: 48 lb.

Colt's Manufacturing LLC (colt.com)

Colt's bolt-action rifles use a Cooper action and offer outstanding accuracy.

M2012

Caliber: .308 Win.
Action: Cooper bolt, short, 3 lugs
Barrel: 22 in., spiral flute, stainless steel, match grade E.R. Shaw
Rifling Twist: RH 1:10 in.
Muzzle Device: Custom Cooper muzzle brake
Action/Barrel Finish: Matte black
Stock: Forged aluminum chassis, adjustable for length of pull and comb height, Magpul pistol grip

Stock Finish: Black
Trigger: Timney single-stage, adjustable
Optic Mount: 20 MOA top rail
Magazine: detachable box, 5-round
Overall Length: 44 in.
Weight: 13.1 lb.
Accuracy: Guarantee 1 MOA 3-shot group at 100 yd.
Features: Similar ergonomics of an AR rifle.
MSRP: $3,799.00

M2012MT308T

Caliber: .308 Win.
Action: Cooper bolt, short, 3 lugs
Barrel: 22 in., spiral flute, stainless steel, match grade E.R. Shaw
Rifling Twist: RH 1:10 in.
Muzzle Device: Custom Cooper muzzle brake
Action/Barrel Finish: Matte black
Stock: Manner composite, aircraft-grade carbon fiber and fiberglass

Stock Finish: Desert tan
Trigger: Timney single-stage, adjustable
Optic Mount: 20 MOA top rail
Magazine: detachable box, 5-round
Overall Length: 44 in.
Weight: 10.25 lb.
Features: Designed as a "crossover" rifle that easily transitions from target shooting to long-range hunting.
MSRP: $3,195.00

M2012LT308G

Caliber: .308 Win.
Action: Cooper bolt, short, 3 lugs
Barrel: 22 in., spiral flute, stainless steel, match grade
E.R. Shaw
Rifling Twist: RH 1:10 in.
Muzzle Device: Custom Cooper muzzle brake
Action/Barrel Finish: Matte black
Stock: Laminated hardwood

Stock Finish: Grey
Trigger: Timney single-stage, adjustable
Optic Mount: 20 MOA top rail
Magazine: detachable box, 5-round
Overall Length: 44 in.
Weight: 8.5 lb.
Features: Designed as a "crossover" rifle that transitions easily from target shooting to long-range hunting.
MSRP: $2,795.00

M2012LT308G

Caliber: .260 Rem.
Action: Cooper bolt, short, 3 lugs
Barrel: 22 in., spiral flute, stainless steel, match grade
E.R. Shaw
Rifling Twist: RH 1:8 in.
Muzzle Device: Custom Cooper muzzle brake
Action/Barrel Finish: Matte black
Stock: Laminated hardwood

Stock Finish: Grey
Trigger: Timney single-stage, adjustable
Optic Mount: 20 MOA top rail
Magazine: detachable box, 5-round
Overall Length: 44 in.
Weight: 8.5 lb.
Features: Designed as a "crossover" rifle that transitions easily from target shooting to long-range hunting.
MSRP: $2,795.00

CZ-USA (cz-usa.com)

Česká zbrojovka a.s. *Uherský Brod* is a Czech firearms manufacturer that was established in 1936. They are known for the excellent CZ 75 pistol line as well as Mauser-style hunting rifles and military small arms. Today CZ-USA offers hunting and military shotguns, rimfire rifles, handguns (including the Dan Wesson brand of 1911s), and hunting, target, and military rifles. Their tactical rifles are built on Mauser-style bolt-actions with control feed and claw extractor.

CZ-USA 550 Urban Counter Sniper (UCS)

Caliber: .308 Win.
Action: Bolt, short, control feed
Barrel: 16 in., cold hammer forged
Rifling Twist: 1:12 in.
Muzzle Device: Surefire muzzle brake , QD suppressor compatible
Action/Barrel Finish: Green Teflon
Stock: Bell & Carson Kevlar-reinforced fiberglass, aluminum bedding block, free-float barrel
Stock Finish: Matte black
Trigger: Single set
Optics Mount: 19mm dovetail
Magazine: Detachable steel box, 10-round
Overall Length: 37 in.
Weight: 8.3 lb.
Accuracy: Not specified
Features: Two-position safety, oversized bolt handle, polished action.
MSRP: $2,530.00

CZ 550 Magnum H.E.T. (High Energy Tactical)

Caliber: .300 RUM, .300 Win. Mag., .338 Lapua Mag.
Action: Bolt, long, control feed
Barrel: 26 in. (.300 RUM, .300 Win. Mag.) or 28 in. (.338 Lapua Mag.), cold hammer forged
Rifling Twist: 1:10 in.
Muzzle Device: Surefire muzzle brake , QD suppressor compatible
Action/Barrel Finish: Matte blue
Stock: Bell & Carson tactical Kevlar-reinforced fiberglass, aluminum bedding block, free-float barrel
Stock Finish: Matte black
Trigger: Single set
Optics Mount: 19mm dovetail
Magazine: fixed box, 4-round (.338 Lapua Mag.), 5-round (.300 RUM, .300 Win. Mag.)
Overall Length: 50.8 in. (.300 RUM, .300 Win. Mag.), 52.6 in. (.338 Lapua Mag.)
Weight: 13 lb. (.300 RUM, .300 Win. Mag.), 13.5 lb. (.338 Lapua Mag.)
Features: Two-position safety, oversized bolt handle, polished action.
MSRP: $3,929.00

CZ 750 Sniper
Caliber: .308 Win. (7.62x51 NATO)
Action: Bolt, short, control feed
Barrel: 25.9 in., 4-groove, hammer forged
Rifling Twist: 1:12 in.
Muzzle Device: muzzle brake
Action/Barrel Finish: Blued
Stock: synthetic thumbhole, adjustable comb height and length of pull, free-float barrel

Stock Finish: Matte black
Trigger: Single stage
Optics Mount: Weaver rail installed or 19mm dovetail
Magazine: Detachable box, 10-round
Overall Length: 48 in.
Weight: 11.9 lb.
Features: Two-position safety, oversized bolt handle, polished action, underside of forend fitted with a 220mm long rail for mounting bipod, mirage shield.
MSRP: $1,999.00

DPMS (dpmsinc.com)

DPMS (Defense Procurement Manufacturing Services) was founded in 1985 by Randy Luth as a small government contract consulting company. Today, DPMS Firearms is part of the Freedom Group and located in St. Cloud, Minnesota, and ranks as the second-largest manufacturer of AR-15 rifles. DPMS firearms and patented accessories are currently in use worldwide by law enforcement agencies, military personnel, and civilians, including US Border Patrol officers and America's top competitive shooters and big game hunters.

Mini SASS
Caliber: 5.56 NATO
Action: Semiautomatic, gas impingement
Barrel: 18 in., fluted bull, Teflon coated 416 stainless steel, threaded muzzle
Rifling Twist: RH 1:8 in.
Muzzle Device: Panther flash hider
Action/Barrel Finish: Matte black
Stock: Magpul PRS, Panther tactical grip, 4-rail free-float handguard

Stock Finish: Matte black
Trigger: JP single stage
Optic Mount: Full length rail on upper receiver with Mangonel folding sights
Magazine: Detachable box, 30-round
Overall Length: 39.5 in.
Weight: 10.25 lb.
Features: Built for precision scenarios, this system is accurate.
MSRP: $1,649.00

LRT-SASS

Caliber: .308 Win./7.62 NATO
Action: Semiautomatic, gas impingement
Barrel: 18 in., fluted, 416 stainless steel, threaded muzzle
Rifling Twist: RH 1:10 in.
Muzzle Device: Panther flash hider
Action/Barrel Finish: Matte black
Stock: Magpul PRS, Panther tactical pistol grip, 4-rail free-float handguard
Stock Finish: Matte black

Trigger: JP two stage
Optic Mount: Full length rail on upper receiver
Magazine: Detachable box, 20-round
Overall Length: 40.25 in.
Weight: 11.45 lb.
Features: The SASS (Semi-Auto Sniper System) was designed for military use and DPMS's version is designed to provide a marksman a weapon that could accomplish both long-range precision and rapid defensive fire when called upon.
MSRP: $2,179.00

NATO REPR (Rapid Engagement Precision Rifle)

Caliber: .308 Win./7.62 NATO
Action: Semiautomatic, gas impingement
Barrel: 20 in., HBAR melonite treated, threaded muzzle
Rifling Twist: RH 1:10 in.
Muzzle Device: ACC flash hider/suppressor adaptor
Action/Barrel Finish: Matte desert tan
Stock: Magpul PRS, lightweight 4-rail free-float handguard, Hogue rubber grip

Stock Finish: Matte desert tan
Trigger: Match two stage
Optic Mount: Full length rail on upper receiver
Magazine: Detachable box, 20-round
Overall Length: 40.25 in.
Weight: 9.75 lb.
Features: Same concept as the SASS (Semi-Auto Sniper System) but lighter weight.
MSRP: $2,589.00

MK 12

Caliber: .308 Win./7.62 NATO
Action: Semiautomatic, gas impingement
Barrel: 18 in., HBAR Teflon coated, 416 stainless, threaded muzzle
Rifling Twist: RH 1:10 in.
Muzzle Device: Panther flash hider
Action/Barrel Finish: Matte black
Stock: B5 Systems adjustable stock, G27 pistol grip, lightweight 4-rail free-float handguard

Stock Finish: Matte black
Trigger: Standard AR-15
Optic Mount: Full length rail on upper receiver with Midwest Industry flip-up sights
Magazine: Detachable box, 20-round
Overall Length: 40.25 in.
Weight: 8.5 lb.
Features: With the collapsible stock the MK 12 can perform carbine and rifle duties. No forward assist.
MSRP: $2,589.00

LR-308

Caliber: .308 Win./7.62 NATO
Action: Semiautomatic, gas impingement
Barrel: 24 in., bull taper, 416 stainless
Rifling Twist: RH 1:10 in.
Muzzle Device: None
Action/Barrel Finish: Matte black
Stock: A2 fixed butt, A2 pistol grip, aluminum free float handguard

Stock Finish: Matte black
Trigger: Standard AR-15
Optic Mount: Rail on upper receiver
Magazine: Detachable box, 20-round
Overall Length: 43.75 in.
Weight: 11.25 lb.
Features: Designed for hunting, this AR has no forward assist or dust cover.
MSRP: $1,199.00

LR-308B

Caliber: .308 Win./7.62 NATO
Action: Semiautomatic, gas impingement
Barrel: 18 in., bull taper, 4140 chrome-moly
Rifling Twist: RH 1:10 in.
Muzzle Device: None
Action/Barrel Finish: Matte black
Stock: A2 fixed butt, A2 pistol grip, aluminum free-float handguard

Stock Finish: Matte black
Trigger: Standard AR-15
Optic Mount: Rail on upper receiver
Magazine: Detachable box, 20-round
Overall Length: 37.75 in.
Weight: 9.75 lb.
Features: Designed for hunting, similar to the LR-308 except with a shorter barrel for better maneuverability.
MSRP: $1,189.00

Long Range Lite

Caliber: .308 Win./7.62 NATO
Action: Semiautomatic, gas impingement
Barrel: 24 in., HBAR, 416 Stainless
Rifling Twist: RH 1:10 in.
Muzzle Device: None
Action/Barrel Finish: Matte black
Stock: A2 fixed butt, Hogue pistol grip, carbon fiber free-float handguard

Stock Finish: Matte black
Trigger: Two-stage match
Optic Mount: Rail on upper receiver
Magazine: Detachable box, 20-round
Overall Length: 43.25 in.
Weight: 10.25 lb.
Features: Designed for hunting and without a forward assist, similar to the LR-308 but two pounds lighter.
MSRP: $1,499.00

24 Special
Caliber: .233 Rem.
Action: Semiautomatic, gas impingement
Barrel: 24 in., fluted bull, 416 stainless
Rifling Twist: RH 1:9 in.
Muzzle Device: None
Action/Barrel Finish: Matte black
Stock: A2 fixed butt, Panther tactical grip, aluminum free-float handguard

Stock Finish: Matte black
Trigger: Standard AR-15
Optic Mount: Rail on upper receiver
Magazine: Detachable box, 30-round
Overall Length: 45.75 in.
Weight: 10.25 lb.
Features: Designed for varmint hunting and/or target shooting, the 24 Special offers a 24-inch barrel to achieve for maximum velocity.
MSRP: $1,229.00

LR-204
Caliber: .204 Ruger
Action: Semiautomatic, gas impingement
Barrel: 24 in., fluted bull, 416 stainless
Rifling Twist: RH 1:12 in.
Muzzle Device: None
Action/Barrel Finish: Matte black
Stock: A2 fixed butt, Panther tactical grip, aluminum free float handguard

Stock Finish: Matte black
Trigger: Standard AR-15
Optic Mount: Rail on upper receiver
Magazine: Detachable box, 30-round
Overall Length: 45.75 in.
Weight: 10.25 lb.
Features: Similar to the 24 Special but chambered in .204 Ruger. It is designed for varmint hunting and/or target shooting.
MSRP: $1,059.00

Bull 24

Caliber: .223 Rem.
Action: Semiautomatic, gas impingement
Barrel: 24 in., bull, 416 stainless
Rifling Twist: RH 1:9 in.
Muzzle Device: None
Action/Barrel Finish: Matte black
Stock: A2 fixed butt, A2 pistol grip, aluminum free-float handguard
Stock Finish: Matte black
Trigger: Standard AR-15
Optic Mount: Rail on upper receiver
Magazine: Detachable box, 30-round
Overall Length: 42.5 in.
Weight: 9.8 lb.
Features: Designed for varmint hunting and/or target shooting with heavy 24-inch bull barrel.
MSRP: $999.00

Bull 20

Caliber: .223 Rem.
Action: Semiautomatic, gas impingement
Barrel: 20 in., bull, 416 stainless
Rifling Twist: RH 1:9 in.
Muzzle Device: None
Action/Barrel Finish: Matte black
Stock: A2 fixed butt, A2 pistol grip,aluminum free float handguard
Stock Finish: Matte black
Trigger: Standard AR-15
Optic Mount: Rail on upper receiver
Magazine: Detachable box, 30-round
Overall Length: 38.5 in.
Weight: 9.5 lb.
Features: Similar to Bull 24 but with shorter 20-inch barrel.
MSRP: $969.00

DSA Inc. (dsarms.com)

D.S. Arms Inc. (DSA) manufactures FN FAL 7.62mm rifle systems in the US utilizing new tooling, improved materials, and modernized processes. DSA FAL rifles are completely interchangeable with the original F.N. metric FAL. They also produce M16 series rifles and components and have been contracted to produce components for M2 .50 caliber, MAG58, and M203 40mm.

SA58 SPR

Caliber: 7.62x51mm NATO
Action: Semiautomatic,gas-operated, tilting bolt
Barrel: 19 in., fluted medium weight, 5/8-24 threaded muzzle
Muzzle Device: Trident flash hider
Action/Barrel Finish: Duracoat matte black

Stock: Fully adjustable side folding PARA S.P.R. stock, SAW pistol grip
Stock Finish: Matte black
Trigger: DS Arms speed trigger
Optics Mount: Picatinny-style rail, folding back-up iron sights
Magazine: Detachable steel box, 10-round
Features: Type 1 receiver, light weight alloy PARA lower.
MSRP: $4,795.00

Drake Associates (drakeassociates.us)

Drake Associates Inc. specializes in developing US and Canadian market opportunities for European Industrial Corporations involved in military and civilian programs. They focus on ammunition and weapon systems from the supply of raw material, production machinery, sub-assemblies, components, spare parts, and finished goods and systems.

Stalker Gen 2

Caliber: .308 Win.
Action: Bolt, Rangemaster Quadlite, short, push feed, 4 lug
Barrel: Heavy, fluted, free floated, 16 in., 5/8x24 threaded muzzle
Rifling Twist: 1:10 in.
Muzzle Device: RPA muzzle brake
Stock: Cadex Strike Dual 30 chassis; folding stock; adjustable length of pull, cheekpiece, recoil pad; modular trigger system; aluminum and polymer construction

Stock Finish: Black
Trigger: X-Mark Pro, two stage, adjustable 1 - 4.5 lb.
Optics Mount: 20 MOA rail
Magazine: AICS detachable steel box, 5- or 10-round
Action/Barrel Finish: Black Cerakote
Overall Length: 36.5 in.
Overall Length Folded: 27.7 in.
Weight: 12.4 lb.
Features: Flush-fit magazine, ambidextrous magazine release, dual tube system with short and long handguards, comes with drag bag.
MSRP: $5,535.50

Stalker Gen 2 Interceptor

Caliber: .308 Win.
Action: Bolt, Rangemaster Quadlite, short, push feed, 4 lug
Barrel: Heavy, fluted, free floated, 26 in., 5/8x24 threaded muzzle
Rifling Twist: 1:10 in.
Muzzle Device: RPA muzzle brake
Stock: Cadex Strike Dual 30 chassis; folding stock; adjustable length of pull, cheekpiece, recoil pad; modular trigger system
Stock Finish: Black
Trigger: X-Mark Pro, two stage, adjustable 1 - 4.5 lb.
Optics Mount: 20 MOA rail
Magazine: AICS detachable steel box, 5- or 10-round
Action/Barrel Finish: Black Cerakote
Overall Length: 36.5 in.
Overall Length Folded: 27.7 in.
Weight: 12.4 lb.
Features: Flush fit magazine, ambidextrous magazine release, dual tube system with short and long handguards, accessory rails, comes with drag bag.
MSRP: $5,535.00

Stalker 300 Strike Dual

Caliber: .300 Win. Mag.
Action: Bolt, Remington 700, long, push feed, 2 lug
Barrel: Heavy, fluted, free floated, 24 in., 5/8x24 threaded muzzle
Rifling Twist: 1:10 in.
Muzzle Device: RPA muzzle brake
Stock: Cadex Strike Dual 33 chassis; folding stock; adjustable length of pull, cheekpiece, recoil pad; modular trigger system
Stock Finish: Black
Trigger: X-Mark Pro
Optics Mount: 20 MOA rail
Magazine: AICS detachable steel box, 5- or 10-round
Action/Barrel Finish: Black Cerakote
Overall Length: 47.5 in.
Overall Length Folded: 25.3 in.
Weight: 12.1 lb.
Features: Ambidextrous magazine release, dual tube system with short and long handguards, accessory rails, comes with drag bag.
MSRP: $7,104.00

Stalker 308 Strike Dual

Caliber: .308 Win.
Action: Bolt, Remington 700, short, push feed, 2 lug
Barrel: Heavy, free floated, 16 in., 5/8x24 threaded muzzle
Rifling Twist: 1:10 in. or 1:11.25 in., 5R rifling
Muzzle Device: RPA muzzle brake
Stock: Cadex Strike Dual 30 chassis; folding stock; adjustable length of pull, cheekpiece, recoil pad; modular trigger system
Stock Finish: Black
Trigger: X-Mark Pro, two stage, adjustable 1–4.5 lb.
Optics Mount: 20 MOA rail
Magazine: AICS detachable steel box, 5- or 10-round
Action/Barrel Finish: Black Cerakote
Overall Length: 36.5 in.
Overall Length Folded: 27.7 in.
Weight: 12.4 lb.
Features: Ambidextrous magazine release, dual tube system with short and long handguards, accessory rails, comes with drag bag.
MSRP: $5,118.00

Stalker 700 Strike Dual

Caliber: .300 Win. Mag.
Action: Bolt, Remington 700, long, push feed, 2 lug
Barrel: Heavy, fluted, free floated, 24 in., 5/8x24 threaded muzzle
Rifling Twist: 1:10 in.
Muzzle Device: RPA muzzle brake
Stock: Cadex Strike Dual 33 chassis; folding stock; adjustable length of pull, cheekpiece, recoil pad; modular trigger system
Stock Finish: Black
Trigger: X-Mark Pro, adjustable
Optics Mount: 20 MOA rail
Magazine: AICS detachable steel box, 5- or 10-round
Action/Barrel Finish: Black Cerakote
Overall Length: 47.5 in.
Overall Length Folded: 25.3 in.
Weight: 12.1 lb.
Features: Ambidextrous magazine release, dual tube system with short and long handguards, accessory rails, comes with drag bag.
MSRP: $7,104.00

Stalker MK13 Strike Dual

Caliber: .300 Win. Mag.
Action: Bolt, Stiller Mk13, long, push feed, 2 lug
Barrel: Heavy, free floated, 24 in., 5/8x24 threaded muzzle
Rifling Twist: 1:10 in.
Muzzle Device: RPA muzzle brake
Stock: Cadex Strike Dual 33 chassis; folding stock; adjustable length of pull, cheekpiece, recoil pad; modular trigger system
Stock Finish: Black
Trigger: Jewel
Optics Mount: 20 MOA rail
Magazine: AICS detachable steel box, 5- or 10-round
Action/Barrel Finish: Black Cerakote
Overall Length: 47.5 in.
Overall Length Folded: 25.3 in.
Weight: 12.1 lb.
Features: Ambidextrous magazine release, dual tube system with short and long handguards, accessory rails, comes with drag bag.
MSRP: $5,885.00

Stalker McMillan 338LM Strike Dual

Caliber: .338 Lapua Mag.
Action: Bolt, McMillan G30, long, push feed, 2 lug
Barrel: Heavy, free floated, 26 in., 5/8x24 threaded muzzle
Rifling Twist: 1:9 in.
Muzzle Device: AAC muzzle brake
Stock: Cadex Strike Dual 33 chassis; folding stock; adjustable length of pull, cheekpiece, recoil pad; modular trigger system
Stock Finish: Black Cerakote
Trigger: Jewel
Optics Mount: 20 MOA rail
Magazine: AICS detachable steel box, 5- or 10-round
Action/Barrel Finish: Black Cerakote
Overall Length: 49.5 in.
Overall Length Folded: 27.3 in.
Weight: 12.7 lb.
Features: Ambidextrous magazine release, dual tube system with short and long handguards, accessory rails, comes with drag bag.
MSRP: $5,885.00

Stalker MK15 Strike Dual 50

Caliber: .416 Barrett, .50 BMG
Action: Bolt, McMillan TCA50, long, push feed, 2 lug
Barrel: Heavy, fluted, free floated, 17.5 in., threaded muzzle
Rifling Twist: 1:14.5 in. (.50BMG)
Muzzle Device: RPA muzzle brake, 3 port
Stock: Cadex Strike Dual 50 chassis; folding stock; adjustable length of pull, cheekpiece, recoil pad; modular trigger system
Stock Finish: Black Cerakote
Trigger: Jewel
Optics Mount: 20 MOA rail
Magazine: CADEX detachable steel box, double stack 5-round
Action/Barrel Finish: Black Cerakote
Overall Length: 44.2 in.
Overall Length Folded: 32.2 in.
Weight: 8.12 lb.
Features: Ambidextrous magazine release, dual tube system with short and long handguards, accessory rails, comes with drag bag, compatible with McMillan magazines.
MSRP: $9,999.00

FNH USA (fnhusa.com)

FNH's story begins in 1897 with a long-standing relationship with gun designer John M. Browning. This Belgium company has produced some of the most iconic pistols, rifles, and shotguns. The FBI purchased the FN SPR A3G precision bolt-action rifle in 2003. Their SPR Series are based on the world-renowned Pre-'64 Model 70-style forged steel action with a three-position safety and massive external claw extractor for controlled round feeding. Both the SPR and TSR series are manufactured in the US.

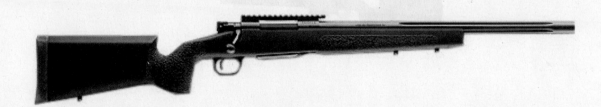

SPR A1

Caliber: .308 Win.
Action: Bolt, Pre-'64 Model 70-style, short, control feed, 2 lug
Barrel: 24 in., cold hammer-forged, chrome lined, free floating
Rifling Twist: RH 1:12 in.
Muzzle Device: None
Stock: McMillan fiberglass tactical

Stock Finish: Black, textured gripping surfaces
Trigger: Model 70-type two-lever adjustable trigger
Optics Mount: 20 MOA rail
Magazine: Detachable box, 4-round
Overall Length: 44 in.
Weight: 11.6 lb.
Features: Three-position safety, knurled bolt handle, multiple steel sling swivel mounting points, recoil pad.
MSRP: $6,499.00

SPR A1a

Caliber: .308 Win.
Action: Bolt, Pre-'64 Model 70-style, short, control feed, 2 lug
Barrel: 20 in., fluted, cold hammer-forged, chrome lined, free floating, muzzle crowned
Rifling Twist: RH 1:12 in.
Muzzle Device: None
Stock: McMillan fiberglass tactical

Stock Finish: Black, textured gripping surfaces
Trigger: Model 70-type two-lever adjustable trigger
Optics Mount: 20 MOA rail
Magazine: Detachable box, 4-round
Overall Length: 40 in.
Weight: 11.8 lb.
Features: Three-position safety, knurled bolt handle, forged steel construction receiver with flat bottom profile, multiple steel sling swivel mounting points, recoil pad.
MSRP: $2,245.00

SPR A3G

Caliber: .308 Win.
Action: Bolt, Pre-'64 Model 70-style, short, control feed, 2 lug
Barrel: 24 in., fluted, cold hammer-forged, chrome lined, free floating, muzzle crowned
Rifling Twist: RH 1:12 in.
Muzzle Device: None
Action/Barrel Finish: Blue
Stock: McMillanA3 fiberglass tactical, adjustable length of pull and comb

Stock Finish: OD green, textured gripping surfaces
Trigger: Model 70-type two-lever adjustable trigger
Optics Mount: One-piece titanium 20 MOA rail
Magazine: Internal box, 5-round, hinged floorplate
Overall Length: 44 in.
Weight: 11.5 lb.
Accuracy: Sub-½ MOA at 100 yards
Features: Three-position safety, knurled bolt handle, forged steel construction receiver with flat bottom profile, multiple steel sling swivel mounting points, receiver hand-bedded with Marine-Tex epoxy, recoil pad.
MSRP: $3,495.00

SPR A5M

Caliber: .308 Win. or .300 WSM
Action: Bolt, Pre-'64 Model 70-style, short, control feed, 2 lug
Barrel: 20in. or 24 in., fluted, cold hammer-forged, chrome lined, free floating, muzzle crowned
Rifling Twist: RH 1:12 in. (.308 Win.), 1:10 in. (.300 WSM)
Muzzle Device: None
Action/Barrel Finish: Matte black
Stock: Fully adjustable McMillan fiberglass, close-radius upright grip, undercut buttstock profile, semi-wide tapered forend, adjustable comb

Stock Finish: Matte black, textured gripping surfaces
Trigger: Model 70-type two-lever adjustable trigger
Optics Mount: One-piece titanium 20 MOA rail
Magazine: Detachable box, 4-,5- or 10-round
Overall Length: 40 in. (20-in. barrel), 43.5 in. – 45 in. (24-in. barrel)
Weight: 11.3 lb. (20-in. barrel), 11.8 lb. (24-in. barrel)
Features: Three-position safety, knurled bolt handle, forged steel construction receiver with flat bottom profile, multiple steel sling swivel mounting points.
MSRP: $2,899.00

TSR XP

Caliber: .308 Win./7.62x51 NATO or .300 WSM
Action: Bolt, Pre-'64 Model 70-style, short, control feed, 2 lug
Barrel: 20 in. or 24 in., fluted, light contour, cold hammer-forged, free floating, target crown
Rifling Twist: RH 1:12 in. (.308 Win.), 1:10 in. (.300 WSM)
Muzzle Device: None
Action/Barrel Finish: Matte black
Stock: Hogue synthetic sporter-style stock with OverMolded rubber surface, full-length aluminum bedding block
Stock Finish: Olive drab
Trigger: Tactical Sport Trigger System, three-lever adjustable
Optics Mount: One-piece aluminum rail
Magazine: Detachable box, 4-round
Overall Length: 40.5 in. (20-in. barrel), 44.5in. (24-in. barrel)
Weight: 8.8 lb. (20-in. barrel), 9.6 lb. (24-in. barrel, .308 Win.), 10.1 lb. (24-in. barrel, .300 WSM)
Features: Three-position safety, knurled bolt handle, forged steel construction receiver with flat bottom profile, multiple steel sling swivel mounting points, recoil pad.
MSRP: $1,199.00

Ballista

Caliber: .308 Win., .300 Win. Mag., .338 Lapua Mag.
Action: Bolt, Pre-'64 Model 70-style, short, control feed, 2 lug
Barrel: 24 in. (.308 Win.) or 26 in. (.300 Win. Mag., .338 Lapua Mag.), fluted, Hammer-forged precision stainless steel, free floating
Rifling Twist: RH 1:11 in. (.308 Win.), 1:10 in. (.300 Win. Mag.) , 1:9 in. (.338 Lapua Mag.)
Muzzle Device: Muzzle brake
Action/Barrel Finish: Olive drab
Stock: Ambidextrous folding stock; adjustable length of pull, butt plate height, comb height, cast-on, cast-off; aluminum and polymer construction
Stock Finish: Olive drab
Trigger: Fully adjustable for single or double-stage release between 3 and 5 lbs.
Optics Mount: One-piece aluminum rail
Magazine: Detachable box, 8- or 15-round (.308 Win.), 6- or 10-round (.300 Win. Mag.), 5- or 8-round (.338 Lapua Mag.)
Overall Length: 49 in.
Overall Length Folded Stock: 37.7 in.
Weight: 15 lb.
Maximum Range: 1,500 m
Features: Modular, multi-caliber bolt-action design, manual thumb safety, grip safety, aluminum alloy receiver, ambidextrous magazine release, barreled receiver is vibration isolated from the stock via elastomeric cushions, barrel may be changed in less than two minutes, each barrel remains true to the receiver's centerline.
MSRP: $6,999.00

FNAR Standard

Caliber: .308 Win. /7.62x51mm NATO
Action: Semiautomatic, gas-operated
Barrel: 16 in., fluted, hammer-forged, hard chromebore, target crown
Rifling Twist: RH 1:12 in.
Muzzle Device: None
Action/Barrel Finish: Olive drab
Stock: Fixed polymer stock, pistol grip, forend; adjustable length of pull, comb height, cast

Stock Finish: Matte black
Length of Pull: 14 in.
Trigger: Single-stage, non-adjustable, set at 4 lb.
Optics Mount: One-piece aluminum rail
Magazine: Detachable box, 10- or 20-round
Overall Length: 37.5 in.
Weight: 8.1 lb.
Features: Two-position safety, removable trigger group, accessory rails.
MSRP: $1,369.00

FNAR Heavy

Caliber: .308 Win. /7.62x51mm NATO
Action: Semiautomatic, gas-operated
Barrel: 20 in., fluted, hammer-forged, hard chrome bore, target crown
Rifling Twist: RH 1:12 in.
Muzzle Device: None
Action/Barrel Finish: Olive drab
Stock: Fixed polymer stock, pistol grip, forend; adjustable length of pull, comb height, cast

Stock Finish: Matte black
Length of Pull: 14 in.
Trigger: Single-stage, non-adjustable, set at 4 lb.
Optics Mount: One-piece aluminum rail
Magazine: Detachable box, 10- or 20-round
Overall Length: 41.5 in.
Weight: 8.7 lb.
Features: Two-position safety, removable trigger group, accessory rails.
MSRP: $1,800.00

MK 20 SSR

Caliber: 7.62x51mm NATO
Action: Selective fire, short-stroke gas piston, rotating bolt
Barrel: 20 in., hammer-forged, chrome lined
Muzzle Device: Flash hider optimized for suppressed fire
Action/Barrel Finish: Matte black
Stock: Fixed, polymer/aluminum construction, pistol grip, adjustable length of pull and comb height
Stock Finish: Flat Dark Earth (FDE)
Optics Mount: One-piece aluminum rail
Magazine: Detachable steel box, 10- or 20-round
Overall Length: 42.5 in.
Weight: 10.6 lb.

Accuracy: Sub-MOA at 1,000 yards
Features: Military sales only, hard-anodized monolithic aluminum receiver, composite polymer trigger module, accessory rails, 600 RPM cyclic rate, extended receiver rail for mounting in-line night vision and thermal devices, adjustable/removable folding front and rear back-up iron sights, barrel can be removed and replaced by the operator to facilitate cleaning and maintenance with negligible impact on previously established zero, ambidextrous selector lever and magazine release, charging handle may be mounted on right or left side, enlarged trigger guard, adjustable gas regulator for use with or without suppressor to maintain felt recoil.
MSRP: . . . . .not published

Fulton Armory (fulton-armory.com)

For over 25 years, Fulton Armory has been building semiauto M14, M1 Garand, M1 Carbine, and AR-15 / AR-10 rifles, receivers, and parts from original USGI receivers in their M1 Garand. Fulton Armory has faithfully recreated Semiautomatic versions of these, and M1 Carbine receivers that meet all USGI material, heat treat, and geometry specifications. Walt Kuleck and Clint McKee wrote the book–three books in fact–on US military rifles: *The M14 Complete Assembly Guide,* *The M1 Garand Complete Assembly Guide* and *The AR-15 Complete Assembly Guide.*

M21 Enhanced Sniper

Caliber: 7.62x51mm NATO/.308 Win.
Action: Semiautomatic, gas-operated pistol, rotating bolt
Barrel: 22 in., GI Contour, chrome-moly, national match or stainless Krieger, threaded muzzle
Rifling Twist: RH 1:11 in. (Krieger barrel)
Muzzle Device: Nation Match flash suppressor with bayonet lug
Action/Barrel Finish: Parkerized
Stock: New walnut, GI contour, adjustable Kydex cheekpiece
Stock Finish: Linseed oil

Trigger: Nation Match trigger
Optics Mount: Side mount Picatinny-style rail, adjustable hooded aperture rear/post front iron sights
Magazine: Detachable steel box, 10-round
Overall Length: 44.3 in.
Weight: 11.6 lb.
Accuracy: Under 1.5 MOA (with Hornady Match ammunition)
Maximum Range: 900 yd.
Features: Civilian version of the US military M14 with numerous custom features available. Enhanced with adjustable stock and match grade barrel.
MSRP: $3,200.00

M25 Peerless Sniper

Caliber: 7.62x51mm NATO/.308 Win.
Action: Semiautomatic, gas-operated pistol, rotating bolt
Barrel: 22 in., medium contour, stainless steel, national match, threaded muzzle
Rifling Twist: RH 1:10 in.
Muzzle Device: Nation Match flash suppressor with bayonet lug
Action/Barrel Finish: Parkerized
Stock: McMillan M2A with adjustable cheekpiece, fiberglass, glass bedded action
Stock Finish: Black

Trigger: Nation Match trigger
Optics Mount: Side mount Picatinny-style rail, adjustable hooded aperture rear/post front iron sights
Magazine: Detachable steel box, 10-round
Overall Length: 44.3 in.
Weight: 11.6 lb.
Accuracy: Sub MOA (with Hornady Match ammunition)
Maximum Range: 900 yd.
Features: Civilian version of the US military M14 with numerous custom features available. Enhanced with adjustable stock and match grade barrel.
MSRP: $4,400.00

M39 EMR
Caliber: 7.62x51mm NATO/.308 Win.
Action: Semiautomatic, gas-operated pistol, rotating bolt
Barrel: 22 in., medium contour, stainless steel, national match, threaded muzzle
Rifling Twist: RH 1:10 in.
Muzzle Device: Nation Match flash suppressor with bayonet lug
Action/Barrel Finish: Parkerized
Stock: Sage Tactical Chassis, Designated Marksman, aluminum, telescoping buttstock with adjustable cheek rest and butt pad
Stock Finish: Black
Trigger: Nation Match trigger
Optics Mount: Side mount Picatinny-style rail, adjustable hooded aperture rear/post front iron sights
Magazine: Detachable steel box, 10-round
Overall Length: 44.3 in.
Weight: 11 lb.
Accuracy: Under 1.5 MOA (with Hornady Match ammunition)
Maximum Range: 900 yd.
Features: M14 Service Rifle fitted with the Fulton Armory Scope Mount, installed in the Sage EBR tactical chassis system with a cut-away 12 o'clock rail to accommodate the scope mount.
MSRP: $3,725.00

Mk14 Mod 2 EBR
Caliber: 7.62x51mm NATO/.308 Win.
Action: Semiautomatic, gas-operated pistol, rotating bolt
Barrel: 22 in., medium contour, stainless steel, national match, threaded muzzle
Rifling Twist: RH 1:10 in.
Muzzle Device: Nation Match flash suppressor with bayonet lug
Action/Barrel Finish: Parkerized
Stock: Sage Tactical Chassis, Precision Marksman Rock Island (PMRI), aluminum, Magpul PRS2 buttstock
Stock Finish: Black
Trigger: Nation Match trigger
Optics Mount: Side mount Picatinny-style rail, adjustable hooded aperture rear/post front iron sights
Magazine: Detachable steel box, 10-round
Overall Length: 42.5 in.
Weight: 12 lb.
Accuracy: Under 1.5 MOA (with Hornady Match ammunition)
Maximum Range: 900 yd.
Features: M14 Service Rifle fitted a direct connect Vortex flash suppressor, and a front sight relocated to the gas cylinder lock (with dovetail), installed in the Sage PMRI (Precision Marksman Rock Island) tactical chassis system which includes an integrated Magpul PRS2 buttstock. A replica of the US Navy's battle rifle recently developed at Rock Island Arsenal.
MSRP: $3,400.00

Harrington & Richardson (hr1871.com)

For over 143 years H&R (Harrington & Richardson) has been making guns that America hunts and shoots with. The single-shot, break action models are simple to operate and accurate.

Ultra Varmint Rifle
Caliber: .223 Rem.
Action: Single-shot, break-action
Barrel: 24 in., bull
Muzzle Device: none
Action/Barrel Finish: Blued
Stock: Laminated American hardwood, Monte Carlo pistol grip, checkered, rubber recoil pad
Stock Finish: Cinnamon

Trigger: Standard
Optics Mount: Weaver-style rail, adjustable hooded aperture rear/post front iron sights
Magazine: n/a
Overall Length: 40 in.
Weight: 8 lb.
Features: Rugged break action operated via a lever, hammer must be cocked manually to fire.
MSRP: . . . .$381.00; $454.00 (thumbhole stock)

Heckler & Koch (HK) (hk-usa.com)

In 1948 after the end of World War II, three former Mauser engineers—Edmund Heckler, Alex Seidel, and Theodor Koch—salvaged what they could from the dismantled arms factory. By 1949 their company, which initially manufactured sewing machine parts and bicycle parts as well as other precision parts, became known as Heckler & Koch GmbH, or more commonly HK. The G3 rifle is perhaps one of the many renowned weapons manufactured by this company. To say this rifle is iconic is an understatement.

PSG1A1
Caliber: 7.62x51mm NATO
Action: Semiautomatic, roller-delayed blowback
Barrel: 25.5 in., heavyweight, polygonal rifling, free-floated, cold-hammer forged
Rifling Twist: RH 1:12 in.
Muzzle Device: None
Action/Barrel Finish: Black
Stock: Adjustable contoured pistol grip with a palm shelf; buttstock adjusts for length of pull, pivoting butt plate, and a vertically adjustable cheekpiece, polymer construction
Stock Finish: Black
Trigger: Factory set at 3 lb., adjustable trigger shoe

Optics Mount: Picatinny-style rail
Magazine: Detachable steel box, 5-, 10- or 20-round
Overall Length: 48.4 in.
Weight: 16.29 lb.
Accuracy: 1 MOA with match grade ammunition
Maximum Range: 800 m
Notes: Military or Law Enforcement sales only, a 12x Schmidt & Bender 3-12x50 telescopic sight is the standard optic, a repositioned "A1" cocking handle ensures no interference with optical sight mounting, service life of barrel is 15,000+ rounds, strengthened receiver to minimize torque, forward assist device for silent loading, accepts HK G3-type magazines.
MSRP: $10,000.00

MSG90 A2

Caliber: 7.62x51mm NATO
Action: Semiautomatic, roller-delayed blowback
Barrel: 23.6 in., heavyweight, polygonal rifling, free-floated, cold-hammer forged, threaded muzzle
Rifling Twist: RH 1:12 in.
Muzzle Device: Flash hider
Action/Barrel Finish: Black
Stock: Adjustable contoured pistol grip with a palm shelf; buttstock adjusts for length of pull, pivoting butt plate, and a vertically adjustable cheekpiece, polymer construction
Stock Finish: Black

Trigger: Factory set at 3 lb., adjustable trigger shoe
Optics Mount: Picatinny-style rail, adjustable front/rear iron sights
Magazine: Detachable steel box, 5-, 10- or 20-round
Overall Length: 46.6 in.
Weight: 15.4 lb.
Accuracy: Sub-MOA with match grade ammunition
Maximum Range: 800 m
Notes: Military or Law Enforcement sales only, similar to PSG1 but lighter weight and suppressor compatible, Anschutz T-way on the forend allows for installation of a bipod or other accessories.
MSRP: $7,000.00

G28

Caliber: 7.62x51mm NATO
Action: Semiautomatic, gas-operated, rotating bolt
Barrel: 16.5 in., cold hammer forged, threaded muzzle, free floated
Rifling Twist: RH 1:12 in.
Muzzle Device: Flash hider
Action/Barrel Finish: Matte black
Stock: HK G28 adjustable cheekpiece buttstock, Falcon Industries ERGO pistol grip
Stock Finish: Black/desert tan

Trigger: Two-stage
Optics Mount: Leupold Picatinny-style rail
Magazine: Detachable steel box, 10- and 20-round
Overall Length: 39.5 in.
Weight: 9.9 lb.
Accuracy: 1 MOA with match grade ammunition
Features: Originally developed from the fully automatic HK417, shipped with Leupold 3-9 VX-R Patrol 3-9x40mm scope, Blue Force Gear sling, shipped in Model 1720 Pelican case.
MSRP: $6,895.00

Howa (legacysports.com)

Since 1940 Howa has been building armament for the Japanese government. In the US they are known for producing accurate, well-made bolt-action rifles under the Howa name as well as brands like Weatherby, Mossberg, and others.

Hogue Kryptek Full Dip Package

Caliber: .223 Rem., .22-250 Rem., .308 Win.
Action: Bolt, short-action, push feed, 2 lug
Barrel: 20 in., hammer forged, heavy #6 contour
Rifling Twist: 1:10 in. (.308 Win.), or 1:12 in. (.223 Rem., .22-250 Rem.)
Muzzle Device: None
Action/Barrel Finish: Kryptek camo (Highlander, Raid, Typhon)

Stock: Hogue Overmolded synthetic, pillar bedded, SuperCell recoil pad
Stock Finish: Kryptek camo (Highlander, Raid, Typhon)
Trigger: HACT, two-stage match
Optics Mount: One-piece rail
Magazine: Detachable box magazine
Overall Length: 40.25 in.
Weight: 9.8 lb. (fluted barrels), 10 lbs. (non-fluted barrels)
Features: Nikko Stirling Targetmaster 4-16x44mm scope with illuminated reticle included.
MSRP: $840.00

Hogue Targetmaster Package

Caliber: .223 Rem., .22-250 Rem., .308 Win.
Action: Bolt, short-action, push feed, 2 lug
Barrel: 20 in., hammer forged, heavy #6 contour, fluted or non-fluted
Rifling Twist: 1:10 in. (.308 Win.), or 1:12 in. (.223 Rem., .22-250 Rem.)
Muzzle Device: None
Action/Barrel Finish: Blue

Stock: Hogue Overmolded synthetic, pillar bedded, SuperCell recoil pad
Stock Finish: Green or black
Trigger: HACT, two-stage match
Optics Mount: One-piece rail
Magazine: Hinged floorplate, 5-round
Overall Length: 40.25 in.
Weight: 9.8 lb. (fluted barrels), 10 lbs. (non-fluted barrels)
Features: Nikko Stirling Targetmaster 4-16x44mm scope included, accepts Howa detachable magazine conversion kit
MSRP: . . .$837.00 (fluted barrels), $787.00 (non-fluted barrels)

Hogue Heavy Barrel Varminter

Caliber: .223 Rem., .22-250 Rem., .308 Win.
Action: Bolt, short-action, push feed, 2 lug
Barrel: 20 in., hammer forged, heavy #6 contour, fluted or non-fluted
Rifling Twist: 1:10 in. (.308 Win.), or 1:12 in. (.223 Rem., .22-250 Rem.)
Muzzle Device: None
Action/Barrel Finish: Blue
Stock: Hogue Overmolded synthetic, pillar bedded, SuperCell recoil pad
Stock Finish: Green or black
Trigger: HACT, two-stage match
Optics Mount: One-piece rail
Magazine: Hinged floorplate, 5-round
Overall Length: 40.25 in.
Weight: 8.25 lb. (fluted barrels), 8.5 lbs. (non-fluted barrels)
Features: Accepts Howa detachable magazine conversion kit.
MSRP: . . . . $717.00 (fluted barrels), $631.00 (non-fluted barrels)

Talon Thumbhole Scope Package

Caliber: .223 Rem., .22-250 Rem., .243 Win., .308 Win.
Action: Bolt, short-action, push feed, 2 lug
Barrel: 20 in. or 24 in., hammer forged, heavy #6 contour, fluted or non-fluted
Rifling Twist: 1:10 in. (.243 Win., .308 Win.), or 1:12 in. (.223 Rem., .22-250 Rem.)
Muzzle Device: None
Action/Barrel Finish: Blue
Stock: Blackhawk Talon, synthetic construction, completely free floated
Stock Finish: Black, desert shadow camo
Trigger: HACT, two-stage match
Optics Mount: One-piece rail
Magazine: Hinged floorplate, 5-round
Overall Length: 40.38 in. (20-in. barrel), 44.38 in. (24-in. barrel)
Weight: 8.9 lb. (20-in. barrel), 9.1 lbs. (24-in. barrel)
Features: Uses Blackhawk recoil reducing stock, includes Nikko Stirling Nighteater 3-10x42mm scope, three-position safety.
MSRP: . . . $1,077.00 (fluted barrels), $993.00 (non-fluted barrels)

Axiom Varminter Scope Package

Caliber: .204 Ruger, .223 Rem., .22-250 Rem., .243 Win., .308 Win.
Action: Bolt, short-action, push feed, 2 lug
Barrel: 20 in. or 24 in., hammer forged, heavy #6 contour, fluted or non-fluted
Rifling Twist: 1:10 in. (.243 Win., .308 Win.), or 1:12 in. (.204 Ruger, .223 Rem., .22-250 Rem.)
Muzzle Device: None
Action/Barrel Finish: Blue
Stock: Blackhawk Axiom, synthetic construction, adjustable length of pull, completely free floated

Stock Finish: Black, desert shadow camo
Trigger: HACT, two-stage match
Optics Mount: One-piece rail
Magazine: Hinged floorplate, 5-round
Overall Length: 38.25-41.25 in. (20-in. barrel), 40.25-45.25 in. (24-in. barrel)
Weight: 10.9 lb. (20-in. barrel), 11.4 lbs. (24-in. barrel)
Features: Uses Blackhawk recoil reducing stock, includes Nikko Stirling Nighteater 3-10x42mm scope, three-position safety.
MSRP: . . .$1,136.00 (camo finish), $993.00 (black finish)

Classic Laminate Varminter

Caliber: .204 Ruger, .223 Rem., .22-250 Rem., .243 Win., .308 Win.
Action: Bolt, short-action, push feed, 2 lug
Barrel: 24 in., hammer forged, heavy #6 contour
Rifling Twist: 1:10 in. (.243 Win., .308 Win.), or 1:12 in. (.204 Ruger, .223 Rem., .22-250 Rem.)
Muzzle Device: None
Action/Barrel Finish: Blue or stainless

Stock: Laminated wood, cooling vents, free floated, dual sling swivel studs in beavertail forearm, raised cheekpiece
Stock Finish: Nutmeg or pepper
Trigger: HACT, two-stage match
Optics Mount: Drilled and tapped for base
Magazine: Hinged floorplate, 5-round
Overall Length: 44.75 in.
Weight: 9.8 lb.
Features: Accepts Howa detachable magazine conversion kit, three-position safety.
MSRP: . . . . $813.00 (blue), $918.00 (stainless)

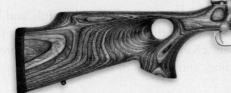

Classic Laminate Thumbhole Varminter

Caliber: .204 Ruger, .223 Rem., .22-250 Rem., .243 Win., .308 Win.
Action: Bolt, short-action, push feed, 2 lug
Barrel: 24 in., hammer forged, heavy #6 contour
Rifling Twist: 1:10 in. (.243 Win., .308 Win.), or 1:12 in. (.204 Ruger, .223 Rem., .22-250 Rem.)
Muzzle Device: None
Action/Barrel Finish: Blue or stainless

Stock: Laminated wood, thumbhole, cooling vents, free floated, dual sling swivel studs in beavertail forearm, raised cheekpiece
Stock Finish: Nutmeg or pepper
Trigger: HACT, two-stage match
Optics Mount: Drilled and tapped for base
Magazine: Hinged floorplate, 5-round
Overall Length: 44.75in.
Weight: 9.8 lb.
Features: Features: Accepts Howa detachable magazine conversion kit, three-position safety.
MSRP: . . . . $813.00 (blue), $918.00 (stainless)

IWI (israel-weapon.com)

IWI was formerly known as Israel Military Industries Ltd. The Galil rifle and its variants are produced by IWI. The Galil rifle was designed by Yisrael Galil and Yaacov Lior in the late 1960s and since 1972 has been in service with Israeli military. The Galil has similar design features as the Soviet AK-47 and Finnish RK 62 rifles.

Galil Sniper SA

Caliber: 7.62x51mm NATO
Action: Selective fire, gas-driven piston, rotating bolt
Barrel: 23 in.
Rifling Twist: RH 1:12 in.
Muzzle Device: Muzzle brake
Action/Barrel Finish: Matte black
Stock: Folding, polymer/aluminum construction, pistol grip with adjustable hand support, monopod
Stock Finish: Black

Trigger: Two-stage
Optics Mount: One-piece aluminum rail with Mil-Spec 10x scope, adjustable front/rear iron sights
Magazine: Detachable steel box, 25-round
Overall Length: 43.3 in.
Overall Length Folded: 33.1 in.
Weight: 16.5 lb.
Maximum Range: 300-500 m
Features: Military sales only, foldable bipod, Muzzle brake reduces recoil and movement by 30 percent.
MSRP: . . . . .n/a

Kimber (kimberamerica.com)

Kimber originated in Oregon in 1979 and has since evolved into a manufacturer of high-quality 1911 pistols and big game hunting rifles. Kimber's tactical rifles are built for real-world law enforcement and military use with models that have specialized features for specific applications. All have match grade barrels, chambers, and triggers. Each features a trued bolt face, hand-finished chamber, hand-lapped lugs, custom glass bedding, and McMillan stock.

Model 84M LPT (Light Police Tactical)
Caliber: .223 Rem., .308 Win.
Action: Bolt, short, fluted, control feed, 2 lug
Barrel: 20 in., fluted, bull contour, match grade chamber, free floating, crowned
Rifling Twist: RH 1:9 in. (.223 Rem.), RH 1:12 in. (.308 Win.)
Muzzle Device: None
Action/Barrel Finish: Matte black
Stock: Laminated wood, pillar bedding, glass bedding, Pachmayr Decelerator recoil pad
Stock Finish: Black epoxy finish
Length of Pull: 13.7 in.
Trigger: Adjustable, factory set at 3-3.5 lb.
Optics Mount: One-piece 1913 Mil-Spec Picatinny rail
Magazine: Internal box, 6-round (.233 Rem.), 5-round (.308 Win.)
Overall Length: 41.2 in.
Weight: 8 lb.
Features: Three-position Model 70-type safety, enlarged bolt handle, front swivel stub for bipod, Mauser-style claw extractor.
MSRP: $1,495.00

Model 8400 Patrol
Caliber: .308 Win.
Action: Bolt, short, fluted, control feed, 2 lug
Barrel: 20 in., fluted, heavy sporter contour, match grade chamber, free floating, crowned
Rifling Twist: RH 1:12 in.
Muzzle Device: None
Action/Barrel Finish: Matte black
Stock: Laminated wood, pillar bedding, glass bedding, Pachmayr Decelerator recoil pad
Stock Finish: Black epoxy finish
Length of Pull: 13.7 in.
Trigger: Adjustable, factory set at 3-3.5 lb.
Optics Mount: One-piece 1913 Mil-Spec Picatinny rail
Magazine: Internal box, 5-round
Overall Length: 39.5 in.
Weight: 8.5 lb.
Features: Three-position Model 70-type safety, enlarged bolt handle, front swivel stub for bipod, Mauser-style claw extractor.
MSRP: $1,495.00

Model 8400 Police Tactical

Caliber: .308 Win., .300 Win. Mag.
Action: Bolt, short or long, fluted (.308 Win.), control feed, 2 lug
Barrel: 20 in. (.308 Win.) or 26 in. (.300 Win. Mag.), fluted, bull contour, match grade chamber, free floating, crowned
Rifling Twist: RH 1:12 in. (.308 Win.), RH 1:10 in. (.300 Win. Mag.)
Muzzle Device: None
Action/Barrel Finish: Matte black
Stock: Laminated wood, pillar bedding, glass bedding, Pachmayr Decelerator recoil pad
Stock Finish: Black epoxy finish
Length of Pull: 13.7 in.
Trigger: Factory set at 3-3.5 lb.
Optics Mount: One-piece 1913 Mil-Spec Picatinny rail
Magazine: Internal box, 5-round (.308 Win.) or 4-round (.300 Win. Mag.)
Overall Length: 43.5 in.
Weight: 8.7 lb.
Features: Three-position Model 70-type safety, enlarged bolt handle, front swivel stub for bipod, Mauser-style claw extractor.
MSRP: $1,495.00

Model 8400 Tactical

Caliber: .308 Win.
Action: Bolt, short, control feed, 2 lug
Barrel: 24 in., bull contour, match grade chamber, free floating, crowned
Rifling Twist: RH 1:12 in.
Muzzle Device: None
Action/Barrel Finish: Matte black
Stock: McMillan A-5 synthetic, glass bedding, Pachmayr Decelerator recoil pad
Stock Finish: Black/gray/green marble, textured gripping surfaces
Length of Pull: 13.6 in.
Trigger: Adjustable, factory set at 3-3.5 lb.
Optics Mount: One-piece 1913 Mil-Spec Picatinny rail
Magazine: Internal box, 5-round
Overall Length: 43.2 in.
Weight: 9.5 lb.
Accuracy: Sub-½ MOA 3-shot group
Features: Three-position Model 70-type safety, enlarged bolt handle, front swivel stub for bipod, Mauser-style claw extractor, hand-lapped lugs, squared bolt face.
MSRP: $1,971.00

Model 8400 Advanced Tactical (camo, black)

Caliber: .308 Win., .300 Win. Mag.
Action: Bolt, short or long, control feed, 2 lug
Barrel: 24 in. (.308 Win.) or 26 in. (.300 Win. Mag.), bull contour, match grade chamber, free floating, crowned
Rifling Twist: RH 1:12 in. (.308 Win.), RH 1:10 in. (.300 Win. Mag.)
Muzzle Device: None
Action/Barrel Finish: Desert tan
Stock: McMillan A-5 synthetic, glass bedding, adjustable length of pull and cheekpiece
Stock Finish: Desert camo, stippled gripping surfaces

Length of Pull: 13.7 in.
Trigger: Adjustable, factory set at 3-3.5 lb.
Optics Mount: One-piece 1913 Mil-Spec Picatinny rail
Magazine: Internal box, 5-round (.308 Win.) or 4-round (.300 Win. Mag.)
Overall Length: 43.2 in.
Weight: 9.8 lb. (.308 Win.) or 10.3 lb. (.300 Win. Mag.)
Accuracy: Sub-½ MOA 3-shot group
Features: Three-position Model 70-type safety, enlarged bolt handle, front swivel stub for bipod, Mauser-style claw extractor.
MSRP: $2,651.00

Knight's Armament (knightarmco.com)

Knight's Armament Company in Titusville, Florida, was founded as a research and development facility more than 30 years ago and has since evolved into a weapons manufacturer offering complete weapon systems, modular accessories, and Knight Vision electro-optics.

SR-15E3 IWS LPR

Caliber: 5.56 NATO
Action: Semiautomatic, gas impingement
Barrel: 18 in., stainless steel, threaded muzzle
Rifling Twist: RH 1:7 in.
Muzzle Device: A2 style flash suppressor
Action/Barrel Finish: Matte black
Stock: Adjustable position
Stock Finish: Matte black

Trigger: Two stage match
Optic Mount: Full length rail on upper receiver
Magazine: Detachable box, 30-round
Overall Length: 35 in. (stock retracted)
Weight: 7.4 lb.
Features: Designed a Light Precision Rifle (LPR) for either competition or LE use. Ambidextrous controls. Multi lug improved E3 bolt.
MSRP $2,499.00

M110

Caliber: 7.62mm NATO/.308 Win.
Action: Semiautomatic, gas impingement
Barrel: 20 in., 5R cut rifling, match grade alloy steel, chrome plated
Rifling Twist: RH 1:11 in.
Muzzle Device: 762QDC flash hider
Action/Barrel Finish: Matte desert tan
Stock: A2 style buttstock and pistol grip, free floated aluminum handguard
Stock Finish: Matte desert tan

Trigger: Two-stage Match
Optic Mount: Full length Picatinny Rail on upper receiver
Magazine: detachable box, 20-round
Overall Length: 46.8 in. (stock retracted)
Weight: 16 lb.
Features: Abundant MIL-STD-1913 rail mounting capabilities, effective sound suppressor system, ambidextrous controls, URX (Upper Receiver Extending) free-float handguard.
MSRP: $17,030.00

M110K1

Caliber: 7.62mm NATO/.308 Win.
Action: Semiautomatic, gas impingement
Barrel: 16 in., 5R cut rifling, match grade alloy steel, chrome plated
Rifling Twist: RH 1:11 in.
Muzzle Device: NAMS muzzle brake
Action/Barrel Finish: Matte desert tan
Stock: 10-position adjustable sliding buttstock, A2 style pistol grip, free-floated aluminum handguard
Stock Finish: Matte desert tan
Trigger: Two-stage Match

Optic Mount: Full length Picatinny Rail on upper receiver
Magazine: detachable box, 20-round
Overall Length: 35.8 in. (stock retracted)
Weight: 8.9 lb.
Features: Compact variant of the full-size M110 featuring a 16 in., URXIII system, ambidextrous controls, carbon cutter bolt carrier, 45° offset micro folding sights.
MSRP: $17,030.00

SR-25 Enhanced Combat Rifle (ECR)
Caliber: 7.62mm NATO/.308 Win.
Action: Semiautomatic, gas impingement
Barrel: 20 in., 5R cut rifling, match grade alloy steel
Rifling Twist: RH 1:11 in.
Muzzle Device: 762QDC flash hider
Action/Barrel Finish: Matte black
Stock: Magpul Adjustable position buttstock, A2-style pistol grip, free-floated aluminum handguard
Stock Finish: Black
Trigger: Two-stage Match
Optic Mount: Full length Picatinny Rail on upper receiver
Magazine: detachable box, 10-round
Overall Length: 39.5 in. (stock retracted)
Weight: 10.4 lb.
Features: Allows use of 762QDC suppressors, boasts an enlarged Ejection Port and Carbon Cutter bolt carrier which allow for improved reliability when firing suppressed or in less than ideal environments, ambidextrous controls, URX (Upper Receiver Extending) free-float handguard, 45° offset sight.
MSRP: $5,719.00

LaRue Tactical (laruetactical.com)

LaRue Tactical is known world-wide for hyper-accurate 7.62mm and 5.56mm rifle systems. They are loacted in Leander, Texas. Don't mess with Texas.

OBR 5.56 20 Inch
Caliber: 5.56mm NATO/.223 Rem.
Action: Semiautomatic, gas impingement
Barrel: 20 in., polygonal rifling
Rifling Twist: RH 1:8 in.
Muzzle Device: A2 flash hider
Action/Barrel Finish: Matte black
Stock: A2-style buttstock, LaRue medium A-PEG Grip pistol grip, free-floated aluminum handguard
Stock Finish: Black
Trigger: Geissele SSA Combat Triggers, two-stage, average 4.5lb pull weight
Optic Mount: Full-length Picatinny Rail on upper receiver
Magazine: detachable box, 20-round
Weight: 8 lb.
Accuracy: Sub MOA (with Federal GMM 77-grain ammo)
Effective Range: 800 m
Features: both the upper and lower are CNC-machined from billet 7075-T6, for the optimum fit and consistency, XTRAXN is a proprietary chamber feature added to reduce frictional forces caused by pressure-expanded cartridge cases bearing against chamber walls. Facilitates reliable extraction through a wide range of temperature / chamber pressure extremes. XTRAXN extends extractor life, while having no effect on the firearm's accuracy.
MSRP: $2,245.00

OBR Complete 7.62 Rifle

Caliber: 7.62mm NATO/.308 Win.
Action: Semiautomatic, gas impingement
Barrel: 16 in., stainless steel
Rifling Twist: RH 1:10 in.
Muzzle Device: A2-style flash hider
Action/Barrel Finish: Matte black
Stock: A2-style buttstock, LaRue medium A-PEG Grip pistol grip, free-floated aluminum handguard
Stock Finish: Black
Trigger: Geissele SSA Combat Triggers, two-stage, average 4.5lb pull weight
Optic Mount: Full length Picatinny Rail on upper receiver
Magazine: detachable box, 20-round
Overall Length: 37.5 in.
Weight: 9.3 lb.

Accuracy: 1 MOA
Effective Range: 800 m
Features: OBR (Optimized Battle Rifle) was built using a newly designed upper-receiver platform, combined with a lower. Both the upper and lower are CNC-machined from billet, for the optimum fit and consistency. Machined from billet 7075-T6, the receiver components are designed with more material in critical areas to alleviate known issues of weakness in 7.62 platforms and to stiffen the receiver. Bolts and Bolt Carriers are hand-polished hard-chrome with max-staked carrier keys. The carrier key contact areas are designed for zero gas leakage. XTRAXN is a proprietary chamber feature added to reduce frictional forces caused by pressure-expanded cartridge cases bearing against chamber walls. Eighteen and 20 in. barrel models available.
MSRP: $3,370.00

LMT (lewismachine.net)

LMT (Lewis Machine & Tool Company) was founded in 1980 to provide the US Military, LE, and government agencies with quality weapons, components, and modular weapons systems.

.308 Modular Weapon System (MWS)

Caliber: 7.62mm NATO/.308 Win.
Action: Semiautomatic, gas impingement
Barrel: 16 in., chrome lined
Rifling Twist: RH 1:10 in.
Muzzle Device: A2-style flash hider
Action/Barrel Finish: Matte black
Stock: SOPMOD buttstock, pistol grip, free-floated aluminum handguard
Stock Finish: Black

Trigger: Two-stage, 9 lb. pull weight
Optic Mount: Full length Picatinny Rail on upper receiver
Magazine: detachable box, 20-round
Overall Length: 35 in. (collapsed stock)
Weight: 9.3 lb.
Features: Complete weapon ships with a sling, operator's manual, tactical adjustable rear sight, tactical front sight, one twenty-round magazine, two heavy duty push button swivels, torque wrench/driver and three rail panels.
MSRP: $3,002.95

LWRC International (lwrci.com)

LWRC International, LLC was founded to pursue the development of a short-stroke gas-piston operated version of the AR15/M16/M4 family of weapons. Their research and development activities have focused on eliminating the inherent shortcomings in the direct impingement operating system. These efforts have resulted in the M6 short-stroke, gas-piston operated rifles and carbines, which improve on the direct impingement system by operating cleaner, quieter, and with greater accuracy and reliability, and longer service life.

R.E.P.R.

Caliber: 7.62mm NATO/.308 Win.
Action: Semiautomatic, short-stroke gas-piston operating system
Barrel: 20 in.
Rifling Twist: RH 1:10 in.
Muzzle Device: A2-style flash hider
Action/Barrel Finish: Black, Flat Dark Earth, Olive Drab Green, Patriot Brown
Stock: Magpul PRS buttstock, pistol grip, free-floated aluminum handguard
Stock Finish: Black
Trigger: Two-stage
Optic Mount: Full length Picatinny Rail on upper receiver

Magazine: detachable box, 20-round
Overall Length: 41.5 in.
Weight: 11.3 lb.
Features: Rapid Engagement Precision Rifle (R.E.P.R.) utilizes a patented self-regulating, short-stroke gas-piston operating system, ensuring unparalleled reliability in the harshest theaters of operation. A side-mounted charging handle allows the shooter to perform reloads without removing their eyes from the target, and prevents any gas blowback to the face when using a suppressor. The ARM-R rails are easily removable and reinstalled with a hex key and provide a 100 percent return to zero for optics and lasers. 16 in. barrel variant available.
MSRP: $3,950.00

Mossberg (Mossberg.com)

Using the ATR as a platform, Mossberg's Night Train comes fully equipped for tactical duty with bipod, scope, and a button rifled barrel. The fully adjustable LBA (Lightening Bolt Action) trigger system adjust down to a two-pound pull. The trigger is creep-free.

ATR Night Train

Caliber: .308 Win.
Action: Bolt, short-action, push feed, 2 lug
Barrel: 22 in., fluted, free floated
Rifling Twist: 1:10 in.
Muzzle Device: None
Action/Barrel Finish: Matte black
Stock: Synthetic
Stock Finish: Black, Multi-cam camo, OD green

Trigger: Lightening Bolt, externally adjustable
Optics Mount: Mounted Picatinny rail
Magazine: Hinged floorplate, 4-round
Overall Length: 42 in.
Weight: 8.5 lb.
Features: Bipod, 4-16x50mm scope with sunshade.
MSRP: $615.00

MVP Predator

Caliber: .223 Rem./5.56mm NATO
Action: Bolt, short-action, push feed, 2 lug
Barrel: 16.3 in., bull, free floated, threaded
Rifling Twist: 1:9 in.
Muzzle Device: Flash suppressor
Action/Barrel Finish: Matte black
Stock: Textured

Stock Finish: Black
Trigger: Lightening Bolt, externally adjustable
Optics Mount: Mounted Picatinny rail
Magazine: Detachable AR box-magazines
Overall Length: 36.5 in.
Weight: 8 lb.
Features: Compatible with AR-15 magazines, comes with 3-9x40mm scope with sunshade.
MSRP: $863.00; $863.00 (7.52mm)

MVP Patrol

Caliber: .223 Rem./5.56mm NATO
Action: Bolt, short-action, push feed, 2 lug
Barrel: 18.5 in., bull, fluted, free floated
Rifling Twist: 1:9 in.
Muzzle Device: None
Action/Barrel Finish: Matte black
Stock: Laminate

Stock Finish: Black/green
Trigger: Lightening Bolt, externally adjustable
Optics Mount: Mounted Picatinny rail
Magazine: Detachable AR box-magazines
Overall Length: 37.5 in.
Weight: 8 lb.
Features: Compatible with AR-15 magazines, comes with 3-9x40mm scope with sunshade.
MSRP: . . . . . . $758.00; $758.00 (20 in. barrel, no scope)

MVP Thunder Ranch

Caliber: .223 Rem./5.56mm NATO
Action: Bolt, short-action, push feed, 2 lug
Barrel: 18.5 in., bull, fluted, free floated, threaded
Rifling Twist: 1:9 in.
Muzzle Device: None
Action/Barrel Finish: Matte black
Stock: Synthetic
Stock Finish: OD green
Trigger: Lightening Bolt, externally adjustable
Optics Mount: Mounted Picatinny rail
Magazine: Detachable 10-round box
Overall Length: 37.5 in.
Weight: 8.2 lb.
Features: Compatible with AR-15 magazines, comes with 3-9x40mm scope with sunshade.
MSRP: $748.00

MVP Flex

Caliber: .223 Rem./5.56mm NATO
Action: Bolt, short-action, push feed, 2 lug
Barrel: 18.5 in., bull, fluted, free floated, 11° crown
Rifling Twist: 1:9 in.
Muzzle Device: None
Action/Barrel Finish: Matte black
Stock: Synthetic Flex, adjustable 6-position
Stock Finish: black
Trigger: Lightening Bolt, externally adjustable
Optics Mount: Mounted Picatinny rail
Magazine: Detachable 10-round box
Overall Length: 35.8 in.
Weight: 7 lb.
Features: Compatible with AR-15 magazines, comes with illuminated reticle 3-9x32mm scope with sunshade.
MSRP: . .$1,142.00; $987.00 (5.56mm or 7.62mm without scope, black or tan)

MVP Varmint

Caliber: .223 Rem./5.56mm NATO
Action: Bolt, short-action, push feed, 2 lug
Barrel: 24 in., bull, fluted, free floated, threaded or non-threaded
Rifling Twist: 1:9 in.
Muzzle Device: None
Action/Barrel Finish: Matte black
Stock: Laminate
Stock Finish: Black/green
Trigger: Lightening Bolt, externally adjustable
Optics Mount: Mounted Picatinny rail
Magazine: Detachable AR box-magazines
Overall Length: 43 in.
Weight: 9.2 lb.
Features: Compatible with AR-15 magazines, comes with 4-16x50mm scope with sunshade and bipod.
MSRP: $897.00

Olympic Arms (olyarms.com)

Olympic Arms, Inc. was founded by Robert C. Schuetz, and began as Schuetzen Gun Works (SGW) in 1956, manufacturing barrels in Colorado Springs, Colorado. Olympic Arms was the first manufacturer to introduce features now seen as commonplace on the AR-15 platform. It was the first company to produce flat-top upper receivers, free-floating aluminum hand guards, pistol caliber conversions, and AR-15-based pistols. Every major component or part is produced in-house.

UM-1P

Caliber: 5.56mm NATO/.223 Rem.
Action: Semiautomatic, gas impingement
Barrel: 24 in., bull ultra match, 416 stainless steel
Rifling Twist: RH 1:10 in. (optional 1:8 in.)
Muzzle Device: none
Action/Barrel Finish: Matte black
Stock: A2-style buttstock, ERGO tactical pistol grip, free-floated aluminum tube handguard
Stock Finish: Black
Trigger: Williams Set Trigger
Optic Mount: Picatinny Rail on upper receiver
Magazine: detachable box, 20-round
Overall Length: 42.3 in.
Weight: 9.5 lb.
Features: Premium target model with AC4 pneumatic recoil buffer, Harris S-series bi-pod installed, ERing system, hand selected premium receivers.
MSRP: $1,623.70

K8

Caliber: 5.56mm NATO/.223 Rem.
Action: Semiautomatic, gas impingement
Barrel: 20 in., bull, button rifled, 416 stainless steel
Rifling Twist: RH 1:9 in. (optional 1:8 in.)
Muzzle Device: none
Action/Barrel Finish: Matte black
Stock: A2-style buttstock and pistol grip, free-floated aluminum tube handguard

Stock Finish: Black
Trigger: Two-stage
Optic Mount: Picatinny Rail on upper receiver
Magazine: detachable box, 20-round
Overall Length: 38.5 in.
Weight: 8.5 lb.
Features: Precision model with optic-ready upper.
MSRP: . . $908.70; $967.20 (.204 Ruger); $1,033.50 (6.8 SPC)

Patriot Ordnance Factory (pof-usa.com)

POF (Patriot Ordnance Factory) builds AR rifles with a regulated short-stroke gas piston operating system allowing the weapon to run cooler and cleaner. Through careful operating rod/piston geometry and regulated gas pressure, all POF rifles and carbines are properly timed and bolt speeds are precisely controlled.

P308 Gen 4

Caliber: 7.62mm NATO/.308 Win.
Action: Semiautomatic, short-stroke gas-piston operating system
Barrel: 20 in.
Rifling Twist: RH 1:10 in.
Muzzle Device: Triple port muzzle brake
Action/Barrel Finish: Black anodized, NP3 coated, OD Cerakote
Stock: Magpul STR/CTR polymer buttstock, Magpul MOE pistol grip, free-floated aluminum monolithic handguard

Stock Finish: Black
Trigger: Single-stage
Optic Mount: Picatinny Rail on upper receiver
Magazine: Magpul PMAG detachable box, 20-round
Overall Length: 42.3 in.(stock extended)
Weight: 8.9 lb.
Features: E² dual extraction technology, ambidextrous bolt catch and magazine release button, receiver tension screws, adjustable gas system, oversized heat sink barrel nut, ETP (Enhanced Trigger Placement) for better trigger control.
MSRP: $3,269.99

PTR Industries (ptr91.com)

PTR builds top quality HK-91 "clone" rifles on original HK tooling and designs from Fabrica Militar of Portugal. PTR produces every part for PTR rifles in the United States.

PTR MSG91
Caliber: 7.62mm NATO/.308 Win.
Action: Semiautomatic, delayed blowback roller-lock system
Barrel: 18 in., match grade, fluted, bull contour
Muzzle Device: muzzle brake
Action/Barrel Finish: Black
Stock: Magpul PRS2 polymer buttstock, H&K Navy type pistol grip, aluminum handguard

Stock Finish: Black
Trigger: Two-stage
Optic Mount: Picatinny Rail
Magazine: Detachable box, 20-round
Overall Length: 42.3 in. (stock extended)
Weight: 12 lb.
Features: Civilian version of famed H&K 91 combat rifle in precision configuration with Harris bi-pod.
MSRP: $2,125.00

PTR MSG91SS
Caliber: 7.62mm NATO/.308 Win.
Action: Semiautomatic, delayed blowback roller-lock system
Barrel: 20 in., match grade, fluted, bull contour, free floated, fully crowned
Muzzle Device: none
Action/Barrel Finish: Black
Stock: Magpul PRS2 polymer buttstock, H&K Navy type pistol grip, aluminum handguard
Stock Finish: Black

Trigger: Two-stage
Optic Mount: Picatinny Rail
Magazine: Detachable box, 20-round
Overall Length: 43.3 in. (stock extended)
Weight: 13 lb.
Features: Civilian version of famed H&K 91 combat rifle in precision configuration with Harris bi-pod, free-floated 20 in. barrel.
MSRP: $2,770.00

PTR MSR

Caliber: 7.62mm NATO/.308 Win.
Action: Semiautomatic, delayed blowback roller-lock system
Barrel: 18 in., match grade, tapered contour, free floated, fully crowned
Muzzle Device: none
Action/Barrel Finish: Earth tone
Stock: Standard fixed polymer buttstock with cheek riser, H&K Navy type pistol grip, aluminum handguard
Stock Finish: Earth tone
Trigger: Two-stage
Optic Mount: Picatinny Rail
Magazine: Detachable box, 5-round
Overall Length: 39.5 in.
Weight: 9.5 lb.
Features: Civilian version of famed H&K 91 combat rifle in MSR configuration with free-floated 18 in. barrel.
MSRP: $1,200.00

Rangemaster Precision Arms (rangemasterprecisionarms.com)

Formerly known as RPA International, it was reorganized in 2011 as Rangemaster Precision Arms. Rangemaster Precision Arms has been building high quality small arms in Kent in the UK for some 40 years. They produce target, hunting and tactical rifles using their proprietary RPA actions; the RPA Quadlock action is a single-shot only, and the RPA Quadlite is used in magazine rifles.

Rangemaster .50 Rifle

Caliber: .50 BMG
Action: Bolt, RPA 4-lug Quadlite action, short, push feed, 4 lug
Barrel: 32 in., fluted, free floating
Rifling Twist: RH 1:15 in.
Muzzle Device: Muzzle brake, 6 ports
Action/Barrel Finish: Matte black
Stock: Folding, composite construction, monopod
Stock Finish: Black
Trigger: Adjustable, factory set at 3.3 lb.
Optics Mount: Picatinny rail
Magazine: Detachable steel box, 5-round
Overall Length: 60 in.
Overall Length Folded: 48 in.
Weight: 37.3 lb.
Maximum Range: 2,000 m
Features: 1.5 millisecond lock time, two-position safety, oversized bolt handle, multiple steel sling swivel mounting points, includes bipod.
MSRP: $8,740.00

Rangemaster .338 Rifle

Caliber: .338 Lapua Mag.
Action: Bolt, RPA 4-lug Quadlite action, short, push feed, 4 lug
Barrel: 28 in., fluted, free floating
Rifling Twist: RH 1:10 in.
Muzzle Device: Muzzle brake, 6 ports
Action/Barrel Finish: Matte black
Stock: Folding, composite construction, monopod
Stock Finish: Black

Trigger: Adjustable, factory set at 3.3 lb.
Optics Mount: Picatinny rail
Magazine: Detachable steel box, 5-round
Overall Length: 51.5 in.
Overall Length Folded: 41.5 in.
Weight: 18.9 lb.
Maximum Range: 1,500 m
Features: 1.5 millisecond lock time, two-position safety, oversized bolt handle, multiple steel sling swivel mounting points, includes bipod.
MSRP: $7,846.00

Rangemaster 7.62

Caliber: .308 Win./7.62x51 NATO
Action: Bolt, RPA 4-lug Quadlite action, short, push feed, 4 lug
Barrel: 26 in., fluted, free floating
Rifling Twist: RH 1:12 in.
Muzzle Device: Muzzle brake, 6 ports
Action/Barrel Finish: Matte black
Stock: Folding, composite construction, monopod
Stock Finish: Black

Trigger: Adjustable, factory set at 3.3 lb.
Optics Mount: Picatinny rail
Magazine: Detachable steel box, 10-round
Overall Length: 48.5 in.
Overall Length Folded: 37.7 in.
Weight: 16.2 lb.
Maximum Range: 1000 m
Features: 1.5 millisecond lock time, two-position safety, oversized bolt handle, multiple steel sling swivel mounting points, includes bipod.
MSRP: $6,773.00

Rangemaster 7.62 STBY

Caliber: .308 Win./7.62x51 NATO
Action: Bolt, RPA 4-lug Quadlite action, short, push feed, 4 lug
Barrel: 16 in., fluted, free floating
Rifling Twist: RH 1:10 in.
Muzzle Device: Muzzle brake, 6 ports
Action/Barrel Finish: Matte black
Stock: Folding, composite construction, monopod
Stock Finish: Black
Trigger: Adjustable, factory set at 3.3 lb.
Optics Mount: Picatinny rail
Magazine: Detachable steel box, 10-round
Overall Length: 37 in.
Overall Length Folded: 28 in.
Weight: 14.5 lb.
Maximum Range: 200–500 m with subsonic ammunition
Features: 1.5 millisecond lock time, two-position safety, oversized bolt handle, multiple steel sling swivel mounting points, includes bipod.

Rangemaster Interceptor Multi-Shot

Caliber: .243 Win., .308 Win./7.62x51 NATO, 7mm-08 Rem.
Action: Bolt, RPA 4-lug Quadlite action, short, push feed, 4 lug
Barrel: 26 in., free floating, threaded muzzle
Rifling Twist: 1:8 in. (.243 Win.), 1:8.5 in. (7mm-08 Rem.), 1:12 in. (.308 Win./7.62x51 NATO)
Muzzle Device: None
Action/Barrel Finish: Matte black
Stock: Fixed, composite construction, adjustable length of pull and comb height
Stock Finish: Black
Trigger: Adjustable, factory set at 3.3 lb.
Optics Mount: Picatinny rail
Magazine: Detachable steel box, 3-round (flush fit) or 10-round
Overall Length: 46 in.
Weight: 11 lb.
Features: 1.5 millisecond lock time, two-position safety, oversized bolt handle, multiple steel sling swivel mounting points.

Remington (remington.com)

Nearly since the time metallic cartridges were invented, Remington has been building centerfire rifles. The Rolling Block single-shot rifle started it off in the late 19th century. The Model 700 and 40-X are legendary for their strength, reliability, and accuracy. The Model 700 is the canvas that many custom rifle builders use to start a custom rifle. It has also been used by the US military in sniper rifles including the M40A1, M40A3, and the M24. The MSR and MX2012 are Remington's latest variants that use the Model 700 action. Law enforcement has also employed Model 700 and Model 40-X actions. Model 40-X actions have been a staple in benchrest competitions for decades. The difference between the Model 700 and Model 40-X is the 40-X has a stiffer receiver and is not cut out for a magazine as is the Model 700. The 40-X comes in single shot and repeater variants from Remington's Custom shop. Repeater 40-Xs use a stripper clip.

Model 700 Sendero SF II

Caliber: 7mm Rem. Mag., .300 Win. Mag., .300 Rem. Ultra Mag.
Action: Bolt, long-action, push feed, 2 lug
Barrel: 26 in., 416 stainless, heavy contour, fluted, free floated, target-style crown
Rifling Twist: 1:9.25 in. (7mm Rem. Mag.), 1:10 in. (.300 Win. Mag., .300 Rem. Ultra Mag.)
Muzzle Device: None
Action/Barrel Finish: Stainless
Stock: H-S Precision, aramid fiber reinforced, aluminum bedding, beavertail forend, ambidextrous finger grooves, palm swell

Stock Finish: Black with gray webbing
Maximum Length of Pull: 13.3 in.
Trigger: X-Mark Pro, externally adjustable, factory Set at 3.5 lb.
Optics Mount: Drilled and tapped for base
Magazine: Hinged floorplate, 3-round
Overall Length: 45.7 in.
Weight: 8.5 lb.
Notes: Long-range hunting rifle
MSRP: $1,451.00

Model 700 SPS Tactical AAC-SD

Caliber: .308 Win.
Action: Bolt, short-action, push feed, 2 lug
Barrel: 20 in., heavy contour, 5/8x24 threaded muzzle
Rifling Twist: 1:10 in.
Muzzle Device: None
Action/Barrel Finish: Matte blue
Stock: Hogue Overmolded, pillar bedded
Stock Finish: Ghillie green

Maximum Length of Pull: 14 in.
Trigger: X-Mark Pro, externally adjustable, factory set at 3.5 lb.
Optics Mount: Drilled and tapped for base
Magazine: Hinged floorplate, 5-round
Overall Length: 39.6 in.
Weight: 7.3 lb.
Features: Accepts AAC and other 5/8-24 threaded flash hiders, muzzle brake and suppressors.
MSRP: $817.00

Model 700 Target Tactical

Caliber: .308 Win.
Action: Bolt, short-action, push feed, 2 lug
Barrel: 26 in., carbon steel, triangular barrel profile with ¼-in. counter-bore,
Rifling Twist: 1:11.25 in., 5R hammer forged rifling
Muzzle Device: None
Action/Barrel Finish: Matte blue
Stock: Bell & Carlson Medalist Varmint/Tactical, composite material construction, adjustable comb and length of pull

Stock Finish: OD green
Maximum Length of Pull: 14 in.
Trigger: X-Mark Pro, externally adjustable, factory set at 3.5 lb.
Optics Mount: Drilled and tapped for bases
Magazine: Steel hinged floorplate, 4-round
Overall Length: 47.5 in.
Weight: 11.7 lb.
Features: Rifling based on M24, tactical bolt knob.
MSRP: $2,117.00

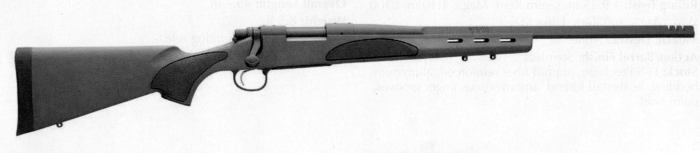

Model 700 VTR

Caliber: .204 Ruger, .223 Rem., .22-250 Rem., .243 Win., .308 Win.
Action: Bolt, short-action, push feed, 2 lug
Barrel: 22 in., carbon steel, triangular contour, target crown
Rifling Twist: 1:9 in. (.223 Rem.), 1:14 in. (.22-250 Rem.), 1:9.5 in. (.243 Win.), 1:12 in. (.204 Ruger, .308 Win.)
Muzzle Device: Integrated muzzle brake
Action/Barrel Finish: Matte blue
Stock: Synthetic Overmold
Stock Finish: Digital desert camo, matte OD green, A-TACS camo

Maximum Length of Pull: 14 in.
Trigger: X-Mark Pro, externally adjustable, factory set at 3.5 lb.
Optics Mount: Drilled and tapped for bases
Magazine: Hinged floorplate, 4-round (.22-250 Rem., .243 Win., .308 Win.), 5-round (.223 Rem.)
Overall Length: 41.7 in.
Weight: 7.5 lb.
Features: Dual front swivel stud for mounting bipod, three forend cooling vents.
MSRP: . . $908.00 (matte OD green), $959 (Desert digital camo, A-TACS camo).

Model 700 XCR Tactical Long Range

Caliber: .223 Rem., .308 Win., .300 Win. Mag., .338 Lapua Mag.
Action: Bolt, short- or long-action, push feed, 2 lug
Barrel: 26 in., stainless steel, varmint contour, target crown, free floated, fluted
Rifling Twist: 1:9 in. (.223 Rem.), 1:10 in. (.300 Win. Mag., .338 Lapua Mag.), 1:12 in. (.308 Win.)
Muzzle Device: Muzzle brake (.338 Lapua Mag.)
Action/Barrel Finish: Black TriNyte
Stock: Bell & Carson, full aluminum bedding block
Stock Finish: OD green
Maximum Length of Pull: 14 in.
Trigger: 40-X, externally adjustable, factory Set at 3.5 lb.
Optics Mount: Drilled and tapped for bases
Magazine: Hinged floorplate, 3-round (.300 Win. Mag.), 4-round (.308 Win.), 5-round (.223 Rem.); detachable box, 5-round (.338 Lapua Mag.)
Overall Length: 45.7 in.
Weight: 8.5 lb.
Accuracy: ½ MOA with match grade ammunition
Maximum Range: 1640 yd. (1500 m)
Features: Dual front swivel stud for mounting bipod, beavertail forend and recessed "thumbhook" behind pistol grip.
MSRP: . . . . $1,510.00; $2,468 (.338 Lapua Mag.)

Model 700 XCR Compact Tactical

Caliber: .223 Rem., .308 Win.
Action: Bolt, short-action, push feed, 2 lug
Barrel: 20 in., stainless steel, heavy contour, fluted, free floated
Rifling Twist: 1:9 in. (.223 Rem.,), 1:12 in. (.308 Win.)
Muzzle Device: None
Action/Barrel Finish: Black TriNyte
Stock: Bell & Carson fiber reinforced
Stock Finish: OD green with black webbing
Maximum Length of Pull: 14 in.
Trigger: 40-X, externally adjustable, factory Set at 3.5 lb.
Optics Mount: Drilled and tapped for bases
Magazine: Hinged floorplate, 4-round (.308 Win.), 5-round (.223 Rem.)
Overall Length: 39.7 in.
Weight: 7.5 lb.
Features: Dual front swivel studs for mounting bipod.
MSRP: $1,510.00

Model 700 SPS Tactical
Caliber: .223 Rem.,.308 Win.
Action: Bolt, short-action, push feed, 2 lug
Barrel: 20 in., hammer forged, carbon steel, heavy contour
Rifling Twist: 1:9 in. (.223 Rem.), 1:10 in., or 1:12 in. (.308 Win.)
Muzzle Device: None
Action/Barrel Finish: Matte blue
Stock: Hogue Overmolded synthetic, pillar bedded, SuperCell recoil pad

Stock Finish: Matte black
Maximum Length of Pull: 14 in.
Trigger: X-Mark Pro, externally adjustable, factory set at 3.5 lb.
Optics Mount: Drilled and tapped for bases
Magazine: Hinged floorplate, 4-round (.308 Win.), 5-round (.223 Rem.)
Overall Length: 39.7 in.
Weight: 7.5 lb.
MSRP: . .$765.00, $817.00 (20-in. barrel, 1:10 in twist rate)

Model 700P
Caliber: .223 Rem., .308 Win., .300 Win. Mag.
Action: Bolt, short- or long-action, push feed, 2 lug
Barrel: 26 in., carbon steel, heavy contour, free floated, crowned muzzle
Rifling Twist: 1:9 in. (.223 Rem.), 1:10 in. (.300 Win. Mag.), 1:12 in. (.308 Win.)
Muzzle Device: None
Action/Barrel Finish: Matte blue
Stock: H-S Precision composite reinforced with Kevlar and fiberglass, aluminum bedding block

Stock Finish: Textured, non-reflective black
Maximum Length of Pull: 14 in.
Trigger: X-Mark Pro, externally adjustable, factory set at 3.5 lb.
Optics Mount: Drilled and tapped for bases
Magazine: Hinged floorplate, 4-round (.223 Rem., .308 Win.), 3-round (.300 Win. Mag.)
Overall Length: 45.7 in.
Weight: 9 lb.
Features: Law Enforcement sales only.

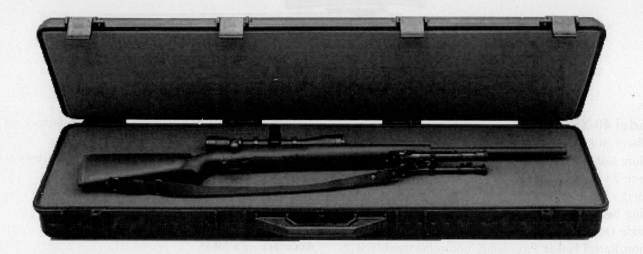

Model 700P Tactical Weapon Systems (TWS)
Caliber: .308 Win.
Action: Bolt, short-action, push feed, 2 lug
Barrel: 26 in., carbon steel, heavy contour, free floated, crowned muzzle
Rifling Twist: 1:12 in.
Muzzle Device: None
Action/Barrel Finish: Matte blue
Stock: H-S Precision composite reinforced with Kevlar and fiberglass, aluminum bedding block
Stock Finish: Textured, non-reflective black

Maximum Length of Pull: 14 in.
Trigger: X-Mark Pro, externally adjustable, factory Set at 3.5 lb.
Optics Mount: Drilled and tapped for bases
Magazine: Hinged floorplate, 4-round
Overall Length: 45.7 in.
Weight: 10.5 lb.
Features: Law Enforcement sales only, includes a Leupold VX-III 3.5-10x40mm scope with a Duplex reticle and flip-open lens covers, Harris bipod, Michaels 1-in. Quick Adjust sling with swivels, Pelican hard case.

Model 40-XB Tactical
Caliber: .308 Win.
Action: Bolt, short-action, push feed, 2 lug
Barrel: 27.2 in., stainless steel with Teflon coating, heavy contour, free floated, crowned muzzle, fluted
Rifling Twist: 1:12 in.
Muzzle Device: None
Action/Barrel Finish: Matte blue
Stock: H-S Precision Pro Series Tactical, composite reinforced with Kevlar and fiberglass, aluminum bedding block, vertical pistol grip

Stock Finish: Black with dark green spider web
Maximum Length of Pull: 14 in.
Trigger: X-Mark Pro, externally adjustable, factory set at 3.5 lb.
Optics Mount: Drilled and tapped for bases
Magazine: Hinged floorplate, 4-round
Overall Length: 45.7 in.
Weight: 10.5 lb.
Accuracy: .5 MOA 5-shots at 100 yd. with match grade ammunition
Features: Law Enforcement sales only.

Model 40-XS

Caliber: .308 Win., .300 Win. Mag., .338 Lapua Mag.
Action: Bolt, Model 40-X action, push feed, 2 lug
Barrel: 24 in., 416 stainless steel, heavy contour, free floated, crowned muzzle
Rifling Twist: 1:12 in. (.308 Win., .300 Win. Mag.)
Muzzle Device: None
Action/Barrel Finish: Proprietary non-reflective black polymer coating
Stock: McMillan A3 or A5 series, adjustable length of pull and comb height
Stock Finish: Black with textured gripping surface
Maximum Length of Pull: 14 in.

Trigger: Model 40-X, externally adjustable, factory set at 3.5 lb.
Optics Mount: Badger Ordnance all-steel Picatinny scope rail and rings
Magazine: Hinged floorplate, 4-round
Overall Length: 45.7 in.
Weight: 10.5 lb.
Accuracy: .75 MOA
Features: Law Enforcement and Custom Shop sales, Sunny Hill heavy duty steel trigger guard, Harris bipod with quick adjust swivel lock, Leupold Mark IV 3.5-10x40mm long-range M1 scope with mil-dot reticle, Turner AWS tactical sling with swivels, Pelican hard case.

M-24 SWS (Sniper Weapon System)

Caliber: .308 Win./7.62x51mm NATO
Action: Bolt, long-action, push feed, 2 lug
Barrel: 24 in., 416R stainless steel, heavy contour, cold-hammer forged, free floated, crowned muzzle
Rifling Twist: 1:11.25 in., 5R rifling
Muzzle Device: None
Action/Barrel Finish: Matte black
Stock: HS Precision, composite construction, adjustable length of pull, aluminum mounting block

Stock Finish: Black
Trigger: Remington M24, adjustable from 3.5-5 lb.
Optics Mount: Drill/tapped for Picatinny-style two-piece bases, OK Weber competition iron sights
Magazine: Hinged floorplate, 5-round
Overall Length: 43 in.
Weight: 11 lb.
Accuracy: .6 MOA at 300 yd.
Effective Range: 800 m
Features: Military sales only, Harris bipod, Leupold Mark 4 M3 10x optic.

M-24-A2

Caliber: .308 Win./7.62x51mm NATO
Action: Bolt, long-action, push feed, 2 lug
Barrel: 24 in., 416R stainless steel, heavy contour, cold-hammer forged, free floated, crowned/threaded muzzle
Rifling Twist: 1:11.25 in., 5R rifling
Muzzle Device: None
Action/Barrel Finish: Matte black
Stock: HS Precision PST-25, composite construction, adjustable length of pull and comb height, aluminum mounting block

M-24-A3

Caliber: .338 Lapua Mag.
Action: Bolt, long-action, push feed, 2 lug
Barrel: 19 in., 416R stainless steel, heavy contour, cold-hammer forged, free floated, crowned/threaded muzzle
Rifling Twist: 1:9 in., 5R rifling
Muzzle Device: OPS Inc 12th Model suppressor
Action/Barrel Finish: Matte black
Stock: Accuracy International chassis, adjustable length of pull and comb height, full aluminum chassis

M24-Rebuild

Notes: Similar to M24. Built from authentic M24 SWS components delivered to the US Army from 1988 through the present day. Complete package.

Stock Finish: Black
Trigger: Remington M24, adjustable from 3.5-5 lb.
Optics Mount: 0 MOA rail
Magazine: Detachable box, 5-round
Overall Length: 43 in.
Weight: 12 lb.
Accuracy: .6 MOA at 300 yd.
Effective Range: 800 m
Features: Military sales only, Harris bipod, Leupold Mark 4 M3 10x optic, improved version of the M24, accepts suppressors, side rails.

Stock Finish: Black
Trigger: Remington M24, adjustable from 3.5-5 lb.
Optics Mount: 30 MOA rail, Badger Ordnance rings
Magazine: Detachable box, 5-round
Overall Length: 41 in.
Weight: 12 lb.
Accuracy: .6 MOA at 300 yd.
Effective Range: 1,200 m
Features: Military sales only, Harris bipod, Leupold Mark 4 M1 LR/T, 8.5-25x50mm optic, improved version of the M24, accepts suppressors, side rails.

MSRP: $3,500.00

MSR (Modular Service Rifle)

Caliber: .308 Win./7.62x51mm NATO, .300 Win. Mag., .338 Norma Mag., .338 Lapua Mag.

Action: Bolt, long-action, push feed, 2 lug

Barrel: 20 in., 22 in., 24 in. or 27 in.; stainless steel, fluted, cold-hammer forged, free floated, threaded muzzle

Rifling Twist: 1:9 in. (.338 Lapua Mag.), 1:11.25 in. (.308 Win./7.62x51mm NATO), 1:10 in. (.300 Win. Mag., .338 Norma Mag.)

Muzzle Device: Muzzle brake and ACC Titan suppressor

Action/Barrel Finish: Cerionite black

Stock: Folding Remington MST full aluminum chassis; adjustable length of pull, comb height, butt plate height, pistol grip, vented handguard

Stock Finish: Matte desert tan/black

Trigger: Remington M24, adjustable from 3.5–5 lb.

Optics Mount: Integral Picatinny rail, Remington UNI-mount rings

Magazine: Detachable box; 5- and 10-round (.338 Norma Mag., .338 Lapua Mag., .308 Win./7.62x51mm NATO), 7-round (.300 Win. Mag.)

Overall Length: 46 in.

Overall Length Folded: 36 in.

Weight: 13 lb.

Accuracy: .7 MOA at 1,000 m (.338 Lapua Mag.)

Effective Range: 1,500 m

Notes: Military sales only, Harris bipod, side rails, suppressor and muzzle brake eliminate 98 percent of muzzle flash and reduces recoil by 60 percent, rails accepts night vision devices.

MSRP: $15,000.00

M700P

Caliber: .308 Win./7.62x51mm NATO

Action: Bolt, short-action, push feed, 2 lug

Barrel: 26 in., carbon steel, heavy contour, cold-hammer forged, free floated, crowned muzzle

Rifling Twist: 1:12 in., 5R rifling

Muzzle Device: None

Action/Barrel Finish: Matte black

Stock: HS Precision, composite construction, aluminum mounting block

Stock Finish: Black

Trigger: Remington X-Mark Pro, adjustable from 3.5-5 lb.

Optics Mount: Badger Ordnance base and 30mm rings

Magazine: Internal box, 4-round

Overall Length: 47.5 in.

Weight: 8 lb.

Features: Military sales only, bipod, Leupold Mark 4 M3 3.5-10x50mm optic, sling, hard case.

USR (Urban Sniper Rifle)

Caliber: .308 Win./7.62x51mm NATO
Action: Bolt, short-action, push feed, 2 lug
Barrel: 20 in., carbon steel, heavy contour, cold-hammer forged, free floated, crowned/threaded muzzle
Rifling Twist: 1:12 in., 5R rifling
Muzzle Device: Muzzle brake
Action/Barrel Finish: Matte black
Stock: HS Precision, composite construction, aluminum mounting block, adjustable length of pull and cheekpiece height

Stock Finish: Black
Trigger: Remington X-Mark Pro, adjustable from 3.5–5 lb.
Optics Mount: Badger Ordnance steel rings, MARS rail
Magazine: Detachable box, 10-round
Overall Length: 40.5 in.
Weight: 9 lb.
Features: Military sales only, bipod, Leupold Mark 4 M3 LR/T 3.5-10x50mm optic, sling, hard case, designed for use with AAC 762-SD suppressor.

700 FED (Federal)

Caliber: .308 Win./7.62x51mm NATO
Action: Bolt, short-action, push feed, 2 lug
Barrel: 24 in., 16R stainless steel, heavy contour, cold-hammer forged, free floated, crowned/threaded muzzle
Rifling Twist: 1:11.25 in., 5R rifling
Muzzle Device: None
Action/Barrel Finish: Matte black
Stock: Accuracy International full aluminum chassis
Stock Finish: Black

Trigger: Remington X-Mark Pro, adjustable from 3.5–5 lb.
Optics Mount: Badger Ordnance steel rings, 0 MOA rail
Magazine: Detachable box, 10-round
Overall Length: 47 in.
Weight: 13.1 lb.
Effective Range: 800–1000 m
Features: Military sales only, Harris bipod, Leupold Mark 4 M1 LR/T 3.5-10x50mm optic with TMR reticle, sling, hard case, designed for use with OPS Inc. 12th model suppressor.

700 LTR (Light Tactical Rifle)

Caliber: .223 Rem., .308 Win./7.62x51mm NATO, .300 Rem. SA Ultra Mag.
Action: Bolt, short-action, push feed, 2 lug
Barrel: 26 in., heavy contour, cold-hammer forged, free floated, fluted, crowned/threaded muzzle
Rifling Twist: 1:12 in. (.308 Win./7.62x51mm NATO), 5R rifling
Muzzle Device: None
Action/Barrel Finish: Matte black

Stock: Composite construction, aluminum bedding block
Stock Finish: Black
Trigger: Remington X-Mark Pro, adjustable from 3.5–5 lb.
Optics Mount: Badger Ordnance steel rings, 0 MOA rail
Magazine: Hinged floorplate box, 4-round (.308 Win./7.62x51mm NATO)
Overall Length: 47.5 in.
Weight: 8 lb.
Features: Military sales only, Harris bipod, Leupold Mark 4 M3 LR/T 3.5-10x50mm optic, sling, hard case.

R11 RSASS (Remington Semi Automatics Sniper System)

Caliber: .308 Win./7.62x51mm NATO
Action: Semiautomatic, gas impingement
Barrel: 16 in. or 18 in., 416R stainless steel, cryogenically treated, threaded muzzle
Rifling Twist: RH 1:10 in.
Muzzle Device: AAC Black Out flash suppressor
Action/Barrel Finish: Matte black
Stock: Magpul PRS, fully adjustable comb and length of pull
Stock Finish: Desert tan
Length of Pull: 13.8-14.8 in.

Trigger: JP Enterprises, adjustable 3.5-5 lb.
Optic Mount: JP Enterprises rail on handguard and upper receiver
Magazine: Detachable box, 20-round
Overall Length: 39.5 in. (without suppressor), 46 in. (with suppressor)
Weight: 12 lb.
Accuracy: sub-MOA to 800 m
Maximum Range: 800–1000 m
Features: Military or Law Enforcement sales only, forged upper and lower receivers, free-floated barrel, hard case, Leupold Mark 4 M3 LR/T, 4.5-14x50mm with TMR reticle, Harris LM-S bipod, ACC Quick Detach suppressor.

XM2010

Caliber: .300 Win. Mag.
Action: Bolt, M24 action, push feed, 2 lug
Barrel: 22 in., heavy contour, cold-hammer forged, free floated, threaded muzzle
Rifling Twist: 1:10 in.
Muzzle Device: AAC TiTan
Action/Barrel Finish: Matte black
Stock: Remington Arms Chassis System (RACS); folding buttstock; adjustable length of pull, recoil pad, cheekpiece height; free-float tubular design, pistol grip, vented handguard, accessory rails
Stock Finish: Desert tan

Trigger: Remington M24, adjustable from 3.5-5 lb.
Optics Mount: 20 MOA monolithic rail, Badger Ordnance steel rings
Magazine: Detachable box, 5-round
Overall Length: 46.5 in. (without suppressor), 52 in. (with suppressor)
Weight: 12 lb.
Accuracy: 1 MOA
Effective Range: 1200 m
Features: Military sales only, Harris bipod, Leupold MKIV ERT 6.5-20x50mm with H-58 reticle optic, hard and soft case.

Rock River Arms (rockriverarms.com)

RRA (Rock River Arms) operates out of Colona, Illinois, producing a full line of rifles, parts, and accessories for AR-style rifles. The US DEA and FBI awarded RRA a 5-year contract as a primary weapons supplier.

LAR-8 Predator HP

Caliber: .308 Win./7.62x51mm NATO
Action: Semiautomatic, gas impingement
Barrel: 20 in., stainless steel HBAR, cryogenically treated
Rifling Twist: RH 1:10 in.
Muzzle Device: None
Action/Barrel Finish: Matte black
Stock: RRA Operator A2 buttstock, Hogue pistol grip, RRA free floated aluminum tube handguard
Stock Finish: Black

Trigger: RRA two-stage
Optic Mount: Picatinny Rail on upper receiver
Magazine: detachable box, 10-round
Overall Length: 40 in.
Weight: 8.6 lb.
Accuracy: 1 MOA @ 100 yds
Features: Designed for big game and predator hunting, uses a unique receiver thread and barrel nut, oversized trigger guard for use with gloved hands.
MSRP: $1,605.00

LAR-8 Varminter A4

Caliber: .308 Win./7.62x51mm NATO
Action: Semiautomatic, gas impingement
Barrel: 26 in., stainless steel, bull, cryogenically treated
Rifling Twist: RH 1:10 in.
Muzzle Device: None
Action/Barrel Finish: Matte black
Stock: A2 buttstock, Hogue pistol grip, RRA free floated aluminum tube handguard
Stock Finish: Black

Trigger: RRA two-stage
Optic Mount: Picatinny Rail on upper receiver
Magazine: detachable box, 10-round
Overall Length: 40 in.
Weight: 11.4 lb.
Accuracy: 1 MOA @ 100 yds
Features: Designed for varmint hunting, uses a unique receiver thread and barrel nut, oversized trigger guard for use with gloved hands.
MSRP: $1,575.00

Ruger (ruger.com)

Sturm, Ruger & Co., Inc. is one of the leading manufacturers of firearms in the US for the commercial sporting market. Ruger builds a full-line of American-made firearms, including single- and double-action revolvers, Semiautomatic pistols, bolt-action rifle, single-shot rifles, and Semiautomatic rifles.

M77 Hawkeye Tactical
Caliber: .223 Rem., .308 Win.
Action: Bolt, short-action, control feed, 2 lug
Barrel: 20 in., 5/8-24 threaded muzzle
Rifling Twist: 1:9 in. (.223 Rem.), 1:10 in. (.308 Win.)
Muzzle Device: Flash hider
Action/Barrel Finish: Alloy steel/matte black or Stainless steel/matte stainless
Stock: Black Hogue OverMold
Stock Finish: Matte black
Trigger: Two-stage, adjustable
Optics Mount: Integral scope mounts
Magazine: Internal box, 5-round (.223 Rem.), 4-round (.308 Win.)
Overall Length: 41.5 in.
Weight: 8.75 lb.
Features: Three-position safety, rubber recoil pad.
MSRP: $1,239.00

M77 Mark II Target
Caliber: .204 Ruger, .22-250 Rem., .223 Rem., 6.5 Creedmoor, .308 Win.
Action: Bolt, short-action, control feed, 2 lug
Barrel: 26 in., heavy taper, hammer forged, target crown
Rifling Twist: 1:12 in. (.204 Ruger), 1:14 in. (.22-250 Rem.), 1:9 in. (.223 Rem.), 1:89 in. (6.5 Creedmoor), 1:10 in. (.308 Win.)
Muzzle Device: None
Action/Barrel Finish: Matte stainless
Stock: Laminate wood with wide forend
Stock Finish: Green/black
Trigger: Two-stage, adjustable
Optics Mount: Integral scope mounts
Magazine: Internal box, 5-round (.204 Ruger, .223 Rem.), 4-round (.22-250 Rem., .6.5 Creedmoor, .308 Win.)
Overall Length: 46 in.
Weight: 9.25 lb.
Features: Three-position safety, rubber recoil pad.
MSRP: $1,029.00

No.1 Varminter
Caliber: .220 Swift
Action: Single shot, falling block
Barrel: 26 in., heavy taper, hammer forged, target crown
Rifling Twist: 1:14 in.
Muzzle Device: None
Action/Barrel Finish: Blued
Stock: Checkered American walnut
Stock Finish: Satin
Trigger: Two-stage

Optics Mount: Integral scope mount blocks
Magazine: n/a
Overall Length: 42.5 in.
Weight: 8.5 lb.
Features: Two-position safety, rubber recoil pad, ejector or can be adjusted to provide extraction only.
MSRP: $1,399.00

SR-556VT
Caliber: 5.56 NATO/.223 Rem.
Action: Semiautomatic, two-stage piston with adjustable regulator
Barrel: 20 in., bull, 416 stainless
Rifling Twist: RH 1:8 in.
Muzzle Device: None
Action/Barrel Finish: Matte black
Stock: A2 fixed butt, Magpul MOE pistol grip, lightweight free-float handguard

Stock Finish: Matte black
Trigger: Two-stage, target style
Optic Mount: Extended Picatinny rail
Magazine: Detachable box, 30-round
Overall Length: 38.25 in.
Weight: 8.5 lb.
Features: Piston gas system provides cleaner and cooler operation, four-position gas regulator can be adjusted, gas system can be closed for use with suppressor.
MSRP: $1,995.00

Mini-14 Target

Caliber: .223 Rem.
Action: Semiautomatic, fixed-piston gas system
Barrel: 22 in., heavy, hammer-forged, 416 stainless
Rifling Twist: RH 1:9 in.
Muzzle Device: Harmonic dampener
Action/Barrel Finish: Matte stainless
Stock: Laminate with thumbhole or Hogue OverMolded
Stock Finish: Black
Trigger: Two-stage

Optic Mount: Integra; scope mounts
Magazine: Detachable box, 5-round
Overall Length: 41.75-43.25 in. (thumbhole stock), 41.5 in. (Hogue stock)
Weight: 8.5 lb. (Hogue stock), 9.5 lb. (thumbhole stock)
Features: Harmonic dampener is adjustable to maximize accuracy for a particular bullet weight or load, thumbhole stock is adjustable for length of pull, uses Garand-style action with breechbolt locking system
MSRP: $1,149.00

Sako (sako.fi)

Sako was established in 1921 and develops world-class military, target, and hunting rifles, as well as cartridges. They are renowned for smooth actions, good triggers, and excellent accuracy.

TRG M10

Caliber: .308 Win., .300 Win. Mag., .338 Lapua Mag.
Action: Bolt, push feed, 3 lug, 60° bolt lift
Barrel: 16 in. (.308 Win.), 20 in. (.308 Win., .338 Lapua Mag.), 23.5 in. (.308 Win., .300 Win. Mag., .338 Lapua Mag.), or 26 in. (.308 Win., .300 Win. Mag., .338 Lapua Mag.); heavy contour, fluted, free floated, M18x1 threaded muzzle
Rifling Twist: 1:10 in. (.338 Lapua Mag.), 1:11 in. (.308 Win., .300 Win. Mag.)
Muzzle Device: Flash hider
Action/Barrel Finish: Matte black
Stock: Folding buttstock; adjustable length of pull, recoil pad, cheekpiece height; free-float tubular design; pistol grip with back strap inserts; vented handguard; accessory rails
Stock Finish: Stealth black, military green and coyote brown

Trigger: Fully adjustable, modular
Optics Mount: 30 MOA Mil-Std-1913 Picatinny rail
Magazine: Detachable steel and polymer box, 11-round (.308 Win.), 7-round (.300 Win. Mag.), 8-round (.338 Lapua Mag.)
Overall Length: 36.8 in. (16-in. barrel), 40.8 in. (20-in. barrel), 44.5 in. (23.5-in. barrel), 46.7 in. (26-in. barrel)
Over Length Stock Folded: 27.1 in. (16-in. barrel), 31.1 in. (20-in. barrel), 34.8 in. (23.5-in. barrel), 36.9 in. (26-in. barrel)
Weight: 12.3 lb. (16-in. barrel), 12.9 lb. (20-in. barrel), 13.5 lb. (23.5-in. barrel), 13.9 lb. (26-in. barrel)
Accuracy: .5 MOA with match grade ammunition
Effective Range: 800 m (.308 Win.), 1,100 m (.300 Win. Mag.), 1,500 m (.338 Lapua Mag.)
Features: Military and Law Enforcement sales only, multi-caliber operator configurable sniper weapon, typically equipped with Zeiss or Schmidt & Bender optic, ambidextrous controls.

TRG-22

Caliber: .308 Win.
Action: Bolt, push feed, 3 lug, 60° bolt lift
Barrel: 20 in. or 26 in., heavy contour, free floated, M18x1 threaded muzzle
Rifling Twist: 1:11 in.
Muzzle Device: None
Action/Barrel Finish: Matte black
Stock: Folding or fixed buttstock; adjustable length of pull, recoil pad, cheekpiece height; free-float tubular design; pistol grip with back strap inserts; vented handguard; accessory rails or fixed with adjustable length of pull and cheekpiece height
Stock Finish: Stealth black, military green and coyote brown
Trigger: Two-stage; adjustable from 2-5 lb.
Optics Mount: Flat or 30 MOA Mil-Std-1913 Picatinny rail
Magazine: Detachable steel and polymer box, 10-round
Overall Length: 39.7 in. (20-in. barrel, fixed stock), 45.7 in. (26-in. barrel, fixed stock), 39.5 in. (20-in. barrel, folding stock), 45.5 in. (26-in. barrel, folding stock)

Over Length Stock Folded: 29.9 in. (20-in. barrel, folding stock), 35.8 in. (26-in. barrel, folding stock)
Weight: 10.5 lb. (20-in. barrel, fixed stock, ITRS short), 10.9 lb. (20-in. barrel, fixed stock, ITRS long), 11.3 lb. (26-in. barrel, fixed stock, ITRS short), 11.8 lb. (26-in. barrel, fixed stock, ITRS long), 12.3 lb. (20-in. barrel, folding stock, ITRS short), 12.8 lb. (20-in. barrel, folding stock, ITRS long), 13.2 lb. (26-in. barrel, folding stock, MMRS variant), 13.6 lb. (26-in. barrel, folding stock, MMRS variant)
Accuracy: .5 MOA with match grade ammunition
Effective Range: 800 m
Features: Military and Law Enforcement sales only, typically equipped with Zeiss or Schmidt & Bender optic, ambidextrous controls, ITRS (Integrated Tactical Rail System) for optics and accessory mounts in either short or long variants, suppressor ready, MMRS (Monolithic Modular Rail System) mounting platform for use with night vision devices and target designators.
MSRP: . $3,084.00 (fixed stock); $5,198.00 (folding stock)

TRG 42

Caliber: .300 Win. Mag., .338 Lapua Mag.
Action: Bolt, push feed, 3 lug, 60° bolt lift, long-action
Barrel: 27 in., heavy contour, free floated, M18x1 threaded muzzle
Rifling Twist: 1:10 in. (.338 Lapua Mag.), 1:11 in. (.300 Win. Mag.)
Muzzle Device: Muzzle brake
Action/Barrel Finish: Matte black
Stock: Folding or fixed buttstock; adjustable length of pull, recoil pad, cheekpiece height; free-float tubular design; pistol grip with back strap inserts; vented handguard; accessory rails
Stock Finish: Black, green or desert tan
Trigger: Two-stage; adjustable from 2-5 lb.
Optics Mount: Flat or 30 MOA Mil-Std-1913 Picatinny rail
Magazine: Detachable steel and polymer box, 7-round (.300 Win. Mag.), 8-round (.338 Lapua Mag.)
Overall Length: 47.2 in. (fixed stock), 47.4 in. (folding stock)
Over Length Stock Folded: 37.9 in.
Weight: 11.9 lb. (fixed stock, ITRS short, .300 Win. Mag.), 12.3 lb. (fixed stock, ITRS long, .300 Win. Mag.), 13.7 lb. (folding stock, ITRS short, .300 Win. Mag.), 14.1 lb. (folding stock, ITRS long, .300 Win. Mag.), 14.6 lb. (folding stock, MMRS variant, .300 Win. Mag.), 11.7 lb. (fixed stock, ITRS short, .338 Lapua Mag.), 12.1 lb. (fixed stock, ITRS long, .338 Lapua Mag.), 13.5 lb. (folding stock, ITRS short, .338 Lapua Mag.), 13.9 lb. (folding stock, ITRS long, .338 Lapua Mag.), 14.4 lb. (folding stock, MMRS variant, .338 Lapua Mag.)
Accuracy: Sub 1 MOA with match grade ammunition
Effective Range: 1,100 m (.300 Win. Mag.), 1,500 m (.338 Lapua Mag.)
Features: Military and Law Enforcement sales only, typically equipped with Zeiss or Schmidt & Bender optic, ambidextrous controls, ITRS (Integrated Tactical Rail System) for optics and accessory mounts in either short or long variants, suppressor ready, MMRS (Monolithic Modular Rail System) mounting platform for use with night vision devices and target designators.
MSRP: . $3,500.00 (fixed stock); $6,289.00 (folding stock)

Savage Arms (savagearms.com)

Savage introduced the Model 110 series of rifles in 1958. Renowned for their accuracy, Savage rifles are built with a fully threaded barrel that is locked into the action via barrel locknut for accuracy. Models with AccuStocks are made with polymer and feature a rigid aluminum rail to free float the barrel—another aid in accuracy. Often copied, the AccuTrigger is easily adjustable, with a crisp release and no creep. The floating bolt head has a few thousandths of an inch of movement to adjust itself when locked into battery. All these features contribute to the rifles' excellent accuracy.

11/111 Long Range Hunter

Caliber: .25-06, .260 Rem., 6.5 Creedmoor, 6.5x284 Norma, 7mm Rem. Mag., .308 Win., .300 WSM, .300 Win. Mag., .338 Lapua Mag.
Action: Bolt, short- or long-action, push feed, 2 lug
Barrel: 24 in. (.260 Rem., 6.5 Creedmoor, .308 Win., .300 WSM) or 26 in. (.25-06, 6.5x284 Norma, 7mm Rem. Mag., .300 Win. Mag., .338 Lapua Mag.), carbon steel, free floated
Rifling Twist: 1:8 in. (.260 Rem., 6.5 Creedmoor, 6.5x284 Norma), 1:9 in. (.338 Lapua Mag.), 1:9.5 in. (7mm Rem. Mag.), 1:10 in. (.25-06, .308 Win., .300 WSM, .300 Win. Mag.)
Muzzle Device: Adjustable muzzle brake, non-adjustable muzzle brake (.338 Lapua Mag.)
Action/Barrel Finish: Matte black
Stock: Karsten, Adjustable comb height
Stock Finish: Black with checkered gripping surfaces

Trigger: AccuTrigger, adjustable from 1.5 - 6 lbs.
Optics Mount: Drilled and tapped for base
Magazine: Hinged floorplate, 2-round (.300 WSM) or 3-round (.25-06, 6.5x284 Norma, 7mm Rem. Mag., .300 Win. Mag.) or 4-round (.260 Rem., 6.5 Creedmoor, .308 Win.); detachable steel box, 5-round (.338 Lapua Mag.)
Overall Length: 45.7 in.
Weight: 8.5 lb. Features: Designed for long-range hunting rifle with adjustable muzzle brake (except in .3338 Lapua Mag.) that helps mitigate recoil. The muzzle brake is rotated to open or close the vent holes. Maximum length of pull is 13.3 in. and the cheekpiece is adjustable.
MSRP: . . . . $1,020.00 (.25-06, .260 Rem., 6.5 Creedmoor, 6.5x284 Norma, 7mm Rem. Mag., .308 Win., .300 Win. Mag.); $1,060.00 (.300 WSM); $1,290.00 (.338 Lapua Mag.)

10 BA

Model: 19125
Caliber: .308 Win.
Action: bolt, push feed, short
Barrel: 24 in. carbon steel
Rifling Twist: RH 1:10 in.
Muzzle Device: Flash Suppressor
Action/Barrel Finish: Matte black
Stock: AccuStock, adjustable Magpul PRS-G3 buttstock (comb/length), adjustable pistol grip
Stock Finish: Matte black

Trigger: AccuTrigger, adjustable from 1.5 - 6 lbs.
Optic Mount: 0 MOA Rail
Magazine: detachable box, 10-round
Overall Length: 45.5 in.
Weight: 13.4 lb.
Features: three-position safety, oversized bolt handle, free floating bolt head, free-floated barrel, sling swivel mounts, grooved black forend, textured pistol grip, adjustable length of pull from 15 to 16.2 in.
MSRP: $2,285.00

10 FCP McMillan

Caliber: .308 Win.
Action: bolt, push feed, short
Barrel: 24 in. carbon steel, heavy contour
Rifling Twist: RH 1:10 in.
Muzzle Device: none
Action/Barrel Finish: Matte black
Stock: McMillan A5 fiberglass
Stock Finish: Matte black, textured finish

Trigger: AccuTrigger, adjustable from 1.5–6 lbs.
Optic Mount: Drilled and tapped for scope mounts
Magazine: detachable box, 4-round
Overall Length: 46.5 in.
Weight: 10 lb.
Features: three-position safety, oversized bolt handle, free floating bolt head, free-floated barrel, sling swivel mounts, rubber butt pad, 13.5 in. length of pull.
MSRP: $1,485.00

10 FCP-K

Caliber: .223 Rem., .308 Win.
Action: bolt, push feed, short
Barrel: 24 in. carbon steel, heavy contour, fluted
Rifling Twist: RH 1:9 in. (.223 Rem.), RH 1:10 in. (.308 Win.)
Muzzle Device: Muzzle brake, threaded (5/8-24)
Action/Barrel Finish: Matte black
Stock: AccuStock

Stock Finish: Matte black
Trigger: AccuTrigger, adjustable from 1.5–6 lbs.
Optic Mount: Drilled and tapped for scope mounts
Magazine: detachable box, 4-round
Overall Length: 46.5 in.
Weight: 9.9 lb. (.223 Rem.), 8.9 lb. (.308 Win.)
Features: three-position safety, oversized bolt handle, free-floating bolt head, free-floated barrel, sling and bipod swivel mounts, rubber butt pad, 13.7 in. length of pull.
MSRP: $975.00

10 FCP-SR

Caliber: .308 Win.
Action: bolt, push feed, short
Barrel: 24 in. carbon steel, heavy contour, fluted
Rifling Twist: RH 1:10 in.
Muzzle Device: none, threaded (5/8-24)
Action/Barrel Finish: Matte black
Stock: AccuStock
Stock Finish: Tan digital camo

Trigger: AccuTrigger, adjustable from 1.5–6 lbs.
Optic Mount: one-piece scope rail
Magazine: detachable box, 10-round
Overall Length: 44.2 in.
Weight: 8.7 lb.
Features: three-position safety, oversized bolt handle, free floating bolt head, free-floated barrel, sling and bipod swivel mounts, rubber butt pad, oversized trigger guard, thread protector, 13.7 in. length of pull.
MSRP: $1,250.00

10 FLCP-K

Caliber: .223 Rem., .308 Win.
Action: bolt, push feed, short
Barrel: 24 in. carbon steel, heavy contour, fluted
Rifling Twist: RH 1:9 in. (.223 Rem.), RH 1:10 in. (.308 Win.)
Muzzle Device: Muzzle brake, threaded (5/8-24)
Action/Barrel Finish: Matte black
Stock: AccuStock
Stock Finish: Matte black

Trigger: AccuTrigger, adjustable from 1.5–6 lbs.
Optic Mount: Drilled and tapped for scope mounts
Magazine: detachable box, 4-round
Overall Length: 46.5 in.
Weight: 9.9 lb. (.223 Rem.), 8.9 lb. (.308 Win.)
Features: left hand version of 10 FCP-K, three-position safety, oversized bolt handle, free-floating bolt head, free-floated barrel, sling and bipod swivel mounts, rubber butt pad, 13.7 in. length of pull.
MSRP: $975.00

10 FP-SR

Caliber: .223 Rem., .308 Win.
Action: bolt, push feed, short
Barrel: 22 in. carbon steel, heavy contour
Rifling Twist: RH 1:9 in. (.223 Rem.), RH 1:10 in. (.308 Win.)
Muzzle Device: none; threaded 5/8-24 (.308 Win.), ½-28 (.223 Rem.)
Action/Barrel Finish: Matte black
Stock: Synthetic

Stock Finish: Matte black
Trigger: AccuTrigger, adjustable from 1.5–6 lbs.
Optic Mount: Drilled and tapped for scope mounts
Magazine: internal box, 4-round
Overall Length: 42.5 in.
Weight: 8.2 lb. (.223 Rem.), 8.2 lb. (.308 Win.)
Features: three-position safety, oversized bolt handle, free floating bolt head, free-floated barrel, sling and bipod swivel mounts, rubber butt pad, 13.7 in. length of pull.
MSRP **$775.00**

10 Precision Carbine

Caliber: .223 Rem., .308 Win.
Barrel: 20 in. carbon steel, heavy contour
Rifling Twist: RH 1:9 in. (.223 Rem.), RH 1:10 in. (.308 Win.)
Muzzle Device: none; threaded 5/8-24 (.308 Win.), ½-28 (.223 Rem.)
Action: bolt, push feed, short
Action/Barrel Finish: Matte black
Stock: AccuStock

Stock Finish: Digital camo
Trigger: AccuTrigger, adjustable from 1.5–6 lbs.
Optic Mount: Drilled and tapped for scope mounts
Magazine: detachable box, 4-round
Overall Length: 40.5 in.
Weight: 8.0 lb. (.223 Rem.), 8.2 lb. (.308 Win.)
Features: three-position safety, oversized bolt handle, free floating bolt head, free-floated barrel, sling and bipod swivel mounts, rubber butt pad, 13.7 in. length of pull.
MSRP: $925.00

10/110 FCP HS Precision
Caliber: .308 Win., .300 Win. Mag., .338 Lapua Mag.
Action: bolt, push feed, short or long
Barrel: 24 in. carbon steel, heavy contour (.308 Win., .300 Win. Mag.); 26 in. fluted, heavy contour (.338 Lapua Mag.)
Rifling Twist: RH 1:10 in. (.308 Win., .300 Win. Mag.); RH 1:9 in. (.338 Lapua Mag.)
Muzzle Device: none (.308 Win., .300 Win. Mag.); muzzle brake (.338 Lapua Mag.)
Action/Barrel Finish: Matte black
Stock: HS Precision PST fiberglass
Stock Finish: Textured matte black

Trigger: AccuTrigger, adjustable from 1.5–6 lbs.
Optic Mount: Drilled and tapped for scope mounts
Magazine: detachable box; 4-round (.308 Win., .300 Win. Mag.), 5-round (.338 Lapua Mag.)
Overall Length: 44.5 in. (.308 Win., .300 Win. Mag.); 49.5 in. (.338 Lapua Mag.)
Weight: 9.0 lb. (.308 Win., .300 Win. Mag.); 10.7 lb. (.338 Lapua Mag.)
Features: three-position safety, oversized bolt handle, free floating bolt head, free-floated barrel, sling and bipod swivel mounts, rubber butt pad, 13.7 in. length of pull
MSRP: $1,230.00 (.308 Win., .300 Win. Mag.), $1,610.00 (.338 Lapua Mag.)

110 BA (RH or LH)
Caliber: .300 Win. Mag., .338 Lapua Mag.
Action: bolt, push feed, long, RH (Right Hand) or LH (Left Hand)
Barrel: 26 in. carbon steel, heavy contour fluted
Rifling Twist: RH 1:10 in. (.300 Win. Mag.); RH 1:9 in. (.338 Lapua Mag.)
Muzzle Device: muzzle brake
Action/Barrel Finish: Matte black
Stock: AccuStock, adjustable Magpul PRS-G3 buttstock (comb/length), adjustable pistol grip

Stock Finish: Matte black
Trigger: AccuTrigger, adjustable from 1.5–6 lbs.
Optic Mount: 20 MOA scope rail
Magazine: detachable box; 5-round
Overall Length: 45.5 in.
Weight: 15.7 lb.
Features: three-position safety, oversized bolt handle, free floating bolt head, free-floated barrel, sling and bipod swivel mounts, rubber butt pad, Picatinny accessory rails, available in left- or right-hand models, length of pull adjusts from 15 to 16.2 in.
MSRP: $2,465.00

25 Walking Varminter

Caliber: .17 Hornet, .204 Ruger, .22 Hornet, .222 Rem., .223 Rem.
Action: bolt, push feed, short-action, 3-lug
Barrel: 22 in. carbon steel, heavy contour fluted
Muzzle Device: none
Action/Barrel Finish: Blued
Stock: Synthetic
Stock Finish: Black
Trigger: AccuTrigger, adjustable from 1.5–6 lbs.
Optic Mount: Drilled and tapped for mounts
Magazine: detachable box; 4-round
Overall Length: 41.8 in.
Weight: 6.9 lb.
Features: Small action scaled to smaller cartridges, two-position safety, 60° bolt handle lift, free floating bolt head, free-floated barrel, sling and bipod swivel mounts, rubber butt pad.
MSRP: . . . . $602.00; $652.00 (camo stock)

25 Lightweight Varminter

Caliber: .17 Hornet, .204 Ruger, .22 Hornet, .223 Rem.
Action: bolt, push feed, short-action, 3-lug
Barrel: 24 in. carbon steel, heavy contour fluted
Muzzle Device: none
Action/Barrel Finish: Blued
Stock: wood laminate
Stock Finish: Natural
Trigger: AccuTrigger, adjustable from 1.5–6 lbs.
Optic Mount: Drilled and tapped for mounts
Magazine: detachable box; 4-round
Overall Length: 43.7 in.
Weight: 8.3 lb.
Features: Small action scaled to smaller cartridges, two-position safety, 60° bolt handle lift, free floating bolt head, free-floated barrel, sling and bipod swivel mounts, rubber butt pad.
MSRP: . . . .$751.00; $800.00 (thumbhole stock)

12 FCV
Caliber: .204 Ruger, .22-250 Rem., .223 Rem.
Action: bolt, push feed, short, two-lug
Barrel: 26 in., carbon steel, heavy contour, fluted
Rifling Twist: RH 1:12 in. (.204 Ruger, .22-250 Rem.); RH 1:9 in. (.223 Rem.)
Muzzle Device: None
Action/Barrel Finish: Blued
Stock: AccuStock synthetic
Stock Finish: Black
Trigger: AccuTrigger, adjustable 6 oz.

Optic Mount: Drilled and tapped for mounts
Magazine: Detachable box; 4-round
Overall Length: 46 in.
Weight: 9 lb.
Features: The Varmint Series features button-rifled, free-floating barrels and a variety of stock configurations. Custom rates of twist to help stabilize heavier bullets during long-range shooting. Extra-heavy, fluted, one-inch diameter barrel with a smaller ejection port provides more rigidity to the receiver and greater precision.
MSRP: $904.00

12 LRPV Left Port
Caliber: .204 Ruger, .22-250 Rem., .223 Rem., 6mm Norma BR
Action: bolt, push feed, short, two-lug
Barrel: 26 in., stainless steel, heavy contour, fluted
Rifling Twist: RH 1:12 in. (.204 Ruger, .22-250 Rem.); RH 1:9 in. (.22-250 Rem., .223 Rem.); RH 1:8 in. (6mm Norma BR); RH 1:7 in. (.223 Rem.)
Muzzle Device: None
Action/Barrel Finish: Matte stainless
Stock: HS Precision with V-Block, synthetic
Stock Finish: Black

Trigger: AccuTrigger, adjustable down to 6 oz.
Optic Mount: Drilled and tapped for mounts
Magazine: Single-shot
Overall Length: 46.25 in.
Weight: 11 lb.
Features: The Varmint Series features button-rifled, free-floating barrels and a variety of stock configurations. Custom rates of twist to help stabilize heavier bullets during long-range shooting. Extra-heavy, fluted, one-inch diameter barrel with a smaller ejection port provides more rigidity to the receiver and greater precision. Left side port for easier loading at the bench.
MSRP: $1,465.00

12 VLP DBM

Caliber: .204 Ruger, .22-250 Rem., .223 Rem., .243 Win., .300 WSM, .308 Win.
Action: bolt, push feed, short, two-lug
Barrel: 26 in., stainless steel, heavy contour, fluted
Rifling Twist: RH 1:12 in. (.204 Ruger, .22-250 Rem.); RH 1:9.25 in. (.300 WSM, .308 Win.); RH 1:9.25 in. (.243 Win.); RH 1:9 in. (.22-250 Rem., .223 Rem.); RH 1:8 in. (6mm Norma BR); RH 1:7 in. (.223 Rem.)
Muzzle Device: None
Action/Barrel Finish: Matte stainless
Stock: Laminated wood
Stock Finish: Natural
Trigger: AccuTrigger, adjustable down to 6 oz.
Optic Mount: Drilled and tapped for mounts
Magazine: Detachable box, 5-round
Overall Length: 46.25 in.
Weight: 10 lb.
Features: The Varmint Series features button-rifled, free-floating barrels and a variety of stock configurations. Custom rates of twist to help stabilize heavier bullets during long-range shooting. Extra-heavy, fluted, one-inch diameter barrel with a smaller ejection port provides more rigidity to the receiver and greater precision.
MSRP: $1,113.00

12 BVSS

Caliber: .22-250 Rem., .223 Rem., .308 Win.
Action: bolt, push feed, short, two-lug
Barrel: 26 in., stainless steel, heavy contour, fluted
Rifling Twist: RH 1:12 in. (.22-250 Rem.); RH 1:10 in. (.308 Win.); RH 1:9 in. (.223 Rem.)
Muzzle Device: None
Action/Barrel Finish: Matte stainless
Stock: Wood laminate
Stock Finish: Natural
Trigger: AccuTrigger, adjustable down to 6 oz.
Optic Mount: Drilled and tapped for mounts
Magazine: internal box; 4-round
Overall Length: 46.25 in.
Weight: 10 lb.
Features: The Varmint Series features button-rifled, free-floating barrels and a variety of stock configurations. Custom rates of twist to help stabilize heavier bullets during long-range shooting. Extra-heavy, fluted, one-inch diameter barrel with a smaller ejection port provides more rigidity to the receiver and greater precision.
MSRP: . . . . $1,081.00; $1,219.00 (Model 12 BTCSS thumbhole stock)

12 Long Range Precision

Caliber: .243 Win., .260 Rem., 6.5 Creedmoor
Action: bolt, push feed, short, two-lug
Barrel: 26 in., carbon steel, heavy contour, fluted
Rifling Twist: RH 1:9.25 in. (.243 Win.); RH 1:8 in. (.260 Rem., 6.5 Creedmoor)
Muzzle Device: None
Action/Barrel Finish: Matte black
Stock: HS Precision fiberglass stock
Stock Finish: Matte black

Trigger: AccuTrigger, adjustable from 1.5–6 lbs.
Optic Mount: Drilled and tapped for mounts
Magazine: detachable box; 4-round
Overall Length: 46.25 in.
Weight: 11 lb.
Features: three-position safety, oversized bolt handle, free floating bolt head, free-floated barrel, sling and bipod swivel mounts, rubber butt pad, side bolt release, oversized bolt knob.
MSRP: $1,170.00

Serbu Firearms (serbu.com)

Serbu Firearms is located in Tampa, Florida, and manufactures single-shot and Semiautomatic .50 BMG rifles.

BFG-50

Caliber: .50 BMG
Action: Bolt
Barrel: 22 in., 29.5 in. or 36 in. (heavy contour), free floating, match grade alloy steel
Rifling Twist: 1:15 in.
Muzzle Device: Shark Brake muzzle brake, 8 port
Action/Barrel Finish: Parkerized (manganese phosphate)
Stock: Fixed, steel construction, recoil pad, ventilated forend
Stock Finish: Parkerized (manganese phosphate)

Trigger: AR-15 trigger, 4 lb. pull weight
Optics Mount: Picatinny-style rail
Magazine: n/a, single-shot
Overall Length: 44 in. (22-in. barrel), 51.5 in. (29.5-in. barrel), 58 in. (36-in. barrel)
Weight: 17 lb. (22-in. barrel), 22 lb. (29.5-in. barrel), 32 lb. (36-in. barrel)
Accuracy: Sub MOA at 100 yd.
Features: Equipped with a bipod, AR-15 safety, custom hammer, spring-loaded firing pin.
MSRP: . . . . $2,395.00; $2,795.00 (36-in. barrel)

BFG-50A

Caliber: .50 BMG
Action: Semiautomatic, gas-operated, 3-lug rotating bolt
Barrel: 26 in., free floating, match grade alloy steel
Rifling Twist: 1:15 in.
Muzzle Device: Shark Brake muzzle brake, 8 port
Action/Barrel Finish: Parkerized (manganese phosphate)
Stock: Fixed, steel construction, recoil pad, ventilated forend
Stock Finish: Parkerized (manganese phosphate)

Trigger: AR-15 trigger, 4 lb. pull weight
Optics Mount: Picatinny-style rail
Magazine: Detachable steel box, 10-round
Overall Length: 52.5 in.
Weight: 25 lb.
Accuracy: Sub MOA at 100 yd.
Features: Compatible with standard 10-round M-82 magazines, gas system similar to that used on a Ljungman AG-42 or MAS 49/56, equipped with a bipod, AR-15 safety, custom hammer, spring-loaded firing pin.
MSRP: $6,700.00

SIG Sauer (sigsauer.com)

The SSG 3000 has the ability to be configured to a shooter's needs. Out-of-the-box is exhibit smooth bolt-action and exceptional long-range accuracy. For the SIG50, SIG partnered with McMillan to make the rifle lighter, more ergonomic on the grip (the pistol grip is similar to SIG's pistols), and with more area on the stock. The TAC2 rifle offers users multi-caliber capability with its modular and compact design and provides maximum portability and rapid deployment for military and law enforcement sniper teams. The Blaser straight-pull bolt-action offers follow-up shot speed unmatched by any other conventional bolt-action rifle on the market. The SIG716 is an AR-based rifle chambered in 7.62 x 51mm that utilizes a short stroke pushrod operating system. The SIG556 features a high-performance two position adjustable gas piston operating rod system and trigger housing that reduces the rifle's weight by one pound and it is designed to accept standard AR magazines.

SSG300 Patrol

Caliber: 7.62x51mm NATO/.308 Win.
Action: Bolt, push feed, 60° bolt lift
Barrel: 18 or 23.5 in., heavy contour, free floated, 5/8x24 in. threaded muzzle
Rifling Twist: 1:11 in.
Muzzle Device: Flash suppressor
Action/Barrel Finish: Matte black
Stock: Composite construction with aluminum bedding; adjustable length of pull andcheekpiece height; free-float design; pistol grip; integral Picatinny accessory rails; bipod attachment

Stock Finish: Matte black
Trigger: Single stage, adjustable factory set at 3.5 lb.
Optics Mount: Integrated zero MOA Mil-Std. 1913 Picatinny rail
Magazine: Detachable box, 5-round
Overall Length: 40 in. (18-in. barrel), 45 in. (23.5-in. barrel)
Weight: 11.5 lb. (18-in. barrel), 12.1 lb. (23.5-in. barrel)
Accuracy: Sub-MOA with match grade ammunition
Features: Round bolt handle, smooth bolt operation.
MSRP: $1,499.00

TAC2

Caliber: .308 Win., .300 Win. Mag., .338 Lapua Mag.
Action: Bolt, push feed, straight pull
Barrel: 24.7 in. (.308 Win.), 25.6 in. (.300 Win. Mag.), 27 in. (.338 Lapua Mag.); heavy contour, free floated, fluted; threaded muzzle
Rifling Twist: 1:11 in. (.308 Win., .300 Win. Mag.), 1:10 in. (.338 Lapua Mag.)
Muzzle Device: Muzzle brake
Action/Barrel Finish: Matte black
Stock: Polymer/aluminum construction; adjustable length of pull, cheekpiece height, spike height; free-float design; pistol grip; vented handguard with Picatinny-style rail; bipod attachment
Stock Finish: Matte black

Trigger: Adjustable, factory set at 2.2–3.3 lb.
Optics Mount: Mil-Std. 1913 Picatinny rail
Magazine: Detachable box, 5-round (.308 Win.), 4-round (.300 Win. Mag.,.338 Lapua Mag.)
Overall Length: 44.5 in. (.308 Win.), 45.5 in. (.300 Win. Mag.), 46.9 in. (.338 Lapua Mag.)
Weight: 11.9 lb. (.308 Win.), 12.1 lb. (.300 Win. Mag.), 12.6 lb. (.338 Lapua Mag.)
Accuracy: Sub-MOA with match grade ammunition
Effective Range: 1,100 m (.300 Win. Mag.), 1,500 m (.338 Lapua Mag.)
Features: Uses Blaser's straight pull action, oversized bolt handle, simple caliber interchangeability with one tool to fire any one of three available calibers.
MSRP: $4,171.00 (.308 Win., .300 Win. Mag.) $4,474.00 (.338 Lapua Mag.)

SIG50

Caliber: .50 BMG
Action: Bolt, push feed
Barrel: 29 in.; heavy contour, free floated, fluted; threaded muzzle
Rifling Twist: 1:15 in.
Muzzle Device: Muzzle brake
Action/Barrel Finish: Desert tan
Stock: Fiberglass construction; adjustable length of pull, cheekpiece height; free-float design; pistol grip; bipod attachment

Stock Finish: Desert tan
Trigger: Single stage, adjustable from 3.5 to 4.5 lb.
Optics Mount: Mil-Std. 1913 Picatinny rail
Magazine: Detachable box, 5-round
Overall Length: 57 in.
Weight: 23.5 lb.
Accuracy: MOA with match grade ammunition
Effective Range: 2,000 m
Features: Heavy duty steel bipod, detachable stock, anti-glare Duracoat coating.
MSRP: $9,825.00

SIG716 Precision

Caliber: 7.62x51mm NATO/.308 Win.
Action: Semiautomatic, short-stroke pushrod with 4-position gas valve
Barrel: 18 in., heavy contour, threaded muzzle
Rifling Twist: RH 1:10 in.
Muzzle Device: None
Action/Barrel Finish: Matte black
Stock: Adjustable Magpul UBR and MIAD grip, aluminum free float handguard with quad rails
Stock Finish: Matte
Trigger: Two-stage Match grade, 5.5 lb. pull weight
Optics Mount: Extended Picatinny-style rail, adjustable/folding iron sights
Magazine: Detachable steel box, 20-round
Overall Length: 38.3 in.
Weight: 11 lb.
Features: Piston system applied to an AR-based rifle, bipod attachment point, equipped with forward assist and dust cover.
MSRP: $2,666.00

SIG556DMR

Caliber: 5.56mm NATO
Action: Semiautomatic, gas-operated, rotating bolt
Barrel: 18 in., match grade, heavy contour
Rifling Twist: RH 1:8 in.
Muzzle Device: None
Action/Barrel Finish: Matte black
Stock: Adjustable Magpul MOA buttstock, aluminum free float handguard with quad rails
Stock Finish: Matte
Trigger: Enhanced single stage target
Optics Mount: Extended Picatinny-style rail
Magazine: Detachable steel box, 20-round
Overall Length: 39.2 in.
Weight: 9.5 lb.
Features: High-performance two position adjustable gas piston operating rod system, accepts standard AR-style magazines, includes Harris bipod.
MSRP: $1,732.00

Springfield Armory (springfield-armory.com)

Located in Illinois, Springfield Armory produces 1911, XD, and XD(M) pistols as well as civilian versions of the M14 called the M1A. They have been in business since 1974 and produce a range of M14 style rifles from match-grade M1As to short-barreled Scout and SOCOM II rifles.

M21 Tactical M1A

Caliber: 7.62x51mm NATO/.308 Win.
Action: Semiautomatic, gas-operated pistol, rotating bolt
Barrel: 22 in., Douglas Premium air-gauged custom heavy match or stainless Krieger, threaded muzzle
Rifling Twist: RH 1:10 in.
Muzzle Device: Flash hider
Action/Barrel Finish: Parkerized
Stock: Fixed, walnut, adjustable cheekpiece
Stock Finish: Matte

Trigger: Two-stage military trigger, factory set at 4.5-5 lb.
Optics Mount: Side mount Picatinny-style rail, adjustable hooded aperture rear/post front iron sights
Magazine: Detachable steel box, 10-round
Overall Length: 44.3 in.
Weight: 11.6 lb.
Maximum Range: 900 yd.
Features: Civilian version of the US military M14 enhanced with adjustable stock and match grade barrel.
MSRP: . . .$3,555.00 (Douglas barrel); $3,975.00 (Krieger barrel)

Stag Arms (stagarms.com)

Stag Arms was founded in May 2003 with the goal to manufacture reliable, 100 percent American-made, competitively priced mil-spec AR-15s. Unique to the AR is their right and left hand ARs. Stag Arms manufactures 80 percent of their rifle parts in house. The parts they do not manufacture are plastic pieces and some of the small springs, which are manufactured in the US by other vendors.

Model 6 (Super Varminter)

Caliber: 5.56 NATO/.223 Rem.
Action: Semiautomatic, gas impingement
Barrel: 24 in., heavy bull profile, 410 stainless, 11° target crown
Rifling Twist: RH 1:8 in.
Muzzle Device: None
Action/Barrel Finish: Matte black, type 3 hard coat anodizing
Stock: A2 style butt, Hogue Overmolded grip, Hogue free-floated aluminum handguard

Stock Finish: Black
Trigger: Two-stage match, factory set at 3.5 lb.
Optic Mount: Picatinny-style rail on upper receiver
Magazine: detachable box, 10-round
Overall Length: 42.5 in.
Weight: 7.8 lb.
Features: Designed for varmint hunting, mil-spec parts, left-handed model (Model 6) available.
MSRP: $1,055.00

Steyr Arms (steyrarms.com)

Steyr began producing weapons in the middle of the 17th century. Throughout the years the company has produced bolt-action rifles and Semiautomatic pistols. Today they produce hunting and sporting weapons. Steyr also produces law enforcement weapons. The Steyr AUG/A3 is an iconic bullpup style rifle. Jeff Cooper worked with Steyr to produce the Scout Rifle, another renowned design. Their bolt-action rifles are in use with LE and military forces around the world.

SSG 08

Caliber: .243 Win., .308 Win., .300 Win. Mag., .338 Lapua Mag.
Action: Bolt, push feed, 2 lug, 70° bolt lift
Barrel: 20 in. (.308 Win.), 23.6 in. (.243 Win., .308 Win., .300 Win. Mag.), heavy contour, free floated, threaded muzzle
Rifling Twist: 1:10 in. (.243 Win., .300 Win. Mag.), 1:12 in. (.308 Win.)
Muzzle Device: Muzzle brake
Action/Barrel Finish: Matte black
Stock: Folding buttstock; aluminum/polymer construction; adjustable length of pull, cheekpiece height, spike height; free-float design; pistol grip with replaceable front-rear grip straps; vented handguard; accessory rails; bipod attachment
Stock Finish: Matte black
Trigger: Adjustable, factory set at 3.52 lb.
Optics Mount: Mil-Std. 1913 Picatinny rail
Magazine: Detachable box, 10-round (.243 Win., .308 Win.), 8-round (.300 Win. Mag.), 6-round (.338 Lapua Mag.)
Overall Length: 43 in. (20 in. barrel), 46.5 in. (23.6 in. barrel)
Over Length Stock Folded: 34.2 in. (20 in. barrel), 37.8 in. (23.6 in. barrel)
Weight: 12.5 lb. (.243 Win.), 11.9 lb. (.308 Win.), 12.8 lb. (.300 Win. Mag.)
Features: Stock folds to left side of weapon allowing user access to action, round bolt handle.
MSRP: $5,895.00

Elite 08

Caliber: .308 Win.
Action: Bolt, push feed, 2 lug, 70° bolt lift
Barrel: 22.4 in., heavy contour, free floated, threaded muzzle
Muzzle Device: Muzzle brake
Action/Barrel Finish: Matte black
Stock: Folding buttstock; aluminum/polymer construction; adjustable length of pull, cheekpiece height, spike height; free-float design; pistol grip with replaceable front-rear grip straps; vented handguard; accessory rails; bipod attachment
Stock Finish: Matte black
Trigger: Adjustable, factory set at 3.52 lb.
Optics Mount: Extended Mil-Std. 1913 Picatinny rail
Magazine: Detachable box, 10-round
Overall Length: 43.9 in.
Over Length Stock Folded: 35.2 in.
Weight: 12.5 lb.
Features: Stock folds to left side of weapon allowing user access to action, same features as the Steyr SSG 08 but is based on the Steyr ELITE system with long Picatinny rail on the housing, tactical bolt knob.
MSRP: $5,999.00

SSG 69 PII

Caliber: .243 Win., .308 Win.
Action: Bolt, push feed, 26 lug, 60° bolt lift
Barrel: 25.6 in., heavy contour, free floated
Rifling Twist: 1:10 in. (.243 Win.), 1:12 in. (.308 Win.)
Muzzle Device: None
Action/Barrel Finish: Matte black
Stock: Traditional synthetic with textured grip areas; adjustable length of pull; free-float design; UIT rail

Stock Finish: Matte black or olive
Trigger: Adjustable from 2.5 to 4.0 lb.
Optics Mount: Drilled and tapped for optic mounts
Magazine: Detachable rotary polymer box, 5-round
Overall Length: 46.8 in.
Weight: 9.2 lb.
Features: Tactical bolt handle, rear locking lugs on bolt.
MSRP: $1,800.00

SSG 69 PIIK

Caliber: .308 Win.
Action: Bolt, push feed, 26 lug, 60° bolt lift
Barrel: 20 in., heavy contour, free floated
Rifling Twist: 1:12 in.
Muzzle Device: None
Action/Barrel Finish: Matte black
Stock: Traditional synthetic with textured grip areas; adjustable length of pull; free-float design; UIT rail

Stock Finish: Matte black or olive
Trigger: Adjustable from 2.5 to 4.0 lb.
Optics Mount: Drilled and tapped for optic mounts
Magazine: Detachable rotary polymer box, 5-round
Overall Length: 41.2 in.
Weight: 8.8 lb.
Features: Tactical bolt handle, rear locking lugs on bolt.
MSRP: $1,800.00

SSG 04

Caliber: .308 Win., .300 Win. Mag.
Action: Bolt, push feed, 2 lug, 70° bolt lift
Barrel: 20 in. (.308 Win.), 23.6 in. (.308 Win., .300 Win. Mag.), heavy contour, free floated, threaded muzzle
Rifling Twist: 1:10 in. (.300 Win. Mag.), 1:12 in. (.308 Win.)
Muzzle Device: Muzzle brake
Action/Barrel Finish: Matte black
Stock: Fixed buttstock; reinforced fiberglass construction; adjustable length of pull, cheekpiece height; free-float design; bipod attachment

Stock Finish: Matte black
Trigger: Fixed
Optics Mount: Integrated Mil-Std. 1913 Picatinny rail
Magazine: Detachable box, 10-round (.308 Win.), 8-round (.300 Win. Mag.)
Overall Length: 42.6 in. (20 in. barrel), 46.3 in. (23.6 in. barrel)
Weight: 10.4 lb. (20-in. barrel), 10.8 lb. (23.6-in. barrel)
Features: Heavy Barrel (HB) or Heavy Barrel Compact (HBC) offered.
MSRP: $1,950.00

SSG 04 A1

Caliber: .308 Win., .300 Win. Mag.
Action: Bolt, push feed, 2 lug, 70° bolt lift
Barrel: 20 in. (.308 Win.), 23.6 in. (.308 Win., .300 Win. Mag.), heavy contour, free floated, threaded muzzle
Rifling Twist: 1:10 in. (.300 Win. Mag.), 1:12 in. (.308 Win.)
Muzzle Device: Muzzle brake
Action/Barrel Finish: Matte black
Stock: Fixed buttstock; reinforced fiberglass construction; adjustable length of pull, cheekpiece height; free-float design; bipod attachment

Stock Finish: Matte black
Trigger: Fixed
Optics Mount: Integrated Mil-Std. 1913 Picatinny rail
Magazine: Detachable box, 10-round (.308 Win.), 8-round (.300 Win. Mag.)
Overall Length: 42.6 in. (20 in. barrel), 46.3 in. (23.6 in. barrel)
Weight: 10.4 lb. (20-in. barrel), 10.8 lb. (23.6-in. barrel)
Features: Heavy Barrel (HB) or Heavy Barrel Compact (HBC) offered, slightly modified version of the SSG 04 with long Picatinny top rail and side accessory rails.
MSRP: $3,195.00

Elite

Caliber: .223 Rem., .308 Win.
Action: Bolt, push feed, 70° bolt lift
Barrel: 22.4 in.
Rifling Twist: 1:9 in. (.223 Rem.), 1:12 in. (.308 Win.)
Muzzle Device: None
Action/Barrel Finish: Matte black
Stock: Aluminum/polymer construction; adjustable length of pull, cheekpiece height; free-float design; integrated bipod
Stock Finish: Matte black
Trigger: Fixed
Optics Mount: Integrated Mil-Std. 1913 Picatinny rail
Magazine: Detachable box, 5-round
Overall Length: 42.9
Weight: 9.7 lb.
Features: 7mm-08 caliber available upon request, oversized bolt knob, 10-round magazine adapter available, set trigger available.
MSRP: $2,299.00

HS .50

Caliber: .50 BMG
Action: Bolt, push feed, 2 lug, 90° bolt lift
Barrel: 33 in.
Rifling Twist: 1:15 in.
Muzzle Device: Muzzle brake
Action/Barrel Finish: Matte black
Stock: Steel construction with polymer pistol grip and rubber recoil pad; free-float design
Stock Finish: Matte black
Trigger: Two stage, factory set at 4 lb.
Optics Mount: Mil-Std. 1913 Picatinny rail
Magazine: n/a
Overall Length: 42.9
Weight: 9.7 lb.
Features: Single-shot, oversized bolt knob, bipod included, available in .460 Steyr as model Steyr HS .460 with twist rate of 1:14 in.
MSRP: $7,560.00

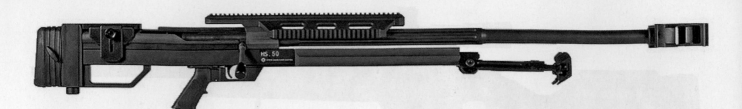

HS .50 M1

Caliber: .50 BMG
Action: Bolt, push feed, 2 lug, 90° bolt lift
Barrel: 33 in.
Rifling Twist: 1:15 in.
Muzzle Device: Muzzle brake
Action/Barrel Finish: Matte black
Stock: Steel construction with polymer pistol grip and rubber recoil pad; buttstock adjustable for length of pull, cheekpiece height, spine; free-float design

Stock Finish: Matte black
Trigger: Two-stage, factory set at 4 lb.
Optics Mount: Extended Mil-Std. 1913 Picatinny rail
Magazine: 5-round
Overall Length: 42.9
Weight: 9.7 lb.
Features: Similar to HS .50 but with longer optic rail, oversized bolt knob, bipod included.
MSRP: $5,299.00

THOR Global Defense Group (thorgdg.com)

THOR manufactures top quality operational equipment ranging from handguns, AR carbines, and suppressors to long-range bolt-action rifles among other equipment. The M408 system is a specialized rifle capable of hard and soft target interdiction. The entire rifle is maintainable at the operator level.

THOR M408

Caliber: .408 CheyTac
Action: Bolt, push feed
Barrel: Krieger fluted match; 30 in.
Rifling Twist: 1:13 in.
Muzzle Device: Muzzle brake
Action/Barrel Finish: Matte desert tan
Stock: Aluminum construction with polymer pistol grip and rubber recoil pad; fully adjustable for length of pull, cheekpiece height, spine; free-float design
Stock Finish: Matte black
Trigger: Two stage

Optics Mount: Integrated Mil-Std. 1913 Picatinny rail
Magazine: Detachable 7-round
Overall Length: 54.5 in.
Overall Length with Stock Collapsed: 48 in.
Weight: 26 lb.
Effective Range: 2,000 m
Features: Takedown rifle system, barrel is removable and replaceable by operator, over-the-barrel bipod system built onto the barrel shroud with carry handle, extended rail available for forward mounted optics, model M375 (.375 CheyTac), model LRIM 338 Lm (.338 Lapua Mag.).
MSRP: $11,495.00

THOR TR375
Caliber: .375 CheyTac
Action: Bolt, push feed
Barrel: 29 in., fluted
Rifling Twist: 1:11 in.
Muzzle Device: Muzzle brake
Action/Barrel Finish: Matte black

Stock: McMillan A5; adjustable for length of pull, cheekpiece height; butt hook; free-float design
Stock Finish: OD green
Trigger: Huber Concepts
Optics Mount: Integrated Mil-Std. 1913 Picatinny rail
Magazine: Detachable 7-round
Features: Fluted bolt with tactical bolt knob, Harris bipod, model TR408 (.408 CheyTac).
MSRP: $9,500.00

THOR TRMA338
Caliber: .338 Lapua Mag.
Action: Bolt, push feed
Barrel: 20 in.
Rifling Twist: 1:10 in.
Muzzle Device: Surefire MB338SS01 muzzle brake
Action/Barrel Finish: Matte black
Stock: Aluminum modular chassis; folding butt; adjustable for length of pull, cheekpiece height; free-float design

Stock Finish: Desert tan
Trigger: Huber Concepts
Optics Mount: Integrated Mil-Std. 1913 Picatinny rail
Magazine: Detachable 7-round
Effective Range: 1,500 m
Features: Accessory rails, Harris bipod, 416R SS action accepts AI/AW magazines.
MSRP: $6,765.00

THOR TRLA300
Caliber: .300 Win. Mag.
Action: Bolt, push feed
Barrel: 20 or 24 in., 4140 Chrome-Moly
Rifling Twist: 1:10 in.
Muzzle Device: Surefire SOCOM muzzle brake
Action/Barrel Finish: Matte black

Stock: Folding butt; aluminum modular chassis; polymer pistol grip; adjustable for length of pull, cheekpiece height; free-float design
Stock Finish: Desert tan
Trigger: Huber Concepts
Optics Mount: Integrated extended Mil-Std. 1913 Picatinny rail
Magazine: Detachable 7-round
Features: Accessory rails, Harris bipod.
MSRP: $6,765.00

THOR TRSA308

Caliber: .308 Win.
Action: Bolt, push feed
Barrel: 20 or 24 in., 4140 Chrome-Moly
Rifling Twist: 1:10 in.
Muzzle Device: Surefire SOCOM muzzle brake
Action/Barrel Finish: Matte black
Stock: Folding butt; aluminum construction; polymer pistol grip; adjustable for length of pull, cheekpiece height; free-float design

Stock Finish: Desert tan
Trigger: Huber Concepts
Optics Mount: Integrated extended Mil-Std. 1913 Picatinny rail
Magazine: Detachable 7-round
Features: Accessory rails, Harris bipod, 416R SS action accepts AI/AW magazines.
MSRP: $5,646.00

THOR XM408

Caliber: .408 CheyTac
Action: Bolt, push feed
Barrel: 30 in., fluted, match grade
Rifling Twist: 1:13 in.
Muzzle Device: Muzzle brake
Action/Barrel Finish: Matte black
Stock: Folding butt; aluminum chassis with polymer pistol grip and rubber recoil pad; fully adjustable for length of pull, cheekpiece height, spine; free-float design
Stock Finish: Matte black
Trigger: Two stage

Optics Mount: Integrated Mil-Std. 1913 Picatinny rail
Magazine: Detachable 5-round
Overall Length: 54.5 in.
Overall Length with Stock Collapsed: 48 in.
Weight: 26 lb.
Accuracy: Sub-MOA
Effective Range: 2,000 m
Features: Takedown rifle system; .50 BMG, .375 CheyTac and .338 Lapua Mag. conversion available; produced with Bill Ritchie, developer of the predecessor Windrunner platform.
MSRP: $5,999.00

THOR XM50

Caliber: .50 BMG
Action: Bolt, push feed
Barrel: 30 in., fluted
Muzzle Device: Shark-style muzzle brake
Action/Barrel Finish: Matte desert tan/matte black

Stock: Aluminum construction with polymer pistol grip and rubber recoil pad; fully adjustable for length of pull, cheekpiece height, spine; free-float handguard
Stock Finish: Matte desert tan
Trigger: Remington-style, factory set at 4 lb.
Optics Mount: Integrated Mil-Std. 1913 Picatinny rail
Magazine: Detachable 5-round
Features: Integrated bipod, quad rail handguard system.
MSRP: $7,999.00

Tikka (tikka.fi)

Tikka rifles are manufactured by Sako in Finland. Tikka rifles are known for having an extremely smooth bolt, crisp trigger, and excellent accuracy. They specialize in hunting and tactical rifles.

T3 Tac

Caliber: .223 Rem., .308 Win., .300 Win. Mag.
Action: Bolt, push feed, 2 lug, 70° bolt lift
Barrel: 20 in. or 23.75 in.; heavy contour, fluted, free floated, threaded muzzle
Rifling Twist: 1:8 or 1:12 in. (.223 Rem.), 1:11 in. (.308 Win., .300 Win. Mag.)
Muzzle Device: none
Action/Barrel Finish: Matte black
Stock: synthetic; adjustable cheekpiece height; free-floated beavertail forend; slings swivels; textures gripping surfaces with palm swell

Stock Finish: Black
Trigger: Single stage, adjustable from 2 to 4 lbs.
Optics Mount: Picatinny rail
Magazine: Detachable single stack box, 6-round (.223 Rem.), 5-round (.308 Win.), 4-round (.300 Win. Mag.)
Overall Length: 43.75 in. (23.75-in. barrel), 40.18 in. (20-in. barrel)
Weight: 8.15 lb. (23.75-in. barrel), 7.75 lb. (20-in. barrel)
Features: Optional single set trigger, cold hammer forged barrel, extra large bolt handle knob, two-position safety.
MSRP: $1,300.00

Tracking Point (tracking-point.com)

In February 2011, TrackingPoint was created to make the world's first Precision Guided Firearms. The optical system and firing system has since been adapted to numerous weapon platforms. The Tag Button, PGF Guided Trigger and the Heads Up Display (HUD) communicates ballistic and environment data to the operator to easily make 1,000-yard shots.

XS1

Caliber: .338 Lapua Mag.
Action: Bolt, push feed, Sturgeon XL
Barrel: 27 in., Krieger, MTU contour, recessed target crown
Rifling Twist: 1:9.35 in.
Muzzle Device: Advanced Armament Corp 90T muzzle brake
Action/Barrel Finish: Matte blue
Stock: Accuracy International AX folding chassis, adjustable length of pull and height of comb
Stock Finish: Matte black

Trigger: PGF guided trigger
Optics Mount: Picatinny rail
Magazine: Detachable box, 5-round
Overall Length: 49 in. (stock open)
Weight: 23.4 lb.
Effective Range: 1,200 yds.
Features: Networked 6-35x Tracking Scope with HUD (Heads Up Display); 200 rounds of Barnes 300-gr. Sierra Open-tip Match XactShot ammunition, Harris bipod, Pelican case, cleaning kit. XS2 and XS3 variants in .300 Win. Mag.
MSRP: $27,500.00

TP 750 300H

Caliber: .300 Win. Mag.
Action: Bolt, push feed
Barrel: 26 in., Remington LTR fluted stainless steel
Muzzle Device: None
Action/Barrel Finish: Black TriNyte PVD coating
Stock: Bell and Carson synthetic
Stock Finish: Spider web green
Trigger: PGF guided trigger
Optics Mount: Picatinny rail

Magazine: Internal box, 3-round
Overall Length: 45.8 in.
Weight: 12 lb.
Effective Range: 1,200 yds.
Features: Networked 6-35x Tracking Scope with HUD (Heads Up Display); Tag Button, Harris bipod, Pelican case, cleaning kit. XS2 and XS3 variants in .300 Win. Mag. Model TP 750 308H in .308 Win. and model TP 750 7mm in 7mm Rem. Mag.
MSRP: $9,995.00

Weatherby (weatherby.com)

The company began in the mid-1940s when a young cartridge "wildcatter" named Roy Weatherby set out to change the world of firearm performance. Contrary to then-popular thinking about heavy bullets pushed at slow speeds, Roy believed that lightweight bullets traveling at super high speeds provided the best combination for one-shot kills. Based upon that philosophy, Weatherby spent the next decade developing propretary high-powered Weatherby Magnum cartridges ranging in calibers from .224 through .460.

Vanguard Series 2 TRR RC

Caliber: .223 Rem., .308 Win.
Action: Bolt, short-action, push feed, 2 lug
Barrel: 22 in., heavy contour, recessed target crown
Rifling Twist: 1:14 in. (.223 Rem.), 1:12 in. (.308 Win.)
Muzzle Device: None
Action/Barrel Finish: Matte blue
Stock: Hand-laminated Monte Carlo composite, aluminum bedding plate, beavertail forearm, Pachmayr Decelerator recoil pad

Stock Finish: Matte black
Maximum Length of Pull: 13.6 in.
Trigger: Match quality, two-stage trigger
Optics Mount: Drilled and tapped for bases
Magazine: Hinged floorplate, 5-round
Overall Length: 42 in.
Weight: 8.7 lb.
Accuracy: Guarantee sub-MOA, 3-shots with premium ammunition
Features: Dual swivel studs allow use of bipod and sling.
MSRP: . . . $765.00 (20-in. barrel); $834.00 (16-in. barrel)

Mark V TRR Custom Magnum

Caliber: .300 Win. Mag., .300 Wby. Mag., .30-378 Wby. Mag., .338 Lapua Mag., .338-378 Wby. Mag.
Action: Bolt, long-action, push feed, 9 lug, 54° bolt lift
Barrel: 26 in. (.300 Win. Mag., .300 Wby. Mag.) or 28 in. (.30-378 Wby. Mag., .338 Lapua Mag., .338-378 Wby. Mag.), heavy contour, free floated, recessed target crown
Rifling Twist: RH 1:9.3 in. (.338 Lapua Mag.), RH 1:10 in. (.300 Win. Mag., .300 Wby. Mag., .30-378 Wby. Mag., .338-378 Wby. Mag.)
Muzzle Device: Accubrake (.30-378 Wby. Mag., .338 Lapua Mag., .338-378 Wby. Mag.)
Action/Barrel Finish: Matte blue
Stock: Composite construction; adjustable length of pull, comb height, drop at heel
Stock Finish: Matte black
Length of Pull: 13.2 in. - 14.7 in.
Trigger: Adjustable trigger, factory set at 3 lb.
Optics Mount: Drilled and tapped for bases
Magazine: Hinged steel floorplate, 3-round (.300 Win. Mag., .300 Wby. Mag.), 2-round (.30-378 Wby. Mag., .338 Lapua Mag., .338-378 Wby. Mag.)
Overall Length: 46 in. (.300 Win. Mag., .300 Wby. Mag.), 48 in. (.30-378 Wby. Mag., .338 Lapua Mag., .338-378 Wby. Mag.)
Weight: 9.2 lb.
Accuracy: Guarantee 1-½-MOA, 3-shots at 100 yds. with premium ammunition
Features: Two-position safety, cocking indicator.
MSRP: $2,800.00

Mark V TRR RC

Caliber: .300 Win. Mag., .300 Wby. Mag., .30-378 Wby. Mag., .338 Lapua Mag., .338-378 Wby. Mag.
Action: Bolt, long-action, push feed, 9 lug, 54° bolt lift
Barrel: 28 in. (.300 Win. Mag., .300 Wby. Mag., .30-378 Wby. Mag., .338 Lapua Mag., .338-378 Wby. Mag.), heavy contour, fluted, free floated
Rifling Twist: RH 1:9.3 in. (.338 Lapua Mag.), RH 1:10 in. (.300 Win. Mag., .300 Wby. Mag., .30-378 Wby. Mag., .338-378 Wby. Mag.)
Muzzle Device: Accubrake
Action/Barrel Finish: Matte blue
Stock: Hand-laminated; CNC 6061 T-6 aluminum bedding system; adjustable for length of pull, drop at heel and cant of the pad
Stock Finish: Desert camo
Length of Pull: 13.2 in.–14.7 in.
Trigger: Adjustable trigger, factory set at 3 lb.
Optics Mount: Drilled and tapped for bases
Magazine: Detachable box, 2-round
Overall Length: 46 in. (.300 Win. Mag., .300 Wby. Mag.), 48 in. (.30-378 Wby. Mag., .338 Lapua Mag., .338-378 Wby. Mag.)
Weight: 9.2 lb.
Accuracy: Guarantee 1-½-MOA, 3-shots at 100 yd. with premium ammunition
Features: Two-position safety, cocking indicator, Stock features a #6 slide for bipod attachment.
MSRP: $2,800.00

Winchester (winchesterguns.com)

Winchester lever-action rifles "won the west" but the Winchester Model 54 bolt-action built in 1925 was the first successful civilian bolt-action rifle for the company. The Model 54 evolved into the widely popular Model 70 which is known as the "Rifleman's Rifle." The exploits of the Model 70 in the hands of hunters like Jack O'Connor and snipers like Carlos Hathcock are legendary.

Model 70 Coyote Light

Caliber: .22-250 Rem., .243 Win., .308 Win., .300 WSM, .270 WSM, .325 WSM
Action: Bolt, short-action, control feed, 2 lug
Barrel: 24 in., fluted, medium heavy, stainless steel, free floating, crowned
Muzzle Device: None
Action/Barrel Finish: Matte stainless
Stock: Bell and Carlson carbon fiber/fiberglass composite with one-piece aluminum bedding, Pachmayr Decelerator recoil pad

Stock Finish: Black
Length of Pull: 13.5 in.
Trigger: MOA trigger system
Optics Mount: Drill and tapped for mounts
Magazine: Internal box, 5-round
Overall Length: 44 in.
Weight: 7.5 lb.
Features: Three-position safety, front swivel stub for bipod, Mauser-style claw extractor, carefully trimmed of any unnecessary bulk.
MSRP: $1,149.00

37. Vintage Precision Rifles

C. Sharps Arms, Inc. (csharpsarms.com)

Model 1874 Bridgeport Sporting Rifle

Caliber: 38-55, 40-65, 40-70 2 1/10 Bottleneck, 40-70 2 1/10 Sharps Straight, 45-70 2 ½ Sharps Straight, 45-90 2 4/10 Sharps Straight, 45-100 2 7/8 Sharps Straight, 45-110 2 7/8 Sharps Straight, 45-120 2 7/8 Sharps Straight, 50-70 Government, 50-90 2 ½ Sharps Straight, 50-100 2 ½ Sharps Straight
Action: Single shot, falling block
Barrel: 26, 28 or 30 in, match grade Badger, heavy tapered round, with cut rifling, hand lapped

Action/Barrel Finish: Case hardened action, blued barrel
Stock: American walnut , straight or pistol grip
Stock Finish: Satin
Trigger: Double set
Sights: Tapped for rear tang, front dovetail for post and hood
Overall Length: 47 in.
Weight: 10 lb.
Features: Multiple caliber, wood and iron sights options. Replica of Sharps Model 1874 rifle.
MSRP: $1,895.00

Model 1875 Target

Caliber: 38-55, 40-65, 40-70 2 1/10 Bottleneck, 40-70 2 1/10 Sharps Straight, 45-70 2 ½ Sharps Straight, or 45-90 2 4/10 Sharps Straight
Action: Single shot, falling block
Barrel: 30-in. match grade Badger, heavy tapered round, with cut rifling, hand lapped
Action/Barrel Finish: Case hardened action, blued barrel
Stock: American walnut w/ pistol grip

Stock Finish: Satin
Trigger: Standard or single set
Sights: Tapped for rear tang, front dovetail for post and hood
Overall Length: 47 in.
Weight: 11 lb.
Features: Multiple wood and iron sights options. Replica of Sharps Model 1875 rifle.
MSRP: $1,325.00

Model 1885 Highwall Sporting Rifle

Caliber: .22 Hornet, .218 Bee, .219 Zipper, 25-35, 30-40 K, 30-30, 32-40, 38-40, 38-55, 405 Winchester, 40-50 Bottleneck, 40-50 Sharps Straight, 40-65, 40-70 2 1/10 Bottleneck, 40-70 2 1/10 Sharps Straight, 45-70 2 ½ Sharps Straight, 45-90 2 4/10 Sharps Straight, 45-100 2 7/8 Sharps Straight, 45-110 2 7/8 Sharps Straight, 45-120 2 7/8 Sharps Straight
Action: Single shot, falling block
Barrel: 26, 28 or 30 in, match grade Badger, heavy tapered round

Action/Barrel Finish: Case hardened action, blued barrel
Stock: American walnut , straight or pistol grip, Schnabel-style forend
Stock Finish: Satin
Trigger: Single, standard
Sights: Tapped for rear tang, front dovetail for post and hood
Overall Length: 47 in. (30-in. barrel)
Weight: 9 lb. 4 oz. (30-in. barrel)
Features: Multiple caliber, wood and iron sights options. Replica of Winchester Model 1885 rifle.
MSRP: $1,750.00

Cimarron (cimarron-firearms.com)

Big Fifty Sharps Rifle

Caliber: 50-90
Action: Single shot, falling block
Barrel: 34 in, octagon to round barrel with cut rifling
Action/Barrel Finish: Case hardened action, blued barrel
Stock: Walnut , pistol grip, Schnabel-style forend
Stock Finish: Satin
Trigger: Double set

Sights: Creedmoor tang rear/ post and hoodfront
Overall Length: 51 in.
Weight: 11.9 lb.
Features: Replica of Sharps Model 1874 rifle. Upgraded wood, hand checkered pistol grip stock, upgraded finish, case hardened receiver, silver German nose cap, Soule Midrange sights, spirit level rear, globe front with inserts.
MSRP: $2,877.51

Billy Dixon Sharps

Caliber: 45-70
Action: Single shot, falling block
Barrel: 32 in, octagon barrel with cut rifling
Action/Barrel Finish: Case hardened action, blued barrel
Stock: Walnut, pistol grip, Schnabel-style forend
Stock Finish: Satin

Trigger: Double set
Sights: Ladder rear/ sliver blade front
Overall Length: 49 in.
Weight: 10.8 lb.
Features: Similar to rifle used by Billy Dixon at Adobe Walls in 1874. Replica of Sharps Model 1874 rifle.
MSRP: $2,141.06

Pride of the Plains Sharps

Caliber: 45-70
Action: Single shot, falling block
Barrel: 30 in., octagon barrel with cut rifling
Action/Barrel Finish: Nickel silver action, blued barrel
Stock: Checkered walnut , pistol grip, Schnabel-style forend
Stock Finish: Satin
Trigger: Double set

Sights: Tang-mount vernier caliper rear/post and hood front
Overall Length: 47 in.
Weight: 11.5 lb.
Features: Hand-checkered walnut stock, coin nickel receiver, high polish blue octagon barrel, Creedmoor sight rear, tunnel sight with front inserts. Replica of Sharps Model 1874 rifle.
MSRP: $2,274.96

Rocky Mountain Sharps

Caliber: 45-70
Action: Single shot, falling block
Barrel: 32 in, octagon barrel with cut rifling
Action/Barrel Finish: Nickel silver action, blued barrel
Stock: Checkered walnut , pistol grip, Schnabel-style forend

Stock Finish: Satin
Trigger: Double set
Optics: 6x Malcolm scope
Overall Length: 49 in.
Weight: 10.8 lb.
Features: Replica of Sharps Model 1874 rifle. Similar to rifle used by Billy Dixon at Adobe Walls in 1874.
MSRP: $2,307.50

Rifle From Down Under Sharps
Caliber: 45-120
Action: Single shot, falling block
Barrel: 34 in.,octagon barrel
Action/Barrel Finish: Case hardened action, blued barrel
Stock: Walnut , straight grip, Schnabel-style forend
Stock Finish: Satin

Trigger: Double set
Sights: Creedmoor tang rear/ post and hoodfront
Overall Length: 51 in.
Weight: 13.2 lb.
Features: Replica of Sharps Model 1874 rifle. Faithful reproduction of the Sharps long-range rifle from the film *Quigley Down Under*.
MSRP: $2,489.20

Adobe Walls Rolling Block
Caliber: 45-70
Action: Single shot, rolling block
Barrel: 30 in, octagon barrel
Action/Barrel Finish: Color case hardened action, blued barrel
Stock: Checkered walnut , pistol grip, Schnabel-style forend
Stock Finish: Satin

Trigger: Double set
Sights: Ladder rear/blade front
Overall Length: 47 in.
Weight: 10.4 lb.
Features: Replica of Remington Rolling Block rifle with hand checkered walnut stock, upgraded walnut hand finished, case hardened receiver, and German silver nose cap.
MSRP: $1,739.36

Deluxe Model 1885 High Wall Sporting Rifle

Caliber: 45-70
Action: Single shot, falling block
Barrel: 30 in.
Action/Barrel Finish: Color case hardened action, blued barrel
Stock: Checkered walnut , pistol grip, Schnabel-style forend
Stock Finish: Satin

Trigger: Double set
Sights: Ladder rear/blade front
Overall Length: 47 in.
Weight: 9.7 lb.
Features: Replica of Winchester Model 1885 rifle with hand checkered walnut stock, upgraded walnut hand finished.
MSRP: . .$1,351.05; $1,250.63 (40-65 caliber, single trigger)

Gibbs Rifle Company, Inc. (gibbsrifle.com)

1903A4-84 Springfield Sniper Rifle

Caliber: .30-06
Action: Bolt, claw extractor, 3 lug
Barrel: 24 in., 4 groove
Muzzle Device: None
Action/Barrel Finish: Light gray/green parkerized
Stock: Old resistant walnut
Stock Finish: Matte
Trigger: Two-stage, military-style

Optics Mount: M84 rifle scope
Magazine: Internal box, 5-round
Overall Length: 43.9 in.
Weight: 8.7 lb.
Features: Replica of Springfield 1903A4 sniper rifle. Improved replica of US Military M84 rifle scope and 7/8 in. top-mounted rings. Blued steel tube with rubber eyepiece, thin crosshair reticle.
MSRP: $1,249.95

Mauser K98k

Caliber: 8mm Mauser (also known as 8x57 JS or 7.9mm)
Action: Bolt, claw extractor, 2 lug
Barrel: 23.5 in.
Rifling Twist: 1:9.24 in.
Muzzle Device: None
Action/Barrel Finish: Blue
Stock: Oil resistant laminated wood
Stock Finish: Matte tan

Trigger: Two-stage, military-style
Optics: 1.5x ZF-41 long eye relief scope
Magazine: Internal box, 5-round
Overall Length: 43.5 in.
Weight: 8.9 lb.
Features: Iron sights with adjustable rear sight, three-position safety, includes long-eye relief replica ZF-41 scope.
MSRP: $1,299.00

Mosin–Nagant 91/30 PU Sniper

Caliber: 7.62mm Russian (also known as 7.62x54R)
Action: Bolt, claw extractor, 2 lug
Barrel: 28.7 in.
Rifling Twist: 1:10 in.
Muzzle Device: None
Action/Barrel Finish: Blue
Stock: Wood

Stock Finish: Matte brown
Trigger: Two-stage, military-style
Optics: 3.5x PU, left-side of receiver mount
Magazine: Internal box, 5-round
Overall Length: 48.5 in.
Weight: 8.8 lb.
Features: Iron sights with adjustable rear sight, 2-position safety, includes genuine Soviet PU military scope.
MSRP: $799.00

Taylor's & Co., Inc. (taylorsfirearms.com)

1874 Sharps Sporting Rifle, Hartford Style
Caliber: 45-70
Action: Single shot, falling block
Barrel: 32 in., octagon barrel
Action/Barrel Finish: Case hardened action, blued barrel
Stock: Walnut, straight grip, Schnabel-style forend
Stock Finish: Satin

Trigger: Double set
Sights: Ladder rear/ sliver blade front
Overall Length: 49 in.
Weight: 10.8 lb.
Features: Similar to rifle used by Billy Dixon at Adobe Walls in 1874. Replica of Sharps Model 1874 rifle.
MSRP: $1,346.00

1885 Single Shot High-Wall
Caliber: 45-70
Action: Single shot, falling block
Barrel: 32 in.
Action/Barrel Finish: Color case hardened action, blued barrel
Stock: Smooth walnut , straight grip

Stock Finish: Satin
Trigger: Single, standard
Sights: Buckhorn rear/blade front
Overall Length: 49 in.
Weight: 10 lb.
Features: Replica of Winchester Model 1885 rifle with walnut stock, upgraded walnut hand finished.
MSRP: $1,109.00

Rolling Block Creedmoor No. 2

Caliber: 45-70
Action: Single shot, rolling block
Barrel: 30 in, round barrel, 1x18 in twist, 6 grooves
Action/Barrel Finish: Coin finish action, blued barrel
Stock: Checkered walnut , pistol grip, Schnabel-style forend
Stock Finish: Satin
Trigger: Double set
Sights: Long range Creedmoor rear/tunnel front
Overall Length: 46.1 in.
Weight: 9.3 lb.
Features: Replica of Remington Rolling Block rifle with hand checkered walnut stock, upgraded walnut hand finished, case hardened receiver and German silver nose cap.
MSRP: $1,739.36

Uberti (uberti.com)

1874 Sharps Deluxe

Caliber: 45-70
Action: Single shot, falling block
Barrel: 34 in, octagon barrel
Action/Barrel Finish: Case hardened action, blued barrel
Stock: AA-grade walnut , straight grip, Schnabel-style forend
Stock Finish: Satin
Trigger: Double set
Sights: Creedmoor tang rear/ post and hoodfront
Overall Length: 51 in.
Weight: 13.2 lb.
Features: Replica of Sharps Model 1874 rifle.
MSRP: $3,129.00

1885 High-Wall Special Sporting

Caliber: 45-70
Action: Single shot, falling block
Barrel: 32 in.
Action/Barrel Finish: Color case hardened action, blued barrel
Stock: Smooth walnut , pistol grip
Stock Finish: Satin
Trigger: Single, standard
Sights: Buckhorn rear/blade front
Overall Length: 49 in.
Weight: 10 lb.
Features: Replica of Winchester Model 1885 rifle with checkered walnut stock.
MSRP: . . $1,239.00; $1,279.00 (45-90 or 45-120 caliber)

38. Scout Rifles

Fulton Armory (fulton-armory.com)

Though technically not true to Cooper's vision, Fulton Armory's scout-type rifles are in the spirit of Scout Rifles with their short overall length, detachable magazine fed firepower and forward mounted optic.

M14 Scout 16
Caliber: 7.62x51mm NATO/.308 Win.
Action: Semiautomatic, gas-operated pistol, rotating bolt
Barrel: 16 in.
Rifling Twist: RH 1:10 in.
Muzzle Device: A2 style flash suppressor
Action/Barrel Finish: Parkerized
Stock: New walnut, GI contour, rubber recoil pad
Stock Finish: Linseed oil
Trigger: Two-stage military trigger

Optics Mount: Handguard Super Scout, 3-Way M1913 Picatinny rail
Magazine: Detachable steel box, 10-round
Overall Length: 37.25 in.
Weight: 8.8 lb.
Accuracy: Under 2.5 MOA (with Hornady Match ammunition)
Features: Short barrel variant of US military M14, tuned gas system, adjustable enlarged aperture rear/post front.
MSRP: $2,900.00

Mk14 Mod 1 EBR
Caliber: 7.62x51mm NATO/.308 Win.
Action: Semiautomatic, gas-operated pistol, rotating bolt
Barrel: 18.5 in.
Rifling Twist: RH 1:10 in.
Muzzle Device: A2 style flash suppressor
Action/Barrel Finish: Parkerized
Stock: Sage Tactical Chassis, CQB, aluminum, Magpul CTR Buttstock
Stock Finish: Black
Trigger: Two-stage military trigger
Optics Mount: Handguard Super Scout, 3-Way M1913 Picatinny rail

Magazine: Detachable steel box, 10-round
Overall Length: 35.25 in.
Weight: 9.9 lb.
Accuracy: Under 1.5 MOA (with Hornady Match ammunition)
Features: The "Chop-Mod" is comprised of Fulton Armory's M14 Service Rifle fitted with an 18.5 in. barrel, direct connect Vortex flash suppressor, and a front sight relocated to the gas cylinder lock (with dovetail), installed in the Sage CQB tactical chassis system with the Magpul CTR buttstock.
MSRP: $3,775.00

Ruger (ruger.com)

Over the years Ruger has made a few Scout Rifles and the latest is a robust carbine that fits into Jeff Cooper's definition.

Gunsite Scout Rifle

Caliber: .308 Win.
Action: Bolt, short-action, control feed, 2 lug
Barrel: 16.5 in. or 18 in., 5/8-24 threaded muzzle
Rifling Twist: 1:10 in.
Muzzle Device: Flash hider
Action/Barrel Finish: Alloy steel/matte black or Stainless steel/matte stainless
Stock: Laminated wood
Stock Finish: Black laminate
Length of Pull: 12.7 in.–14.2 in.
Trigger: LC6, two-stage, adjustable
Optics Mount: Integral scope mounts, Picatinny-style rail, adjustable ghost ring rear/protected front post
Magazine: Detachable steel box, 3-, 5- or 10-round
Overall Length: 41 in.
Weight: 7 lb. (16.5-in. barrel), 7.1 lb. (18-in. barrel)
Features: Three-position safety, rubber recoil pad with three ½-in. spacers
MSRP: $1,039.00 (16-in. barrel); $1,099.00 (18-in. barrel)

Savage (savagearms.com)

Using their Model 10 short-action, Savage has created a Scout Rifle that is lightweight and provides plenty of firepower.

10 FCM Scout

Caliber: .308 Win., 7.62x39mm
Action: bolt, push feed, short
Barrel: 20.5 in. carbon steel
Rifling Twist: RH 1:10 in.
Muzzle Device: none
Action/Barrel Finish: Matte black
Stock: AccuStock
Stock Finish: Matte black
Length of Pull: 13.7 in.
Trigger: AccuTrigger, adjustable from 1.5 – 6 lbs.
Optic Mount: Barrel-mounted scope mount, ghost ring rear/ramp front sights
Magazine: detachable box, 4-round
Overall Length: 39.7 in.
Weight: 6.6 lb.
Features: three-position safety, oversized bolt handle, free-floating bolt head, free-floated barrel, sling swivel mounts, rubber butt pad.
MSRP: $865.00

Springfield Armory (springfield-armory.com)

Though technically not true to Cooper's vision, Springfield Armory's scout-type rifles are in the spirit of Scout Rifles with their short overall length, detachable magazine fed firepower, and forward mounted optic.

SOCOM 16 M1A

Caliber: 7.62x51mm NATO/.308 Win.
Action: Semiautomatic, gas-operated pistol, rotating bolt
Barrel: 16.2 in.
Rifling Twist: RH 1:11 in.
Muzzle Device: Muzzle brake
Action/Barrel Finish: Parkerized
Stock: Fixed, polymer
Stock Finish: Matte black

Trigger: Two-stage military trigger, factory set at 5-6 lb.
Optics Mount: Weaver-style rail forward of the action
Magazine: Detachable steel box, 10-round
Overall Length: 37.25 in.
Weight: 8.8 lb.
Features: Civilian version of the US military M14, shortest barrel allowed for civilian-owned rifle, re-tuned gas system, adjustable enlarged aperture rear/post front.
MSRP: . . . $1,893.00 (black composite stock); $1,905.00 (green composite stock)

SOCOM II M1A

Caliber: 7.62x51mm NATO/.308 Win.
Action: Semiautomatic, gas-operated pistol, rotating bolt
Barrel: 16.2 in.
Rifling Twist: RH 1:11 in.
Muzzle Device: Muzzle brake
Action/Barrel Finish: Parkerized
Stock: Fixed, polymer
Stock Finish: Matte black
Trigger: Two-stage military trigger, factory set at 5-6 lb.

Optics Mount: Weaver-style rail forward of the action
Magazine: Detachable steel box, 10-round
Overall Length: 37.2 in.
Weight: 8.8 lb.
Features: Civilian version of the US military M14, shortest barrel allowed for civilian-owned rifle, re-tuned gas system, Cluster Rail System accommodate optics, lights, or other accessories designed to fit a standard Picatinny rail, adjustable aperture rear/post front with Tritium insert iron sights.
MSRP: . . . . . $2,176.00; $2,286.00 (extended Cluster rail)

Scout Squad M1A

Caliber: 7.62x51mm NATO/.308 Win.
Action: Semiautomatic, gas-operated pistol, rotating bolt
Barrel: 18 in.
Rifling Twist: RH 1:11 in.
Muzzle Device: Muzzle brake
Action/Barrel Finish: Parkerized
Stock: Fixed, polymer
Stock Finish: polymer matte black or Mossy Oak camo or walnut

Trigger: Two-stage military trigger, factory set at 5–6 lb.
Optics Mount: Weaver-style rail forward of the action
Magazine: Detachable steel box, 10-round
Overall Length: 37.2 in.
Weight: 8.8 lb.
Features: Civilian version of the US military M14, military-style adjustable aperture rear/national matchfront blade iron sights.
MSRP: . . . $1,761.00 (black composite stock); $1,848.00 (Mossy Oak camo stock) ; $1,893.00 (walnut stock)

Steyr Arms (steyrarms.com)

When Steyr presented Jeff Cooper with a prototype of the Scout Rifle, Cooper did not look any further. The caliber, weight, ergonomics, and other features make this the original Scout Rifle.

Mannlicher Scout

Caliber: .223 Rem., .243 Rem., 7 mm-08 Rem., .308 Win.
Action: Bolt, push feed, 2 lug, 70° bolt lift
Barrel: 19 in., lightweight, fluted, free floated
Rifling Twist: 1:8.6 in. (7mm-08), 1:9 in. (.223 Rem., .243 Win.), 1:10 in. (.308 Win.)
Muzzle Device: None
Action/Barrel Finish: Matte black

Stock: Polymer construction; adjustable length of pull; integrated bipod in forearm; additional magazine can be stored in buttstock well; integrated rail
Stock Finish: Matte black or grey
Trigger: Single set or direct, adjustable
Optics Mount: Mil-Std. 1913 Picatinny rail
Magazine: Detachable box, 5- or 10-round
Overall Length: 38.6 in.
Weight: 6.6 lb.
Features: Classic Jeff Cooper Scout Rifle, uses same action as Elite.
MSRP: $2,099.00

39. Suppressors

Advanced Armament Corp. (advanced-armament.com)

M4-2000

Caliber: 5.56mm NATO
Overall Length: 6.62 in.
Length Added: 5.1 in.
Diameter: 1.5 in.
Weight: 17.6 oz.
Sound Reduction: 32-34 dB
Mounting: 51T ratchet

Cyclone

Caliber: 7.62mm NATO, .300 BLK
Overall Length: 9.5 in.
Length Added: 8.75 in.
Diameter: 1.5 in.
Weight: 22.4 oz.
Material: Inconel 718, 316L SS

Hunter

Caliber: 7.62mm NATO, .300 BLK
Overall Length: 7.3 in.
Length Added: 6.5 in.
Diameter: 1.5 in.
Weight: 21.4 oz.
Material: Inconel 718, 316L SS

762-SDN-6

Caliber: 7.62mm NATO, .300 BLK
Overall Length: 7.6 in.
Length Added: 6.1 in.
Diameter: 1.5 in.
Weight: 20 oz.
Material: Inconel 718, 316L SS

300-TM

Caliber: 7.62mm NATO, .300 Win. Mag.
Overall Length: 9.3 in.
Length Added: 8.7 in.
Diameter: 1.5 in.
Weight: 15 oz.
Material: Grades 5 & 9 titanium

Finish: Cerakote
Features: Patent pending fast-attach Ratchet-Mount to provide precision accuracy with minimal and repeatable zero-shift. Compact size and light weight manufactured with high-temperature aerospace alloy. Back-pressure lowering design of the silencer aids in shooter comfort, reduces weapon fouling, and minimizes cyclic rate increase.
MSRP: $1,050.00

Sound Reduction: 30-33 dB
Mounting: 5/8-24, M18x1
Finish: Cerakote
Features: Rigid and simple threaded mounting design provides reliable precision accuracy with minimal and repeatable zero-shift for extraordinary sound and recoil reduction.
MSRP: $750.00

Sound Reduction: 227-29 dB
Mounting: 5/8-24, M18x1
Finish: Cerakote
Features: The rigid direct-thread interface and accuracy-driven design of the baffle cores helps enhance accuracy and repeatable zero-shift.
MSRP: $650.00

Sound Reduction: 25 dB (7.62mm NATO), 39 dB (.300 BLK)
Mounting: 51T ratchet
Finish: Cerakote
Features: Compact fast-attach sound and flash suppressor is 1.25 inches shorter than the 762-SD and features a fully welded all-Inconel baffle stack and front end cap to maximize durability on select fire 7.62mm SBRs.
MSRP: $1,050.00

Sound Reduction: 28-33 dB
Mounting: 5/8-24 or M18x1 thread
Finish: Cerakote
Features: Based on the military tested and adopted Mk13-SD, the 300-TM is a thread mounting suppressor for 7.62mm NATO and .300 Winchester Magnum rifles constructed of titanium.
MSRP: $1,195.00

MK13-SD
Caliber: 7.62mm NATO, .300 Win. Mag., .300 BLK
Overall Length: 9.5 in.
Length Added: 8.9 in.
Diameter: 1.5 in.
Weight: 13.9 oz.
Material: Grades 5 & 9 titanium

MG-SD
Caliber: 5.56 NATO and 7.62mm NATO
Overall Length: 7.6 in.
Length Added: 5.2 in.
Diameter: 2 in.
Weight: 31 oz.
Material: Inconel 718, 316L SS
Sound Reduction: 25 dB (5.56 NATO), 26 dB (7.62 NATO)

Titan-TI
Caliber: .338 Lapua Mag. and lower
Overall Length: 10 in.
Length Added: 8 in.
Diameter: 1.8 in.
Weight: 21 oz.
Material: Grades 5 & 9 titanium

Titan-QD
Caliber: .338 Lapua Mag.
Overall Length: 10 in.
Length Added: 8.4 in.
Diameter: 1.8 in.
Weight: 20 oz.
Material: Grades 5 & 9 titanium

Cyclops
Caliber: .50 BMG
Overall Length: 15.75in.
Length Added: 12.65 in.
Diameter: 2.5 in.
Weight: 4 lb. 12 oz.
Material: Alloy steel

Sound Reduction: 28-33 dB
Mounting: 90T ratchet
Finish: Gun-Kote
Features: Military chosen Mk13-SD is an ultra-light-weight, fast-attach, high performance sound and flash suppressor for bolt-action rifles. Grade 5 Titanium monolithic baffle core and Grade 9 Titanium tube.
MSRP: $1,795.00

Mounting: 90T ratchet taper mount
Finish: Cerakote
Features: Military adopted MG-SD is a single unit solution for reducing the signature of 5.56mm and 7.62mm light machine guns. Designed to handle the unrelenting heat and abrasive blasting of sustained burst firing, the MG-SD features a rugged monolithic core of heat treated Inconel 718.
MSRP: $2,295.00

Sound Reduction: 34 dB
Mounting: Thread
Finish: Gun-Kote
Features: Incorporates Hyposone monolithic baffle module and CNC fusion welding, light-weight 100 percent titanium.
MSRP: $1,695.00

Sound Reduction: 32 dB
Mounting: 90T ratchet
Finish: Gun-Kote
Features: Features monolithic Hyposone baffle module and is assembled via fully CNC automated fusion welding. Selected as the silencer for the Army's XM2010 sniper rifle.
MSRP: $1,995.00

Sound Reduction: 32 dB
Mounting: Ratchet
Finish: Gun-Kote
Features: Designed to reduce the sound, felt recoil, environmental disturbances and visible flash signature of bolt-action and single shot rifles chambering the .50 BMG cartridge.
MSRP: $2,500.00

AWC Systems Technology (awcsystech.com)

Thundertrap
Caliber: .22 to .50 Beowolf
Overall Length: 10.25 in.
Length Added: 8.25 in.
Diameter: 1.6 in.
Weight: 30 oz.

PSR
Caliber: .22 to .50 Beowolf
Overall Length: 8 in.
Diameter: 1.6 in.
Weight: 30 oz.
Material: Stainless
Sound Reduction: not published
Mounting: Thread

T.H.O.R. Thundertrap
Caliber: .22 to .50 Beowolf
Overall Length: 8 in.
Length Added: 8.25 in.
Diameter: 1.6 in.
Weight: 19.2 oz.

T.H.O.R. PSR
Caliber: .22 to .50 Beowolf
Overall Length: 8 in.
Diameter: 1.6 in.
Weight: 16 oz.
Material: Titanium

Turbodyne
Caliber: .50 BMG
Overall Length: 16.5 in.
Length Added: 15 in.
Diameter: 2 in.
Material: Stainless

Material: Stainless
Sound Reduction: not published
Mounting: Thread
Finish: Matte black, tan, olive drab
Features: Retains spent gases for a longer period causing the sound emitted to be a soft hiss rather than a pop.
MSRP: $955.00

Finish: Matte black, tan, olive drab
Features: Designed for the US Special Operations Command's Precision Sniper Rifle solicitation by AWC in partnership with Surgeon Rifles. The PSR suppressor mounts over our muzzle brake for a faster attachment method that maintains the accuracy and repeatability. The muzzle brake by itself is an effective recoil reducer.
MSRP: $1,095.00

Material: Titanium
Sound Reduction: not published
Mounting: Thread
Finish: Matte black, tan, olive drab
Features: Shorter, lighter, and astonishingly quiet suppressor, 5th generation of the Thundertrap.
MSRP: $1,595.00

Sound Reduction: not published
Mounting: Thread
Finish: Matte black, tan, olive drab
Features: One of the lightest suppressors on the market to achieve minimal point-of-impact shift.
MSRP: $1695.00

Sound Reduction: not published
Mounting: Thread
Finish: Matte black, tan, olive drab
Features: Constructed of 100 percent stainless steel and 360 degree circumferentially welded, produces less noise than a .22 Long Rifle.
MSRP: $1,895.00

AR Screw-On
Caliber: .223 Rem.
Overall Length: 7.38 in.
Diameter: 1.5 in.
Weight: 26 oz.

Sound Reduction: not published
Mounting: Thread
Finish: Matte black
Features: Designed for use on AR-15 weapons.
MSRP: $1,095.00

EliteIron (eliteiron.net)

Bravo 1

Alpha
Caliber: .50 BMG
Overall Length: 14 in.
Diameter: 2 in.
Weight: 4 lb. 9 oz.
Sound Reduction: 38 dB

Mounting: 1-14 or 7/8-14 thread
Finish: Matte olive drab
Features: For light weight .50 BMG caliber rifles (such as the Barrett 99), user will feel a slight increase in felt recoil.
MSRP: $1,600.00

Bravo
Caliber: .30 caliber
Overall Length: 9.5 in.
Diameter: 1.6 in.
Weight: 30 oz.
Material: 4140 chrome-moly

Sound Reduction: 34.5 dB
Mounting: 5/8-24 thread
Finish: Matte black
Features: Can be used on a large variety of rifles and in many calibers. Those include 6.5x284, .300 Win. Mag., and .300 RUM.
MSRP: $750.00

Bravo 1

Caliber: .30 caliber
Overall Length: 8 in.
Diameter: 1.6 in.
Weight: 25.5 oz.
Material: 4140 chrome-moly

Bravo SD

Caliber: .30 caliber
Overall Length: 10 in.
Length Added: 6 in.
Diameter: 1.6 in.
Weight: 28 oz.
Material: 4140 chrome-moly

Sierra SD

Caliber: .338 caliber
Overall Length: 12 in.
Length Added: 8 in.
Diameter: 1.6 in.
Weight: 33 oz.

Sierra

Caliber: .338 Lapua Mag.
Overall Length: 9.5 in.
Diameter: 1.6 in.
Weight: 30 oz.

Windtalker

Caliber: .375, .408 and .416
Overall Length: 12 in.
Diameter: 2 in.
Weight: 3 lb. 15 oz.
Material: 4140 chrome-moly

GemTech (gem-tech.com)

Sound Reduction: 33.5 dB
Mounting: 5/8-24 thread
Finish: Matte black
Features: Designed for the AR-10 gas system rifle in .308 Win., 3-piece system: suppressor, brake and thread protector.
MSRP: $750.00

Sound Reduction: 34-35 dB
Mounting: 5/8-24 thread
Finish: Matte desert tan
Features: Two-stage suppressor, a high and low section that can be used in both a bolt and gas rifle, built for no larger than a .308 caliber rifle.
MSRP: $1,125.00

Material: 4140 chrome-moly
Sound Reduction: 33 dB
Mounting: ¾-24, ¾-20 or M18-1 thread
Finish: Matte desert tan
Features: Made for a variety of calibers including 7mm Rem. Mag., .300 Win. Mag., and all .338 cartridges.
MSRP: $1,125.00

Material: 4140 chrome-moly
Sound Reduction: not published
Mounting: ¾-24, ¾-20 or M18-1 thread
Finish: Matte black
Features: Much quieter than other .308 Win. suppressors.
MSRP: $925.00

Sound Reduction: 38 dB
Mounting: 7/8-24, 7/8-20, 7/8-14 or 1-14 thread
Finish: Matte black
Features: Built to take the extreme pressures of these ultra high velocity rounds.
MSRP: $1,520.00

HALO

Caliber: 5.56 NATO, .223 Rem.
Overall Length: 7.2 in.
Diameter: 1.5 in.
Weight: 21 oz.
Material: 300 Series stainless steel
Sound Reduction: not published
Mounting: Thread
Finish: Matte black
Features: Requires no modification to the host weapon, utilizing a simple, patented, no-tools mounting system

G5

Caliber: 5.56 NATO, .223 Rem.
Overall Length: 7 in.
Length Added: 5.5 in.
Diameter: 1.5 in.
Weight: 18.8 oz.
Materials: Stainless steel, Inconel, titanium
Sound Reduction: not published

Sandstorm

Caliber: 7.62 NATO/.308 Win.
Overall Length: 7.8 in.
Diameter: 1.5 in.
Weight: 13.3 oz.
Materials: Ttitanium

Quicksand

Caliber: 7.62 NATO/.308 Win.
Overall Length: 9.2 in.
Diameter: 1.5 in.
Weight: 17.5 oz.

HVT-THD

Caliber: 7.62 NATO/.308 Win.
Overall Length: 8.2 in.
Diameter: 1.5 in.
Weight: 24 oz.
Materials: Welded stainless steel
Sound Reduction: not published
Mounting: 5/8-24 (2A) threads
Finish: Optically flat black oxide

that slips over most NATO weapon 5.56mm flash hiders. It may be swapped between many different weapons easily, including the M16, M4, HK416, and M249. The patented mounting system utilizes the 22mm standard NATO-specification birdcage type flash hider as used by the military worldwide. Mounting or removal can be performed without the use of tools in less than thirty seconds.
MSRP: $750.00

Mounting: Quickmount adapter
Finish: Matte black oxide
Features: Attaches to weapon via GemTech's Quickmount flash hider–a push and twist that may be done wearing gloves, in any weather condition, and in total darkness. The mount provides repeatable POI shift each time it is mounted.
MSRP: $875.00

Sound Reduction: not published
Mounting: 5/8-24 (2A) thread
Finish: Bead-blasted low reflective grey/natural titanium
Features: Light weight to lessened point of impact shift, less harmonic disturbance to the barrel, and faster cooling.
MSRP: $1,125.00

Materials: Ttitanium
Sound Reduction: not published
Mounting: Quickmount
Finish: Bead-blasted low reflective grey/natural titanium
Features: Quick-detach version of the Sandstorm
MSRP: $1,300.00

Features: Unusually quiet sound signature that is indistinguishable from, and masked by, the bullet flight noise, making it ideal for both urban and rural tactical operations. Recoil and visual signature (flash, dust) are reduced greatly along with the audible signature. The high-accuracy/low-blowback baffle was designated by the US Navy as "highly favorable" in limiting rate-of-fire increase. Suitable on automatic rifles as well as bolt-action precision rifles.
MSRP: $750.00

HVT-QM

Caliber: 7.62 NATO/.308 Win.
Overall Length: 9.2 in.
Diameter: 1.5 in.
Weight: 28 oz.
Materials: Welded stainless steel
Sound Reduction: not published
Mounting: Quickmount
Finish: Optically flat black oxide

Knight's Armament (knightarmco.com)

762QDC

Caliber: 7.62 NATO/.308 Win.
Overall Length: 7.78 in.
Weight: 19.6 oz.

SR-25

Caliber: 7.62 NATO/.308 Win., .300 BLK
Overall Length: 12.25 in.
Weight: 29.9 oz.

M110

Caliber: 7.62 NATO/.308 Win., .300 BLK
Overall Length: 14.12 in.
Diameter: 1.37 in.

SRT Arms (srtarms.com)

Hurricane

Caliber: .223 Rem.
Overall Length: 6.2 in.
Diameter: 1.5 in.
Weight: 22 oz.
Materials: Stainless steel

Features: Quickmount version. Unusually quiet sound signature that is indistinguishable from, and masked by, the bullet flight noise, making it ideal for both urban and rural tactical operations. Recoil and visual signature (flash, dust) are reduced greatly along with the audible signature. The high-accuracy/low-blowback baffle was designated by the US Navy as "highly favorable" in limiting rate-of-fire increase. Suitable on automatic rifles as well as bolt-action precision rifles.
MSRP: $850.00

Sound Reduction: 28 dB
Mounting: Quick Disconnect Mount
Finish: Matte black
MSRP: . . . . .not published

Sound Reduction: not published
Mounting: Gate latch connector
Finish: Matte black
Features: Connects to M110 flash hider
MSRP: . . . . .not published

Weight: 2 lb.
Sound Reduction: not published
Mounting: Quick Detach Mechanism
Finish: Matte tan
MSRP: . . . . .not published

Sound Reduction: 33–37dB
Mounting: ½-28 thread
Finish: Matte black
Features: Designed for use with all ammunition and rated for burst full-automatic fire.
MSRP: $585.00

Hurricane Ti

Caliber: .223 Rem.
Overall Length: 6.2 in.
Diameter: 1.5 in.
Weight: 11 oz.
Materials: Titanium

Hurricane XL

Caliber: .223 Rem., .22-250 Rem.
Overall Length: 7.5 in.
Diameter: 1.5 in.
Weight: 25 oz.
Materials: Stainless steel

Hurricane XL Ti

Caliber: .223 Rem., .22-250 Rem.
Overall Length: 7.5 in.
Diameter: 1.5 in.
Weight: 13 oz.
Materials: Stainless steel

Shadow

Caliber: .308 Win.
Overall Length: 8 in.
Diameter: 1.5 in.
Weight: 28 oz.

Shadow Ti

Caliber: .308 Win., .300 RUM
Overall Length: 8 in.
Diameter: 1.5 in.
Weight: 14 oz.

Shadow XL

Caliber: .308 Win., .300 RUM
Overall Length: 9.3 in.
Diameter: 1.5 in.
Weight: 32 oz.

Shadow XL Ti

Caliber: .308 Win., .300 RUM
Overall Length: 9.2 in.
Diameter: 1.5 in.
Weight: 16 oz.

Shadow LM

Caliber: .338 Lapua Mag.
Overall Length: 10.5 in.
Diameter: 1.5 in.
Weight: 34 oz.

Sound Reduction: 32–36 dB
Mounting: ½-28 thread
Finish: Matte black
Features: Designed for use with all ammunition and rated for burst full-automatic fire.
MSRP: $945.00

Sound Reduction: 35–38 dB
Mounting: ½-28 thread
Finish: Matte black
Features: Designed for use with all ammunition and rated for burst full-automatic fire.
MSRP: $690.00

Sound Reduction: 36-40 dB
Mounting: ½-28 thread
Finish: Matte black
Features: Designed for use with all ammunition and rated for burst full-automatic fire.
MSRP: $1,075.00

Materials: Stainless steel
Sound Reduction: 27–31 dB
Mounting: ½-28 thread
Finish: Matte black
Features: Designed for optimum accuracy.
MSRP: $685.00

Materials: Grade 9 titanium, 6A1-4V aluminum
Sound Reduction: 29–33 dB
Mounting: ½-28 thread
Finish: Matte black
Features: Designed for optimum accuracy.
MSRP: $1,095.00

Materials: Stainless steel
Sound Reduction: 33–37 dB
Mounting: ½-28 thread
Finish: Matte black
Features: Designed for optimum accuracy.
MSRP: $795.00

Materials: Titanium
Sound Reduction: 31–35 dB
Mounting: ½-28 thread
Finish: Matte black
Features: Designed for optimum accuracy.
MSRP: $1,245.00

Materials: 304 and 316 stainless steel
Sound Reduction: 35 dB
Mounting: ½-28 thread
Finish: Matte black
Features: Designed for optimum accuracy.
MSRP: $995.00

Shadow LM Ti
Caliber: .338 Lapua Mag.
Overall Length: 10.5 in.
Diameter: 1.5 in.
Weight: 17 oz.

Liberty Suppressors (libertycans.net)

Victory
Caliber: 7.62 NATO
Overall Length: 10 in.
Diameter: 1.5 in.
Weight: 15.7 oz.
Materials: Titanium with stainless steel blast baffle
Sound Reduction: 32 dB

Freedom
Caliber: 7.62 NATO
Overall Length: 10 in.
Diameter: 1.5 in.
Weight: 22.5 oz.
Materials: Titanium with stainless steel blast baffle

Constitution
Caliber: 5.7x28mm, 5.56 NATO, .22 LR
Overall Length: 6.35 in.
Diameter: 1.6 in.
Weight: 22.1 oz.
Materials: Alloy steel

Triumph
Caliber: 5.56 NATO
Overall Length: 7 in.
Diameter: 1.5 in.
Weight: 12 oz.
Materials: Titanium, stainless steel, Inconel
Sound Reduction: 30 dB

Materials: Titanium
Sound Reduction: 35 dB
Mounting: ½-28 thread
Finish: Matte black
Features: Designed for optimum accuracy.
MSRP: $1,650.00

Mounting: 5/8-24 thread
Finish: Matte black
Features: Titanium is used for all the components except for the blast chamber which is lined with stainless steel to eliminate ablative sparking and baffle erosion in the blast area.
MSRP: $1,195.00

Sound Reduction: 31 dB
Mounting: 5/8-24 thread
Finish: Matte black
Features: Uses the innovative square bore technology that Liberty developed for their Pandora line of suppressors.
MSRP: $830.00

Sound Reduction: 30 dB
Mounting: ½-28 thread
Finish: Matte black
Features: Designed for use on .223 Rem. AR-15s and on .22 LR AR uppers without lead buildup issues of the .22 LR.
MSRP: $545.00

Mounting: ½-28 thread
Finish: Matte black
Features: Produces suppression in excess of 30 dB of noise reduction and is lighter weight due to the use of titanium in the construction of the core. It also has an inconel blast baffle for durability and use in full auto applications.
MSRP: $799.00

Torch

Caliber: .223 Rem.
Overall Length: 8 in.
Diameter: 1.5 in.
Weight: 21.7 oz.
Materials: Stainless steel

Sound Reduction: 35 dB
Mounting: ½-28 thread
Finish: Matte black, green, stainless
Features: All stainless construction for AR-15 style rifles, thread mounted to maintain maximum alignment with the bore.
MSRP: $495.00

Torch QA

Caliber: .223 Rem.
Overall Length: 8 in.
Diameter: 1.5 in.
Weight: 23 oz.
Materials: 300 stainless steel

Sound Reduction: 35 dB
Mounting: Quick Attachment
Finish: Matte black
Features: QA version of the Torch is a rapid attachment design intended for quick deployment.
MSRP: $680.00

Freedom Magnum Quick Attach

Caliber: .300 Win. Mag.
Overall Length: 11 in.
Diameter: 1.5 in.
Weight: 24.4 oz.
Materials: Titanium, stainless

Sound Reduction: not published
Mounting: Quick Attachment
Finish: Matte stainless
Features: Rapid thread attachment requires only three turns to install on the weapon.
MSRP: $1,045.00

Freedom Magnum

Caliber: .30 caliber up to .300 Win. Mag.
Overall Length: 11 in.
Diameter: 1.5 in.
Weight: 22.5 oz.
Materials: Titanium, stainless

Sound Reduction: not published
Mounting: 5/8-24 thread
Finish: Matte black
Features: Mounts via traditional thread mounting for better accuracy and repeatability.
MSRP: $930.00

The Hoosier

Caliber: .308 Win. and smaller
Overall Length: 10 in.
Diameter: 1.5 in.
Weight: 22 oz.
Materials: Titanium, stainless steel

Sound Reduction: not published
Mounting: 5/8-24 thread
Finish: Matte black
Features: Designed for the .358 Hoosier cartridge, but compatible with .308 family and smaller.
MSRP: $830.00

Victory Mag

Caliber: .300 Win. Mag.
Overall Length: 11 in.
Diameter: 1.5 in.
Weight: 18.5oz.
Materials: Titanium, stainless steel blast baffle
Sound Reduction: 34 dB
Mounting: 5/8-24 thread
Finish: Matte black

Features: The core of the suppressor is a monolithic design where all the baffles as well as the front of the suppressor are made from a single homogeneous piece of Grade 5 (6Al/4V) Heat Treated Titanium alloy, giving strength as well as eliminating baffle spin which can be a problem with traditional stack baffle designs. The monolithic design also enables simple yet repeatable setups since the baffles cannot move inside the suppressor.
MSRP: $1,395.00

OPS Inc. (opsinc.us)

3rd Model 5.56mm
Caliber: 5.56 NATO/.223 Rem.
Overall Length: 7.3 in.
Length Added: 5 in.
Diameter: 1.5 in.
Weight: 24 oz.

12th Model SPR MBS (MK12)
Caliber: 5.56 NATO/.223 Rem.
Overall Length: 8.875 in.
Length Added: 6.25 in.
Diameter: 1.5 in.
Weight: 21 oz.

3rd Model .30 Caliber
Caliber: 7.62mm/.30 caliber
Overall Length: 12.5 in.
Length Added: 7.25 in.
Diameter: 1.5 in.
Weight: 31 oz.
Materials: 300 stainless steel

12th Model PSS / AR-10 /SR-25 Medium-weight Barrel MBS
Caliber: 7.62mm/.30 caliber
Overall Length: 11 in.
Length Added: 7 in.
Diameter: 1.5 in.

3rd Model .408 Caliber MBS
Caliber: .408 Chey-Tac
Materials: 300 stainless steel
Sound Reduction: not published
Mounting: Muzzle brake adaptor

3rd Model 50 Caliber MBS
Caliber: .12.7mm/.50 BMG
Overall Length: 21 in.
Length Added: 9 in.
Diameter: 2.5 in.

Materials: 300 stainless steel
Sound Reduction: not published
Mounting: 1/2-28 thread
Finish: Matte black
Features: Meets SOPMOD objective of 30,000 rounds under various firing schedules.

Materials: 300 stainless steel
Sound Reduction: 40dB
Mounting: Muzzle brake adaptor
Finish: Matte black
Features: Mounts via threads on the outside of the muzzle brake centering on the adapter fitting. A 20 degree taper on the adapter locks the silencer onto the barrel.

Sound Reduction: 40dB
Mounting: Muzzle brake adaptor
Finish: Matte black
Features: Once the barrel is machined for the suppressor, no tools are required to remove or install the MBS to the weapon. An average increase in accuracy of .25 MOA as well as a 20 to 50 feet per second increase in velocity was measured during testing of this suppressor.

Weight: 28 oz.
Materials: 300 stainless steel
Sound Reduction: 40dB
Mounting: Muzzle brake adaptor
Finish: Matte black
Features: Designed for use on semi- and full-automatic weapons.

Finish: Matte black
Features: Designed for the .408 Chey-Tac. Suppressor threads back over the barrel locking onto a machined fitting that is used with a threaded muzzle to align and secure the device to the weapon. No tools are required to remove or install the MBS to the weapon.

Weight: 6 lb. 10 oz.
Materials: 300 stainless steel
Sound Reduction: not published
Mounting: Muzzle brake adaptor
Finish: Matte black
Features: Designed for the .50 BMG weapons.

Silencerco (silencerco.com)

SPECWAR 556
Caliber: 5.56 NATO/.223 Rem.
Overall Length: 7.3 in.
Diameter: 1.5 in.
Weight: 19.5 oz.
Materials: 718 Inconel, stainless steel

Sound Reduction: not published
Mounting: ASR quick detach mount
Finish: Matte black
Features: Active Spring Retention design allows for installation and removal in seconds.
MSRP: $799.00

5.56 Saker
Caliber: 5.56 NATO
Overall Length: 6.758 in.
Diameter: 1.5 in.
Weight: 18.02 oz.
Materials: Stainless steel

Sound Reduction: 32–34 dB
Mounting: Trifecta RS Flash Hider mount
Finish: Matte black
Features: Interchangeable front cap for different purposes such as a flash hider.
MSRP: $1,200.00

Smith Enterprise (smithenterprise.com)

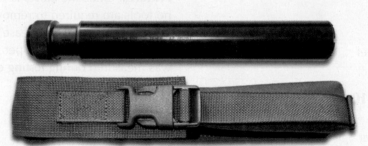

SEI M14DC Wind Talker
Caliber: .30 caliber
Overall Length: 11.2 in.
Length Added: 8.9 in.
Diameter: 1.5 in.
Weight: 1 lb. 14 oz.
Materials: 300 series stainless steel, titanium, aluminum

Sound Reduction: not published
Mounting: Quick detach mount using Vortex DC flash hider/interface
Finish: Black oxide
Features: Quick detachable and rebuildable suppressor for Vortex-equipped .30 cal. / 6.8 mm weapons, safety certified by US Navy.

SEI 5.56mm M4DC Wind Talker
Caliber: 5.56mm
Overall Length: 9.2 in.
Diameter: 1.5 in.
Weight: 26 oz.
Materials: 300 series stainless steel, titanium, aluminum

Sound Reduction: not published
Mounting: Quick detach mount using VortexG6A2 flash hider/interface
Finish: Black oxide
Features: Quick detachable and rebuildable suppressor for Vortex-equipped weapons.

SOCOM556-RC

Caliber: 5.56mm/.223 Rem.
Overall Length: 6.2 in.
Length Added: 4 in.
Diameter: 1.5 in.
Weight: 17 oz.
Materials: Stainless steel
Sound Reduction: not published
Mounting: Fast-Attach lock ring
Finish: Cerakote black or dark earth
Features: Selected for the M4 and Mk18 carbines by US Special Operations Command after placing first in the most extensive and rigorous suppressor testing ever conducted; it also received the USSOCOM official safety verification in support of fielding. Core design reduces back pressure, suppressed cyclic rate, and gas blowback.
MSRP: $1,375.00

SOCOM556-MONSTER

Caliber: 5.56mm/.223 Rem.
Overall Length: 6.5 in.
Length Added: 4 in.
Diameter: 1.5 in.
Weight: 17.5 oz.
Materials: Stainless steel
Sound Reduction: not published
Mounting: Fast-Attach lock ring
Finish: Cerakote black or dark earth
Features: Suppressor has serrated teeth on the front plate.
MSRP: $1,425.00

SOCOM762-RC

Caliber: 7.62mm/.308 Win.
Overall Length: 8.4 in.
Diameter: 1.5 in.
Weight: 19.5 oz.
Materials: Stainless steel
Sound Reduction: not published
Mounting: Fast-Attach lock ring
Finish: Cerakote black or dark earth
Features: This compact and lightweight suppressor—mounted to the Mk13 sniper rifle in .300 Win. Mag.—recently won the Mk13 contract award with US Special Operations Command.
MSRP: $1,799.00

SOCOM762- MINI

Caliber: 7.62mm/.308 Win.
Overall Length: 6.2 in.
Diameter: 1.5 in.
Weight: 17 oz.
Materials: Stainless steel
Sound Reduction: not published
Mounting: Fast-Attach lock ring
Finish: Cerakote black or dark earth
Features: Optimized for use with 7.62x39 and 7.62x35 caliber rifles and will also adequately suppress 7.62x51 NATO caliber rifles with a barrel length of sixteen inches or longer.
MSRP: $1,799.00

Thompson Machine (thompsonmachine.net)

The SIXTEEN
Caliber: .223 Rem./5.56 NATO
Overall Length: 8.5 in.
Diameter: 1.5 in.
Weight: 27 oz.
Materials: Alloy steel

Sound Reduction: not published
Mounting: ½-28 thread
Finish: Matte parkerized
Features: Designed for AR or bolt rifles in 5.56 NATO or .223 Rem. as well as .22 rimfire. Easily disassembles for cleaning.
MSRP: $679.00

The THIRTY
Caliber: .30 caliber up to .308 Win., 7.62x39 and similar
Overall Length: 8.375 in.
Diameter: 1.5 in.
Weight: 27 oz.
Materials: Steel alloy

Sound Reduction: not published
Mounting: 5/8-24thread
Finish: Matte parkerized
Features: Monocore suppressor that reduces .308 Win. sound signature to .22 Long Rifle. Quickly and easily disassembled for cleaning.
MSRP: $679.00

Thunder Beast Arms Corporation (TBAC) (thunderbeastarms.com)

Ultra-9
Caliber: .30 caliber up to .300 Win. Mag.
Overall Length: 9 in.
Diameter: 1.5 in.
Weight: 16 oz.
Materials: Titanium
Sound Reduction: not published
Mounting: 5/8-24, M18-1, or M18-1 thread

Finish: Black Cerakote, OD green or FDE
Features: Designed around .308 for maximum flexibility and is rated up to .300 Winchester Magnum. Also suitable for competitive mid-sized cartridges for long-range shooting such as .243 Winchester, .260 Remington, 6.5 Creedmoor, 6.5x47 Lapua, 6.5-284 Norma, and 7mm Remington Magnum and 7mm WSM.
MSRP: $1,145.00

Model 338BA
Caliber: .338 caliber up to .338 Lapua Mag. or .338 RUM
Overall Length: 10.4 in.
Diameter: 1.8 in.
Weight: 23.4 oz.
Materials: Titanium
Sound Reduction: not published

Mounting: 5/8-24, ¾-20, ¾-24, ¾-28, M18-1, or M18-1.5 thread
Finish: Black Cerakote, OD green or FDE
Features: Effectively suppresses the extreme muzzle blast of .338 magnums down to levels similar to suppressed .308 Win.
MSRP: $1,795.00

Yankee Hill Machine (YHM) (yhm.net)

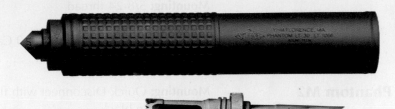

.30 Cal Phantom LT
Caliber: up to .308 Win.
Overall Length: 7.625 in.
Diameter: 1.5 in.
Weight: 20 oz.
Materials: 300 series stainless steel, Inconel 718

.30 Cal Phantom LTA
Caliber: up to .308 Win.
Overall Length: 7.625 in.
Diameter: 1.5 in.
Weight: 20 oz.
Materials: 300 series stainless steel, Inconel 718
Sound Reduction: 35 dB
Mounting: Q.D. flash hider

Titanium Q.D. Phantom 5.56
Caliber: .223 Rem./5.56 NATO
Overall Length: 6.875 in.
Diameter: 1.5 in.
Weight: 12 oz.
Materials: Titanium, Inconel 718

Titanium .30 Cal. Q.D. Phantom
Caliber: .30 cal./7.62mm
Overall Length: 8.5 in.
Diameter: 1.5 in.
Weight: 15 oz.
Materials: Titanium, Inconel 718

Sound Reduction: 35 dB
Mounting: Q.D. flash hider
Finish: Matte black
Features: The Phantom .30 LT (Light Tactical) and LTA (Light Tactical, Aggressive) are smaller, lighter versions of the Phantom M2.
MSRP: $789.00

Finish: Matte black
Features: The Phantom .30 Cal. LT (Light Tactical) and LTA (Light Tactical, Aggressive) are smaller, lighter versions of the Phantom M2. Similar to Phantom .30 Cal. LT, but with an aggressive end with sharp tips that can be used to break glass, position the firearm for breaching, or can be used in hand-to-hand situations.
MSRP: $825.00

Sound Reduction: 35 dB
Mounting: Q.D. flash hider
Finish: Natural matte
Features: Rated for limited full auto use and should be allowed time to cool in between magazines.
MSRP: $1,068.00

Sound Reduction: 32 dB
Mounting: Q.D. flash hider
Finish: Natural matte
Features: Offers the same sound reduction as the standard Phantom model but in a much lighter package.
MSRP: $1,177.00

Titanium .30 Cal. Thread-On Phantom
Caliber: .30 cal./7.62mm
Overall Length: 8.5 in.
Diameter: 1.5 in.
Weight: 15 oz.
Materials: Titanium, Inconel 718
Sound Reduction: 32 dB
Mounting: 5/8-24 thread
Finish: Natural matte
Features: Screw on version of .30 Cal Q.D. Phantom.
MSRP: $1,088.00

Stainless .30 Cal. Q.D. Phantom M2
Caliber: .30 cal./7.62mm
Overall Length: 8.5 in.
Diameter: 1.625 in.
Weight: 25 oz.
Materials: 300 series stainless steel, Inconel 718
Sound Reduction: 32 dB
Mounting: Quick Disconnect with flash hider
Finish: Matte black
Features: Designed for use with a Phantom 5.56mm flash hider on a 5.56mm rifle; allows users to purchase one sound suppressor and use it on .30 caliber and 5.56mm rifles. For safety the 5.56mm sound suppressor will not fit onto a 7.62mm flash hider.
MSRP: $800.00

Stainless .30 Cal. Thread-On Phantom
Caliber: .30 cal./7.62mm NATO
Overall Length: 8.5 in.
Diameter: 1.625 in.
Weight: 28 oz.
Materials: 300 series steel, Inconel 718
Sound Reduction: 32 dB
Mounting: 5/8-24 thread
Finish: Matte black
Features: Screw on version of .30 Cal Q.D. Phantom.
MSRP: $800.00

Q.D. Phantom .338
Caliber: .338 Lapua Mag.
Overall Length: 10.15 in.
Diameter: 1.625 in.
Weight: 33 oz.
Materials: Chrome-Moly steel
Sound Reduction: 28 dB
Mounting: Quick Disconnect
Finish: Matte black
Features: Phantom Q.D. Mount System holds the sound suppressor firmly in place by hand tightening and allows the sound suppressor to be removed by hand when no longer needed. A gas seal keeps the threads clean so the suppressor will not bind.
MSRP: $800.00

40. Tactical Rifle Scopes

Barrett (barrett.net)

BORS

Magnification: n/a
Objective Lens: n/a
Field of View: n/a
Height: 2.5 in.
Width: 3.2 in.
Weight: 13 oz
Range: n/a
Features: Barrett Optical Ranging System (BORS) is an integrated ballistics computer that mounts directly on the rifle scope and couples to the elevation knob. BORS instantly takes care of the data work by drawing from several tables and taking into account a number of real-time external factors. Compatible with Leupold, Schmidt & Bender, and NightForce optics. Waterproof and fogproof. Uses one CR-123 battery; thirty-hour battery life.
MSRP: $1,399.00

Burris (burrisoptics.com)

C4 Plus 4.5-14x42mm

Magnification: 4.5-14x
Objective Lens: 42mm
Reticle: C4 Wind MOA
Finish: Matte black
Field of View: 22 ft (low)/7.5 ft (high) @ 1000 yds
Exit Pupil: 9mm (low)/3mm (high)
Click Value: ¼ MOA
Adjustment Range: 66 MOA

Eye Relief: 3.1-3.8 in.
Tube Diameter: 30mm
Length: 13 in.
Weight: 18 oz
Features: The C4 (Cartridge, Calibrated, Custom Clicker) matches elevation to cartridge trajectory. Customized WindMap tells how many MOA tick marks on the reticle to hold into the wind from 1 mph to 10 mph wind speed. Waterproof, shockproof, and fogproof.
MSRP: $499.00; $299.00 (3-9x40mm)

Eliminator III 4-16x50mm

Magnification: 4-16x
Objective Lens: 50 mm
Reticle: X96
Finish: Matte black
Field of View: 26 ft (low)/7 ft (high) @ 1000 yds
Exit Pupil: 12.5 mm (low)/3.1 mm (high)
Click Value: 1/8 MOA
Adjustment Range: 40 MOA
Eye Relief: 3.5-4 in.

Tube Diameter: n/a
Length: 15.5 in.
Weight: 30.4 oz
Features: Variable power scope with built-in laser rangefinder that ranges out to 1,200 yards depending on reflectivity of target. Trajectory compensation is calculated to ammunition and range. Uses one CR123A battery with a 5,000-cycle battery life. Adjustable parallax. Built-in mounting rail. Waterproof, shockproof, and fogproof.
MSRP: . . . . $1,499.00; $1,199.00(3-12x44mm)

MSR 4.5-14x42mm

Magnification: 4.5-14x
Objective Lens: 42 mm
Reticle: Ballistic Plex
Finish: Matte black
Field of View: 22 ft (low)/7.5 ft (high) @ 1000 yds
Exit Pupil: 9 mm (low)/3 mm (high)
Click Value: ¼ MOA
Adjustment Range: 42 MOA

Eye Relief: 3.1-3.8 in/
Tube Diameter: 30mm
Length: 13 in.
Weight: 18 oz
Features: Designed for AR-style rifles, the Ballistic Plex reticle is configured to the .223 Rem. cartridge loads. Index-matched lenses are multi-coated for glare elimination and maximum contrast in low light situations. Waterproof, shockproof, and fogproof.
MSRP: $249.00; $199.00 (3-9x40mm)

XTRII 8-40x50mm

Magnification: 48-40x
Objective Lens: 50 mm
Reticle: F-Class MOA, illuminated, FFP
Finish: Matte black
Field of View: 13.2 ft (low)/2.8 ft (high) @ 1000 yds
Exit Pupil: 6.2 mm (low)/1.2 mm (high)
Click Value: 1/8 MOA
Adjustment Range: 70 MOA elevation/30 MOA windage
Eye Relief: 3.5-4.2 in.

Bushnell (bushnell.com)

Tube Diameter: 34 mm
Length: 16.7 in.
Weight: 31.4 oz
Features: 5x zoom system with 25 percent thicker tube construction, dimensionally-matched precision adjustment knobs, and Zero Click Stop technology. Hi-Lume multi-coated lenses, optimizing target resolution, contrast, and low-light performance. Waterproof, shockproof, and fogproof.
MSRP: . $1,199.00; $1,199.00 (5-25x50mm, G2B mil-dot reticle); $799.00 (2-10x42mm, G2B mil-dot reticle)

LRS 10x40mm SFP

Magnification: 10x
Objective Lens: 40 mm
Reticle: mil-dot
Finish: Matte black
Field of View: 11 ft @ 100 yds
Exit Pupil: 4 mm
Click Value: ¼ MOA

Adjustment Range: 80 MOA
Eye Relief: 3.5 in.
Tube Diameter: 1 in.
Length: 11.5 in.
Weight: 80 oz
Features: Fixed power. SFP (Second Focal Plane) reticle, ultra wide band coating. Waterproof and fogproof.
MSRP: $390.95

SMRS 1-8.5x24mm

Magnification: 1-8.5x
Objective Lens: 24 mm
Reticle: Illum. BTR-2
Finish: Matte black
Field of View: 105 ft (low)/14 ft (high) @ 100 yds
Exit Pupil: 13.2 mm (low)/3.2 mm (high)
Click Value: .1 Mil
Adjustment Range: 60 MOA

Eye Relief: 3.5 in.
Tube Diameter: 34 mm
Length: 10.2 in.
Weight: 23 oz
Features: Variable power, fixed parallax adjustment, FFP (First Focal Plane) reticle, fully multi-coated lenses, T-Lok turrets, 11 reticle illumination settings. Waterproof and fogproof.
MSRP: $2,149.00

LRS 3-12x44mm

Magnification: 3-12x
Objective Lens: 44 mm
Reticle: mil-dot, Illum. mil-dot or BTR-Mil
Finish: Matte black
Field of View: 34 ft (low)/8.9 ft (high) @ 100 yds
Exit Pupil: 12.1 mm (low)/3.7 mm (high)
Click Value: .1 Mil

Adjustment Range: 25 MOA
Eye Relief: 3.7 in.
Tube Diameter: 30 mm
Length: 13.4 in.
Weight: 24.4 oz
Features: Variable power, side focus parallax adjustment, FFP (First Focal Plane) reticle, fully multi-coated lenses. Waterproof and fogproof.
MSRP: $1,407.95

HDMR 3.5-21x50mm

Magnification: 3.5-21x
Objective Lens: 50 mm
Reticle: Horus H-59 or Horus TRMR2
Finish: Matte black
Field of View: 25.3 ft (low)/5.1 ft (high) @ 100 yds
Exit Pupil: 10.4 mm (low)/2.4 mm (high)
Click Value: .1 Mil

Adjustment Range: 50 MOA
Eye Relief: 3.7 in.
Tube Diameter: 34 mm
Length: 13.2 in.
Weight: 32.5 oz
Features: Variable power, side focus parallax adjustment, FFP (First Focal Plane) reticle, fully multi-coated lenses. Waterproof and fogproof.
MSRP: $1,599.00

Yardage Pro

Magnification: 4-12x
Objective Lens: 42 mm
Reticle: mil-dot
Finish: Matte black
Field of View: 26 ft (low)/8.5 ft (high) @ 100 yds
Click Value: ¼ in.
Eye Relief: 3.5 in.

Tube Diameter: n/a
Length: 13 in.
Weight: 25 oz
Features: Variable power with built-in laser rangefinder with a ranging capability from 30 to 800 yards and bullet-drop compensator. Integral Weaver-style mount. Waterproof and fogproof.
MSRP: $709.99

ERS 6-24x50mm

Magnification: 6-24x
Objective Lens: 50 mm
Reticle: mil-dot, Illum. mil-dot, G2, or Illum. BTR-Mil
Finish: Matte black, flat dark earth (3.5-21x50mm)
Field of View: 17.5 ft (low)/4.5 ft (high) @ 100 yds
Exit Pupil: 7.5 mm (low)/2.1 mm (high)
Click Value: ¼ in.
Adjustment Range: 70 MOA

Eye Relief: 4 in.
Tube Diameter: 30 mm
Length: 13.5 in.
Weight: 27 oz
Features: Variable power, side focus parallax adjustment, FFP (First Focal Plane) or SFP (Second Focal Plane) reticle, fully multi-coated lenses. Waterproof and fogproof.
MSRP: . . . .$1,300.00; $979.00 (4.5-30x50mm); $1,949.00 (matte black, 3.5-21x50mm); $1,999.00 (flat dark earth, 3.5-21x50mm)

XRS 4.5-30x50mm

Magnification: 4.5-30x
Objective Lens: 50 mm
Reticle: G2
Finish: Matte black
Field of View: 24 ft (low)/3.6 ft (high) @ 100 yds
Exit Pupil: 9 mm (low)/1.7 mm (high)
Click Value: .1 Mil
Adjustment Range: 50 MOA

Eye Relief: 3.7 in.
Tube Diameter: 34 mm
Length: 10.2 in.
Weight: 37 oz
Features: Variable power, side focus parallax adjustment, FFP (First Focal Plane) reticle, fully multi-coated lenses. T-Lok locking target turrets with Z-Lok zero stop. Waterproof and fogproof.
MSRP: $2,149.00

AR Optics 4.5-18x40mm

Magnification: 4.5-18x
Objective Lens: 40 mm
Reticle: Drop Zone-223 BDC
Finish: Matte black
Field of View: 22 ft (low)/7.3 ft (high) @ 100 yds
Exit Pupil: 8.6 mm (low)/2.3 mm (high)
Click Value: ¼ in.

Adjustment Range: 25 MOA
Eye Relief: 3.7 in.
Tube Diameter: 1 in.
Length: 12.4 in.
Weight: 21.5 oz
Features: Variable power, side focus parallax adjustment, SFP (Second Focal Plane) reticle calibrated to .223 Rem. cartridge. Waterproof and fogproof.
MSRP: $149.99

Counter Sniper (countersniperoptics.com)

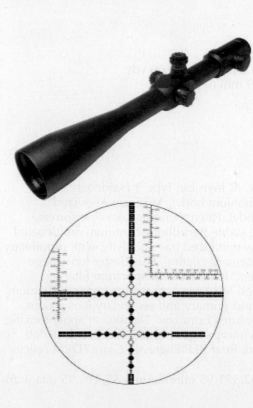

10/40-56R

Magnification: 10-40x
Objective Lens: 56 mm
Reticle: TDRM
Finish: Matte black
Field of View: 10 ft (low)/2.5 ft (high) @ 100 yds
Exit Pupil: 5.6 mm (low)/1.4 mm (high)
Click Value: 1/8 MOA
Adjustment Range: 65 MOA
Eye Relief: 3.2-4.1 in.
Tube Diameter: 35 mm
Length: 17.7 in.
Weight: 2 lb 2.4 oz
Features: Variable power, parallax side focus, SFP (Second Focal Plane) tri-color illuminated reticle. Bertrillium-Zantitium multicoated optics for dusk/dawn/shadow enhanced transmissivity, with proprietary HydroShear water/ice displacement coating, DustCaster Ion-charge for ant-static dust displacement, InfraShield IR spectrum filtering coating, TitaniStar 68 Rockwell Mil-spec anti-scratch coating. Aluminum or titanium body.Waterproof and fogproof.
MSRP: . . . . $3,001.95 (aluminum); $6,046.95 (titanium)

2.5/10-56
Magnification: 2.5-10x
Objective Lens: 56 mm
Reticle: 2nd Gen mil-dot
Finish: Matte black
Field of View: 44.1 ft (low)/8.4 ft (high) @ 100 yds
Exit Pupil: 12.2 mm (low)/3 mm (high)
Click Value: 1/8 MOA
Adjustment Range: 95 MOA
Eye Relief: 5.9-4.2 in.
Tube Diameter: 35 mm
Length: 15 in.
Weight: 2 lb 4 oz
Features: PermaLax optics provide razor focus as depth of field expands with zoom range. IR Invisible Type 3 Hardcoat Anodized Body and Rings (Titanium body), Mil-Spec Anodized (T6160 Aircraft Aluminum body). Patent Pending Lockable Turrets, Proprietary-230-+485 degree stable Bertrillium-Zantitium multicoated optics for dusk/dawn /shadow enhanced transmissivity, with proprietary HydroShear water/ice displacement coating, DustCaster Ion-charge for ant-static dust displacement, InfraShield™ IR spectrum filtering coating, TitaniStar 68 Rockwell Mil-Spec anti-scratch coating. Titanium versions feature aspheric hybrid primary and secondary lens groups, Aircraft Aluminum features Extra Low Dispersion apochromatic lenses. Waterproof and fogproof.
MSRP: . . . . $1,520.95 (aluminum); $3,337.95 (titanium)

2/16-44
Magnification: 2-16x
Objective Lens: 44 mm
Reticle: TDRM
Finish: Matte black
Field of View: 55.4 ft (low)/6.3 ft (high) @ 100 yds
Exit Pupil: 14.8 mm (low)/2.9 mm (high)
Click Value: ¼ MOA
Adjustment Range: 85 MOA
Eye Relief: 6.51-3.5 in.
Tube Diameter: 30 mm
Length: 13 in.
Weight: 1 lb 11.9 oz
Features: Side Focus parallax, IR Invisible Type 3 Hardcoat Anodized Body and Rings (Titanium body), Mil-Spec Anodized (T6160 Aircraft Aluminum body). Patent Pending Lockable Turrets, Proprietary-230-+485 degree stable Bertrillium-Zantitium multicoated optics for dusk/dawn /shadow enhanced transmissivity, with proprietary HydroShear water/ice displacement coating, DustCaster Ion-charge for ant-static dust displacement, InfraShield IR spectrum filtering coating, TitaniStar 68 Rockwell Mil-Spec anti-scratch coating. Titanium versions feature aspheric hybrid primary and secondary lens groups, Aircraft Aluminum version features Extra Low Dispersion apochromatic lenses. Proprietary rare earth/nitrogen gas purged, hard earth sealed, Variable Tri-Color Illuminated, Rear RFP Engraved Glass TDRM reticle. Waterproof and fogproof.
MSRP: . . . . $2,371.95 (aluminum); $5,416.95 (titanium)

3/12-50

Magnification: 3-12x
Objective Lens: 50 mm
Reticle: 2nd Gen mil-dot
Finish: Matte black
Field of View: 33.2 ft (low)/7.2 ft (high) @ 100 yds
Exit Pupil: 14.2 mm (low)/3 mm (high)
Click Value: ¼ MOA
Adjustment Range: 95 MOA
Eye Relief: 4.84-3.9in.
Tube Diameter: 30 mm
Length: 15.3 in.
Weight: 1 lb 11.9 oz

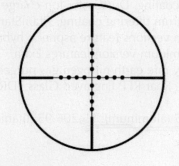

Features: PermaLax optics provide razor focus as depth of field expands with zoom range. IR Invisible Type 3 Hardcoat Anodized Body and Rings (Titanium),MIL Spec Anodized in T6160 Aircraft Aluminum. Patent Pending Lockable Turrets, Proprietary-230-+485°F stable Bertrillium-Zantitium multicoated optics for dusk/dawn/shadow enhanced transmissivity, with proprietary HydroShear water/ice displacement coating, DustCaster Ion-charge for ant-static dust displacement, InfraShield IR spectrum filtering coating, TitaniStar 68 Rockwell Mil-spec anti-scratch coating. Titanium versions feature aspheric hybrid primary and secondary lens groups, Aircraft Aluminum features Extra Low Dispersion apochromatic lenses. Proprietary rare earth/nitrogen gas purged, hard earth sealed, standard mil-dot .25-1.0 Milliradian Marked rear plane reticles.Waterproof and fogproof.
MSRP: . . . . $1,447.95 (aluminum); $3,316.95 (titanium)

4/16-42

Magnification: 4-16x
Objective Lens: 42 mm
Reticle: 2nd Gen mil-dot
Finish: Matte black
Field of View: 25.2 ft (low)/6.3ft (high) @ 100 yds
Exit Pupil: 10.5 mm (low)/2.6 mm (high)
Click Value: ¼ MOA
Adjustment Range: 75 MOA
Eye Relief: 5.11-3.5 in.
Tube Diameter: 30 mm
Length: 16.3 in.
Weight: 1 lb 12.7 oz

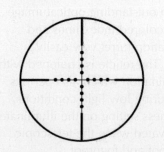

Features: Side Focus parallax, IR Invisible Type 3 Hardcoat Anodized Body and Rings (Titanium body), Mil-Spec Anodized (T6160 Aircraft Aluminum body). Patent Pending Lockable Turrets, Proprietary-230-+485 degree stable Bertrillium-Zantitium multicoated optics for dusk/dawn /shadow enhanced transmissivity, with proprietary HydroShear water/ice displacement coating, DustCaster Ion-charge for ant-static dust displacement, InfraShield IR spectrum filtering coating, TitaniStar 68 Rockwell Mil-Spec anti-scratch coating. Titanium versions feature aspheric hybrid primary and secondary lens groups, Aircraft Aluminum version features Extra Low Dispersion apochromatic lenses. Proprietary rare earth/nitrogen gas purged, hard earth sealed, Variable Tri-Color Illuminated, Rear RFP Engraved Glass TDRM reticle. Waterproof and fogproof.
MSRP: . . . . $1,363.95 (aluminum); $3,347.95 (titanium)

6/25-56

Magnification: 6-25x
Objective Lens: 56 mm
Reticle: 2nd Gen mil-dot
Finish: Matte black
Field of View: 18.6 ft (low)/4.9 ft (high) @ 100 yds
Exit Pupil: 9.2 mm (low)/2.4 mm (high)
Click Value: 1/8 MOA
Adjustment Range: 25 MOA
Eye Relief: 4.21-3.31 in.
Tube Diameter: 30 mm
Length: 15.9 in.
Weight: 2 lb 2.6 oz
Features: Side Focus parallax, IR Invisible Type 3 Hardcoat Anodized Body and Rings (Titanium body), Mil-Spec Anodized (T6160 Aircraft Aluminum body). Patent Pending Lockable Turrets, Proprietary-230-+485 degree stable Bertrillium-Zantitium multicoated optics for dusk/dawn /shadow enhanced transmissivity, with proprietary HydroShear water/ice displacement coating, DustCaster Ion-charge for ant-static dust displacement, InfraShield IR spectrum filtering coating, TitaniStar 68 Rockwell Mil-Spec anti-scratch coating. Titanium versions feature aspheric hybrid primary and secondary lens groups, Aircraft Aluminum version features Extra Low Dispersion apochromatic lenses. Proprietary rare earth/nitrogen gas purged, hard earth sealed, Variable Tri-Color Illuminated, Rear RFP Engraved Glass TDRM reticle. Waterproof and fogproof.
MSRP: . . . . $1,835.95 (aluminum); $5,206.95 (titanium)

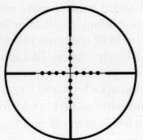

Hensoldt (eurooptic.com)

Hensoldt ZF 3-12x56 FF

Magnification: 3-12x
Objective Lens: 56 mm
Reticle: Illum. mil-dot
Finish: Matte black
Field of View: 34 m (low)/117 m (high) @ 1000 m
Click Value: .1 MRAD
Tube Diameter: 34 mm
Length: 12.8 in.
Weight: 28.2 oz

Features: Available with a reticle in the first and second focal plane. They deliver an outstanding optical image. Bullet drop compensation; colored index lines and numeric values on the elevation turret very easily indicate the current setting. The reticle is equipped with continuously variable illumination which also permits precise target acquisition during low light conditions. The previously used brightness setting on the illuminated reticle is automatically activated when the telescopic sight is turned on. Waterproof and fogproof.
MSRP: $3,160.00

Hensoldt ZF 6-24x56 mil-dot

Magnification: 6-24x
Objective Lens: 56 mm
Reticle: Illum. mil-dot
Finish: Matte black
Field of View: 61 m (low)/17 m (high) @ 1000 m
Click Value: .05 MRAD
Tube Diameter: 30 mm
Length: 15.2 in.
Weight: 29.9 oz

Features: Available with a reticle in the first and second focal plane. They deliver an outstanding optical image. Bullet drop compensation; colored index lines and numeric values on the elevation turret very easily indicate the current setting. The reticle is equipped with continuously variable illumination which also permits precise target acquisition during low light conditions. The previously used brightness setting on the illuminated reticle is automatically activated when the telescopic sight is turned on. Waterproof and fogproof.
MSRP: $3,350.00; $3,570.00 (6-24x72mm)

Hensoldt ZF 6-24x72 SAM

Magnification: 6-24x
Objective Lens: 72 mm
Reticle: Illum. mil-dot
Finish: Matte black
Field of View: 61 m (low)/17 m (high) @ 1000 m
Click Value: .05 MRAD

Tube Diameter: 30 mm
Length: 15.2 in.
Weight: 29.9 oz
Features: SAM (Sniper Auxiliary Module) has built-in ballistic calculator and sensor in the mount. Can be used on a weapon with different types of ammunition since values are saved in the module. Waterproof and fogproof.
MSRP: $11,982.00

Top-Angle Pro 30mm

Magnification: 7-30x
Objective Lens: 50 mm
Reticle: mil-dot
Finish: Matte black
Field of View: 10.6 ft (low)/3.5 ft (high) @ 100 yds
Click Value: ¼ in.

Tube Diameter: 30 mm
Length: 17.2 in.
Weight: 29.8 oz
Features: Big and bright DiamondTuff fully multi-coated 50mm lenses and Top-Angle parallax adjustment and positive Fast Focus large diameter ocular lens. Waterproof and fogproof.
MSRP: $449.00; $349.00 (3-12x50mm)

Uni-Dial 2.5-10x44mm

Magnification: 2.5-10x
Objective Lens: 44 mm
Reticle: mil-dot
Finish: Matte black
Field of View: 47.2 ft (low)/11.9 ft (high) @ 100 yds
Click Value: ¼ in.
Tube Diameter: 1 in.
Length: 13.2 in.
Weight: 15.3 oz
Features: Using a series of ten moveable indicators or flags, the shooter can set the range zero points. The dial is calibrated in minutes so that the flags can be set according to the ballistic data. Once set, the flags are locked in place and the dial is operated in a conventional manner. The vertical dial has a 0.5 minute click adjustment and the windage knob has 0.25 minute clicks. Both adjustments have a tope to prevent the shooter from getting lost as to where his or her zero is. But both adjustments can be unlocked from the stops to permit zeroing. Waterproof and fogproof.
MSRP: . . . .$249.00; $285.99 (4-16x50mm, 30mm tube); $341.00 (7-30x50mm)

Camputer ART M-1000

Magnification: 2.5-10x
Objective Lens: 44 mm
Reticle: mil-dot
Finish: Matte black
Field of View: 47.2 ft (low)/11.9 ft (high) @ 100 yds
Click Value: ¼ in.
Tube Diameter: 1 in.
Length: 13.2 in.
Weight: 25.2 oz
Features: When the shooter frames an 18 inch or 1 meter target using the brackets on the reticle, the scope will automatically range the target and compensate for bullet trajectory for distances of 250 to 1,000 meters. No holdover or guesswork. The cam of the new generation 2.5-10x44mm ART (Auto Ranging Trajectory) system, which was invented and designed by Jim Leatherwood for military snipers in Vietnam during the 1960s, has been redesigned by using one trajectory cam that is incrementally adjustable and can be calibrated for most centerfire rifle cartridge, from .223 Rem. to .50 BMG. Waterproof and fogproof.
MSRP: $358.99

Malcolm Vintage Style

Magnification: 6x
Objective Lens: 16 mm
Reticle: fine crosshairs
Finish: blued
Field of View: 12 ft @ 100 yds
Click Value: n/a
Tube Diameter: ¾ in.
Length: 18 in.
Weight: 18 oz
Features: Malcolm is the oldest name in scope manufacturing, established in 1855. True to the originals, the long-tube model features a graduated "rabbit-eared" rear mount; the short-tube model a "caged" rear mount. Both are adjustable for the windage and elevation. Reproduction vintage style rifle scopes available in three basic models cover scoping needs, from late percussion muzzle-loaders through the black powder cartridge rifle era and for the early "smokeless cartridge" rifle models. Both the long 1860s–1870s-style "Wm. Malcolm" scope and the shorter late 1880s–1890s-style models come with appropriate and authentically styled mounts of those periods.
MSRP: . $286.99; $266.99 (17-in. length); $368.99 (long)

Malcolm 8x USMC Sniper

Magnification: 8x
Objective Lens: 31 mm
Reticle: fine crosshairs
Finish: blued
Field of View: 11 ft @ 100 yds
Exit Pupil: 4.2 mm
Click Value: n/a

Eye Relief: 3.15 in.
Tube Diameter: ¾ in.
Length: 23 in.
Weight: 25.4oz
Features: Scopes of this design with micrometer click external adjustment were once favored by long-range precision shooters. A reproduction of the famed Unertl 8x scope used by USMC snipers during the Vietnam War.
MSRP: $521.55

M73 WWII Sniper Scope

Magnification: 2.5x
Objective Lens: 16 mm
Reticle: fine crosshairs
Finish: blued
Field of View: 24.1 ft @ 100 yds
Exit Pupil: 4 mm
Click Value: ½ in
Adjustment Range: 60 MOA
Eye Relief: 3.5 in.
Tube Diameter: ¾ in.

Length: 11.8 in.
Weight: 8.3oz
Features: Replica of scope used during World War II on US sniper rifles. In 1942 the US Army adopted the M1903A4 as the first standardized US sniper rifle and this scope is the spitting image of the original. Internally, this scope is superior with improvements that include a modern erector tube and quality multi-coated lenses for superior light transmission, more windage and elevation adjustment than the original with a total of 60 MOA with either windage or elevation.
MSRP: $341.00

Konus (konuspro.com)

KonusPro M-30 8.5-32x52mm

Magnification: 8.5-32x
Objective Lens: 52 mm
Reticle: Engraved Dual illuminated mil-dot
Finish: Matte black
Field of View: 13 ft (low)/3.3 ft (high) @ 100 yds
Exit Pupil: 6.1 mm (low)/1.6 mm (high)
Click Value: 1/10 Mil
Adjustment Range: 50 in.
Eye Relief: 3.9 in.

Tube Diameter: 30 mm
Length: 17 in.
Weight: 29.9 oz
Features: Unbreakable glass engraved, red and blue dual illuminated reticle. Fully multi-coated lenses for optimum light gathering. Features level-bubble for the utmost in precision at long range. Side focus wheel that removes parallax from 10 yards to infinity. Waterproof and fogproof.
MSRP: $679.99; $599.99 (4.5-16x40mm); $669.99 (3-12x56mm); $369.99 (1-4x24mm)

Kruger (krugeroptical.com)

6-24x50 TacDriver T4i

Magnification: 6-24x
Objective Lens: 50 mm
Reticle: LRR
Finish: Matte black
Field of View: 11.3 ft (low)/3.5 ft (high) @ 100 yds
Exit Pupil: 5.3 mm (low)/2 mm (high)
Click Value: ¼ MOA
Adjustment Range: 50 MOA

Eye Relief: 3.2 in.
Tube Diameter: 30 mm
Length: 17 in.
Weight: 27.5 oz
Features: Glass-etched, illuminated reticles, a first-in-class, two-button illumination control system on most models, and locking windage and elevation knobs. Waterproof and fogproof.
MSRP: $470.99

Leupold

(leupold.com)

Mark 4 ER/T 8.5-25x50mm

Magnification: 8.5-25x
Objective Lens: 50 mm
Reticle: mil-dot or TMR
Finish: Matte black
Field of View: 11.2 ft (low)/4.4 ft (high) @ 100 yds
Exit Pupil: 4.6 mm (low)/1.5 mm (high)
Click Value: ¼ MOA
Adjustment Range: 50 MOA
Eye Relief: 3.7-5.3 in.
Tube Diameter: 30 mm
Length: 14.5 in.
Weight: 22.5oz
Features: ER/T (Extended Range/Tactical) M1 and M5 Front Focal rifle scopes are designed for long-range work; the M5's mil-based adjustments complement the mil-based reticles to make long-range shot placement quicker and easier. Index Matched Lens System, using index matched glass with wavelength specific lens coatings designed to optimize the transmission of low-light wavelengths. DiamondCoat 2, an ion-assist lens coating, for higher light transmission and high level of abrasion resistance that exceeds military standards for hardness and durability. Twin bias spring erector system, super Fast-Focus, and lockable eyepiece, 3:1 zoom ratio.Waterproof, shockproof, and fogproof.
MSRP: . . . . . . $2,364.99; $2,124.99 (6.4-20x50mm, M1 or M5 reticle); $2,999.99 (6.4-20x50mm, M5A2 reticle); $1,999.99 (4.5-14x50mm, M1,M3, or M5 reticle)

Mark 4 LR/T 8.5-25x50mm

Magnification: 8.5-25x
Objective Lens: 50 mm
Reticle: Illum. M1 or M5
Finish: Matte black
Field of View: 11.2 ft (low)/4.4 ft (high) @ 100 yds
Exit Pupil: 5.9 mm (low)/2 mm (high)
Click Value: ¼ MOA
Adjustment Range: 70 MOA
Eye Relief: 3.7-5.3 in.
Tube Diameter: 30 mm
Length: 14.4 in.
Weight: 22.5 oz
Features: LR/T (Long Range/Tactical) uses Xtended Twilight Lens System to deliver superior resolution in low-light situations. Side focus parallax adjustment can be used from any shooting position to remove parallax. Finger-adjustable click windage and elevation dials. Adjustment dials utilize durable, dependable wear and corrosion proof parts and a precision anti-backlash mechanism with a dual erector spring to provide positive windage and elevation adjustments. The lowest two illumination settings are compatible with night vision devices. Waterproof, shockproof, and fogproof.
MSRP: . . . . $1,999.99; $1,749.99 (non-illum. M1reticle); $1,874.99 (6.5-20x50mm, illum. M1 reticle); $1,749.99 (4.5-14x50mm, illum./non-illum. M1 reticle); $1,749.99 (10x40mm, M1 reticle); $1,874.99 (3.5-10x40mm, Illum. M2 reticle)

VX-R Patrol 3-9x40mm

Magnification: 3-9x
Objective Lens: 40 mm
Reticle: Illum. FireDot TMR
Finish: Matte black
Field of View: 33.6 ft (low)/13.6 ft (high) @ 100 yds
Exit Pupil: 12.1 mm (low)/4.7 mm (high)
Click Value: 1/10 Mil
Adjustment Range: 60 MOA
Eye Relief: 3.7-4.2 in.
Tube Diameter: 30 mm

Length: 12.6 in.
Weight: 15.3 oz
Features: VX-R Patrol series features an illuminated FireDot reticle and Index Matched lens coatings for bright and crisp sight picture, with instant on fiber optic illumination. A single touch of the button activates the illumination with eight different intensity settings. Automatically switches to "stand by" mode after five minutes of inactivity. Reactivates whenever the weapon is moved. Waterproof, shockproof, and fogproof.
MSRP: $749.99; $724.99 (1.25-4x20mm)

Mark 4 2.4-8x36mm MR/T

Magnification: 2.4-8x
Objective Lens: 36 mm
Reticle: Illum. TMR
Finish: Matte black
Field of View: 35.5 ft (low)/13.6 ft (high) @ 100 yds
Exit Pupil: 14.4 mm (low)/4.5 mm (high)
Click Value: ½ MOA
Adjustment Range: 90 MOA

Eye Relief: 3 in.
Tube Diameter: 30 mm
Length: 11.3 in.
Weight: 16 oz
Features: MR/T (Mid Range Tactical) series features tactical turrets and range estimating reticles. The TS 30 A2 model is a unique version of the Mark 4 MR/T scope configured for a specific military customer. Waterproof, shockproof, and fogproof.
MSRP: $1,374.99; $1,124.99 (1.25-5x20mm, M2 reticle)

Mark AR MOD 1 3-9x40mm

Magnification: 3-9x
Objective Lens: 40 mm
Reticle: Illum. FireDot TMR, Duplex or mil-dot
Finish: Matte black
Field of View: 33.5 ft (low)/14.1 ft (high) @ 100 yds
Exit Pupil: 13.3 mm (low)/4.45 mm (high)
Click Value: 1/10 Mil
Adjustment Range: 52 MOA windage, 56 MOA elevation

Millett (millettsights.com)

Eye Relief: 3.6-4.2 in.
Tube Diameter: 1 in.
Length: 12.6 in.
Weight: 12.4 oz
Features: Uses tactical P5 elevation turret with 1/10 Mil adjustments and is calibrated for .223 Rem./5.56mm NATO 55-grain projectiles at a velocity of 3100 fps. Waterproof, shockproof, and fogproof.
MSRP: . . . $299.99 (Duplex); $349.99 (mil-dot); $449.99 (Illum. FireDot)

Tactical TRS-1 4-16x50mm

Magnification: 4-16x
Objective Lens: 50 mm
Reticle: Illum. mil-dot
Finish: Matte black
Exit Pupil: 12.5 mm (low)/3.5 mm (high)
Click Value: 1/10 Mil
Eye Relief: 3.5 in.

Tube Diameter: 30 mm
Length: 15 in.
Features: TRS (Tactical Rifle Scope)rifle scopes have multi-coated lenses with an adjustable green illuminated reticle; the mil-dot bar reticle system functions as a standard mil-dot with the addition of a thin line for easier alignment for rangefinding and holdover.
MSRP: $324.99

Tactical LRS 6-25x56mm
Magnification: 6-25x
Objective Lens: 56 mm
Reticle: Illum. mil-dot Bar
Finish: Matte black
Click Value: ¼ MOA
Eye Relief: 3 in.
Tube Diameter: 35 mm

Length: 17 in.
Features: LRS (Long Range Scope) rifle scopes features a one-piece 35mm tube and 56mm objective and delivers superior brightness and outstanding repeatable accuracy with the largest long-range weapons, including those chambered for the .50 BMG and .338 Lapua. Precision controls with 140 MOA adjustment.
MSRP: $489.99

Night Force (nightforceoptics.com)

5-25x56 ATACR
Magnification: 5-25x
Objective Lens: 56 mm
Reticle: Illum. Mil-R or MOAR, SFP
Finish: Matte black
Field of View: 17.9 ft (low)/4.9 ft (high) @ 100 yds
Exit Pupil: 10.5 mm (low)/2.3 mm (high)
Click Value: ¼ MOA/.1 Mil-Rad
Adjustment Range: 120 MOA elevation/60 MOA windage
Eye Relief: 3.5 in.

Tube Diameter: 34 mm
Length: 14.3 in.
Weight: 38oz
Features: The ATACR (Advanced Tactical Rifle scope) features 120 MOA/34.9 Mils of elevation adjustment, 20 percent more than the NXS series, and uses fully multi-coated ED glass for light transmission values of over 90 percent, brilliant images and exceptional color contrast. ZeroStop turrets. Waterproof, shockproof, and fogproof.
MSRP: $2,328.00

5-25x56 B.E.A.S.T.

Magnification: 5-25x
Objective Lens: 56 mm
Reticle: FFP, Illum. Mil-R, MOAR, MD2.0, TReMoR 2, or H59
Finish: Matte black
Field of View: 18.7 ft (low)/4.9 ft (high) @ 100 yds
Exit Pupil: 8.3 mm (low)/2.3 mm (high)
Click Value: ¼ MOA and ½ MOA/.1 and .2 Mil-Rad
Adjustment Range: 120 MOA elevation/80 MOA windage
Eye Relief: 3.3-3.5 in.

Tube Diameter: 34 mm
Length: 15.3 in.
Weight: 39oz
Features: The B.E.A.S.T. (Best Example of Advanced Scope Technology) uses a FFP (First Focal Plane) reticle with i4F intelligent four-function elevation control. Initial adjustments with the primary elevation knob are lightning fast, in .50 MOA/.2 Mil-Radian increments. An integral fine adjustment lever provides additional elevation adjustments in .25 MOA/.1 Mil-Radian increments. Waterproof, shockproof, and fogproof.
MSRP: $3,298.00

2.5-10x32 NXS Compact

Magnification: 2.5-10x
Objective Lens: 32 mm
Reticle: Illum. mil-dot, MOAR, IHR, or Velocity 600
Finish: Matte black
Field of View: 44 ft (low)/11 ft (high) @ 100 yds
Exit Pupil: 13.3 mm (low)/3.3 mm (high)
Click Value: ¼ MOA/.1 Mil-Rad
Adjustment Range: 100 MOA
Eye Relief: 3.7 in.
Tube Diameter: 30 mm

Length: 12 in.
Weight: 19 oz
Features: NXS Compact series has an objective lens assembly that focuses light rays more precisely for exceptional image clarity and color accuracy. Also features multi-coated lenses, resettable tactical turrets, and a detachable power throw level that attaches directly to the power selection ring. Waterproof, shockproof, and fogproof.
MSRP: . . . $1,609.00; $1,329.00 (1-4x24mm); $1,746.00 (2.5-10x42mm)

8-32x56 NXS

Magnification: 8-32x
Objective Lens: 56 mm
Reticle: Illum. MOAR, MOAR-T, NP-R1, NP-R2, NP-2DD, MLR, or Mil-dot
Finish: Matte black
Field of View: 12.1 ft (low)/3.1 ft (high) @ 100 yds
Exit Pupil: 7 mm (low)/1.8 mm (high)
Click Value: 1/8, ¼ MOA/.1 Mil-Rad
Adjustment Range: 65 MOA elevation/45 MOA windage
Eye Relief: 3.8 in.
Tube Diameter: 30 mm
Length: 15.9 in.
Weight: 34oz

Nikon (nikonsportoptics.com)

Features: NXS rifle scopes are subjected to abuse during product development that would destroy lesser optics. Pre-production scopes are tested in a pressure tank simulating 100 feet of water for 24 hours, ensuring absolute waterproof integrity. Thermal tested by freezing them to -80° F, then heating them to 200° F within a one-hour period. Function is checked at both temperature extremes. Recoil and impact testing for positive and negative forces is conducted at 1,250 Gs. Every rifle scope is completely inspected and checked at 70 to 130 different points, depending on the model. Waterproof, shockproof, and fogproof.
MSRP: . . . . $1,899.00; $1,959.00 (5.5-22x56mm); $2,025.00 (5.5-22x56mm, Velocity reticle); $1,798.00-2,467.00 (3.5-15x50mm, depending on features)

M-308

Magnification: 4-16x
Objective Lens: 42 mm
Reticle: BDC 800 or Nikoplex
Finish: Matte black
Field of View: 25.2 ft (low)/6.3 ft (high) @ 100 yds
Exit Pupil: 10.5 mm (low)/2.3 mm (high)
Click Value: ¼ MOA
Adjustment Range: 40 MOA
Eye Relief: 3.5 in.
Tube Diameter: 1 in.
Length: 13.5 in.

Weight: 19oz
Features: The M-308 is designed for long-range precision on the .308 AR platform with features like fully multi-coated lenses, Ultra ClearCoat optical system that delivers image clarity and resolution. The NikoPlex reticle model features Rapid Action Turrets that are calibrated for the trajectory of the .308 Win./7.62 NATO round with 168-grain HPBT bullets; the BDC 800 reticle model features tactical turrets with ¼ MOA click adjustment and holdover points out to 800 yards calibrated to .308 Win. 168-grain bullets. Waterproof, shockproof and fogproof.
MSRP: . . . . $429.00 (Nikoplex); $449.95 (BDC 800)

5-25x56 PM II/LP

Magnification: 5-25x
Objective Lens: 56 mm
Reticle: P3L, P4L, P4L fein, Police, Klein, H2CMR or H37 (FFP); P3L, P4L, P4L fein (SFP)
Finish: Matte black
Field of View: 5.3 m (low)/1.5 m (high) @ 100 m
Exit Pupil: 10.9 mm (low)/2.3 mm (high)
Click Value: ¼ MOA/.1 MRAD
Adjustment Range: 65 MOA
Eye Relief: 3.3 in.
Tube Diameter: 34 mm

Length: 16.4 in.
Weight: 38.1oz
Features: PM (Police Marksman) II offers an exceptionally wide field of view and precision shots out to 2,000 meters. It is equipped with parallax compensation, illuminated reticle and two turns in the elevation adjustment (Double Turn). Parallax compensation may be adjusted starting at 10 meters and reaching to infinity. The scope may be supplied with the reticle in the first or in the second focal plane. Waterproof, shockproof, and fogproof.
MSRP: $3,739.00

5-25x56 PM II/LP/MTC/LT

Magnification: 5-25x
Objective Lens: 56 mm
Reticle: P3L, P4L, P4L fein, Police, Klein, H2CMR or H37 (FFP); P3L, P4L, P4L fein (SFP)
Finish: RAL8000
Field of View: 5.3 m (low)/1.5 m (high) @ 100 m
Exit Pupil: 10.9 mm (low)/2.3 mm (high)
Click Value: ¼ MOA/.1 MRAD
Adjustment Range: 64 MOA
Eye Relief: 3.3 in.
Tube Diameter: 34 mm
Length: 16.4 in.

Weight: 40.5oz
Features: The PSR (Precision Sniper Rifle) turret was designed specifically to the requirements of SOCOM (US Special Operations Command) for target interdiction to 1500 meters and beyond. It features tactile clicks at each .1 MRAD and a more pronounced feel at every full MRAD or ten clicks in the case of MRAD scopes. When the turret moves to its 2nd revolution a round rings rises on the top of the turret allowing the shooter to feel that he is in the 2nd revolution. Both windage and elevation turrets offer a locking ring which prevents inadvertent turret movement after the scope is adjusted. Waterproof, shockproof and fogproof.
MSRP: . . $3,729.00–$4,079.00 (depending on reticle type)

3-27x56 PM II/LP/LT

Magnification: 3-27x
Objective Lens: 56 mm
Reticle: P3L, P4L, P4L fein, Police, Klein, H2CMR or H37 (FFP); P3L, P4L, P4L fein (SFP)
Finish: Matte black, RAL8000 or Pantone
Field of View: 13 m (low)/1.4 m (high) @ 100 m
Exit Pupil: 10.9 mm (low)/2.3 mm (high)
Click Value: ¼ MOA/.1 MRAD
Adjustment Range: 65 MOA

Eye Relief: 3.5 in.
Tube Diameter: 34 mm
Length: 15.5 in.
Weight: 39.8 oz
Features: 9x zoom scope for versatile shooting situations, tested and selected by the elite USSOCOM, completely waterproof up to 25 meters, large adjustment range for ultra long-range shooting, locking MTC turrets, ultra high accuracy and shock resistant for large calibers, rugged military design. Waterproof, shockproof, and fogproof.
MSRP: . . . $6,159.00–$6,999.00 (depending on features)

10x42 PM II

Magnification: 10x
Objective Lens: 42 mm
Reticle: P3 mil-dot (FFP)
Finish: Matte black
Field of View: 1 ft @ 100 yds
Click Value: .36 MOA
Eye Relief: 3.3 in.

Tube Diameter: 30 mm
Length: 13.3 in.
Weight: 21 oz
Features: Simple, rugged, and reliable, this fixed 10x power provides some of the highest light transmission levels, yet presents a low profile. The P3 Mil-dot reticle is standard.
MSRP: $1,949.00

Steiner (steiner-optics.com)

M5Xi Military 5-25x56
Magnification: 5-25x
Objective Lens: 56 mm
Reticle: G2B mil-dot or MSR
Finish: Matte black
Field of View: 23.6 ft (low)/4.9 ft (high) @ 100 yds
Exit Pupil: 9.8 mm (low)/2.2 mm (high)
Click Value: .1 Mil-Rad
Adjustment Range: 26 mils elevation/6 mils windage

Eye Relief: 3.5 in.
Tube Diameter: 34 mm
Length: 16.6 in.
Weight: 36.3oz
Features: M5Xi series features true 25x magnification, etched glass G2B mil-dot reticle, patented DuoScale elevation with second-rotation scale that's hidden when inactive. Waterproof, shockproof, and fogproof.
MSRP: . . . $3,599.99; $2,989.99 (1-5x24mm); $3,329.99 (3-15x50mm)

Trijicon (trijicon.com)

TARS
Magnification: 3-15x
Objective Lens: 50 mm
Reticle: Illum. TARS101, TARS102, TARS103 or TARS104
Finish: Matte black
Field of View: 37.4 ft (low)/7.5 ft (high) @ 100 yds
Exit Pupil: .66 mm (low)/.13 mm (high)
Click Value: ¼ MOA/.1 Mil
Adjustment Range: 150 MOA elevation/120 MOA windage; 44 Mil elevation/36 Mil windage
Eye Relief: 3.3 in.
Tube Diameter: 34 mm

Length: 13.9 in.
Weight: 47oz
Features: TARS is a rugged variable power rifle scope that features a first focal plane reticle with 10 illumination settings, including two for night vision, oversized target adjusters feature 150 MOA/44 mil total elevation adjustment and 30 MOA/10 mil adjustments per revolution as well as a mechanism to prevent unintentional adjuster rotation. Combined with an elevation Return to Zero feature, allows for rapid zeroing on a target no matter the distance. Waterproof, shockproof, and fogproof.
MSRP: $4,058.00

U.S. Optics (usoptics.com)

SR-6 1.5-6x

Magnification: 1.5-6x
Objective Lens: 28 mm
Reticle: JNG MIL
Finish: Matte black
Field of View: 64.6 ft (low)/25.3 ft (high) @ 100 yds
Exit Pupil: 18.6 mm (low)/4.6 mm (high)
Click Value: .1 Mil
Adjustment Range: 27.8 Mil elevation/23 Mil windage
Eye Relief: 3.5 in.
Tube Diameter: 30 mm

Length: 11 in.
Weight: 22.4 oz
Features: Ideal for engaging targets at distances from point blank out to 600+ yards. Uses an illuminated JNG MIL reticle to facilitate quick center-mass target acquisition in any lighting condition via the outer ring and .5 MIL hash marks on the stadia lines. Dual elevation and windage rebound springs will insure decades of reliable and accurate adjustments. Waterproof, shockproof, and fogproof.
MSRP: $1,505.00

ER-25 5-25x

Magnification: 5-25x
Objective Lens: 58 mm
Reticle: mil-dot
Finish: Matte black Type III Hard Anodizing
Field of View: 16.6 ft (low)/5.3 ft (high) @ 100 yds
Exit Pupil: 2.7 mm (high)
Click Value: .1 Mil
Adjustment Range: 95 MOA
Eye Relief: 3.5 in.
Tube Diameter: 34 mm
Length: 18 in.
Weight: 2 lbs 8 oz

Features: ER-25 series features a Turret Parallax Adjustment Locater (TPAL) system for sharp image resolution throughout the 5-25x power magnification range and at distances past 2,000 yards. The reticle has twelve illumination settings. Erector Repositioning Elevation Knob (EREK) system maximizes gross elevation travel adjustment for maximum elevation adjustment where traditional turrets leave off beyond 2,000 yards. MIL, MOA and Horus reticle options are available. Dual elevation and windage rebound springs ensure reliable and accurate adjustments.Waterproof, shockproof, and fogproof.
MSRP: $3,301.00

MR-10 1.8-10x

Magnification: 1-8x
Objective Lens: 37 mm
Reticle: mil-dot
Finish: Matte black Type III Hard Anodizing
Field of View: 41.6 ft (low)/12.8 ft (high) @ 100 yds
Exit Pupil: 4 mm (high)
Click Value: .1 Mil
Adjustment Range: 32 Mil elevation/23 Mil windage
Eye Relief: 2.7 in.
Tube Diameter: 30 mm
Length: 13 in.
Weight: 30.5 oz
Features: MR-10 series has a Turret Parallax Adjustment Locator (TPAL) system for the sharpest image resolution possible throughout the 1.8-10X power magnification range, a 12-position illuminated reticle system, an Erector Repositioning Elevation Knob (EREK) system that maximizes gross elevation travel adjustment for maximum elevation adjustment where traditional turrets leave off, and MIL and MOA reticle options. Waterproof, shockproof, and fogproof.
MSRP: $2,341.00

LR-17 3.2-17x

Magnification: 1-8x
Objective Lens: 44 mm
Reticle: mil-dot
Finish: Matte black Type III Hard Anodizing
Field of View: 25.3 ft (low)/8.3 ft (high) @ 100 yds
Exit Pupil: 3 mm (high)
Click Value: .1 Mil
Adjustment Range: 23 Mil elevation/21 Mil windage
Eye Relief: 2.7 in.
Tube Diameter: 30 mm
Length: 16.5 in.
Weight: 32.2 oz
Features: The LR-17 series provides a decisive advantage when engaging targets beyond 1,500 yards. A 44mm objective lens sits in front of a Turret Parallax Adjustment Locator (TPAL) system for sharp image resolution throughout the 3.2-17x power magnification range. When weather and light conditions are less than optimal the 12-position illuminated reticle system provides another advantage. All LR-17 scopes feature an Erector Repositioning Elevation Knob (EREK) system that maximizes gross elevation travel adjustment for maximum elevation adjustment where traditional turrets leave off. MIL, MOA, and Horus reticle options are available. Dual elevation and windage rebound springs will insure decades of reliable and accurate adjustments. Waterproof, shockproof, and fogproof.
MSRP: $2,746.00

Viper PST 6-24x50 FFP

Magnification: 6-24x
Objective Lens: 50 mm
Reticle: EBR-1 (MOA or MRAD), EBR-2C (MOA or MRAD)
Finish: Matte black
Field of View: 17.8 ft (low)/5.1 ft (high) @ 100 yds
Click Value: ¼ MOA
Adjustment Range: 65 MOA
Eye Relief: 4 in.

Tube Diameter: 30 mm
Length: 15.5 in.
Weight: 23.4 oz
Features: The Viper PST (Precision Shooting Tactical) rifle scope boasts features associated with top-tier rifle scopes. Matching reticle and turret measurements allow accurate, fast dialing of shots. Waterproof, shockproof, and fogproof.
MSRP: . . . . . $1,049.00; $999.00 (4-16x50 FFP); $899.00 (2.5-10x32 ΓFP); $849.00 (6-24x50); $799.00 (4-16x50); $699.00 (2.5-10x44); $599.00 (1-4x24)

Razor HD Gen II 4.5-27x56

Magnification: 4.5-27x
Objective Lens: 56 mm
Reticle: EBR-1C (MRAD), EBR-2C (MOA or MRAD)
Finish: Matte black
Field of View: 25.3 ft (low)/4.4 ft (high) @ 100 yds
Click Value: .1 MRAD
Adjustment Range: 33 MRAD elevation/13 MRAD windage

Eye Relief: 3.7 in.
Tube Diameter: 34 mm
Length: 15.5 in.
Weight: 14.4 oz
Features: Gen II Razor series feature a 6x zoom range, a 34mm single-piece aircraft-grade aluminum tube, and the L-Tec turret system. Waterproof, shockproof, and fogproof.
MSRP: $2,999.00; $2,599.00 (3-18x50); $1,899.00 (1-6x24)

Razor HD 5-20x50 (MOA)

Magnification: 5-20x
Objective Lens: 50 mm
Reticle: EBR-1 (15 MOA turrets or 25 MOA turrets), EBR-2B (25 MOA turrets)
Finish: Matte black
Field of View: 22 ft (low)/5.8 ft (high) @ 100 yds
Click Value: ¼ MOA
Adjustment Range: 125 MOA

Eye Relief: 3.9 in.
Tube Diameter: 35 mm
Length: 15.8 in.
Weight: 35.2oz
Features: Razor HD 5-20x50 is built on a solid 35mm one-piece tube and packed with more than a dozen unique performance and optical features—including a precision-etched first focal plane reticle. Waterproof, shockproof, and fogproof.
MSRP: . . . . $2,499.00; $2,499.00 (5-20x50 MRAD)

Weaver (weaver-mounts.com)

Tactical 4-20x50

Magnification: 4-20x
Objective Lens: 50 mm
Reticle: MilDot, CIRT or EMDR
Finish: Matte black
Field of View: 25.1 ft (low)/5 ft (high) @ 100 yds
Exit Pupil: 9.5 mm (low)/2.4 mm (high)
Click Value: ¼ MOA
Adjustment Range: 55 MOA
Eye Relief: 3.9 in.
Tube Diameter: 30 mm

Length: 14.88 in.
Weight: 28oz
Features: Tactical series features reset-to-zero turrets, side focus parallax adjustment, fully multi-coated lenses with an extra hard coating on the exterior lenses, and first focal plane reticles. Waterproof, shockproof, and fogproof.
MSRP: . . . .$1,247.95; $1,234.49 (3-15x50); $1,117.95 (3-15x50); $1,069.95(1-5x24); $1,247.95 (4-20x50); $1,197.95 (2-10x36)

41. Tactical Binoculars

Bushnell (bushnell.com)

Elite 10x42mm
Magnification: 10x
Objective Lens: 42mm
Field of View: 314 ft @ 1000 yds
Height: 5.6 in.
Width: 5.1 in.
Weight: 25.7 oz
Features: Roof prism design use BaK-4 glass, phase-coated glass. Multi-coated ED-glass lenses Rubber-armored magnesium housing, center focus, and twist-up eyecups. Black finish. Waterproof and fogproof.
MSRP: $699.00; $677.00 (8x42mm)

Legend Ultra HD10x42mm
Magnification: 10x
Objective Lens: 42mm
Field of View: 340 ft @ 1000 yds
Height: 5.5 in.
Width: 5 in.
Weight: 22.5 oz
Features: Roof prism design uses BaK-4 glass, multi-coated glass. Soft-touch rubber-armored magnesium housing, center focus, and twist-up eyecups. Black finish. Waterproof and fogproof.
MSRP: . . . . $413.00; $435.00 (camo)

Fraser Optics (Fraser-optics.com)

14x40 Stedi-Eye Observer Stabilized LE Edition
Magnification: 14x
Objective Lens: 40 mm
Field of View: 223 ft @ 1000 yds
Height: 8.2 in.
Width: 7.5 in.
Weight: 72 oz
Features: Uses gyro stabilization technology to correct up to 98 percent of image motion caused by hand tremor and platform motion. Proprietary compound optical coatings minimize unwanted reflections and maximize light transmission through the optical channels, resulting in enhanced image brightness and contrast. CCD recording device attaches to an ocular of any Stedi-Eye series binocular and transmits 512x492 video for remote monitoring or recording. Waterproof and fogproof.
MSRP: $5,600.00

14x40 Stedi-Eye PM25 Stabilized LE Edition

Magnification: 14x
Objective Lens: 40 mm
Field of View: 223 ft @ 1000 yds
Height: 8.2 in.
Width: 7.5 in.
Weight: 72 oz
Features: Uses gyro stabilization technology to correct up to 98 percent of image motion caused by hand tremor and platform motion. Proprietary compound optical coatings minimize unwanted reflections and maximize light transmission through the optical channels, resulting in enhanced image brightness and contrast. CCD recording device attaches to an ocular of any Stedi-Eye series binocular and transmits 512x492 video for remote monitoring or recording. Features sighting reticle, weatherproof/buoyant housing, fully multicoated optics, and supplemental external power supply. Waterproof and fogproof.
MSRP: $6,500.00

Leica (us.leica-camera.com)

Geovid 10x42 HD-B

Magnification: 10x
Objective Lens: 42mm
Field of View: 342 ft @ 1000 yds
Height: 6.8 in.
Width: 4.8 in.
Weight: 34.7 oz
Range: 10–2,000 yds
Features: Geovid HD-B combines a binocular with a laser rangefinder (LFR). The LFR accesses an internal database with ballistic curves for most standard calibers plus users can upload their own specific parameters for hand-loaded or special ammunition from a microSD memory card. Point of aim correction for various reticles and ASV (rapid reticle adjustment). Perger Porro prisms, AquaDura coating for easier cleaning. Waterproof, shockproof, and fogproof.
MSRP: . . . . $2,999.99; $479.99 (MIL-L reticle)

Leupold (leupold.com)

BX-2 Tactical 10x42mm

Magnification: 10x
Objective Lens: 42mm
Field of View: 267 ft @ 1000 yds
Height: 5.5 in.
Width: 5.5 in.
Weight: 23.1 oz
Features: Lightweight roof prism design. Waterproof, shockproof and fogproof.
MSRP: . . . . $399.99; $479.99 (MIL-L reticle)

Meopta (meoptasportsoptics.com)

MeoStar B1 42mm HD
Magnification: 10x
Objective Lens: 42mm
Field of View: 330 ft @ 1000 yds
Height: 5.5 in.
Width: 5.2 in.
Weight: 31.6 oz
Features: Roof prism design using an aluminum chassis. Protective rubber armor with sculpted thumb pockets help reduce hand fatigue and improve grip. Extra-low dispersion, fluorite objective lens eliminate chromatic aberration (CA) or color fringing in challenging lighting conditions and deliver pin point resolution, increased contrast, and vivid color fidelity. Waterproof, shockproof, and fogproof.
MSRP: $987.00

MeoStar B1 56mm
Magnification: 10x
Objective Lens: 56mm
Field of View: 333 ft @ 1000 yds
Height: 8.3 in.
Width: 5.6 in.
Weight: 39.5 oz
Features: Massive roof prism design using an aluminum chassis with rubber armor. Ergonomic to reduce hand fatigue and improve grip. Extra-low dispersion, fluorite objective lens eliminate chromatic aberration (CA) or color fringing Extra large 7mm exit pupils to provide better light gathering capability. Proprietary MB5501TM ion assisted lens multi-coatings deliver maximum light transmission in dusk to nighttime conditions to ensure brightness and resolution. Waterproof, shockproof, and fogproof.
MSRP: $1,125.00

Steiner (steiner-optics.com)

T42 Tactical 10x42mm
Magnification: 10x
Objective Lens: 42mm
Field of View: 317 ft @ 1000 yds
Height: 6.6 in.
Width: 4.9 in.
Weight: 26.4 oz
Features: Roof prism design uses military grade rubber armor to protect lenses, reduce noise and provide a sure grip. Waterproof, shockproof, and fogproof.
MSRP: $575.00

T24 Tactical 8x24mm

Magnification: 8x
Objective Lens: 24mm
Field of View: 317 ft @ 1000 yds
Height: 4.2 in.
Width: 4.8 in.
Weight: 12.6 oz
Features: Lightweight, roof prism design uses military grade rubber armor to protect lenses, reduce noise and provide a sure grip. Fast-CloseFocus feature require minimal focus wheel movement for quick adjustment. Waterproof, shockproof, and fogproof.
MSRP: $345.00

MM50 Military/Marine 10x50mm

Magnification: 10x
Objective Lens: 50mm
Field of View: 302 ft @ 1000 yds
Height: 5 in.
Width: 8.1 in.
Weight: 35.3 oz
Features: Porro prism design with high magnification and larger objectives for better performance in low-light conditions. The Makrolon housing is a durable polycarbonate with NBR long life rubber armor. Waterproof, shockproof, and fogproof.
MSRP: $660.00

M50rc Commander Military 7x50mm rc

Magnification: 7x
Objective Lens: 50mm
Field of View: 392 ft @ 1000 yds
Height: 8.1 in.
Width: 5.5 in.
Weight: 39.7 oz
Features: This porro prism design integrates an illuminated HD stabilized compass and a MIL ranging reticle. Waterproof, shockproof, and fogproof.
MSRP: $1,260.00

M80 Military 20x80mm

Magnification: 20x
Objective Lens: 80mm
Field of View: 195 ft @ 1000 yds
Height: 11.6 in.
Width: 8.9 in.
Weight: 68.1 oz
Features: Porro prism design built for image acuity; this high-power binocular offers clarity and sharpness with extended viewing comfort. Waterproof, shockproof, and fogproof.
MSRP: $1,700.00

Swarovski (swarovskioptik.com/hunting)

EL8.5x42 W B

Magnification: 8.5x
Objective Lens: 42mm
Field of View: 399 ft @ 1000 yds
Height: 6.3 in.
Width: 4.8 in.
Weight: 29.5 oz
Features: Roof prism design uses the EL wrap-around grip for extended viewing. Use of high-precision fluoride-containing HD lenses and prisms results in razor-sharp, high-contrast images with maximum color fidelity. Waterproof, shockproof, and fogproof.
MSRP: . . . . $2,810.00;$2,866.00 (10x42mm)

Vortex (vortexoptics.com)

Razor HD 12x50

Magnification: 12x
Objective Lens: 50mm
Field of View: 285 ft @ 1000 yds
Height: 6.8 in.
Width: 5.1 in.
Weight: 28.7 oz
Features: Roof prism design with premium HD extra-low dispersion glass. Open hinge with magnesium chassis with rubber armor coating. Waterproof, shockproof, and fogproof.
MSRP: $1,499.00; $1,489.00 (10x50mm); $1,299.00 (10x42mm); $1,279.00 (8x42mm)

Conquest HD 10x42

Magnification: 10x
Objective Lens: 42mm
Field of View: 345 ft @ 1000 yds
Height: 6.5 in.
Width: 4.7 in.
Weight: 28 oz
Features: Roof prism design. HD lens system provides true and neutral color fidelity with Carl Zeiss T* multi-layer coated lenses. Focus system with the large focusing wheel ensures easy handling, optimum grip, and precise focusing even when wearing gloves.Waterproof, shockproof, and fogproof.
MSRP: $1,299.00; $1,279.00 (8x42mm)

20x60 T* S Image Stabilization

Magnification: 20x
Objective Lens: 60mm
Field of View: 156 ft @ 1000 yds
Height: 10.8 in.
Width: 6.3 in.
Weight: 58.6 oz
Features: Roof prism design. Mechanical image stabilization system with gimbal-mounted spring joint and magnetic damping action works at the touch of a button, noiselessly and without battery power. Rubber armor over the metal casing protects the internal optics and mechanics. Waterproof, shockproof, and fogproof.
MSRP $6,999.99

Victory 8x32 T* FL

Magnification: 8x
Objective Lens: 32mm
Field of View: 420 ft @ 1000 yds
Height: 4.6 in.
Width: 4.6 in.
Weight: 19.8 oz
Features: Roof prism design with wide field of view. Lenses are made of fluoride glass to minimize chromatic aberrations and ensure high image definition. Waterproof, shockproof, and fogproof.
MSRP: $2,166.99; $2,222.99 (10x32mm); $2,555.99 (10x42mm); $2,722.99 (10x56mm)

42. Tactical Spotting Scopes

Bushnell (bushnell.com)

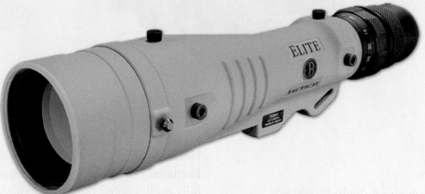

LMSS 8-40x60mm
Magnification: 8-40x
Objective Lens: 60 mm
Field of View: 83 ft (low)/50 ft (high) @ 100 yds
Exit Pupil: 5 mm (low)/1.5 mm (high)
Eye Relief: 30 mm
Focus: 30 ft (low)
Length: 12.7 in

Weight: 37.1 oz
Finish: Sand
Features: 5x magnification ratio, ED prime glass for vivid details, fully multi-coated optics for the brightest images, rubber-armored aluminum body, RainGuard HD water-repellent lens coating, twist-up eyecups, waterproof/fogproof.
MSRP: $2,417.95

Legend Ultra HD 12-36x50mm
Magnification: 12-36x
Objective Lens: 50 mm
Field of View: 179 ft (low)/90ft (high) @ 100 yds
Exit Pupil: 4.2 mm (low)/1.4 mm (high)
Eye Relief: 17 mm
Focus: 15 ft (low)
Length: 10.5 in

Weight: 36.3 oz
Finish: Black
Features: ED Prime extra-low dispersion glass, 2-speed dual focus controls, RainGuard HD water-repellent lens coating, waterproof/fogproof, BaK-4 prisms, fully multi-coated optics,compact porro prism design, long eye relief, close focusing, zoom eyepiece.
MSRP: . . $444.95 (straight body); $466.95 (angled body)

Elite 15-45x60mm

Magnification: 15-45x
Objective Lens: 60 mm
Field of View: 125 ft (low)/65 ft (high) @ 100 yds
Exit Pupil: 4 mm (low)/1.3 mm (high)
Eye Relief: 30 mm
Focus: 30 ft (low)
Length: 12.7 in

Kowa

kowa-usa.com

Weight: 26.5 oz
Finish: Black
Features: PC-3 phase-corrected BaK-4 roof prisms with fully multi-coated optics for extra-sharp, extra-bright and brilliant color resolution at the longest ranges, waterproof/fogproof.
MSRP: $652.95; $1,402.95 (20-60x80mm, straight body); $1,444.95 (20-60x80mm, angled body)

TSN-883 88mm with TE-10Z 20-60x Zoom Eyepiece

Magnification: 20-60x
Objective Lens: 88 mm
Field of View: 38.4 ft (low)/18.3ft (high) @ 1000 yds
Exit Pupil: 19.4 mm (low)/2.3 mm (high)
Eye Relief: 17-16.5 mm
Focus: 30 ft (low)
Length: 13.5 in
Weight: 53.5 oz
Finish: green/gray
Features: Fluorite Crystal lenses with ultra-low dispersion properties to reduce chromatic aberration, or color blur.

The housing is waterproof and filled with dry nitrogen gas to prevent internal fogging to ensure image clarity. The dual focus mechanism has smooth movement at high magnifications for pinpoint accuracy in image display. The quick focus can easily shift from infinity to 5m in two revolutions with the large knob. The fine focus moves fluidly to create pinpoint accuracy and is extremely useful at high magnifications and with digiscoping systems. Magnesium alloy body is constructed by a process called thixotropic molding to give the strength and feel from a traditional metal body, but with much lighter weight, yet rugged.
MSRP: . . . $2,725.00 (straight or angled body) + $670.00 (TE-10Z 20-60x eyepiece)

Kruger Optical (krugeroptical.com)

7-25x50 Lynx
Magnification: 7-25x
Objective Lens: 50 mm
Field of View: 241 ft (low)/104 ft (high) @ 1000 yds
Exit Pupil: 7.1 mm (low)/2 mm (high)
Eye Relief: 30 mm
Focus: 10 m to infinity
Length: 11 in
Weight: 53.5 oz
Finish: Black

Features: Hand-held scope designed for quick and accurate target acquisition. Available with or without an illuminated mil-dot ranging reticle. A single button controls the brightness of the illuminated reticle, with 10 distinct brightness settings. Reticle can be removed from the field of view, for a clear view of the target. Designed with an ambidextrous hand strap and thumb grip for convenient one-handed operation with either hand, as well as a tripod mount on the bottom of the scope. Shockproof, waterproof, and fogproof.
MSRP: $1,470.00; $1,599.00 (14-50x60mm)

Leica (us.leica-camera.com)

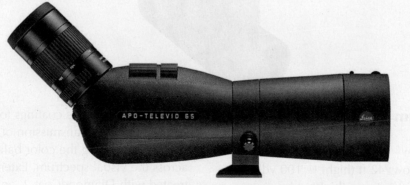

APO-Televid 65
Magnification: 25-50x
Objective Lens: 65 mm
Field of View: 123 ft (low)/84 ft (high) @ 1000 yds
Focus: 9.5 ft (low)
Length: 11.8 in
Weight: 39.6 oz

Finish: Black
Features: Fluorite lens deliver an image with excellent color fidelity and sharpness with maximum contrast. Magnesium-alloy chassis has rubber armoring. Waterproof/fogproof/shockproof.
MSRP: . . . $2,099.99 (straight or angled body) + $900.00 (25-50x eyepiece)

GR 10-20x40mm Compact

Magnification: 10-20x
Objective Lens: 40 mm
Field of View: 199 ft (low)/136ft (high) @ 1000 yds
Exit Pupil: 4 mm (low)/2 mm (high)
Eye Relief: 17.2-18.5 mm
Focus: 5.5 ft (low)
Length: 7.5 in
Weight: 15.8 oz
Finish: Black

Features: Xtended Twilight Lens System matches coatings to glass indices to achieve the best possible transmission of the blue/violet spectrum, without sacrificing the color balanced light transmission across the visual spectrum. Exterior lens surfaces are treated with DiamondCoat 2, an ion-assist lens coating, for higher light transmission and greater levels of abrasion resistance. Smooth focusing, armor coated body, waterproof/fogproof.
MSRP: . . . $439.99;$1,249.99 (12-40x60mm); $1,749.99 (12-40x60mm HD Kit); $499.99 (15-30x50mm Compact)

Mark 4 12-40x60mm Tactical

Magnification: 12-40x
Objective Lens: 60 mm
Field of View: 121 ft (low)/42 ft (high) @ 100 yds
Exit Pupil: 4.1 mm (low)/1.3 mm (high)
Eye Relief: 30 mm
Focus: 36 ft (low)
Length: 15.5 in
Weight: 61.8 oz
Finish: Black
Features: Choice of reticles allow spotter and sniper to view the same targets the same way. Xtended Twilight

Lens System matches coatings to glass indices to achieve the best possible transmission of the blue/violet spectrum, without sacrificing the color balanced light transmission across the visual spectrum. Exterior lens surfaces are treated with DiamondCoat 2, an ion-assist lens coating, for higher light transmission and greater levels of abrasion resistance. Smooth focusing, armor coated body, waterproof/fogproof.
MSRP: $2,124.99 (TMR, Post & Duplex reticle);$2,999.99 (H-36, H-32, Inverted H-36, Inverted H-32)

Mark 4 20-60x80mm Tactical

Magnification: 20-60x
Objective Lens: 80 mm
Field of View: 16.8 ft (low)/5.2 (high) @ 100 yds
Exit Pupil: 4.8 mm (low)/1.5 mm (high)
Eye Relief: 1.18 in
Focus: 36 ft (low)
Length: 12.4 in
Weight: 37 oz
Finish: Black
Features: With either a mil-dot reticle or Tactical Milling Reticle (TMR) the spotting scope enables a sniper and

spotter to view the same targets the same way. Xtended Twilight Lens System matches coatings to glass indices to achieve the best possible transmission of the blue/violet spectrum, without sacrificing the color balanced light transmission across the visual spectrum. Exterior lens surfaces are treated with DiamondCoat 2, an ion-assist lens coating, for higher light transmission and greater levels of abrasion resistance. Smooth focusing, armor coated body, waterproof/fogproof.
MSRP: $2,999.99

Meopta (meoptasportsoptics.com)

MeoStar S2 82 HD Angled

Magnification: 20-70x
Objective Lens: 82 mm
Eye Relief: 18 mm
Focus: 5.5 ft (low)
Length: 13.4 in
Weight: 55.4 oz
Finish: Black/green
Features: Extra-low dispersion HD glass lenses for maximum light gathering ability and color fidelity. Lens

elements are fully multicoated with Meopta's proprietary MeoBright 5501 anti-reflective coating, to maximize light transmitted and enhance contrast. Exposed lens surfaces are also finished with layers of Meopta's MeoDrop moisture-repellant and MeoShield scratch-resistant coatings. CentricDrive focus wheel is oversized and textured, objective housing is nitrogen-purged and gasket-sealed, magnesium and aluminum chassis provides a shock-resistant foundation for the optical system.
MSRP: $2,199.99

Nightforce (nightforceoptics.com)

TS-82 Xtreme Hi-Def

Magnification: 20-70x
Objective Lens: 82 mm
Field of View: 48.7 ft (low)/23 ft (high) @ 1000 yds
Exit Pupil: 4.1 mm (low)/1.1 mm (high)
Eye Relief: 18 mm
Focus: 4.6 ft (low)
Length: 16.4 in
Weight: 67 oz
Finish: Black/gray

U.S. Optics (nightforceoptics.com)

Features: Proprietary Nightforce coatings result in superb contrast and brightness, plus a hydrophobic coating that sheds water without leaving residue and repels fingerprints and smudges, keeping your images crisp and clean. APO fluorite glass. Allows attachment of iPhone 4 or 5 to take high resolution photos. Aluminum body provides ruggedness and thermal stability, and it's shockproof and waterproof. Large center focus ring is highly precise, comfortable to use, and extremely fast.
MSRP: . . . . $2,522.00 (angled or straight body)

Field Observation scope 15-40x

Magnification: 15-40x
Objective Lens: 60 mm
Field of View: 8.5 ft (low)/2.7 ft (high) @ 100 yds
Eye Relief: 2.5 in
Length: 14.4 in
Weight: 32 oz
Finish: Black
Features: Based on the SSOT requirements set forth by the USMC as a Field Observation Scope (FOS). The FOS

is engineered to provide generous eye relief for all-day glassing without causing strain to the observer's eyes. The ERGO parallax adjustment bell provides the sharpest image possible when glassing in the field throughout the 15-40X power magnification range. Reticle options are available to pair the FOS with certain ER series, MR series, and LR series rifle scopes.
MSRP: $1,075.00

Viper HD 20-60x80

Magnification: 20-60x
Objective Lens: 80 mm
Field of View: 110 ft (low)/50 ft (high) @ 1000 yds
Exit Pupil: 4 mm (low)/1.3 mm (high)
Eye Relief: 20-15 mm
Focus: 22 ft (low)

Length: 17.5 in
Weight: 67 oz
Finish: Green/black
Features: HD (High Density) extra-low dispersion glass for impressive resolution and color fidelity and XR fully multi-coated lenses for maximum brightness. Fogproof and waterproof.
MSRP: . . . .$1,099.00 (angled or straight body)

Zeiss (sportsoptics.zeiss.com)

Victory DiaScope 65 T* FL

Magnification: 15-56x
Objective Lens: 65 mm
Field of View: 156 ft (low)/63 ft (high) @ 1000 yds
Exit Pupil: 4.3 mm (low)/1.2 mm (high)
Focus: 13.1 ft (low)
Length: 11.1 in
Weight: 39 oz
Finish: Black

Features: FL lens construction consists of multiple thin lenses and high-performance fluoride glass. Dual Speed Focus (DSF) combines two focusing speeds in one knob. If the knob is turned quickly beyond the fine focus range, the system operates in rapid mode and the focus point is quickly adjusted to the appropriate distance. LotuTec coating on the lens and eyepiece ensures they are waterproof. The Carl Zeiss T* multi-layer coating provides bright, high-contrast images in all conditions.
MSRP: . . .$2,900.00 (angled or straight body); $3,499.00 (85T* FL, straight or angled body)

43. Tactical Rangefinders

Bushnell (bushnell.com)

FUSION 1 Mile ARC 10x42mm
Magnification: 10x
Objective Lens: 42mm
Field of View: 305 ft @ 1000 yds
Height: 6.0 in
Width: 5.5 in
Weight: 31 oz
Range: 10–1760 yds
Features: The Fusion 1 Mile ARC combines a binocular with a rangefinder with fully multi-coated lenses and BaK-4 glass prisms. Features ARC bow mode for "shoots-like" horizontal distance, and ARC rifle mode provides bullet-drop and holdover with Sight-In option. Modes include scan, bullseye, and brush targeting. Waterproof and fogproof.
MSRP: $1,199.00; $999.00 (8x32mm); $1,299.00 (12x50mm)

Elite 1 Mile ARC
Power: 7x
Measurement Range: 5–1,760 yds
Accuracy: ± .5 yds
Weight: 12.1 oz
Length: 5.1 in
Width: 3.7 in
Display: Vivid Display Technology (VDT)
Power Source: 1 x 3V/CR123
Finish: Tan and black
Features: Ranging distance depends on reflectivity of target, i.e.,tree 1,000 yards, deer 500 yards. Rifle Mode provides bullet-drop/holdover in CM, IN, MOA & MIL; BullsEye, Brush, and Scan modes; built-in tripod mount. Waterproof.
MSRP: $784.95

G-Force 1300 ARC

Power: 6x
Measurement Range: 5–1,760 yds
Accuracy: ± .5 yds
Weight: 8 oz
Length: 5.1 in
Width: 3.7 in
Display: Vivid Display Technology (VDT)
Power Source: 1 x 3V/CR123
Finish: black or camo
Features: Ranging distance depends on reflectivity of target, i.e.,tree 900 yards, deer 600 yards. Bow Mode provides true horizontal distance from 5–99 yards; Rifle Mode gives bullet-drop/holdover in CM, IN, MOA & MIL; BullsEye, Brush, and Scan modes. Waterproof.
MSRP: $399.99

Scout DX 1000 ARC

Power: 6x
Measurement Range: 5–1,000 yds
Accuracy: ± .5 yds
Weight: 6.6 oz
Length: 3.5 in
Width: 3 in
Display: Vivid Display Technology (VDT)
Power Source: 1 x 3V/CR2
Finish: Black or Realtree XTRA camo
Features: Ranging distance depends on reflectivity of target, i.e., tree 650 yards, deer 325 yards. Three modes: BullsEye, Brush, and Scan. Features aiming circle reticle and Angle Range Compensation (ARC) in both bow and rifle modes to provide true-angle compensation by accounting for the terrain angle when calculating distance, giving exact distance. Rifle mode has bullet-drop, variable sight-in distance, and holdover in both MOA and MIL with Variable Sight-In (VSI) distance technology for the exact zeroed range of weapon. Built-in tripod mount.Waterproof.
MSRP: . . . . $299.99 (black); $319.99 (Realtree XTRA camo)

Leupold (leupold.com)

RX-1000i TBR with DNA

Power: 6x
Measurement Range: 5–1,000 yds
Field of View: 320 ft @ 1000 yds
Exit Pupil: 3.6 mm
Eye Relief: 16 mm
Weight: 7.8 oz
Length: 3.8 in
Width: 2.8 in
Display: LED

Power Source: 1 x 3V/C2
Finish: Black/gray or Mossy Oak Break-Up
Features: Ranging distance depends on reflectivity of target, i.e., tree 700 yards, deer 600 yards. Combines True Ballistic Ranging (TBR) technology with lightning-fast Digitally eNhanced Accuracy (DNA) engine. TBR matches incline, range to target, and ballistics information.
MSRP: . . . . . . $399.99 (Black/gray); $419.99 (Mossy Oak Break-Up)

Leica Sport Optics (leica-sportoptics.com)

Rangemaster CRF 1600-B

Power: 7x
Measurement Range: 10–1,600 yds
Accuracy: ± 2 yds @ 800 yds
Field of View: 347 ft @ 1000 yds
Exit Pupil: 3.4 mm
Eye Relief: 15 mm
Weight: 7.8 oz
Length: 4.5 in

Width: 2.2 in
Display: LED, red
Power Source: 1 x 3V/Lithium-type C2R
Battery Life: Approx. 3,000 measurements
Finish: Black
Features: Displays the temperature, angle, and atmospheric pressure, features 12 ballistics curves that will match most cartridge trajectories. Waterproof and fogproof.
MSRP: $799.99

358 • Shooter's Bible Guide to Tactical Firearms   www.skyhorsepublishing.com

Nikon (nikonsportoptics.com)

Monarch Gold Laser 1200
Power: 7x
Measurement Range: 11–1,200 yds
Exit Pupil: 3.6 mm
Eye Relief: 18.6 mm
Weight: 9.8 oz
Length: 5.7 in
Width: 3.2 in
Display: LCD
Power Source: 1 x 3V/Lithium-type CR2

Finish: Realtree Hardwoods Green
Features: Tru-Target ranging system provides flexible viewing with first target priority mode, distant target priority mode and scanning capability to find trophies in the field. Continuous ranging feature allows ranging of moving or multiple targets. Automatically powers down after 8 seconds to reduce battery use. Waterproof and fogproof except battery compartment.
MSRP: $479.95

Steiner (steiner-optics.com)

M30r LRF Military 8x30mm LRF
Magnification: 8x
Objective Lens: 30mm
Field of View: 319 ft @ 1000 yds
Height: 4.5 in
Width: 6.7 in

Weight: 26.5 oz
Features: The porro prism design combines a LRF (Laser Range Finder) feature with arranging capability from 27 to 1,860 yards. Built with a durable polycarbonate Makrolon housing it can withstand impacts up to 11 Gs. Waterproof, shockproof, and fogproof.
MSRP: $2,588.00

Laser Guide 8x30B

Power: 8x
Measurement Range: 15-1,600 yds
Accuracy: ± 1 yd
Field of View: 408 ft @ 1000 yds
Exit Pupil: 3.8 mm
Weight: 13.2 oz
Length: 4.7 in
Width: 3.9 in
Display: LCD
Power Source: 1 x 3V/Lithium-type CR2
Battery Life: Approx. 1,000 measurements

Finish: green
Features: Monocular laser range-finder has SWAROBRIGHT coating for enhanced light transmission and ultra-crisp images. The eye-safe class-1 laser delivers ±1-yard accuracy on reflective objects up to 1,500 yards away, even in poor weather and light conditions. LCD display has an aiming circle reticle for rapid target acquisition and displays ranges in yards or meters. Scan mode feature displays constant target readings while panning. Waterproof and fogproof.
MSRP: $999.99

EL Range 8x42 W B

Magnification: 8x
Objective Lens: 42mm
Field of View: 411 ft @ 1000 yds
Height: 6.5 in
Width: 4.6 in
Weight: 32.1 oz

Features: Roof prism design with integrated LRF (Laser Range Finder) with a range of 33 to 1,500 yards. Uses the EL wrap-around grip for extended viewing and high-precision fluoride-containing HD lenses and prisms results in razor-sharp, high-contrast images with maximum color fidelity. Waterproof, shockproof, and fogproof.
MSRP: $3,477.00; $3,532.00 (10x42mm)

Vortex (vortexoptics.com)

Ranger 1000

Power: 6x
Measurement Range: 11–1,000 yds
Accuracy: ± 3 yds @ 1000 yds
Field of View: 315 ft @ 1000 yds
Eye Relief: 17 mm
Weight: 7.7 oz
Length: 3.9 in
Width: 3 in
Display: LED, red
Power Source: 1 x 3V/Lithium-type C2R

Battery Life: Approx. 2,000 measurements
Finish: Black/green
Features: Ranging distance depends on reflectivity of target, i.e., tree 1000 yards, deer 500 yards. HCD (Horizontal Component Distance) mode displays an angle-compensated distance reading. Line of Sight (LOS) mode displays actual line of sight range. Scan mode displays continual distance readings when panning across a landscape or tracking a moving animal. Waterproof.
MSRP: $499.00

Zeiss (sportsoptics.zeiss.com)

Victory 8x45 T* RF

Magnification: 8x
Objective Lens: 45mm
Field of View: 375 ft @ 1000 yds
Height: 6.6 in
Width: 5.3 in
Weight: 35 oz
Features: Roof prism design with LRF (Laser Range Finder) with range from 10 to 1,300 yards. The Ballistic Information System (BIS) gives all the information needed to correct the holdover point quickly and precisely. Rubber armor over the metal casing protects the internal optics and mechanics. Waterproof, shockproof, and fogproof.
MSRP: $2,999.99; $3,111.99 (10x45mm); $3,666.99 (10x56mm)

Victory 8x26 T* PRF

Power: 8x
Measurement Range: 10–1,300 yds
Field of View: 330 ft @ 1000 yds
Eye Relief: 17.5 mm
Weight: 10.9 oz
Length: 5.07 in
Width: 3.8 in

Display: LED, red
Power Source: 1 x 3V/Lithium-type CR2
Battery Life: Approx. 2,000 measurements
Finish: Black
Features: The Ballistic Information System (BIS) software uses the selected ballistics curve, the caliber and the distance measurement to find the appropriate correction value for the shot. Waterproof.
MSRP: $699.00

44. Ammunition

ASYM Precision Ammunition (store.chencustom.com)
Stan Chen Customs is a division of Legacy Custom Products, Inc. They are a custom gunsmithing shop specializing in 1911s. In 2010 ASYM Precision Ammunition was started to manufacture precision, match grade ammunition for tactical, defensive, and competition purposes. New brass and boxer primed. Made in USA.

Caliber	Bullet Weight (grains)	Bullet Type	Velocity (fps)	Muzzle Energy (ft. lbs.)	Cartridges Per Box
5.56mm	55	FMJ-BT	3050	1136	1000
.223 Rem.	68	OTM	2800	1184	50
.223 Rem.	75	OTM	2630	1152	50
.223 Rem.	77	OTM	2610	1165	50
.308 Win.	168	Sierra MatchKing	2660	2640	20
.308 Win.	175	Sierra MatchKing	2625	2678	200

ARMSCOR USA ammunition is made in the USA. The company is ISO 9001 Certified and complies with the SAAMI and CIP standards. Made with new brass and boxer primers.

Caliber	Bullet Weight (grains)	Bullet Type	Velocity (fps)	Muzzle Energy (ft. lbs.)	Cartridges Per Box
.223 Rem.	55	FMJ	3050	1136	20

Atomic Ammunition (atomicammunition.com)

Atomic produces the most affordable, minute of angle (MOA) accurate service rifle ammunition and bonded, match grade defensive hollow point handgun ammunition in the world. They are American owned, American staffed, and every component use to manufacture their cartridges is supplied by American companies. Cartridges are made with new brass and boxer primed.

Caliber	Bullet Weight (grains)	Bullet Type	Velocity (fps)	Muzzle Energy (ft. lbs.)	Cartridges Per Box
.308 Win.	140	Nosler HPBT Custom Competition	2500	1943	100
.308 Win.	168	Nosler HPBT Custom Competition	2600	2522	100

Australian Outback (outbackammo.com.au)

Australian Outback produces ammo for military and civilian use. Their proprietary BTI (Ballistic Temperature Independence) process ensures the ammo delivers consistent levels of performance no matter what the outside temperature from scorching heat to freezing cold. Constructed with new brass and boxer primers. Made in Australia.

Caliber	Bullet Weight (grains)	Bullet Type	Velocity (fps)	Muzzle Energy (ft. lbs.)	Cartridges Per Box
.223 Rem.	69	Sierra HPBT MatchKing	2959	1342	20
.308 Win.	168	Sierra HPBT MatchKing	2791	2906	20

Bear (dkgtrading.com)

Bear ammunition has been produced in Russia since 1869 and manufactures ammo for military and civilian use. It is one of the largest supplies of cartridges in Russia. It is loaded to military specifications. Silver Bear ammunition is new production ammo manufactured with Berdan primed non-reloadable, highly polished zinc coated steel cases that offer long shelf life and sure-fire ignition.

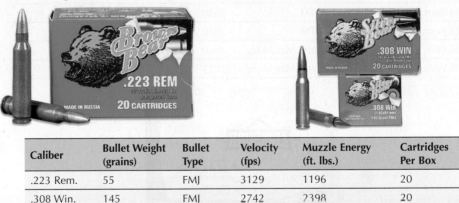

Caliber	Bullet Weight (grains)	Bullet Type	Velocity (fps)	Muzzle Energy (ft. lbs.)	Cartridges Per Box
.223 Rem.	55	FMJ	3129	1196	20
.308 Win.	145	FMJ	2742	2398	20

Brown Bear ammunition is new production ammo manufactured with non-reloadable, lacquered steel cases with Berdan primers.

Caliber	Bullet Weight In Grains	Bullet Type	Velocity In fps	Muzzle Energy in ft. lbs.	Cartridges Per Box
.223 Rem.	55	FMJ	3130	1197	20
.308 Win.	145	FMJ	2749	2434	20

Black Hills Ammunition (black-hills.com)

All branches of the US Military and Law enforcement agencies nationwide use Black Hills ammo, as well as firearms manufacturers during weapon development. It is new production, non-corrosive, in Boxer primed, reloadable brass cases.

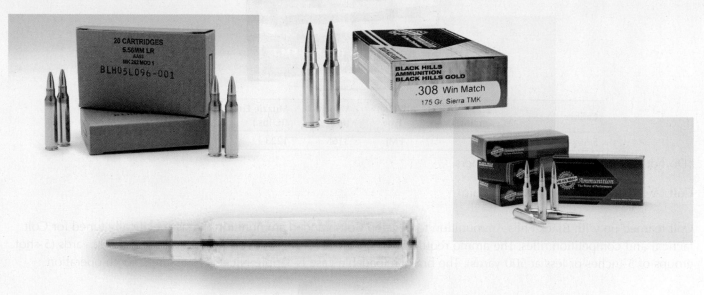

Caliber	Bullet Weight (grains)	Bullet Type	Velocity (fps)	Muzzle Energy (ft. lbs.)	Cartridges Per Box
.223 Rem.	52	Match HP	3250	1219	20
.223 Rem.	55	FMJ	3200	1250	20
.223 Rem.	68	Heavy Match HP	2850	1227	20
.223 Rem.	69	Sierra MatchKing	2850	1245	20
.223 Rem.	75	Heavy Match HP	2750	1259	20
.223 Rem.	77	Sierra MatchKing	2750	1293	20
.308 Win.	168	Match HP	2650	2620	20
.308 Win.	175	Match HP	2600	2627	20
.300 Win. Mag.	190	Match HP	2950	3672	20
.338 Lapua Mag.	250	Sierra MatchKing	2950	4831	20
.338 Lapua Mag.	300	Sierra MatchKing	2800	5223	20
.338 Norma Mag.	300	Sierra MatchKing	2725	4946	20

Black Hills Remanufactured ammunition reloads once-fired brass for rounds suitable for training.

Caliber	Bullet Weight (grains)	Bullet Type	Velocity (fps)	Muzzle Energy (ft. lbs.)	Cartridges Per Box
.223 Rem.	52	Match HP	3250		20
.223 Rem.	55	FMJ	3200		20
.223 Rem.	68	Heavy Match HP	2850		20
.223 Rem.	69	Sierra MatchKing	2850		20
.223 Rem.	75	Heavy Match HP	2750		20
.223 Rem.	77	Sierra MatchKing	2750		20

Century Arms International (centuryarms.com)

The HotShot M193 uses brass cases/boxer primed and are non-corrosive. It is made in Poland to NATO M193 specifications.

Caliber	Bullet Weight (grains)	Bullet Type	Velocity (fps)	Muzzle Energy (ft. lbs.)	Cartridges Per Box
5.56x45mm M193	55	FMJ	3166	1223	20

*Do not use in .223 Rem.-only chambers.

Colt (Available through midwayusa.com)

Colt teamed up with Black Hills Ammunition to develop Colt-branded ammunition that is specifically tuned for Colt tactical and competition rifles. The ammo requirement specified consistent five-shot MOA groups at 500 yards (5-shot groups of 5-inches or less at 500 yards). The brass, reloadable case is "Triple Nickel" to assure smooth operation.

Caliber	Bullet Weight (grains)	Bullet Type	Velocity (fps)	Muzzle Energy (ft. lbs.)	Cartridges Per Box
5.56x45mm	55	Sierra MatchKing HPBT	3200	1250	20
5.56x45mm	77	Sierra MatchKing HPBT	2750	1293	20

CorBon (corbon.com)

CorBon offers a variety of ammunition for specific scenarios. It is all new production, non-corrosive, loaded in Boxer-primed, reloadable brass cases. CorBon DPX is new manufacture ammunition that uses reloadable brass cases and boxer primers. DPX ammunition reliably penetrates hard barriers, while it only penetrates to what is considered safe depths of 14 to18 inches in ballistic gelatin. Penetrates hard barriers like auto glass and steel. Made in America. American owned.

Caliber	Bullet Weight (grains)	Bullet Type	Velocity (fps)	Muzzle Energy (ft. lbs.)	Cartridges Per Box
.223 Rem.	53	DPX	3000	1059	20
.223 Rem.	62	DPX	2750	1041	20
.308 Win.	130	TIP DPX	3000	2599	20
.308 Win.	168	TIP DPX	3125	3643	20
.300 Win. Mag.	180	TIP DPX	3000	3598	20
.338 Lapua Mag.	225	TIP DPX	3100	4802	20
.338 Lapua Mag.	265	TIP DPX	2800	4614	20

CorBon Performance Match Ammunition is new manufacture loaded with match-grade components for accuracy and reliability.

Caliber	Bullet Weight (grains)	Bullet Type	Velocity (fps)	Muzzle Energy (ft. lbs.)	Cartridges Per Box
.223 Rem.	55	Match FMJ	3000	1099	20
.223 Rem.	69	Match HPBT	3000	1379	20
.223 Rem.	77	Match HPBT	2800	1341	20
.308 Win.	155	Performance Match Scenar	2900	2895	20
.308 Win.	168	Match HPBT	2700	2720	20
.308 Win.	175	Match HPBT	2650	2730	20
.308 Win.	185	Performance Match FMJ-RBT Subsonic	1000	411	20
.308 Win.	190	Performance Match HPBT	2600	2853	20
.300 Win. Mag.	190	Performance Match HPBT	2900	3549	20
.338 Norma Mag.	300	Performance Match HPBT	2750	5038	20
.338 Lapua Mag.	250	Performance Match HPBT	3000	4997	20
.338 Lapua Mag.	300	Performance Match FMJ-RBT Subsonic	1000	666	20
.338 Lapua Mag.	300	Performance Match HPBT	2800	5224	20

DoubleTap (doubletapammo.com)

DoubleTap ammunition is new manufacture using reloadable brass, Boxer primed, and loaded with a variety of bullet types for defensive applications.

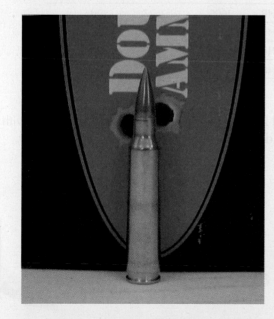

Caliber	Bullet Weight (grains)	Bullet Type	Velocity (fps)	Muzzle Energy (ft. lbs.)	Cartridges Per Box
.223 Rem.	55	FMJ-BT	3300	1330	50
.223 Rem.	62	FMJ-BT	3200	1410	50
.223 Rem.	69	Match HPBT	3000	1379	20
.223 Rem.	77	Match HPBT	2855	1394	20
.223 Rem.	80	Match HPBT	2825	1418	20

Federal Premium (federalpremium.com)

American Eagle ammo is new production that uses reloadable brass and Boxer primers. Good choice for training.

Caliber	Bullet Weight (grains)	Bullet Type	Velocity (fps)	Muzzle Energy (ft. lbs.)	Cartridges Per Box
.223 Rem. (5.56x45mm)	55	FMJ-BT	3240	1282	20
.223 Rem. (5.56x45mm)	62	FMJ-BT	3020	1255	20
.308 Win. (7.62x51mm) (5.56x45mm)	150	FMJ-BT	2820	2648	20
.308 Win. (7.62x51mm) (5.56x45mm)	168	OTM	2650	2619	20

Gold Medal cartridges use Sierra MatchKing bullets. It is new production that uses reloadable brass and Boxer primers. For reliability and consistency for competition this is a good choice.

Caliber	Bullet Weight (grains)	Bullet Type	Velocity (fps)	Muzzle Energy (ft. lbs.)	Cartridges Per Box
.223 Rem. (5.56x45mm)	69	Sierra MatchKing BTHP	2950	1333	20
.223 Rem. (5.56x45mm)	77	Sierra MatchKing BTHP	2720	1265	20
.308 Win. (7.62x51mm) (5.56x45mm)	168	Sierra MatchKing BTHP	2650	2619	20
.308 Win. (7.62x51mm) (5.56x45mm)	175	Sierra MatchKing BTHP	2600	2627	20
.300 Win. Mag.	190	Sierra MatchKing BTHP	2900	3548	20
.338 Lapua Mag.	250	Sierra MatchKing BTHP	2950	4830	20
.338 Lapua Mag.	300	Sierra MatchKing BTHP	2850	4434	20

Fiocchi (fiocchiusa.com)

The Exacta Rifle Match line of ammunition is designed for competition and long-range shooting. Cartridges are loaded with Sierra Hollow Point MatchKing bullets. It is a new manufacture with reloadable brass and Boxer primers. Made in Italy.

Caliber	Bullet Weight (grains)	Bullet Type	Velocity (fps)	Muzzle Energy (ft. lbs.)	Cartridges Per Box
.223 Rem.	69	Sierra MatchKing BTHP	2735	1145	20
.223 Rem.	77	Sierra MatchKing BTHP	2660	1209	20
.308 Win.	168	Sierra MatchKing BTHP	2650	2619	20
.308 Win.	175	Sierra MatchKing BTHP	2595	2616	20
.308 Win.	180	Sierra MatchKing BTHP	2595	2616	20
.300 Win. Mag.	190	Sierra MatchKing BTHP	2900	3548	20

The Shooting Dynamics line of ammunition is designed for training. It is a new manufacture with new, reloadable brass, Boxer primers, and a variety of bullet weights and velocities.

Caliber	Bullet Weight (grains)	Bullet Type	Velocity (fps)	Muzzle Energy (ft. lbs.)	Cartridges Per Box
.223 Rem.	55	FMJ-BT	3240	1281	20
.223 Rem.	62	FMJ-BT	3000	1238	20
.308 Win.	168	FMJ-BT	2890	2781	20

Fiocchi Canned Heat ammunition is packed in a sealed can with desiccant to protect the cartridges from moisture. Rounds use new, reloadable brass and Boxer primers.

Caliber	Bullet Weight (grains)	Bullet Type	Velocity (fps)	Muzzle Energy (ft. lbs.)	Cartridges Per Box
.223 Rem.	56	FMJ	3314	1355	50
.223 Rem.	62	FMJ	3117	1375	50
.308 Win.	150	FMJ	2641	2629	20

GECO (geco-munition.de/en)

GECO incorporates a wide range of products which includes pistol/revolver ammunition, air gun pellets, small caliber ammunition, shotshells, and rifle cartridges, and has recently introduced explosive cartridges and blank cartridges. Reloadable brass, Boxer primed. Made in Germany.

Caliber	Bullet Weight (grains)	Bullet Type	Velocity (fps)	Muzzle Energy (ft. lbs.)	Cartridges Per Box
.223 Rem.	55	FMJ-BT	3240	1281	50
.223 Rem.	62	FMJ-BT	3000	1238	50
.308 Win.	150	FMJ-BT	2890	2781	20

Hornady (hornady.com)

Hornady Steel Match ammo is new manufacture designed specifically for training and competition. Ammunition is loaded in polymer-coated steel cases. Made in USA.

Caliber	Bullet Weight (grains)	Bullet Type	Velocity (fps)	Muzzle Energy (ft. lbs.)	Cartridges Per Box
.223 Rem.	52	BTHP	3250	1220	20
.223 Rem.	55	HP	3240	1282	50
.223 Rem.	75	HPBT	3240	1282	50
.308 Win.	155	BTHP	2610	2344	50

Hornady Match Ammunition is loaded to strict standards for proper ignition and provide consistent, match-winning, pin-point accuracy shot-after-shot. This ammunition is new production, non-corrosive, in boxer primed, reloadable brass cases.

Caliber	Bullet Weight (grains)	Bullet Type	Velocity (fps)	Muzzle Energy (ft. lbs.)	Cartridges Per Box
.223 Rem.	75	BTHP	2790	1296	20
.308 Win.	155	OTM	2775	2650	20
.308 Win.	168	BTHP	2700	2719	20
.308 Win.	178	BTHP	2600	2627	20
.300 Win. Mag.	195	BTHP	2930	3717	20
.338 Lapua Mag.	250	BTHP	2900	4668	20
.338 Lapua Mag.	285	BTHP	2745	4768	20
.50 BMG	750	A-MAX	2820	1324	10

Hornady SUPERFORMANCE ammunition is loaded with proprietary propellants that increase the velocity ratings up to 200 feet per second compared to other ammunition brands. Because there is no increase in pressure, regardless of the caliber, there is no increase in felt recoil but there is an increase in efficiency and high speed performance. Ammo is loaded in new, reloadable, boxer primed brass.

Caliber	Bullet Weight (grains)	Bullet Type	Velocity (fps)	Muzzle Energy (ft. lbs.)	Cartridges Per Box
.223 Rem.	75	HPBT	2930	1429	20
5.56 NATO	75	BTHP	2910	1410	20
.308 Win.	178	BTHP	2775	3043	20

Each round of Hornady Custom ammunition is built to the tightest tolerances for peak performance. This ammunition is new production, non-corrosive, in boxer primed, reloadable brass cases.

Caliber	Bullet Weight (grains)	Bullet Type	Velocity (fps)	Muzzle Energy (ft. lbs.)	Cartridges Per Box
.223 Rem.	68	BTHP	2960	1323	20
.223 Rem.	55	FMJ-BT	3240	1282	50

Hornady Training ammo is new manufacture designed specifically for training and competition. Ammunition is loaded in reloadable brass cases. Made in USA.

Caliber	Bullet Weight (grains)	Bullet Type	Velocity (fps)	Muzzle Energy (ft. lbs.)	Cartridges Per Box
.223 Rem.	55	FMJ Brass	3240	1282	50

Lapua (lapua.com)

Lapua has been manufacturing ammunition since 1923. They have a reputation for producing high quality ammunition for use in competition, hunting, and military/LE applications. Ammo is brass case, boxer primed. Made in Finland.

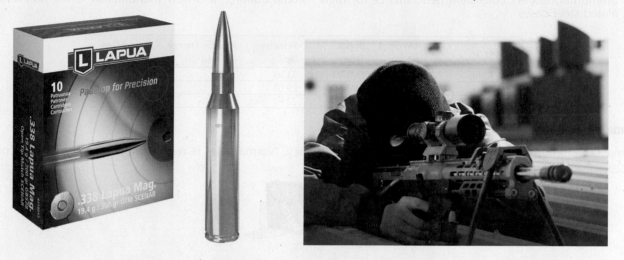

Caliber	Bullet Weight (grains)	Bullet Type	Velocity (fps)	Muzzle Energy (ft. lbs.)	Cartridges Per Box
.223 Rem.(5.56x45mm)	55	FMJ	3130	1196	20
.223 Rem.(5.56x45mm)	69	Scenar-L	2723	1143	50
.308 Win. (7.62x51mm)	123	FMJ	2935	2361	20
.308 Win. (7.62x51mm)	150	Lock Base	2790	2592	20
.308 Win. (7.62x51mm)	155	Scenar	2820	2621	20
.308 Win. (7.62x51mm)	165	Armor Piercing	2850	2975	20
.308 Win. (7.62x51mm)	167	Scenar	2756	2867	50
.308 Win. (7.62x51mm)	170	Lock Base	2756	2867	20
.308 Win. (7.62x51mm)	185	Scenar	2475	2518	50
.308 Win. (7.62x51mm)	185	FMJ-BT	2490	2549	20
.308 Win. (7.62x51mm) Subsonic	200	FMJ-BT	1066	506	20
.308 Win. (7.62x51mm)	175	Scenar-L	2602	2630	50
.308 Win. (7.62x51mm)	170	Lock Base	2756	2867	20
.338 Lapua Mag.	250	Scenar	2970	4896	10
.338 Lapua Mag.	250	Lock Base	2953	4840	10
.338 Lapua Mag.	248	Armor Piercing	2970	4866	
.338 Lapua Mag.	253	Armor Piercing Incendiary	2935	4840	20
.338 Lapua Mag.	300	Scenar	2723	4938	10
.338 Lapua Mag.	300	Armor Piercing	2723	4938	20

Magtech (magtechammunition.com)

Magtech ammunition is new manufacture using reloadable brass and boxer primers. Made in Brazil.

Caliber	Bullet Weight (grains)	Bullet Type	Velocity (fps)	Muzzle Energy (ft. lbs.)	Cartridges Per Box
.223 Rem.	55	FMJ-BT	3241	1281	20
.308 Win.	150	FMJ-BT	2820	2649	20
.50 BMG M33	624	FMJ			10

MFS (ruag-usa.com/brands/mfs)

MFS ammunition offers consistent performance for high volume training. It is new manufacture using non-reloadable zinc plated steel cases.

Caliber	Bullet Weight (grains)	Bullet Type	Velocity (fps)	Muzzle Energy (ft. lbs.)	Cartridges Per Box
.223 Rem.	55	FMJ-BT	3130	1196	20
.223 Rem.	62	FMJ-BT	2910	1166	20
.308 Win.	145	FMJ	2750	2434	20

Norma (norma-usa.com)

Norma Tac ammunition is designed for competition accuracy. Norma brass is renowned for its quality and longevity allowing for multiple reloads. Made in Sweden.

Caliber	Bullet Weight (grains)	Bullet Type	Velocity (fps)	Muzzle Energy (ft. lbs.)	Cartridges Per Box
.223 Rem.	55	FMJ	3250	1290	20
.223 Rem.	77	HPBT	2790	1331	20
.308 Win.	150	FMJ	2660	2357	20
.308 Win.	168	Sierra MatchKing	2720	2761	20
.338 Lapua Mag.	300	Sierra HPBT	2660	4715	20

Nosler (nosler.com)

Founded in 1948, Nosler was a family-owned company when it started in 1948. It is known for big game hunting bullets like the Partition and Ballistic Tip. They manufacture bullets, brass, ammunition, and semi-custom rifles. Made in USA. Nosler Match Grade Ammunition consists of Nosler's precisely-designed Custom Competition bullet along with Nosler brass.

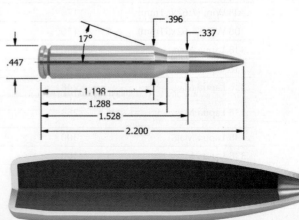

Caliber	Bullet Weight (grains)	Bullet Type	Velocity (fps)	Muzzle Energy (ft. lbs.)	Cartridges Per Box
.223 Rem.	52	HPBT	3250	1219	20
.223 Rem.	69	HPBT	2700	1116	20
.223 Rem.	77	HPBT	2550	1111	20
.308 Win.	155	HPBT	2850	2795	20
.308 Win.	168	HPBT	2750	2820	20
.308 Win.	175	HPBT	2500	2428	20
.338 Lapua Mag.	300	HPBT	2650	4677	20

PMC (pmcammo.com)

All PMC Ammunition is loaded in new brass cases with boxer primers. PMC ammunition is non-corrosive. Made in South Korea. PMC's X-TAC line uses Sierra bullets in the .223 Remington and .308 Winchester cartridges. It comes in reloadable brass cases and suitable for competition.

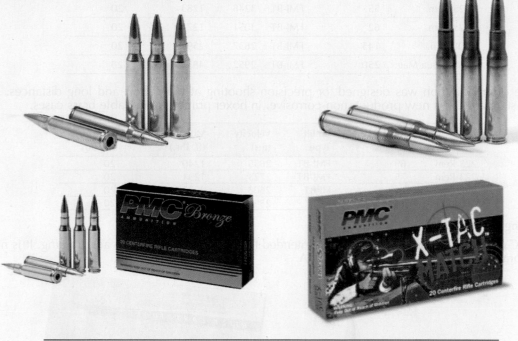

Caliber	Bullet Weight (grains)	Bullet Type	Velocity (fps)	Muzzle Energy (ft. lbs.)	Cartridges Per Box
.223 Rem.	77	OTM	2790	2561	20
.308 Win.	168	OTM	2700	2503	20
.50 BMG	740	Solid Brass	2830	2728	20

PMC Bronze line is new production manufactured with a variety of bullet types. It uses reloadable brass cases and is suitable for practice and training.

Caliber	Bullet Weight (grains)	Bullet Type	Velocity (fps)	Muzzle Energy (ft. lbs.)	Cartridges Per Box
.223 Rem.	55	FMJ-BT	3200	2833	20
.308 Win. (7.62 NATO)	147	FMJ-BT	2780	2575	20
.50 BMG	660	FMJ-BT	3080	2854	10

Prvi Partizan (prvipartizan.com)

Prvi Partizan (PPU) has been producing ammunition for eighty years, since it was founded in 1928. PPU has supplied Serbian Army and Police and many foreign armies and also produces hunting and sporting ammunition. Made in Serbia.

Caliber	Bullet Weight (grains)	Bullet Type	Velocity (fps)	Muzzle Energy (ft. lbs.)	Cartridges Per Box
.223 Rem.	55	FMJ-BT	3248	1283	20
.223 Rem.	62	FMJ-BT	3051	1275	20
.308 Win.	145	FMJ-BT	2837	2596	20
.338 Lapua Mag.	250	FMJ-BT	2952	4838	20

PPU's Match line of ammunition was designed for precision shooting at both short and long distances. Ammunition meets all SAAMI standards. It is new product, non-corrosive, in boxer primed, reloadable brass cases.

Caliber	Bullet Weight (grains)	Bullet Type	Velocity (fps)	Muzzle Energy (ft. lbs.)	Cartridges Per Box
.223 Rem.	69	FMJ-BT	2855	1249	20
.223 Rem.	75	FMJ-BT	2723	1231	20
.308 Win.	168	HPBT	2608	2537	20
.308 Win.	175	FMJ	2591	2610	20

Remington (remington.com)

Remington's UMC is new manufacture ammunition intended for high volume practice and training. It is manufactured with reloadable brass and boxer primed. Made in USA.

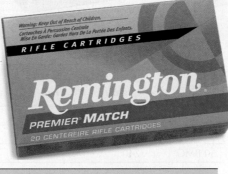

Caliber	Bullet Weight (grains)	Bullet Type	Velocity (fps)	Muzzle Energy (ft. lbs.)	Cartridges Per Box
.223 Rem.	55	FMJ	3240	1282	20
.223 Rem.	62	Closed Tip Flat Base	3100	1323	20
.308 Win.	150	FMJ	2820	2648	20
.308 Win.	175	FMJ	2591	2610	20

Remington's Premier Match ammo is new manufacture ammunition and employs special loading practices to ensure world-class performance and accuracy with every shot. It is manufactured with reloadable brass and boxer primed. Made in USA.

Caliber	Bullet Weight (grains)	Bullet Type	Velocity (fps)	Muzzle Energy (ft. lbs.)	Cartridges Per Box
.223 Rem.	62	JHP	3025	1260	20
.223 Rem.	69	Sierra MatchKing BTHP	3000	1379	20
.223 Rem.	77	Sierra MatchKing BTHP	2788	1329	20
.308 Win.	168	Sierra MatchKing BTHP	2608	2537	20
.308 Win.	175	Sierra MatchKing BTHP	2609	2644	20

Right To Bear Ammo (right2bearammo.com)

Right To Bear Ammo ammunition is manufactured for training.

Caliber	Bullet Weight (grains)	Bullet Type	Velocity (fps)	Muzzle Energy (ft. lbs.)	Cartridges Per Box
.223 Rem.	75	BTHP	2790	1296	20
.308 Win.	150	BTHP	2700	2427	200

RWS (ruag-usa.com)

RUAG Ammotec's heritage is in competition. They produce rimfire, centerfire and pellets. The ammo is new manufacture with reloadable brass and boxer primed. Made in Germany.

RWS Target Elite cartridges are precision match and designed for target shooting.

Caliber	Bullet Weight (grains)	Bullet Type	Velocity (fps)	Muzzle Energy (ft. lbs.)	Cartridges Per Box
.308 Win.	154	BTHP	2986	3054	20
.308 Win.	168	BTHP	2625	2573	20
.308 Win.	190	BTHP	2461	2551	20
.308 Win.	154	BTHP	2986	3054	20

RWS Target Elite Plus cartridges are designed for target shooting and use a double step loading process to ensure the highest quality and consistency.

Caliber	Bullet Weight (grains)	Bullet Type	Velocity (fps)	Muzzle Energy (ft. lbs.)	Cartridges Per Box
.308 Win.	168	BTHP	2641	2603	20

Sellier & Bellot (sellierbellot.us)

Sellier & Bellot Training ammunition is designed for high volume training. Cartridges are new brass and boxer primed. Made in Czech Republic.

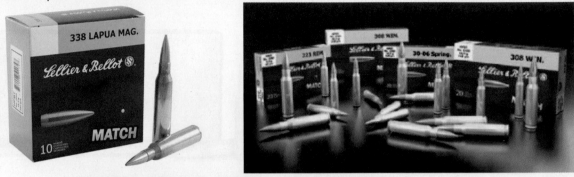

Caliber	Bullet Weight (grains)	Bullet Type	Velocity (fps)	Muzzle Energy (ft. lbs.)	Cartridges Per Box
.223 Rem.	55	FMJ	3300	1344	20
.308 Win.	147	FMJ	2812	2581	20
.308 Win.	180	FMJ	2411	2331	20

Sellier & Bellot Match ammo is made for competition shooting. Cartridges are new brass and boxer primed.

Caliber	Bullet Weight (grains)	Bullet Type	Velocity (fps)	Muzzle Energy (ft. lbs.)	Cartridges Per Box
.223 Rem.	52	Sierra BTHP	3412	1340	20
.223 Rem.	69	Sierra BTHP	3018	1404	20
.308 Win.	168	Sierra BTHP	2628	2579	20
.308 Win.	180	Sierra BTHP	2507	2519	20
.300 Win. Mag.	168	Sierra BTHP	3018	3402	20
.338 LapuaMag.	250	Sierra BTHP	2878	4599	10

SSA (ssarmory.com)

Silver State Armory (SSA) is a manufacturer of custom brass cases and ammunition. Made in USA.

Caliber	Bullet Weight (grains)	Bullet Type	Velocity (fps)	Muzzle Energy (ft. lbs.)	Cartridges Per Box
.223 Rem.	55	FMJ	2975	1081	20
.223 Rem. M855	62	FMJ	3000	1265	20
.223 Rem.	69	SSA HPBT	2830	1243	20
.223 Rem.	77	SSA HPBT	2650	1239	20
.223 Rem.	77	Sierra HPBT	2650	1239	20
5.56mm	55	FMJ	2975	1081	20
5.56mm	62	FMJ	3025	1236	20
5.56mm	77	Sierra HPBT	2650	1239	20
5.56mm	77	SSA HPBT	2650	1239	20
.308 Win. M80 Ball	147	FMJ	2840	2656	20
.308 Win.	168	Sierra HPBT	2600	2600	20
.308 Win.	175	Sierra HPBT	2620	2630	20
.308 Win.	168	SSA HPBT	2600	2600	20
.308 Win.	175	SSA HPBT	2620	2630	20
.308 Win.	150	Sierra MatchKing HPBT	2620	2630	20
7.62x51mm	168	Sierra HPBT	2600	2600	20
7.62x51mm	168	SSA HPBT	2600	2600	20
7.62x51mm	175	Sierra HPBT	2620	2630	20
7.62x51mm	175	SSA HPBT	2620	2630	20

Swiss P (ruag-usa.com/brands/swiss-p)

The Swiss P family of rifle cartridges was developed specifically for sniper use. Made in Switzerland. Swiss P Target is designed for match use, training, or combat.

Caliber	Bullet Weight (grains)	Bullet Type	Velocity (fps)	Muzzle Energy (ft. lbs.)	Cartridges Per Box
.223 Rem.	69	FMJHC	2920	1306	50
.308 Win.	168	HPBT	2641	2603	20
.300 Win. Mag.	200	HP	2854	3617	10
.338 Lapua Mag.	250	HPBT	2838	4470	20
.338 LapuaMag.	300	HPBT	2690	4821	20

Swiss P Ball uses FMJ bullets. Swiss P STYX is designed for fatal shots against soft targets.

Caliber	Bullet Weight (grains)	Bullet Type	Velocity (fps)	Muzzle Energy (ft. lbs.)	Cartridges Per Box
.223 Rem.	64	FMJ	2969	1247	20
.308 Win.	176	FMJ	2592	1887	20
.300 Win. Mag.	198	Styx	2887	3670	20
.338 Lapua Mag.	252	FMJ	2805	4394	20

Swiss P STYX is designed for fatal shots against soft targets. Swiss P Tactical is for precision shots against target behind glass. Made in Switzerland.

Caliber	Bullet Weight (grains)	Bullet Type	Velocity (fps)	Muzzle Energy (ft. lbs.)	Cartridges Per Box
.223 Rem.	69	HPBT	2920	1306	20
.308 Win.	167	HPBT	2657	2618	20
.338 Lapua Mag.	247	Styx	2854	4467	20

Swiss P Tactical is for precision shots against target behind glass. Made in Switzerland.

Caliber	Bullet Weight (grains)	Bullet Type	Velocity (fps)	Muzzle Energy (ft. lbs.)	Cartridges Per Box
.223 Rem.	55	FMJ	3300	1344	20
.308 Win.	164	FNBT	2690	2628	20
.300 Win. Mag.	187	Solid FNBT	2887	3456	20
.338 LapuaMag.	250	FNBT	2822	4420	20

Tulammo (tulammousa.com)

Tula Cartridge Works was founded in 1880 and is the leading producer of small arms ammunition in Russia. This is new manufacture with polymer coated steel case that is non-reloadable, non corrosive, boxer primed. Good for high volume training.

Caliber	Bullet Weight (grains)	Bullet Type	Velocity (fps)	Muzzle Energy (ft. lbs.)	Cartridges Per Box
.223 Rem.	55	FMJ*	3241	1223	20
.223 Rem.	62	FMJ*	3025	1275	20
.308 Win.	150	FMJ*	2800	2522	20

*Bimetal jacket

Ultramax (ultramaxammunition.com)

Ultramax uses previously fired brass cases. This is remanufactured ammunition that goes through a 10-Step quality assurance process and is suitable for high volume training and practice.

Caliber	Bullet Weight (grains)	Bullet Type	Velocity (fps)	Muzzle Energy (ft. lbs.)	Cartridges Per Box
.223 Rem.	55	FMJ	3000	1099	50
.223 Rem.	62	FMJ	2925	1178	50
.223 Rem.	68	Match HP	2900	1270	50
.308 Win.	168	Match HP	2680	2679	20

Winchester (winchester.com)

Olin Corporation owns the Winchester Ammunition brand. Olin has been in the powder and munitions business since 1892. The ammo is new brass and boxer primed. Made in USA.

Match ammunition offers accuracy and consistency for competitive shooting.

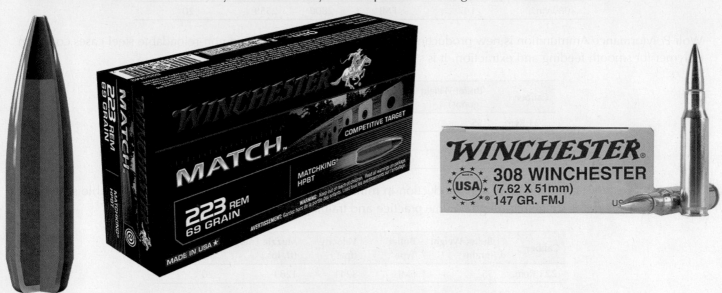

Caliber	Bullet Weight (grains)	Bullet Type	Velocity (fps)	Muzzle Energy (ft. lbs.)	Cartridges Per Box
.223 Rem.	69	Match	3060	1282	20
.308 Win.	168	Match	2680	2559	20
.338 Lapua Mag.	250	Sierra MatchKing BTHP	2900	4668	20

Winchester USA ammo is made with FMJ bullets and designed for training. It is new production loaded in reloadable brass.

Caliber	Bullet Weight (grains)	Bullet Type	Velocity (fps)	Muzzle Energy (ft. lbs.)	Cartridges Per Box
.223 Rem.	55	FMJ	3600	1282	20
.223 Rem.	62	FMJ	3100	1323	20
.308 Win.	147	FMJ	2800	2559	20

Wolf Performance Ammunition (wolfammo.com)

Wolf Ammo produces a number of brands of ammo designed for high volume shooting and training. Made in Russia.

Wolf Gold Ammunition is new production in reloadable brass cases. Good for high volume training.

Caliber	Bullet Weight (grains)	Bullet Type	Velocity (fps)	Muzzle Energy (ft. lbs.)	Cartridges Per Box
.223 Rem. (M193)	55	FMJ	3250	1290	20
.223 Rem.	75	Match HP	2750	1260	20
.308 Win.	147	FMJ	2800	2559	20

Wolf Polyformance Ammunition is new production using Full Metal Jacket (FMJ) in non-reloadable steel cases coated in polymer for smooth feeding and extraction. It is suitable for practice and training.

Caliber	Bullet Weight (grains)	Bullet Type	Velocity (fps)	Muzzle Energy (ft. lbs.)	Cartridges Per Box
.223 Rem.	55	FMJ	3241	1283	20
.223 Rem.	62	FMJ	2750	1041	20
.308 Win.	150	FMJ	2800	2559	20

Wolf Military Classic ammunition is new production in military calibers manufactured with non-reloadable steel cases coated in polymer. It is suitable for high volume practice and training.

Caliber	Bullet Weight (grains)	Bullet Type	Velocity (fps)	Muzzle Energy (ft. lbs.)	Cartridges Per Box
.223 Rem.	55	FMJ	3241	1283	20

45. Tactical Shooting Gear

BALLISTIC CALCULATORS —ANALOG

Accuracy First (accuracy1stdg.com)

Civilian—Whiz Wheel

Features: Custom made to order using operator's ammunition, rifle barrel twist rate, scope's height above the centerline of the bore, mean velocity as measured from a chronograph, and distance of the muzzle to the chronograph. Operates in MOA or MILS; yards or meters.

MSRP: $34.95

Ballisticard Systems (ballisticards.com)

A2 & D2 Tactical Ballisticards

Features: Custom designed around user's caliber choice, cards provide horizontal trajectory to 500 yards (Military models to 1,000 yards), uphill/downhill trajectories for various angles, scope clicks (come-ups) for changing zero if desired, wind deflection at 5 and 10 mph (adaptable to other speeds), and moving target leads. "Alpha 2" (A2) 500 yard format designed for use from 25 yards to 500 yards, in 25 yard increments, with a 100 yard zero. "Delta 2" (D2) 1,000 yard format designed for use from 50 to 1,000 yards, in 50 yard increments, with a 100 yard zero.

MSRP: $17.95

Delta Max

Features: Custom designed around user's caliber choice. Data for multiple temperatures adaptable from 0°–120°F, calculated for 2,000 feet, adaptable to altitude changes from 0–10,000 feet; range is from 50–1000 yards, in 50 yard increments, with 100 yard zero; data is in Inches, Mils and MOA for both Elevation and 10 mph Wind; moving Target Leads to 600 yards (four speeds—leads in Inches and Mils); and up/Down angle cosines and simple instructions for application.

MSRP: $22.95

Mildot Master (mildot.com)

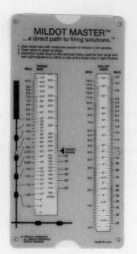

Mildot Master

Features: Designed along the same principle as a slide rule, utilizing logarithmic and inverse logarithmic scales developed specifically for performing the following operations: Rapid and simple calculation of range to target, rapid and simple calculation of the amount of sight correction necessary to compensate for bullet drop and/or wind drift for a given range, angle of fire for uphill or downhill shots.

MSRP: $7.99

Slope Doper (slopedoper.com)

Slope Doper

Features: Determine the slope to your target, read off a range conversion factor, and successfully hit that target.

MSRP: $25.95

U.S. Tactical Supply (ustacticalsupply.com)

One Shot Package

Features: Design around user's caliber choice. Includes: Modular data book and 6-ring binder, data book cover, Mildot Master, Slope Doper, MILSPEC-XR FDAC Field Density Altitude Compensator, tactical all-weather pen, and custom USTS Sniper Template.

MSRP: . . . . $147.77–$232.09 (depending on caliber)

BALLISTIC CALCULATORS—DIGITAL

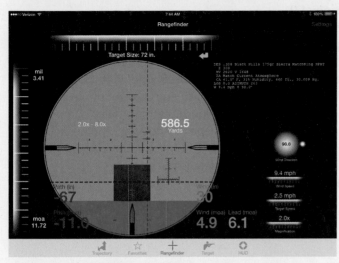

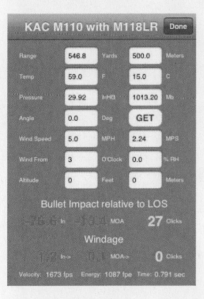

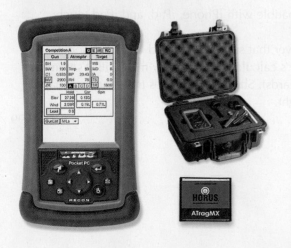

Ballistic: Standard Edition

Version: 5.0.5
Size: 9.7 MB
Requirements: iOS 4.3 or later; compatible with iPhone, iPad, and iPod touch; optimized for iPhone 5
Features: Compensate for atmospheric conditions, Coriolis effect, gyroscopic spin drift, and more. It's also much more than an advanced trajectory calculator. With a vast library of nearly 4,000 projectiles and factory loads, rangefinder, and range log.
MSRP: $12.99

BulletFlight

Version: 4.0.0
Size: 0.9 MB
Requirements: Compatible with iPhone, iPod touch, and iPad; requires iOS 4.2 or later.
Features: Level M, Military-grade version. Dynamically gives user the solution needed to make that shot. Current weather conditions including temperature, pressure, humidity, wind speed, and wind direction can be input, as well as angles to the target as measured by the built-in accelerometer. The app then provides highly detailed solutions out to 3000 meters.
MSRP: $29.99

Horus PDA with ATragMX

Dimensions: 6.5 in x 3.7 in
Weight: 17 oz
Power Source: 2 AA
Features: ATragMX ballistics software loaded onto a rugged PDA. Provides accurate aiming data out to 2,500 yards. Features USB ports, memory card slots.
MSRP: $2,000.00

iSnipe

Round

Load Projectile »

Ammo Name	Lapua Scenar HPBT	
Caliber	0.338	in.
Bullet Weight	250	grain
Ballistic Coef.	0.669	G1
Muzzle Velocity	2970	ft/sec

Save... Load »

Firearm

Firearm Desc.	AR-30A1	
Zero Distance	300	yards
Sight Height	1.5	in.

Compute More Compute

iSnipe
Version: 4.0
Size: 9.7 MB
Requirements: iOS 4.3 or later; compatible with iPhone, iPad, and iPod touch; optimized for iPhone 5
Features: Landscape support for iPhone/iPod, "Zero Conditions" feature that allows entry/saving of weather conditions while zeroing your firearm for later computation, "Optimize Point Blank Range" calculator. Updates include: solving Engine to be more accurate and precise, graphing engine, Unit Selections, details screen.
MSRP: $14.99

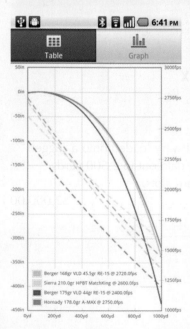

Shooter
Version: 1.2.6
Size: 3.6 MB
Requirements: iOS 4.3 or later; compatible with iPhone, iPad, and iPod touch; optimized for iPhone 5, Android.
Features: Uses a custom ballistics solver that supports G1 and G7 drag models. It is very fast and highly accurate. Shooter's calculations normally match JBM's numbers within round-off error (0.1" at 1000 yards). Shooter calculates trajectory, windage, lead, velocity, energy, and time of flight.
MSRP: $9.99

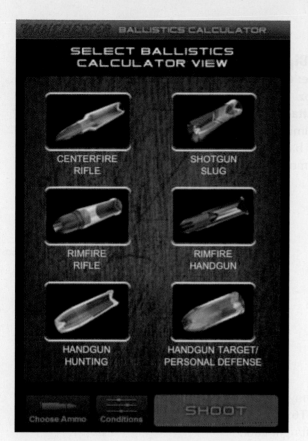

Winchester Ballistics Calculator

Version: 2
Size: 4.8 MB
Requirements: iOS 3.1 or later; compatible with iPhone, iPad, and iPod touch
Features: Compare up to three Winchester Ammunition products, view product information and product images, adjust wind speed and direction, adjust outside air temperature, adjust sight height, adjust sight-in range, adjust max range, view flight time, drop, wind drift and velocity, interact with charts and graphs of the bullet point of impact and trajectory.
MSRP: . . . . Free

BIPODS

Accu-Shot (accu-shot.com)

BT10-Atlas Bipod

Height Range: 4.75–9 in
Weight: 11 oz
Method of Attachment: Picatinny rail
Features: Leg positions: stowed back or forward, 90° straight down, 45° forward; ±15° of preloaded pan and cant.
MSRP: . . . $219.95; $219.95 (BT10-NC, no clamp); $279.95 (BT10-LW17, ADM 170-S lever)

Ashbury Precision Ordnance (ashburyprecisionordnance.com)

Anypoint Bipod-Tripod
Height Range: 6–9 in
Weight: 14 oz
Method of Attachment: sling swivel stud
Features: Aluminum alloy with steel parts, hard rubber leg caps, hinged base has tension adjustment and buffer springs to eliminate tremor or looseness. Anodized black/tan finish.
MSRP: $687.50

Allied Precision (alliedprecisionarms.com)

DMS
Height Range: 9–12 in
Weight: 11 oz
Method of Attachment: Picatinny rail
Features: Made of billet 6061-T6 alloy, Type III Mil-Spec anodized black finish, 5-position locking legs, 20° left/right cant.
MSRP: $159.00

AR-50
Height Range: 17 in
Method of Attachment: direct
Features: Made of steel, black oxide finish, adjustable lockable cant, ski feet.
MSRP: $269.00

BlackHawk (blackhawk.com)

Sportster Pivot
Height Range: 6–9 in
Method of Attachment: Sling stud
Features: Pivot eliminates rifle canting on uneven terrain, rapid-adjust pivot lever, no-rust anodized legs with increased spring tension, spring-return telescoping legs.
MSRP: . . . . . . $69.00; $69.00 (9-13 in); $69.99 (13.5-23 in); $84.99 (14.5-29.2 in)

Sportster

Height Range: 6–9 in
Method of Attachment: Sling stud
Features: No-rust anodized legs with increased spring tension, spring-return telescoping legs.
MSRP: . . . . $48.99; $48.99 (9-13 in); $51.99 (13.5-23 in); $59.99 (14.5-29.2 in)

Sportster Traversetrack

Height Range: 6–9 in
Method of Attachment: Sling stud
Features: All-metal construction, horizontal traverse for smooth target acquisition and tracking, pivot action for level shooting on uneven terrain, rapid-adjust lever lock, spring-return telescoping legs.
MSRP: . . . . $74.99; $74.99 (9-13 in, 13.5-23 in); $84.99 (14.5-29.2 in)

Caldwell (battenfeldtechnologies.com)

AR Bipods

Height Range: prone
Method of Attachment: Picatinny rail
Features: Built-in systems for both pivot and cant movement gives maximum range of alignment without having to reposition the bipod. Internal spring system is low profile and quiet. Leg adjustment mechanism is fast and secure, no-wobble height positioning and rubber feet ensure good grip on all surfaces. Anodized aluminum construction. Available in Matte Black or Desert Tan finish.
MSRP: . . . . $59.00 (prone); $92.00 (sitting)

XLA Bipods

Height Range: 6–9 in
Weight: 9 oz
Method of Attachment: Sling stud
Features: Lightweight aluminum with legs that spring out to the shooting position with the touch of a button.Black or camo finish.
MSRP: $54.99; $59.99 (9-13 in); $64.99 (13-23 in); $79.99 (13.5-27 in); $64.99–92.99 (pivot model)

Clutch Bipods

Height Range: prone or sitting
Method of Attachment: Sling stud
Features: Aluminum design, built-in swivel pan feature left or right 20° combined with an 18° bi-directional cant. Black finish.
MSRP: . . . . $69.99 (prone); $84.99 (sitting)

GG&G (gggaz.com)

Accu-Force QD System
Provides Quick On-Off
Capability

Bipod Head Pans
20 Degrees Left And
Right Of Center And
Cants 25 Degrees Left
And Right Of Center

Bipod Legs Will Lock
45 Degrees Forward To
Accommodate The Terrain

Replacement Bipod
Feet Are Available
For Purchase

XDS-2 Quick Detach

Height Range: 8–10.2 in
Weight: 15.4 oz
Method of Attachment: Picatinny rail
Features: Quick detach head that cants 25°, pans 20° (swivels left to right 20°), a leg locking system that allows the bipod legs to lock forward at a 45° angle for difficult terrain, and rubber feet that grip more surfaces and are replaceable.
MSRP: . . . .$219.00; $199.00 (non-quick detach)

25 Degrees Of Cant In Either
Direction Of Center

Legs Extend From
7" To 9.5"

Standard XDS

Height Range: 7–9.5 in
Weight: 11.5 oz
Method of Attachment: Picatinny rail
Features: Affords 25° of cant in either direction of center. Manufactured from aircraft grade 6061 T6 aluminum alloy.
MSRP: . . . . $179.00; $199.95 (quick detach)

Accu-Force QD System Provides Quick On-Off Capability

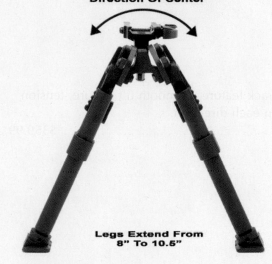

Pivot System Provides 25 Degrees Of Cant In Either Direction Of Center

Legs Extend From 8" To 10.5"

Heavy Duty XDS

Height Range: 8–10.5 in
Weight: 17 oz
Method of Attachment: Picatinny rail
Features: Affords 25 degrees of cant in either direction of center. Manufactured from aircraft grade 6061 T6 aluminum alloy. Designed for the M14, AR-10, and other large caliber rifles.
MSRP: . . . .$209.00; $229.95 (quick detach)

Harris Bipods (harrisbipods.com)

S-BRM

Height Range: 6–9 in
Weight: 13 oz
Method of Attachment: Sling stud
Features: Lightweight aluminum with legs that spring out to the shooting position. Anodized black finish. Leg notch model with legs that are spring loaded and when the release button is depressed, they kick out to maximum height.
MSRP: . . . $106.99; $89.99–129.99 (9–13 in, 13.5–23, depending on lock model type); $110.77–151.09 (12–25 in, 13.5–27 in, depending on lock model type)

S-BR

Height Range: 6–9 in
Weight: 14 oz
Method of Attachment: Sling stud
Features: Friction lock model feature a friction lock or set screw to adjust height; set screw has a large knurled knob for easy operation, loosen the friction lock to extend leg and tighten to lock in place.
MSRP: $106.99

S-L
Height Range: 9-13 in
Weight: 19 oz
Method of Attachment: Sling stud
Features: Swivel model with hinged base has tension adjustment and buffer springs to eliminate tremor or looseness. Available in Friction Lock or Leg Notch models.
MSRP: $106.99

Sierra 7 Bipods (sierra7bipods.com)

S7
Method of Attachment: Picatinny rail
Features: Rugged, reliable, have a smooth pan and track feature, a smooth tilt feature, tension adjustment until lock for both; 90° of panning, 45° in each direction.
MSRP: $359.99

Smith Enterprises (smithenterprise.com)

Lightweight QD
Height Range: 7-9 in
Weight: 16 oz
Method of Attachment: Picatinny rail
Features: 4140 chrome-moly steel and 304 stainless steel construction; spring-loaded legs are precision cut for detents with positive locking notches; ski feet.
MSRP: $265.00

CHEEK RESTS

BlackHawk (blackhawk.com)

Ammo Cheek Pad

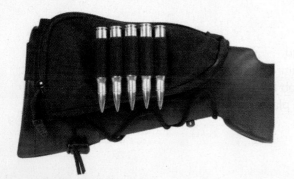

Features: Made of non-slip HawkTex fabric, 5 cartridge loops, zippered utility pouch, attaches to buttstock via a tie-down system.
MSRP: $34.99

HawkTex Tactical Cheek Pad (Adjustable)
Features: Constructed of non-slip HawkTex for positive cheek weld, height-adjustable inserts, three adjustable straps, end retaining strap to prevent forward slip.
MSRP: $29.99

Rifle Cheek Pad
Features: 1000 denier nylon and closed-cell foam aids eye relief efficiency, prevents slipping, and reduces recoil. Attaches to buttstock by a tie-down system, ensuring proper fit to all rifle stocks.
MSRP: $19.99

Urban Warfare Cheekpad
Features: 1000 denier nylon and closed-cell foam construction, 5 cartridge loops, zippered utility pouch, attaches to buttstock by a tie-down system, ensuring proper fit to all rifle stocks.
MSRP: $44.99

Bradley Cheek Rest (bradleycheekrest.com)

B 24
Features: Fits most bolt-action rifles. Ambidextrous with ¾ in to 7/8 in rise. Made of Kydexcarbon fiber that is durable and non-flexible.
MSRP: $94.99

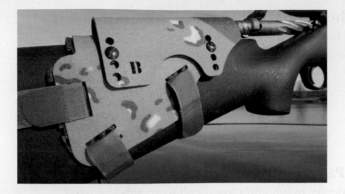

Bradley Adjustable Cheek Rest

Features: Cheek Rest can be used as a one piece 3/8 inch rise cheek rest, or, can be adjusted up to 1-½ inch of comb height, made of Kydex, comes our heavy duty non-slip pad for a perfect non-slip mount and fit.

MSRP . . . . $112.89–$124.89 (depending on finish)

VooDoo Tactical (voodootactical.net)

Cheek Rest for Fixed Rifle Stocks

Features: Ambidextrous cheek rest fits most fixed rifle stocks. Features hook-n-loop straps, removable ¼ in padded insert. Made out of 600D polyester. Coyote tan, black or OD green.

MSRP: $16.95

DATA BOOKS

Brownells (brownells.com)

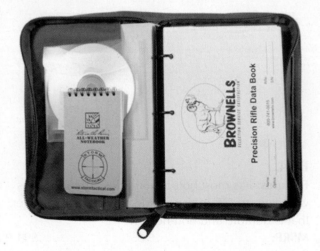

Brownells Rifle and Sniper Modular Data Books

Features: Plastic cover, metal binder rings. Sniper models have a Coyote tan nylon, zippered outer cover. Large—5½" x 8½". 3-ring binder. 90 lb. card stock pages. Small—4-5/8" x 7". 6-ring binder. Rite-in-the-Rain pages, plus 3" x 5" spiral bound note pad and permanent ink pen.

MSRP: $74.99

Impact Data Book (impactdatabooks.com)

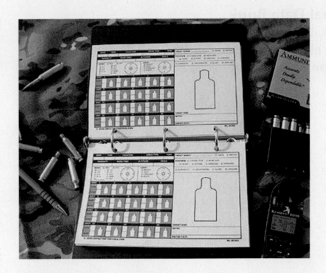

Modular Data Book

Features: Customized for individual shooting needs with choices of book size, paper type, binder color and data collection pages. Book measures in at 9-1/8 in x 6-½ in.

Choice of paper: Standard 80 weight executive stock paper or Rite in the Rain water resistant paper. Durable plastic three-ring binder in tan or black.

MSRP: $42.00

Storm Tactical (stormtactical.com)

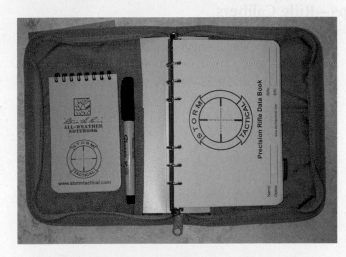

"Rite in Rain" 6-Ring Mini Binder Modular Sniper Kit

Features: Rite in Rain tan paper modular data book with CDROM, Rite in Rain tan zipper Cordura outer cover, black Sharpie ultra fine point permanent marker, 3 in x 5 in tan notebook. Coyote tan, OD green, multicam.

MSRP: $70.00

U.S. Tactical (ustacticalsupply.com)

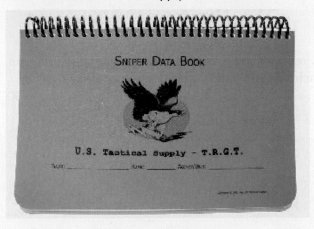

Sniper Data Book

Features: Already in operational use. Mil-Spec materials and construction. Printed 20 lb. bond, tactical green "Rite-in-the-Rain" paper. Cover made of polydura plastic with black plastic spiral ring. 128 leaves, 256 pages of data book. 14 pages of formulas, conversion tables, and charts on range estimation, wind, moving targets, and angle fire. Data sheets for zero summaries, cold bore shots, zeroes, bullseye, stationary, unknown distance, and moving targets. Various mission sheets and a barrel log included. For 7.62 mm NATO/.308 and .300 Win. rifles.

MSRP: $42.00

Voodoo Tactical (voodootactical.net)

Operational Data Book

Features: Spiral notebook includes charts and formulas, including windage and elevation. 84 pages in a hardcover spiral-bound format that can be laid flat or folded back on it. Dimensions 4 in x 5 in.

MSRP: $16.95

DUMMY TRAINING AMMUNITION

A-Zoom (azoomsnapcaps.com)

Aluminum Snap Caps—Rifle Calibers

Features: Metal Snap Caps Protect weapon from spring fatigue and damage to firing pins from dry firing. Practice sight control, trigger squeeze, and check the weapons cycling.

MSRP: . . . .$9.98–$13.00 (depending on caliber)

Traditions Performance Firearms (traditionsfirearms.com)

Snap Caps-Rifle-Plastic

Features: Made to protect your firearms by relieving the stress on your firing pins and firing pin springs. Practice dry firing your guns to teach safe gun handling, improve your shooting skills.

MSRP: $8.99

Snap Caps-Rifle-Aluminum

Features: Aluminum snap caps are made to protect a firearm by relieving the stress on the firing pins and firing pin springs. Safe to dry fire.
MSRP: $9.99

Rifle Training Cartridges

Features: Meet all SAAMI specifications for dummy ammunition, weighted like real ammunition, will cycle like an actual loaded cartridge, durable brass cases and rims so they will not become damaged like plastic dummies rounds, rubber insert to make it a snap cap, perfect for function testing, firearms instructors/students as teaching and training aids, new shooters who are learning to safely load and unload their firearms, malfunction drills, and dry-fire practice.
MSRP: . . . .$7.98–$13.98

Triple K (triplek.com)

Plastic Snap Caps—Rifle Calibers

Features: Plastic snap caps cycle through magazines. Excellent training aids as well as protection for your firing pin when dry firing.
MSRP: . . . . $7.79–$14.29 (depending on caliber)

SHOOTING MATS & DRAG BAGS

Barrett (Barrettrifles.com)

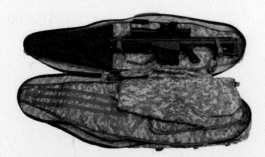

Drag Bag

Material: 1000 Denier Cordura
Color: ACU, black, coyote, OD green
Overall Length: 60 in.
Features: Fully padded; built-in shoulder straps and waist harness; fits model 99, 95 and 82A1.
MSRP: $525.00

Drag Bag/Shooting Mat

Material: Nylon
Color: OD green
Unrolled Dimensions: 60.5 x 52 in.
Rolled Dimensions: 44.5x18x2.5 in.
Features: Fits model 95, 82A1/M107.
MSRP: $550.00

Blackhawk (blackhawk.com)

Pro-Shooters Mat

Material: 1000 Denier nylon and closed cell foam
Color: Black, desert tan, olive drab
Unrolled Dimensions: 83 x 28 in.
Features: Hydration-compatible pouch with tube routing system, HawkTex shooting surface, shoulder strap, wraparound handles.
MSRP: $165.00

Stalker Drag Mat

Material: 1000 Denier nylon and .5 in. closed cell foam
Color: Black, olive drab
Unrolled Dimensions: 50.5 x 32 in.
Features: Detachable shoulder strap with HawkTex pad, interior weapon-securing straps, elastic loops hold 10 rounds of .308 ammo with protective flap, wraparound carry handles, internal data book pocket.
MSRP: $160.00

Crosstac (crosstac.com)

Elite Survival Systems (elitesurvival.com)

Long Gun Mat

Material: 1000 Denier nylon and closed cell foam
Color: Black, desert tan, olive drab
Unrolled Dimensions: 49 x 28 in.
Features: Wraparound carry handles; silent YKK zipper and sliders; hard, plastic, protective crown cover lined with closed-cell foam; concealable backpack harness straps and belt; elasticized sternum strap; fits all rifles up to 50-inch long; freefall and static-line jumpable, compatible with BLACKHAWK! Hydration System.
MSRP: $250.00

Precision Long Range Shooting Mat

Material: 1000 Denier PVC Coated Polyester
Color: Multicam, coyote brown
Unrolled Dimensions: 79x36 in.
Rolled Dimensions: 36 x 3 in.
Features: Integral bipod rail; mat folds, unfolds, and deploys flat instantly.
MSRP: $160.00

Epsilon Shooting Mat System

Material: heavy-duty 1000 denier nylon
Color: Black or coyote tan
Case Dimensions: 36 in x 14 in
Shooting Mat Dimensions: 72 in x 42 in
Weight: 7 lb
Features: Wide handle wrap and four buckles keep collapsed form secure, large, non-slip Toughtek areas on shooting surface, Velcro loop areas on hold Hook & Loop Accessory Pouches, MOLLE panel and pocket for accessories and storage, zippered front pocket, covered D-rings for attachment of backpack/shoulder straps, padded with 3/8 in closed-cell foam.
MSRP: $199.95

Ultimate Sniper Drag Bag
Material: heavy-duty 1000 denier nylon
Color: Coyote tan
Case Dimensions: 51 in
Weight: 8 lb
Features: Internal cleaning rod pouch and utility compartment, adjustable tie-down system to secure weapon, reinforced drag handle, loops for Ghillie attachment, two exterior zippered cargo pockets with full internal MOLLE compatibility for attaching modular pouches, flat exterior zippered pocket, removable and adjustable S-shaped backpack straps which can be tucked away when not in use, straps can also be reversed to carry case inverted.
MSRP: $249.95

Galati Gear (galatiinternational.com)

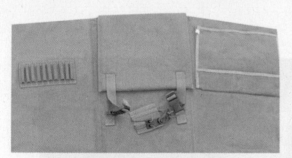

Tactical Rifle Cover Case and Shooting Mat
Material: Cordura nylon
Color: Olive drab
Case Dimensions: 10 x 49 in.
Shooting Mat Dimensions: 31 x 49 in.
Weight: 3 lb.
Features: A muzzle guard and clip assembly keeps the firearm secure; elastic ammo loops; accessory pocket; fold-out flap on the shooting mat functions as a knee pad and also helps secure the weapon during transport.
MSRP: $100.00

Roll Up Shooters Mat
Material: Cordura nylon
Color: Black, olive drab
Unrolled Dimensions: 67 x 51 in.
Rolled Dimensions: 27 x 13 in.
Weight: 4 lb.
Features: Additional flap folds out on each side to provide extra space.
MSRP: $85.00

Deluxe Shooters Mat

Material: Cordura nylon
Color: Black, olive drab, tan
Case Dimensions: 48 x 11.5 in.
Mat Dimensions: 66 x 37 in.
Weight 10 lb.
Features: Holds guns up to 48-in. long, heavy-duty YKK dual slider zipper; laces are sewn on the outside of the case to secure a tie-down camouflage system; numerous accessory loops to attach items to the case by ALICE clips; reinforced carry handles; padded back-pack straps; two drag loops.
MSRP: $250.00

Elite Sniper Shooter Mat

Material: Cordura nylon
Color: Olive drab, tan
Case Dimensions: 55 x 12 in.
Mat Dimensions: 72 x 40 in.
Weight: 14 lb.
Features: Designed for large caliber rifles; holds guns up to 50-in. long; bipod, silencer/accessory, and bolt pouches, heavy-duty YKK dual slider zipper; laces are sewn on the outside of the case to secure a tie-down camouflage system; numerous accessory loops to attach items to the case by alice clips; reinforced carry handles; padded back-pack straps.
MSRP: $280.00

Triad Tactical (triadtactical.com)

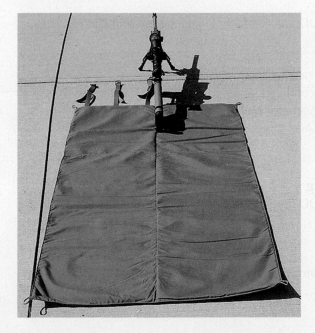

Triad Padded Shooting Mat

Material: Two layers of Codura and .125-in. foam padding
Color: Multicam, coyote, khaki, range green, olive drab, A-TACS, A-TACS FG , black
Unrolled Dimensions: 57 x 36.6 in.
Rolled Dimensions: 18 x 5.5 in.
Weight: 2.5 lb.
Features: 19-in. section of non-slip, durable material to set elbows and buttstock on.
MSRP: $95.00

VooDoo Tactical (voodootactical.net)

Pro Series Competition Shooting Mat

Material: Cordura nylon

Color: Olive Drab, desert tan, black, ACU digital camo

Features: Carry handle; full backpack-like shoulder harness; exterior padded pouch for spotting scope (fits up to an 80mm objective lens); large padded pouch for

SLINGS

Blue Force Gear (blueforcegear.com)

electronics, binoculars, rangefinders or other accessories; drag handles on the nose; multiple exterior surfaces have MOLLE Webbing; unfolds into three sections, a fold-out leg panel at one end and a fold-out extension on the front to keep muzzle blast from throwing up dust; anti-skid pads for bipod; holds a rifle up to 48 inches long.

MSRP: $190.00

NSN Vickers Sling

Color: OD green

Material: Nylon

Style: 2-point

Width: 1.25 in.

Details: Developed to meet the requirements of former 1st SFOD-Delta operational member Larry Vickers. Over 100,000 Vickers Combat Applications Slings are in use by every branch of service in the United States.

MSRP: $55.00

Vickers PB Sling

Color: Coyote brown, OD green, black, foliage green, multicam

Material: Nylon

Style: 2-point

Width: 1.25 in., 1.5 in. or 2 in. (padded)

Details: VCAS-PB sling combines American-made push button swivels with the Vickers Sling, Acetal or metal hardware.

MSRP: . . . . . . $77.00 (Acetal hardware); $87.00 (padded); $135.00 (metal hardware)

Vickers Cobra Sling

Color: Coyote brown, OD green, black, foliage green, multicam

Material: Nylon

Style: 2-point

Width: 1.25 in.

Details: Steel triglides and matching black machined aluminum adjuster.

MSRP: . . . . $107.00; $120.00 (padded)

Quick-Set Latigo Sling

Color: Tan, matte black, gloss black
Material: Leather
Style: 2-point
Width: 1 or 1.25 in.
Details: Fast quick set sling, with or without swivels
MSRP: .$49.99; $59.99 (1-in. with QD swivels); $79.99 (1.25-in. with QD swivels)

Competitor Plus Sling

Color: Tan, black
Material: Leather
Style: 2-point
Width: 1.25 in.
Details: Reproduction of the original 1907 Military Sling.
MSRP: . . . . $66.99 (tan); $69.99 (black)

Tactical Plus Sling

Color: Black, brown, OD green
Material: BioThane
Style: 2-point
Width: 1.25 in.
Details: Based on the 1907 Military Sling, urethane-coated nylon material is weather resistant.
MSRP: . . . .$64.99 (brown); $59.99 (black, OD green)

Specter Gear (spectergear.com)

CST 3 Point Tactical Sling
Color: Coyote tan, black, olive drab, foliage green
Material: Nylon
Style: Cross Shoulder Transition (CST), 3-point
Width: 1.25 in.
Details: Designed to fit various model rifles and carbines; ambidextrous; available with or without an Emergency Release Buckle (ERB); supplied with a stirrup type rear adapter and wrap around front adapter.
MSRP: $34.13

SOP 3 Point Tactical Sling
Color: Coyote tan, black, olive drab, foliage green
Material: Nylon
Style: Special Operations Patrol (SOP), 3-point
Width: 1.5 in.
Details: Designed for various rifles and carbines; available with or without an Emergency Release Buckle (ERB); Transition Release Buckle (TRB) provides cross shoulder transition.
MSRP: $34.13

Tactical Intervention Specialists (tacticalintervention.com)

Quick Cuff Model M24 US Military Precision Rifle Sling
Color: Olive, black, tan
Material: Nylon
Style: 2-point
Width: 1.45 in.
Details: Developed for sniper rifles; includes swivels; as used by US Army Special Forces, Rangers, US Navy Seals, The US Marine Corps, USMC Snipers, and Canadian Special Forces.
MSRP: $75.00

Slip Cuff Quick Release Sling
Color: Olive, black, tan
Material: Nylon
Style: 2-point
Width: 1.45 in.
Details: Can be used on both precision and CQB weapons, available with or without swivels.
MSRP: . . .$60.00; $65.00 (with heavy duty QD swivels or AI type hooks); $75.00 (with heavy duty flush cup swivels)

Viking Tactics (vikingtactics.com)

MK2 With Cuff assembly
Color: Coyote, black
Material: Nylon
Style: 2-point
Width: 1 in.
Details: Quick adjust portion of the sling gives user the ability to wear the cuff, snap in and adjust the sling quickly to the necessary length. Cuff comes equipped with a small snap shackle that allows user to attach or detach quickly. The VTAC-MK2-WC sling is a modified VTAC MK2 sling that includes an arm cuff as well as two HDQD swivels.
MSRP: $82.12

SUPPRESSOR COVERS

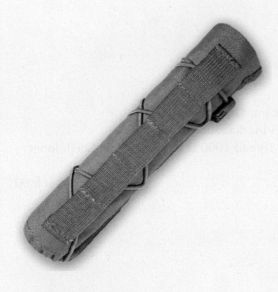

Armageddon (armageddongear.com)

Suppressor Cover
Retention: Bungee cord
Color: Coyote Brown, Multicam, ATACS, Foliage Green, Black, and Ranger Green.

Size: All 1.5x9 in. suppressors
Details: Cover design ensures NO contact areas between nylon shell and hot suppressor.
MSRP: $69.95

SA—Suppressor Cover Anti-Mirage Shield
Retention: Velcro
Color: Coyote Brown, Multicam, OD Green, Black
Size: Up to 1.75 in. dia., 1.75 in. dia. and larger
Details: Opens down the length of the suppressor and is held closed with a strip of velcro-like material.
MSRP: $62.00

SASR
Retention: Bungee cord
Color: Coyote Brown, Multicam, OD Green, Black
Size: Up to 1.75in. dia., 1.75 in. dia. and larger
Details: Sewn with NOMEX Thread 1000 D Cordura Outer Shell. Inner shell can withstand 1800°F.
MSRP: $68.00

WIND METERS

Caldwell (battenfeldtechnologies.com)

Wind Wizard
Features: Reads wind and temperature in Celsius and Fahrenheit; Wind speed measures in mph, ft/min, km/h, m/s, or knots; Wind chill display; LCD backlight.
MSRP: $39.99

4000 Pocket Weather Meter

Dimensions: 5.0 in x 1.8 in
Weight: 3.6 oz
Features: Wind and weather monitoring functions plus data storage, graphing functions, and computer interface technology. Tracks barometric pressure, pressure trend, altitude, relative humidity, heat stress index, dewpoint, wet bulb temperature, density altitude, wind chill, temperature (air, water, and snow), current wind speed, average wind speed, maximum wind gust.
MSRP: . . . . $249.00; $259.00 (night vision); $339.00 (Bluetooth); $354.00 (Bluetooth, NV)

4500NV Applied Ballistics Meter

Dimensions: 5.0 in x 1.8 in
Weight: 3.6 oz
Features: Wind and weather monitoring functions plus data storage, graphing functions, and computer interface technology. Tracks barometric pressure, pressure trend, altitude, relative humidity, heat stress index, dewpoint, wet bulb temperature, density altitude, wind chill, temperature (air, water, and snow), current wind speed, average wind speed,maximum wind gust. Built-in Applied Ballistics software with Litz library of G1 and G7 referenced Ballistic Coefficients (BC's), custom drag curve modeling, ballistic calibration, PC Loader software to build firearm profiles on computer and transfer them via wire or Bluetooth. Olive drab or tan.
MSRP: . . . . $589.00; $689.00 (Bluetooth)

4500NV Horus ATrag Ballistics

Dimensions: 5.0 in x 1.8 in
Weight: 3.6 oz
Features: Combines the Kestrel 4500 with Night Vision and Horus ATrag Ballistics software. Olive drab or tan.
MSRP: . . . .$589.00; $389.00 (Bluetooth, NV)

References

Abril de Fontcuberta, Eduardo. *100+ Sniper Exercises*. Boulder, CO: Paladin Press, 2013.

Brophy, William S. *The Springfield 1903 Rifles*. Harrisburg, PA: Stackpole Books, 1985.

Cooper, Jeff. *The Art of the Rife*. Boulder, CO: Paladin Press, 1997.

Craig, William. *Enemy at the Gates: The Battle for Stalingrad*. New York, NY: E.P. Dutton & Co., Inc., 1973.

Doherty, Glen and Webb, Brandon. *Navy Seal Sniper: An Intimate Look at the Sniper of the 21st Century*. New York, NY: Skyhorse Publishing, 2013.

Fjestad, S.P. *Blue Book of Gun Values*. Minneapolis: Blue Book Publications, Inc., 2009.

Gebhardt, James F., trans. *Nastavleniye po strelkovoma delu: 7.62mm Snayperskaya Vintovka obr. 1891/30 g. s opticheskim priselom PU I pribory nablyudeniya—The Official Mosin–Nagant Sniper Rifle Manual*. Boulder, CO: Paladin Press, 2010.

Grossman, Dave. *On Killing*. New York, NY: Back Bay Books, 2009.

Henderson, Charles. *Marine Sniper: 93 Confirmed Kills*. New York, NY: Berkley Caliber Books, 1986.

Kyle, Chris with McEwen, Scott and DeFelice, Jim. *American Sniper*. New York, NY: Harper, 2012.

McKenney, Lt. Col. Tom C. *The Sniper Anthology:, Snipers of the Second World War*. Louisiana: Pelican Publishing Company, Inc., 2012.

O'Connor, Jack. *The Art of Hunting Big Game in North America*. New York, NY: Outdoor Life, 1967.

Pastor, John L. *The Ultimate Sniper*, Boulder, CO: Paladin Press, 2006.

Poyer, Joe *The Model 1903 Springfield Rifle and its Variations*. Tusin, CA: North Cape Publications, Inc., 2008.

Sasser Charles W. and Roberts, Craig. *One Shot—One Kill*. New York, NY: Pocket Star Books, 1990.

Sellers, Frank. *Sharps Firearms*. North Hollywood, CA: Beinfield Publishing, Inc., 1978.

Senich, Peter. *The German Sniper 1914–1945*. Boulder, CO: Paladin Press, 1997.

Sharpe, Phillip B. *The Rifle in America*. New York, NY: Funk & Wagnalls Company, 1953.

Venturino, Mike. *Shooting Buffalo Rifles of the Old West*. Livingston, MT: MLV Enterprises, 2002.

Wigginton, Eliot, ed. *Foxfire 5*. Garden City, New York: Anchor Press/Doubleday, 1979.

US Navy, *U.S. Navy Seal Sniper Training Program*. New York, NY: Skyhorse Publishing, 2011.

Appendix A — Rifleman's Creed

Rifleman's Creed

This is my rifle. There are many like it, but this one is mine.

My rifle is my best friend. It is my life. I must master it as I must master my life.

My rifle, without me, is useless. Without my rifle, I am useless. I must fire my rifle true. I must shoot straighter than my enemy who is trying to kill me. I must shoot him before he shoots me. I will . . .

My rifle and I know that what counts in this war is not the rounds we fire, the noise of our burst, or the smoke we make. We know that it is the hits that count. We will hit . . .

My rifle is human, even as I, because it is my life. Thus, I will learn it as a brother. I will learn its weaknesses, its strength, its parts, its accessories, its sights and its barrel. I will keep my rifle clean and ready, even as I am clean and ready. We will become part of each other. We will . . .

Before God, I swear this creed. My rifle and I are the defenders of my country. We are the masters of our enemy. We are the saviors of my life.

So be it, until victory is America's and there is no enemy, but peace!

—Written by Major General William H. Rupertus between late 1941 and early 1942

Appendix B – Military Sniper Kill Counts

WORLD WAR I		
NAME	**COUNTRY (SERVICE BRANCH)**	**KILLS**
Francis Pegwahmagabow	Canada	378
Billy Sing	Australia (AIF)	202 / 98*
Henry Norwest	Canada	115
Herbert W. McBride	Canada/USA	100+
Ottavio Bottecchia	Italy	100+
Neville Methven	South Africa	100
Johnson Paudash	Canada	88
Philip McDonald	Canada	70
Herman Davis	USA	60
L. Greener	Canada	54
P. Riel	Canada	30
S.D. Richey	Canada	13+

* kills unconfirmed

WORLD WAR II		
NAME	**COUNTRY**	**KILLS**
Simo Häyhä	Finland	542
Ivan Sidorenko	USSR	500
Nikolay YakovlevichIlyin	USSR	494
Ivan Nikolayevich Kulbertinov	USSR	487
V. N. Pchelintsev	USSR	456
Mikhail Budenkov	USSR	437
Fyodor Matveevich Okhlopkov	USSR	429
Fyodor Djachenko	USSR	425
Vasilij Ivanovich Golosov	USSR	422
Afanasy Gordienko	USSR	417
Stepan Petrenko	USSR	412
Erwin Konig[1]	Germany	400
Vasily Zaytsev	USSR	400
Pyotr Alexeyevich Goncharov	USSR	380

WORLD WAR II CONT.		
Semen D. Nomokonov	USSR	367
Ivan Petrovich Antonov	USSR	362
Abdulkhani Idrisov	USSR	349
Philipp Yakovlevich Rubaho	USSR	346
Matthaus Hetzenauer	Germany	345
Ivan Ivanovich Larkin	USSR	340
Victor Ivanovich Medvedev	USSR	331
E. Nicolaev	USSR	324
Leonid Yakovlevich Butkevich	USSR	315
Nikolai Ilyin	USSR	315
Lyudmila M. Pavlichenko[F]	USSR	309
Alexander Pavlovich Lebedev	USSR	307
Ivan Pavlovich Gorelikov	USSR	305
Ivan Petrovich Antonov	USSR	302
Heinz Thorvald[1]	Germany	300
Gennadij Iosifovich Velichko	USSR	300
Moisej Timofeyevich Usik	USSR	300
Nataly V. Kovshova[F] & Maria Polivanova[F, 2]	USSR	300
Ivan Filippovich Abdulov	USSR	298
Yakov Mikhajlovich Smetnev	USSR	279
Liba Rugova	USSR	274
Anatolij Chekhov	USSR	265
Zhambyl Evscheyevich Tulaev	USSR	262
Josef' Sepp' Allerberger	Germany	257
Fyodor Kuzmich Chegodaev	USSR	250
Ivan Ivanovich Bocharov	USSR	248
Mikhail Ignatievich Belousov	USSR	245
Maxim Passar	USSR	237
David Teboevich Doev	USSR	226
Vasilij Shalvovich Kvac hantiradze	USSR	215

Bruno Sutkus	Germany	209
Mikhail Stepanovich Sokhin	USSR	202
Friedrich Pein	Germany	200
Noj Petrovich Adamia	USSR	200
M.A. Abbasov	USSR	200
Gefreiter Meyer	Germany	180
Yekaterina Zuranova[F]	USSR	155
Vladimir Ptchelinzev	USSR	152
Inna Semyonovna Mudretsova[F]	USSR	143
Joseph Pilyushin	USSR	136
Feodosy Smeljachkov	USSR	125
I. Merkulov	USSR	125
H. Andruhaev	USSR	125
Oleh Dir	Germany	120
Tatiana Igantovna Kostyrina[F]	USSR	120
Janis Roze	USSR	116
N.P. Petrova[F]	USSR	107
V. N. Pchelintsev	USSR	102
Yelizaveta Mironova[F]	USS.R	100+
Aliya Moldagulova[F]	USSR	91
Nina Lobkovskaya[F]	USSR	89
Lidiya Gudovantseva[F]	USSR	76
Helmut Wirnsberger	Germany	64
Alexandra Shlyakhova[F]	USSR	63
P. Grjaznov	USSR	57
Roza Shanina[F]	USSR	54
A.P. Medvedeva-Nazarkina[F]	USSR	43
Marie Ljalkova[F]	Czech Army	30
James Bedford MacArthur	Canada	9

* kills unconfirmed
[F]Female
[1]Controversy whether German snipers Konig or Thorvald ever existed and were ever sent to Stalingrad to eliminate Soviet sniper Zaytsev.
[2]Female sniper

KOREAN WAR		
NAME	**COUNTRY (SERVICE BRANCH)**	**KILLS**
Zhang Taofang	China	214
Richard Crawford	USA (Army)	14 / 29*

* kills unconfirmed

VIETNAM WAR		
NAME	**COUNTRY (SERVICE BRANCH)**	**KILLS**
Adelbert Waldron III	USA (Army)	109
Charles B. Mawhinney	USA (USMC)	103
Eric R. England	USA (USMC)	98
Carlos Hathcock	USA (USMC)	93
Ronnie Shinya Marshall	USA (Army)	77
Thomas R. Leonard	USA (USMC)	74
Steve Suttles	USA (USMC)	63
Joseph T. Ward	USA (USMC)	63
George Filyaw	USA (USMC)	56 / 20*
Philip G. Moran	USA (Army)	53
Raymond W. Westphal	USA (USMC)	49 / 19*
Terry Mathis	USA (Army)	48
James C. Peters	USA (Army)	43 / 11*
T.R. Graves	USA (USMC)	43
Lynn Bushnell	USA (USMC)	43
Daniel L. Greene	USA (Navy)	42 / 12*
Joe York	USA (Navy)	42
Tom "Moose" Ferran	USA (USMC)	41
James Gularte	USA (USMC)	40
Ronald D. Bundy	USA (USMC)	40
Michael E. Duncan	USA (Army)	39
Chester Clarke	USA (Army)	39
William Lucas	USA (USMC) / USA (Army)	38 / 1
Bob Jones	USA (Army)	38
John M. Perry	USA (USMC)	37 / 5*
Dennis Oscier	USA (USMC)	36 / 20*
Bill E. Nation	USA (USMC)	35
Jay Taylor I	USA (USMC)	28 / 18*
Clifford L. Wallace	USA (USMC)	27
Ed W. Eaton	USA (Army)	27
Craig McGary	USA (Navy)	26 / 8*
Mike Brewton	USA (Army)	23

VIETNAM WAR CONT.

Lloyd Crow	USA (USMC)	23
Bobby J. Lee	USA (USMC)	18
Craig Roberts	USA (USMC)	18 35*
Ed Kugler	USA (USMC)	17
Gary J. Brown	USA (Navy)	17 4*
Karl H. Grosshans	USA (USMC)	16
Greg Kraljev	USA (USMC)	15
Leonard J. Wilson	USA (USMC)	14 5*
Timothy Dunn	USA (USMC)	14
Thomas R. "Tommy" Cohenour	USA (Army)	13
Ron Szpond	USA (USMC)	12 12*
William B. Martin	USA (USMC)	12
John L. Brooks	USA (USMC)	11 6*
Gary Lefebvre	USA (USMC)	11
Bill Koch	USA (Army)	8 3*
Michael McMillan	USA (Army)	5
Gary M. White	USA (USMC)	4 5*
Gabriel J. Gradney	USA (USMC)	4 1*
David W. Lee	USA (Army)	3 4*
Alan Bruce Hartung	USA (USMC)	3 3*
Colin McGee	USA (USMC)	3
Robert Miles	USA (Army)	2
Ralph E. Stevenson	USA (Army)	1

* kills unconfirmed

GRENADA

NAME	COUNTRY (SERVICE BRANCH)	KILLS
Scott Burkett	USA (USMC)	3 4*
Patrick McFadden[3]	USA (USMC)	3
John H. Hackenberg	USA (USMC)	1

GRENADA CONT.

E. Tribull	USA (USMC)	3*

* kills unconfirmed
[3]McFadden served in Grenada and Somalia

PANAMA

NAME	COUNTRY (SERVICE BRANCH)	KILLS
Jeffrey N. Tucker[4]	USA (USMC)	3
Bobby L. King[4]	USA (USMC)	3 2*
Tweed Almond	USA (Army)	3
Robert Kirts	USA (Army)	4*

* kills unconfirmed
[4]Tucker and King served in Panama and Desert Storm

DESERT STORM

NAME	COUNTRY (SERVICE BRANCH)	KILLS
Frank Grieci	USA (USMC)	15
Scott Dennison[5]	USA (Army)	14 2*
Jeffrey N. Tucker[4]	USA (USMC)	3 13
Joseph McElheny	USA (USMC)	13
Alexander K. Sheppard	USA (USMC)	11
Robert H. Stiles	USA (Army)	5 3*
Douglas Parker	USA (USMC)	4 2*
Jose Macias	USA (USMC)	4
Dave Dayter	USA (USMC)	3
Grady Snell	USA (USMC)	3
Bobby L. King[6]	USA (USMC)	2 1*
Robert Rocha	USA (USMC)	2 3*
Steven A Schirman	USA (USMC)	2

* kills unconfirmed
[4]Tucker and King served in Panama and Desert Storm
[5]Dennison served in Bosnia and Desert Storm
[6]King served in Panama and Desert Storm

SOMALIA

NAME	COUNTRY (SERVICE BRANCH)	KILLS
John Fuger	USA (USMC)	6
Cory Smith	USA (USMC)	6
Stephen Tyson	USA (USMC)	6
Chase Hamilton	USA (USMC)	5
Patrick McFadden[3]	USA (USMC)	3
Eldon Noble	USA (USMC)	3
David E. Galloway	USA (USMC)	3
Chris Mark	USA (USMC)	2
Julio A. Garcia	USA (USMC)	1
Bill Cook	USA (USMC)	1*
John Henry Davis III	USA (Army)	0

* kills unconfirmed

SOMALIA

NAME	COUNTRY (SERVICE BRANCH)	KILLS
Scott Dennison[5]	USA (Army)	4 1*

* kills unconfirmed
[5]Dennison served in Bosnia and Desert Storm
IRAQ OperationIraqi Freedom(OIF) and Operation Enduring Freedom (OEF)

IRAQ (OIF, OEF, OND)

NAME	COUNTRY (SERVICE BRANCH)	KILLS
Chris Kyle[7]	USA (Navy)	160 95*
Timothy L. Kellner	USA (Army)	78 4*
Jack Coughlin[7]	USA (USMC)	63
Ian "Duke" Crune[7]	USA (US SOCOM)	21 13*
Ethan Place	USA (USMC)	19
Jonathan "Juan" Warren7	USA (US SOCOM)	18 15*
Randall Davis	USA (Army)	8 2*
Skyler Ford	USA (Army)	8
John Giehm	USA (USMC) & USA (Army)	7 2*
Spencer Hisatake & Ian Yee	USA (Army)	6
David *****	U.K. (Royal Marine Commandos)	5

NAME	COUNTRY (SERVICE BRANCH)	KILLS
Ross *****	U.K. (Royal Marine Commandos)	4
Ryan Mish	USA (Army)	3 1*
Matthew Pickar	USA (Army)	3 1*
Justin Cooper	USA (USMC)	3
Ethan Caduff	USA (Army)	2 2*
Ryan Barna	USA (Army)	2
Christopher Lochner	USA (Army)	2
Benjamin Redus	USA (Army)	1 3*
Joe LeBleu	USA (Army)	1 3*
Beau Babbitt	USA (Army)	1

* kills unconfirmed
[7]Kyle, Coughlin, Crune, and Warren served in OIF and OEF

AFGHANISTAN

NAME	COUNTRY (SERVICE BRANCH)	KILLS
Mark Osmond	U.K.	44
Tom Potter	U.K.	31
Robert Furlong	Canada (C.A.F.)	1+
Arron Perry	Canada (C.A.F.)	1+

OTHER CONFLICTS

NAME	COUNTRY (SERVICE BRANCH)	KILLS
Gregory S. Bartlett[H]	USA (USMC)	5
Patrick Simpson[H]	USA (USMC)	2 3*
Robert K. Canfield[B]	USA (USMC)	2
Jason Ferrand[L]	USA (USMC)	1 2*
Roger Griffith[L]	USA (USMC)	1 1*

* kills unconfirmed
[H]Honduras
[B]Beruit
[L]Liberia

Special thanks to snipercentral.com for use of this data.

Appendix C – Rifle Scope Reticles

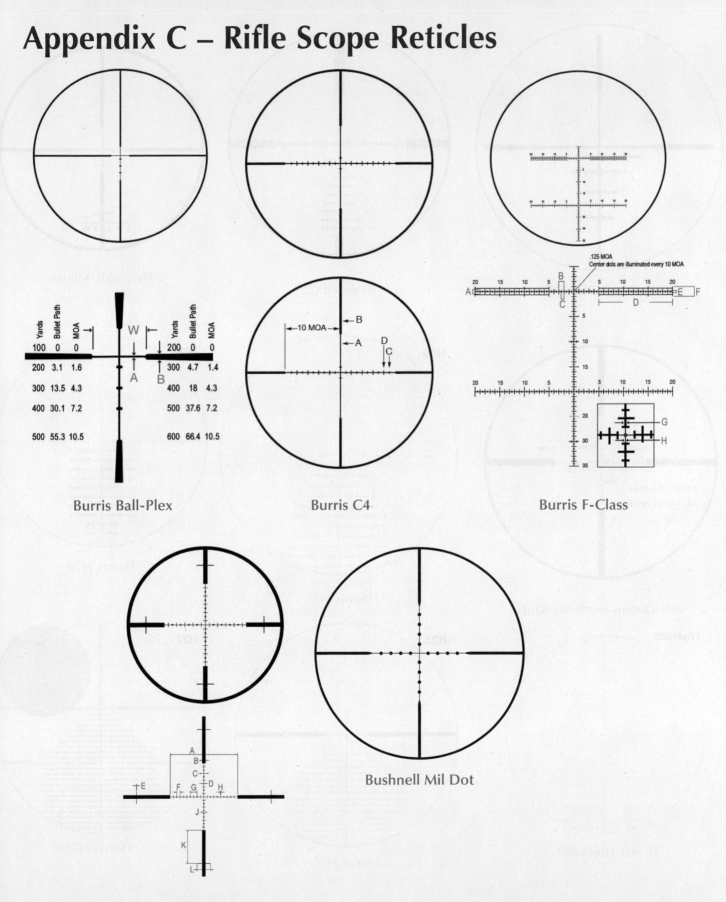

Burris Ball-Plex

Yards	Bullet Path	MOA		Yards	Bullet Path	MOA
100	0	0		200	0	0
200	3.1	1.6		300	4.7	1.4
300	13.5	4.3		400	18	4.3
400	30.1	7.2		500	37.6	7.2
500	55.3	10.5		600	66.4	10.5

Burris C4

Burris F-Class

.125 MOA
Center dots are illuminated every 10 MOA

Burris G2B

Bushnell Mil Dot

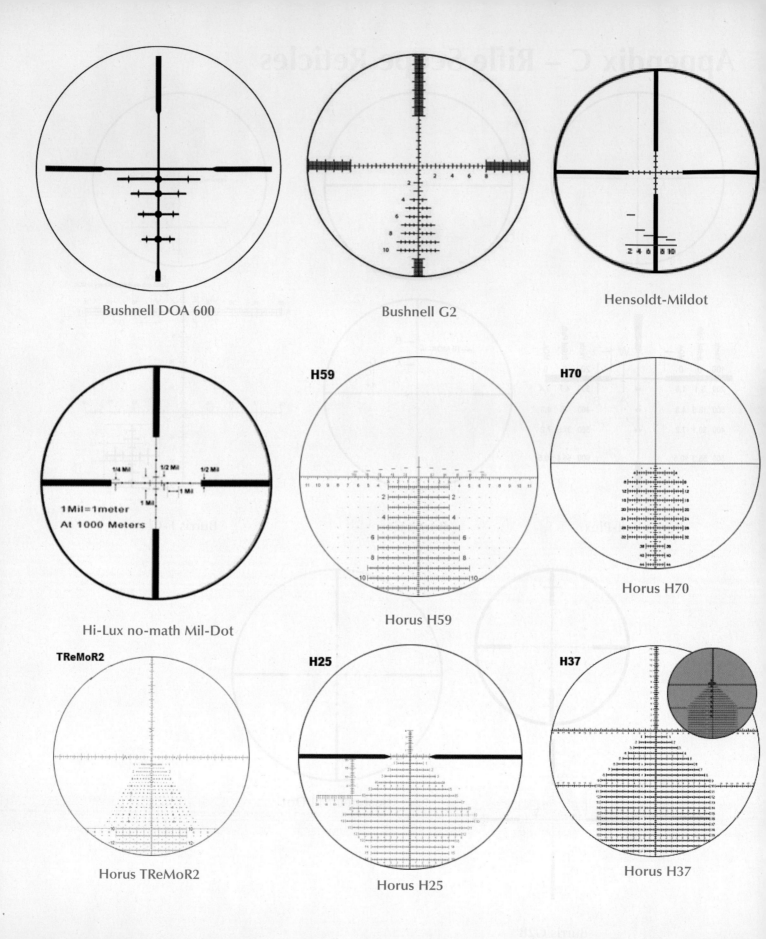

Bushnell DOA 600

Bushnell G2

Hensoldt-Mildot

Hi-Lux no-math Mil-Dot

Horus H59

Horus H70

Horus TReMoR2

Horus H25

Horus H37

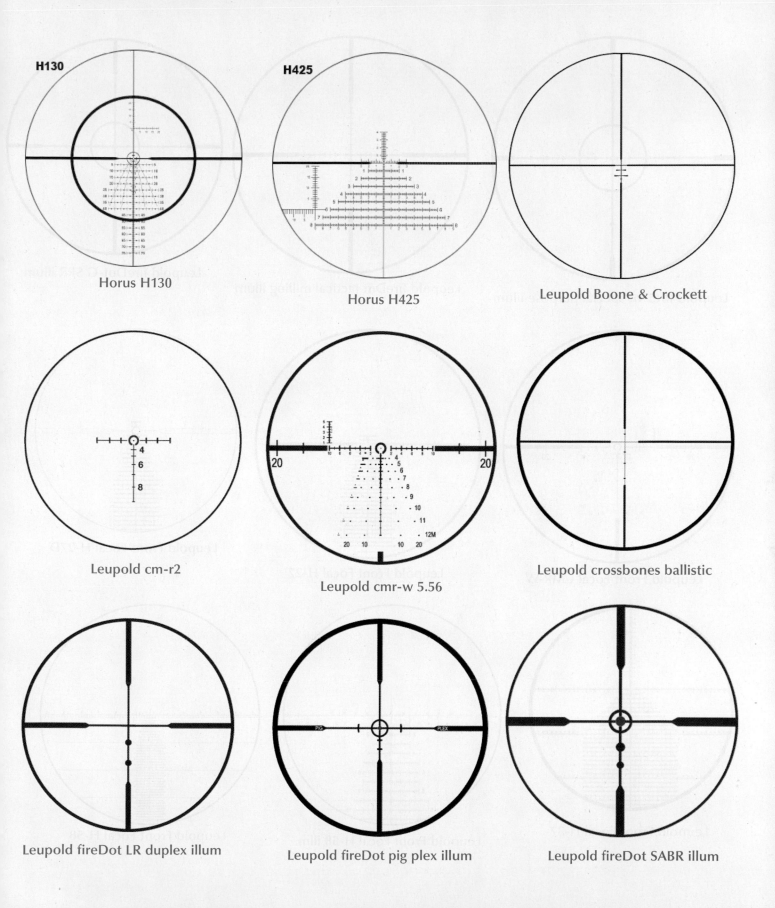

Horus H130

Horus H425

Leupold Boone & Crockett

Leupold cm-r2

Leupold cmr-w 5.56

Leupold crossbones ballistic

Leupold fireDot LR duplex illum

Leupold fireDot pig plex illum

Leupold fireDot SABR illum

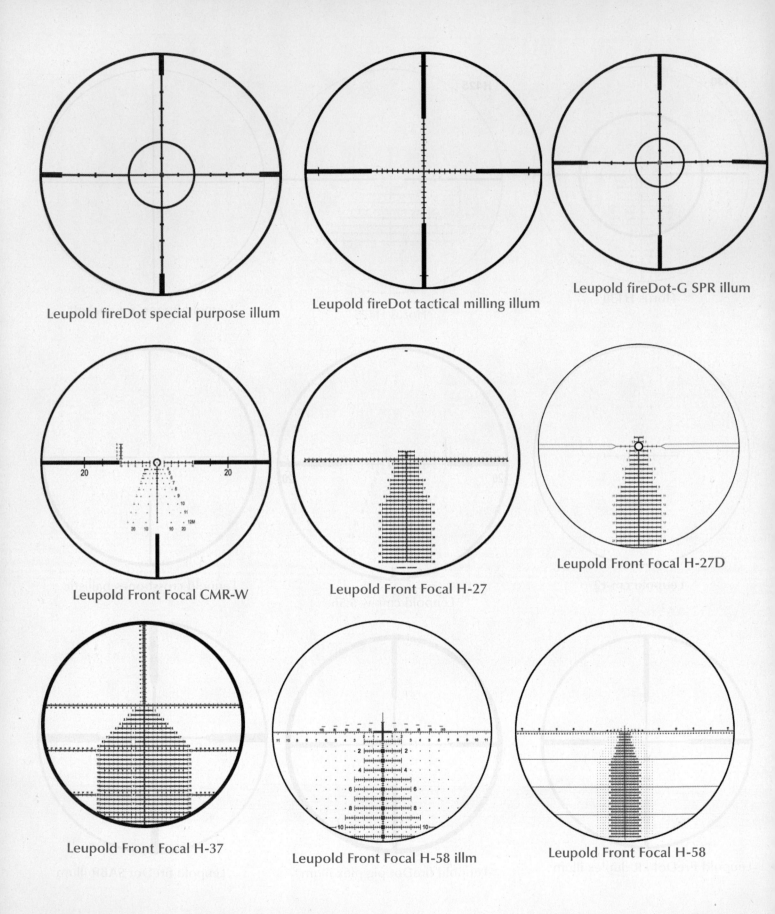

Leupold fireDot special purpose illum

Leupold fireDot tactical milling illum

Leupold fireDot-G SPR illum

Leupold Front Focal CMR-W

Leupold Front Focal H-27

Leupold Front Focal H-27D

Leupold Front Focal H-37

Leupold Front Focal H-58 illm

Leupold Front Focal H-58

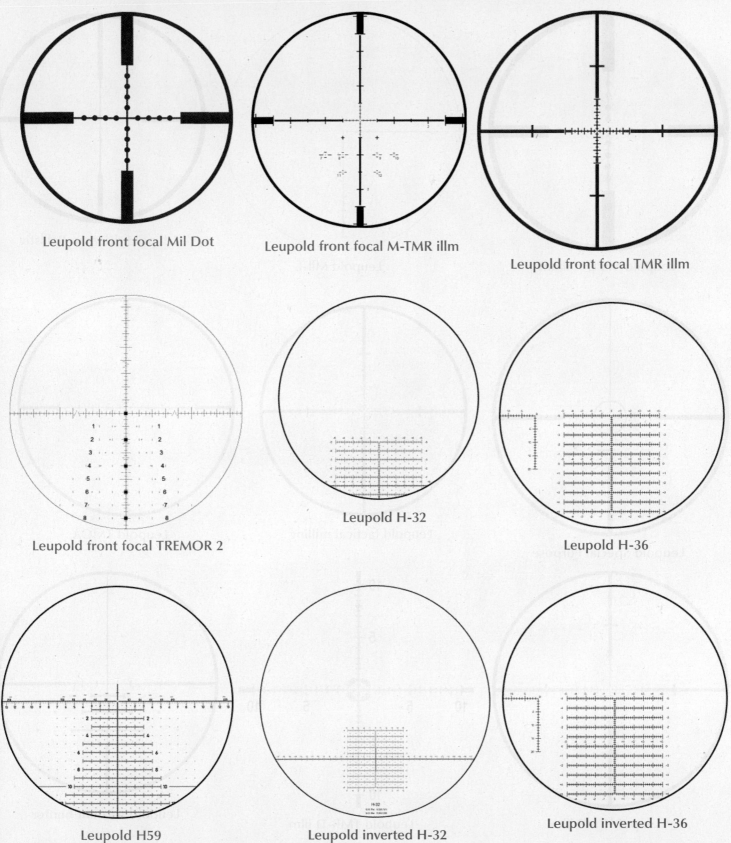

Leupold front focal Mil Dot

Leupold front focal M-TMR illm

Leupold front focal TMR illm

Leupold front focal TREMOR 2

Leupold H-32

Leupold H-36

Leupold H59

Leupold inverted H-32

Leupold inverted H-36

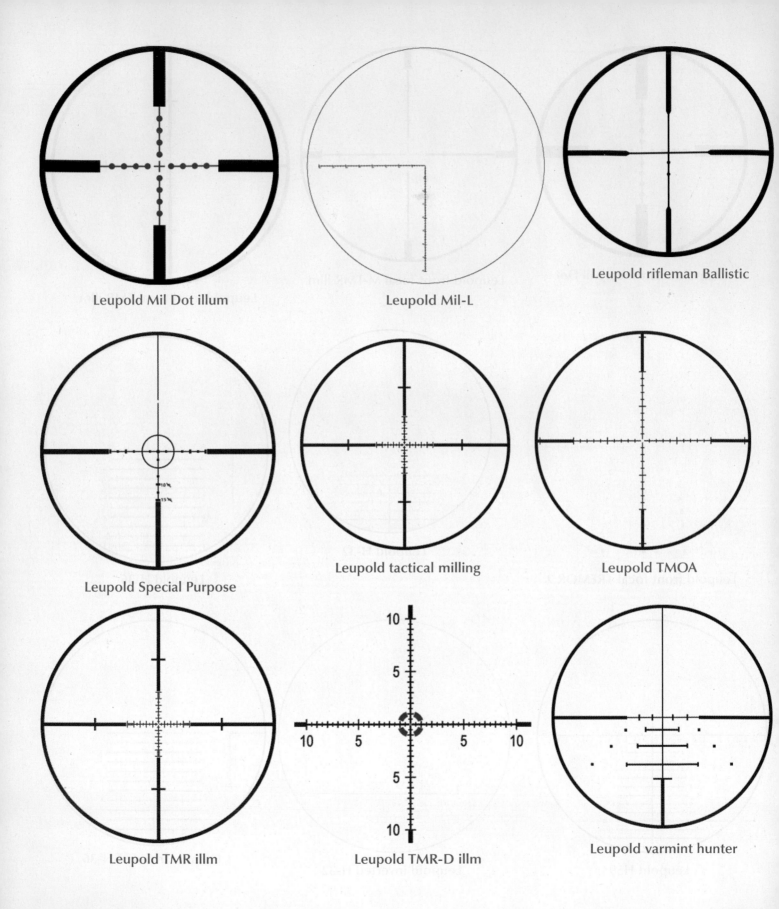

Leupold Mil Dot illum

Leupold Mil-L

Leupold rifleman Ballistic

Leupold Special Purpose

Leupold tactical milling

Leupold TMOA

Leupold TMR illm

Leupold TMR-D illm

Leupold varmint hunter

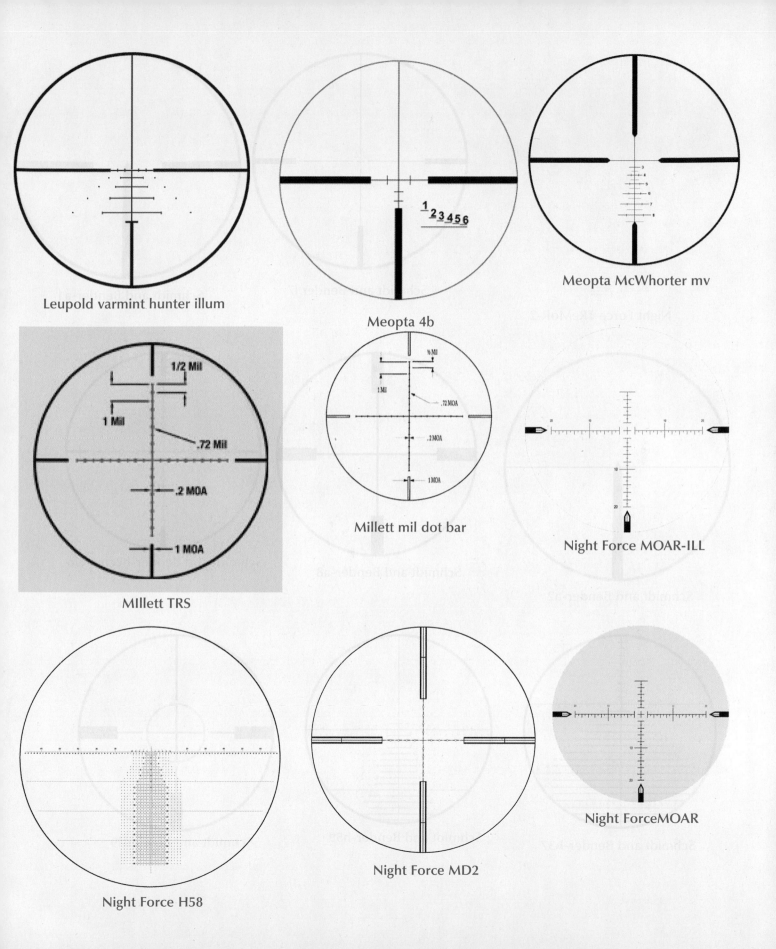

Leupold varmint hunter illum

Meopta 4b

Meopta McWhorter mv

MIllett TRS

Millett mil dot bar

Night Force MOAR-ILL

Night Force H58

Night Force MD2

Night ForceMOAR

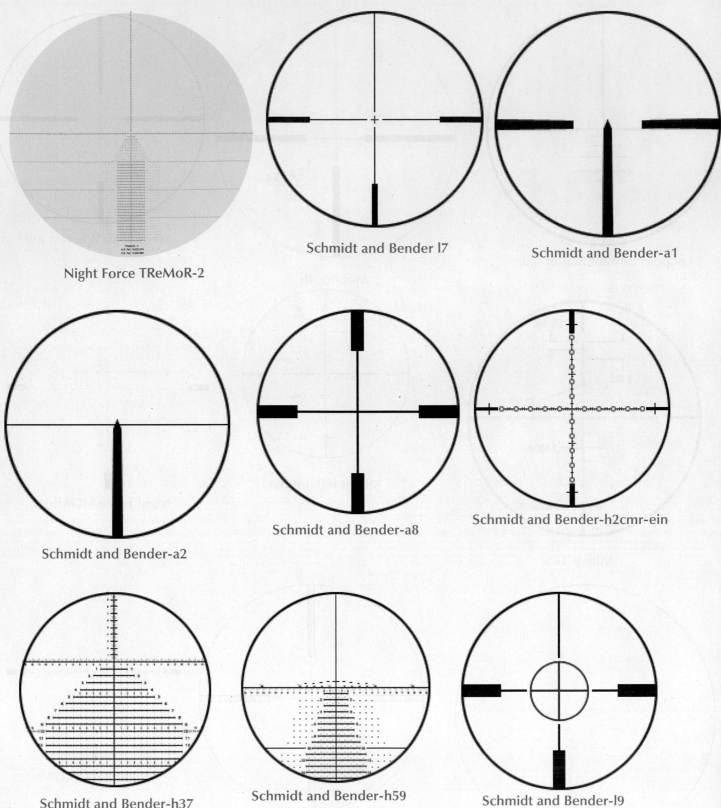

Night Force TReMoR-2

Schmidt and Bender l7

Schmidt and Bender-a1

Schmidt and Bender-a2

Schmidt and Bender-a8

Schmidt and Bender-h2cmr-ein

Schmidt and Bender-h37

Schmidt and Bender-h59

Schmidt and Bender-l9

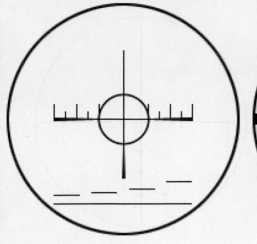

Schmidt and Bender-p1-bryant-1be

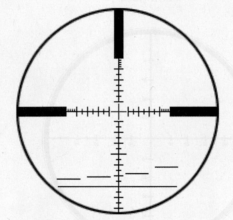

Schmidt and Bender-p3

Schmidt and Bender-p3-2be

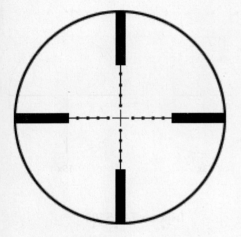

Schmidt and Bender-p3l-mildot-1be

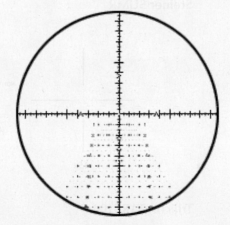

Schmidt and Bender-p4l-1be

Schmidt and Bender-p4l-1be-fein

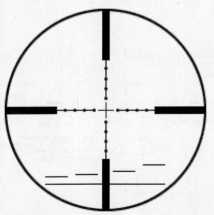

Schmidt and Bender-police-ein

Schmidt and Bender-tremor2

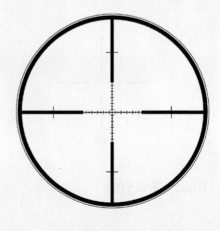

Steiner Mil-Dot

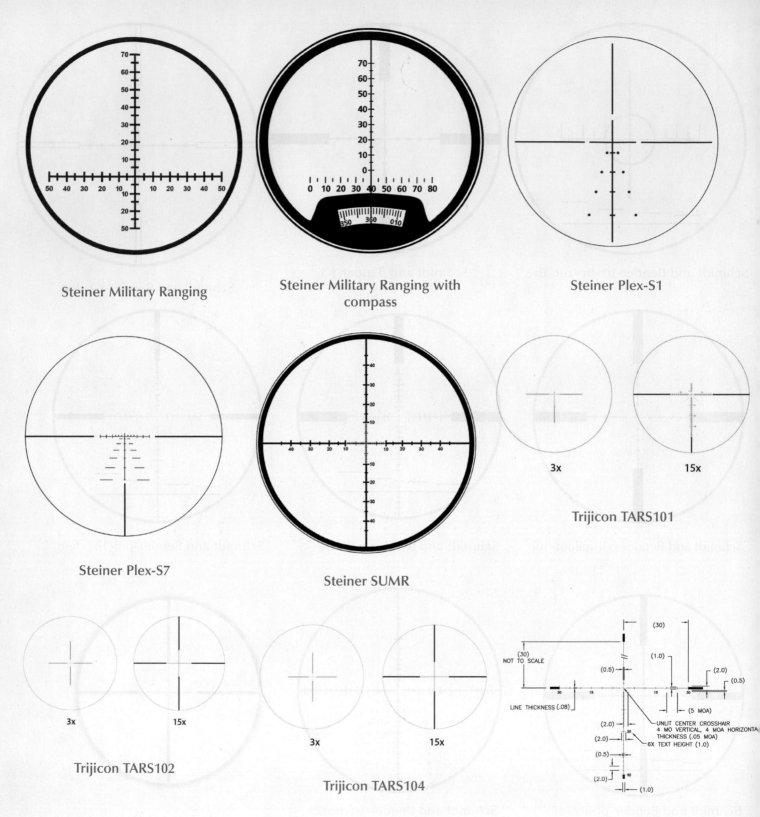

Steiner Military Ranging

Steiner Military Ranging with compass

Steiner Plex-S1

Steiner Plex-S7

Steiner SUMR

Trijicon TARS101

3x   15x

Trijicon TARS102

3x   15x

Trijicon TARS104

3x   15x

U.S. Optics RDP MOA

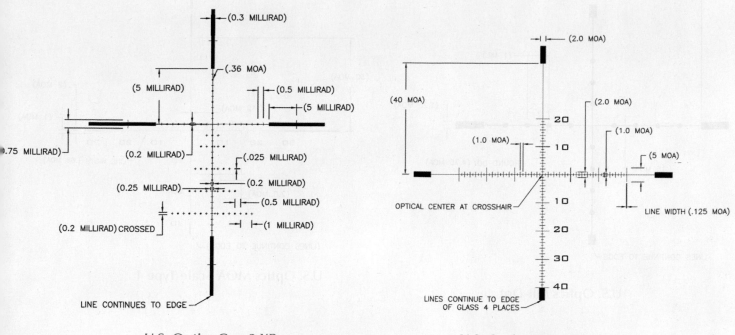

U.S. Optics Gen 2 XR

U.S. Optics MDMOA

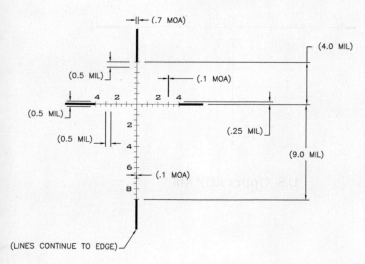

U.S. Optics Mil Scale GAP

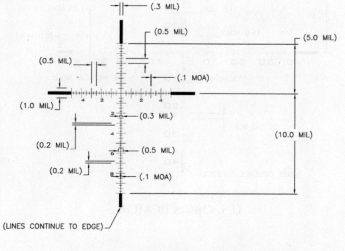

U.S. Optics Mil Scale MPR

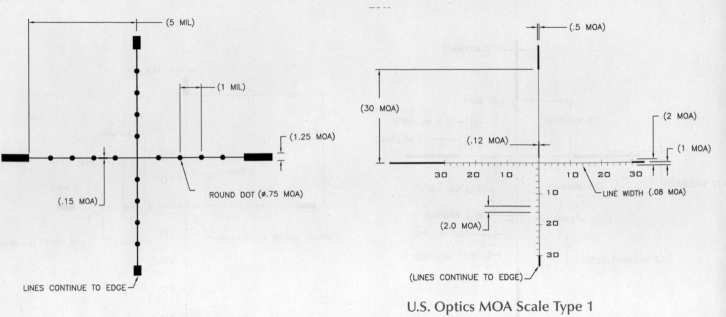

U.S. Optics Mil-Dot

U.S. Optics MOA Scale Type 1

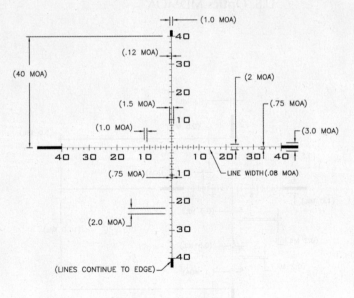

U.S. Optics PCMOA

U.S. Optics RDP Mil

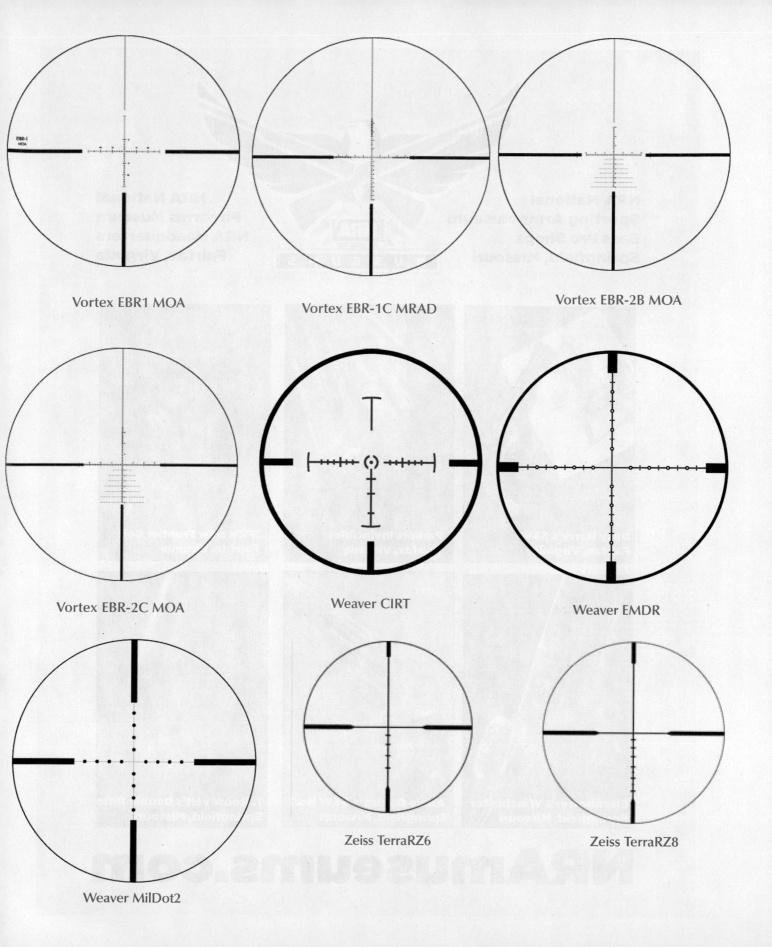

Vortex EBR1 MOA

Vortex EBR-1C MRAD

Vortex EBR-2B MOA

Vortex EBR-2C MOA

Weaver CIRT

Weaver EMDR

Weaver MilDot2

Zeiss TerraRZ6

Zeiss TerraRZ8